Tove H. Malloy (ed.)
Minority Issues in Europe: Rights, Concepts, Policy
Volume 1

Minority Issues in Europe: Rights, Concepts, Policy

Volume 1

Edited by

Tove H. Malloy

Verlag für wissenschaftliche Literatur

Umschlagabbildung: networking © vege – Fotolia.com

ISBN 978-3-86596-543-1

© Frank & Timme GmbH Verlag für wissenschaftliche Literatur
Berlin 2013. Alle Rechte vorbehalten.

Das Werk einschließlich aller Teile ist urheberrechtlich geschützt.
Jede Verwertung außerhalb der engen Grenzen des Urheberrechtsgesetzes ist ohne Zustimmung des Verlags unzulässig und strafbar.
Das gilt insbesondere für Vervielfältigungen, Übersetzungen,
Mikroverfilmungen und die Einspeicherung und Verarbeitung in
elektronischen Systemen.

Herstellung durch das atelier eilenberger, Taucha bei Leipzig.
Printed in Germany.
Gedruckt auf säurefreiem, alterungsbeständigem Papier.

www.frank-timme.de

Table of Contents

Acknowledgements 9
List of Abbreviations 10
Introduction 13
    The Aim of the Book 13
    The Problem of a Definition 14
    A Note on Approach and Method 18
    Notes 21

PART I

Chapter 1: European History of Minority Relations 27
RAUL CÂRSTOCEA

    Introduction 27
    Early beginnings: religious freedoms 28
    The Enlightenment and the emergence of nationalism 31
    The Congress of Berlin (1878) and the establishment
    of minority rights obligations 33
    World War I and its aftermath: the new international order
    and the Minority Treaties 36
    The functioning of the League of Nations and its limitations 41
    Key points 46
    Further reading 47
    Notes 48

Chapter 2: European International Law 51
TOVE H. MALLOY

    Introduction 51
    The Council of Europe 52
    The Congress of Local and Regional Authorities 62
    The European Union 65
    The European Approach 69
    Key Points 69
    Further reading 70
    Notes 71

Chapter 3: Europeanisation 75
TAMARA HOCH JOVANOVICH

Introduction 75
The concept of Europeanisation 76
Europeanisation and minority rights 80
EU internal frameworks and minority rights 86
Key points 98
Further reading 98
Notes 99

PART II

Chapter 4: Ethnicity, Culture and Language: Individuals and Groups 107
FEDERICA PRINA

Introduction 107
Ethnicity, Culture and Language 108
The State, Society and its Groups 112
Recognition 113
The Group and its Members 114
From Ethnic Characteristics to Rights 116
Protection and Promotion of Cultural and Linguistic Pluralism 120
Limitations to Minority Protection 122
Intra-group and inter-group dynamics 123
Key Points 124
Further reading 125
Notes 126

Chapter 5: Conflict and Unity 131
HANNA VASILEVICH

Introduction 131
Defining conflict and unity 132
Minority demands 136
Minority demands and interstate relations 138
Forms of ethnic conflict regulation 140
Key points 154
Further reading 155
Notes 155

Chapter 6: Transnationalism 161
ZORA POPOVA

- Introduction 161
- Brief History of the Concept 163
- Definitions of Transnationalism 165
- Key Approaches to Transnationalism 169
- Transnationalism and Minority Issues 176
- Are Roma Transnational? 181
- Key Points 181
- Further Reading 182
- Notes 183

Chapter 7: Late Modernity 189
TOVE H. MALLOY

- Introduction 189
- Late Modernity 191
- External Forces and Social Change 194
- Ontological Diversity 198
- Debates 202
- Public Space Issues 208
- Key Points 213
- Further reading 214
- Notes 214

PART III

Chapter 8: Conflict mitigation policies 221
KIRYŁ KAŚCIAN

- Introduction 221
- UN mechanisms 222
- Charter-based mechanisms 224
- Treaty-based mechanisms 228
- OSCE mechanisms 232
- The High Commissioner on National Minorities 233
- NATO and minority-related conflict mitigation 238
- Key Points 240
- Further reading 241
- Notes 242

Chapter 9: Democracy, participation, and empowerment 247
ANDREEA CÂRSTOCEA

Introduction 247
General Considerations 248
Descriptive representation 255
Representation in practice 262
Social movements and Roma participation 266
Key points 268
Further reading 269
Notes 270

Chapter 10: Diversity management 273
ALEXANDER OSIPOV

Introduction 273
Practical conceptualizations of diversity 276
Major frames of diversity management 280
Goals and objectives 284
Strategies, norms and policies 287
Areas of application 290
Limits of state interventionism 294
Key points 295
Further reading 296
Notes 296

Bibliography 301

Index 325

Notes on Contributors 347

Acknowledgements

Since 2011, the research staff at the European Centre for Minority Issues (ECMI) has been teaching a winter semester course in minority issues at Flensburg University as part of the University's MA Programme in European Studies. The course is taught in English, and the students come from all over the world with many from the former Soviet Union and Eastern Europe. The aim of the course is to introduce the students to a multi-disciplinary approach to understanding minority issues in Europe. In preparing the course, we soon realized that relevant teaching material was as diverse as the topic. Not only did it we draw on the literature of a number of academic disciplines in the social and political sciences as well as law, we also brought in new materials not generally known to the sub-discipline of minority studies. Occasionally, there was an overlap in that the same material was assigned for differing topics. Thus, assigning a general textbook proved rather challenging. To fill the gap, we set out to draw up an outline and divided the writing tasks between the teaching staff. Thankfully, both our co-operation partner, Prof. Dr. Charlotte Gaitanides at Flensburg University and the ECMI Executive Board supported the idea.

In preparing the typescript we have incurred many debts. As editor, I would like to thank the contributors for their co-operation and forbearance in responding to queries and corrections even during holiday periods. And thank you to our former ECMI colleague, Thomas Parker, who acted as language editor with great precision. I would also like to thank the Centre's technical and administrative staff, ECMI Librarian William McKinney, intern Tinatin Genebashvili and Project Assistant Oana Musteata, who helped with style issues and prepared the Bibliography and the Index. A great debt and special thanks is owed to my PA, Tamari Bulia, for supervising the technical preparation of the entire typescript. Tamari is an alumna of the MA Programme and without her efficiency and dedication, the volume would not have been a reality. Our editor at Frank & Timme Publishers, Ms. Astrid Matthes, provided important assistance in the final stages of the preparation for which we are thankful. Finally, we would like to thank our local partner, Sydbank Germany, for supporting the project financially.

Flensburg, August 2013   Tove H. Malloy

List of Abbreviations

AC	Advisory Committee
CEDAW	Committee on the Elimination of Discrimination against Women
CEE	Central and Eastern Europe
CERD	Committee on the Elimination of Racial Discrimination
CoE	Council of Europe
EBLUL	European Bureau for Lesser-Used Languages
ECHR	European Convention on Human Rights
ECJ	European Court of Justice
ECMI	European Centre for Minority Issues
ECPR	European Consortium for Political Research
ECRI	European Commission on Racism and Intolerance
ECRML	European Charter for Regional or Minority Languages
EGTC	European Grouping of Territorial Cooperation
ENP	European Neighbourhood Policy
EP	European Parliament
ERA	European Research Area
ERDF	European Regional Development Fund
ETS	European Treaty Series
EU	European Union
EURAC	European Academy of Bozen/Bolzano
EUROREG	European Institute for Regional and Local Development
FCNM	Framework Convention for the Protection of National Minorities
FGM	Female Genital Mutilation
FRA	Fundamental Rights Agency
HCNM	High Commissioner on National Minorities
ICESCR	International Covenant on Economic, Social and Cultural Rights
IMER	International Migration and Ethnic Relations
IMISCOE	International Migration, Integration and Social Cohesion
InIIS	Institute for Intercultural and International Studies
IPMS	Indigenous Peoples and Minorities Section

ISCA	Institute of Social and Cultural Anthropology
MEP	Member of the European Parliament
NAACP	National Association for the Advancement of Colored People
NATO	North Atlantic Treaty Organization
NGO	Non-Governmental Organization
OED	Oxford English Dictionary
OHCHR	Office of the High Commissioner for Human Rights
OSCE	Organization for Security and Co-operation in Europe
OSI	Open Society Institute
TEU	Treaty on European Union
TFEU	Treaty on the Functioning of the European Union
UDHR	Universal Declaration of Human Rights
UN	United Nations
UNESCO	United Nations Educational, Scientific and Cultural Organization
USSR	Union of Soviet Socialist Republics

Introduction

Tove H. Malloy

The Aim of the Book

This book aims to assist advanced students in understanding minority issues as these have developed during the modern era in Europe. We do not propose to cover all aspects of minority existence in Europe, nor do we attempt to cover all disciplines. The book is meant as an introduction providing the starting points from which students may delve deeper into specific aspects and issues of their interest. We believe the field of minority studies is expanding rapidly, in many directions and over many sub-fields of academic exploration. While this is a welcomed development, it requires stocktaking from time to time. Minorities have been part of European history and politics since ancient Greece, and from the middle of the 16th Century they have been objects of policy-making. Early on religious minorities were seen as obstacles to state-building and later, national and language minorities came to be seen as a threat to nation-building. Immigrants who left Europe for the New World experienced less pressure as cultural minority groups but were nevertheless met with lack of acceptance and respect. In the 20th Century, minorities in Europe became the object of major bellicose conflicts and protracted international mediation. At times they were seen as an anomaly of international relations, a 'fifth column.' Domestically, traditional minorities had to fight their own way to be able to remain in their homelands while newcomers were received with rejection and were expected to return home. At the same time, personal identity became a public domain item; minority groups emerged and formed on the basis of identity and difference. Whether 'old Europe' or the New World, minorities have often been seen as a threat to peace and security and mostly as outsiders who do not fit in. In the early 21st Century of inter-connected societies and hyper-mobility, minorities are also seen as a threat to social cohesion and the common public goods of the welfare state.

The period covered in this book, basically from the Peace of Augsburg (1555) to the second Lisbon Treaty (in force 2009), represents essentially four minority discourses aimed at governing minority issues.[1] The first and most powerful, the security discourse, formed during the Reformation around the need to protect the freedom of religion of minority groups living in homelands governed by a different religious creed. Later in Europe's history, the security discourse expanded to include national and ethnic minorities, and it remains a vital part of European intergovernmental politics around the Helsinki Process, especially in areas where so-called 'frozen' conflicts have stalled the possibility to protect minorities. Early on these issues were governed by inter-state treaties and later by the League of Nations; today, they are monitored mainly by the dialogue mandate of the Organization for Security and Co-operation in Europe (OSCE). The second discourse, the justice discourse, emerged as a result of the atrocities committed against minorities during World War II, and formed first around the United Nations (UN) system's peace mandate in the immediate aftermath of the War, and later around the Council of Europe's democratization mandate. The justice discourse regulates the human rights domain, and minority rights have ironically by default also become part of this discourse—by default because initially minority rights were not included in the UN system. The third discourse, the cohesion discourse formed around the European Economic Community, now the European Union (EU), in the 1980s, when the Single Act (1986) laid the foundation for greater cohesion among member states, and thus eventually for the cohesion of the European Continent, with the number of member states growing after the opening up of the Soviet bloc.[2] This discourse has regulated minority protection through two main instruments: the conditionality track for new members of the EU and the social inclusion track for all member states. Finally, the fourth discourse, the European citizenship discourse, emerged during the drafting of the Maastricht Treaty (adopted 1991) and the conceptualization of the EU transition from being mainly an economic integration project to becoming a political project. This discourse has grappled with seminal issues, such as a common European identity in light of the EU's so-called 'democratic deficit.' The European citizenship discourse incorporates mainly two strands of articulations with regard to minorities: One is on dual/multiple and transnational citizenship and the other on active citizenship and participation. While these discourses have different starting points, they exist today in parallel as well as overlapping within the field of minority issues.

The Problem of a Definition

The concern of this book is minority groups and their individual members. Finding a definition of a 'minority' has, however, been fraught with controversy for decades. This is to the consternation of most international lawyers because it is difficult to argue litigation without knowing who the defendant is. The UN Sub-Committee on the Prevention of Discrimination and Protection of Minorities has grappled with the issue almost since its establishment, and a number of prominent experts has been asked to seek a solution to the problem.[3] The problem of a legal definition in international law is a question of whether a universal definition of minorities can be properly articulated. Inasmuch as international law instruments must apply to a wide range of states, a definition would by necessity have to be broad and general. That is near impossible in contemporary circumstances where minorities self-identify according to particular characteristics and a hybrid of diverse affiliations. Moreover, seeking a definition runs into the dilemma of whether to use objective or subjective criteria.[4] Objective criteria may result in discrimination; subjective criteria could lead to segregation. This is why in the legal context experts will have to work from the premise that a minority is a matter of fact, not law. Thus, it has been suggested that minorities are voluntary associations,[5] and most human rights instruments aimed at protecting minorities provide that belonging to a minority is a free choice.[6] This does not, however, allow for the innate bonds that many cultures foster. Finally, it could be argued that each case is unique. The characteristics and contexts vary from minority to minority and from country to country. Thus, in other academic fields, such as the social and political sciences, scholars operate with analytical definitions; that is, working definitions that possess the sole purpose of analysing a phenomenon. Whether one works on the basis of positivistic or hermeneutical/interpretist methods, a dependent variable is usually necessary.[7]

For analytical purposes, and only for analytical purposes, minority studies apply a dichotomy system of two categories of minorities in Europe: the so-called 'old' and 'new' minorities. Old minorities refer to minorities who have traditionally been a minority for many years, whereas new minorities indicate a group which has been present in a territory for a shorter period. These vague rules are, of course, only guidelines; it is difficult to define exactly what constitutes many years versus a few? This question will always invite arbitrary responses. This is why scholars prefer to argue that the question of a definition is unique to each case. Notwithstanding this dilemma, there are scholars outside the realm of law, who have volunteered definitions over the years; they have usually combined objective and subjective criteria.[8] The problem of the objective and/or subjective views is related to the issue of pre-determination versus self-determination. Where self-determination allows minorities to manifest themselves, pre-determination requires advanced decisions on the identity of minorities.[9] Therefore, a combination of the two may at times be the best solution.

Due to the long history of old minorities in Europe, the scientific debate on a definition has focused mainly on these groups. Although they may possess several characteristics of belonging, i.e. religion, language and national allegiances, they are often jumbled together under the rubric of 'national minorities'. Will Kymlicka has suggested a short-hand version holding that national minorities are "groups who formed functioning societies on their historical homelands prior to being incorporated into a larger state."[10] More recently Jennifer Jackson Preece has put forth a detailed definition which holds that a national minority is

… a group numerically inferior to the rest of the population of a state, in a non-dominant position, well-defined and historically established on the territory of the state, whose members—being nationals of the state— possess ethnic, religious, linguistic or cultural characteristics differing from those of the rest of the population and show, if only implicitly, a sense of solidarity, directed towards preserving their culture, traditions, religion, or language.[11]

As a working tool, this definition is helpful. However, national minorities are a specific type of minority group; they are autochthonous.[12] While not entirely uncontroversial,[13] the term *autochthonous* refers to a minority that is native to a particular region, in this case certain regions of Europe that were once either independent or belonged to another sovereign, often neighbouring state. An autochthonous minority's status is a result of incorporation into another sovereign unit through the change of borders after major conflicts in the modern era. Most notably this has happened after bellicose conflicts, such as the Napoleonic Wars, World War I and II, but also after the breakup of the USSR.[14] Thus, one could argue that national minorities of autochthonous status in Europe are in essence the groups that have inadvertently found themselves 'on the wrong side of the border'. Important to note is that these minorities have not had any instrumental reasons, such as economic or political, for changing national allegiance. In fact, they have not been in the position to make a choice.

Autochthonous minorities include, but are not limited to, ethnic Hungarian speakers in Slovakia, Romania, Slovenia, Serbia and the Ukraine; ethnic Turks in Bulgaria and the Balkans; ethnic Albanians in Kosovo and Macedonia; ethnic Rusyns, Russians, Romanians, Slovaks, and Belarusians in the Ukraine; ethnic Moravians in the Czech Republic; German speaking Austrians in northern Italy; ethnic Italians in southern Austria and Slovenia; German speakers in southern Denmark; Danish speakers in northern Germany, and Russian speakers in the Baltic states. While the territorial criterion for the autochthonous status of most of these groups is usually quite clear, the criteria of time and language are less so. Whereas the Hungarians had been in the Danube basin for many centuries prior to the demise of the Austro-Hungarian Empire, the Russians in the Baltic states have migrated fairly recently. But they were migrating within the territory of their own state in much the same way the Turkish people had migrated into Bulgaria and other parts of the Balkans during the Ottoman Empire. Hence, the elimination of empires resulted in national groups residing away from what became their 'nation-state' due to the change of borders within which they had at some point migrated. Moreover, autochthonous national minorities also include other old minorities, such as the Bretons in France, the Basques and the Catalans in Spain, the Welsh, the Scots and the Irish in the United Kingdom. In fact, these autochthonous national minorities might well be seen as autochthonous in a stronger sense inasmuch as they have been national groups attached to territory over an even longer period and some of which have held independence at one time. Except perhaps for the Scots, most of these minorities did not choose to become minorities.

Unlike old minorities, new minorities have usually made a conscious choice to start out a new life as a member of a minority. This does not mean that they accept the idea of minority status, but for analytical purposes the rational decision to leave a homeland in favour of another territory has been characterized as voluntary no matter what reasons may have led to the move.[15] Political refugees are not included in this group mainly because they did not have a 'free' choice, and they are protected under different international law provisions than minorities.[16] Nevertheless, once they have arrived in the settlement country, they are often seen and treated as immigrants, and in the analysis of new minorities it is very difficult to distinguish the two categories. Analytical definitions of immigrant groups vary considerably from continent to continent due to different push and pull factors that have led to the migration.[17] Often migration happens in waves, but with the onset of hyper-mobility due to mass transportation as well as regional conflict patterns, the periods between waves have virtually disappeared. In Europe, most migration patterns are due mainly to decolonization or economic conditions in Africa and Asia as well as the more recent political conditions in the Middle East. Some immigrant groups may be edging closer to the definition of an old minority in terms of timeframe. These are immigrants from the colonies as well as immigrants from Turkey and Central Asia who came in the mid-20th Century. The immigrants from the colonies where allowed entry for moral reasons, whereas immigrants from Central Asia were invited to work in the new mass production sectors in the more industrialized countries. Their decision to come to Europe was for the most part a free choice based on instrumental reasons.

A third category of minorities in Europe may be termed social minorities. This is also an analytical category which the literature on minorities often either overlooks or jumbles together with the broad understanding of a minority. Social minorities are characterized by gender, age, sexual orientation, or physical or mental handicaps. They may also include specific types of vulnerability which requires special attention by the majority society. These groups are not the focus of this book.

It should be clear that it is not wise to promote one particular definition of what constitutes a minority. We return to the issue of definition from time to time in this book; however, without any prejudices one way or the other. Our scholarly aim is to provide the reader with the foundation to undertake analytical precision because we believe this is required to understand the many ways that different issues, events, and phenomena are related, or thought to be related in the area of minority studies.

A Note on Approach and Method

This book is multi-disciplinary in its approach to studying minority issues within European states and inter-state relations. We cover the relevant disciplines for our topics according to available literature. The study of minority existence in Europe has mainly been the focus of historians as well as legal and international relations scholars.[18] The approach of most of these studies is normative. It has only been within the last few decades that political scientists have turned their attention to the role of minorities as political actors in developed democracies.[19] While much of this literature focuses on the political and institutional accommodation of minorities in terms of self-government or self-administration, such as collective autonomy within unitary and federated states, it also takes a normative view. This literature is not only informed by both the security and the justice discourses but has also remained frozen in its focus on the national state due to the substantial number of minorities that gained collective autonomy rights within European states during the 20th Century.[20] One off-shoot of this literature has placed minorities in the perspective of European integration and speculated whether autonomous minority regions might be mobilizing within the politics of multi-level governance in the EU.[21] With a few exceptions in the study of Euro-regions, little has been written about minorities as political actors with regard to cross-border issues.[22] Even these studies focus mainly on the institutionalisation of Euro-regions and less on the how national minorities have been involved in these types of regions. The social science literature has focused primarily on immigrant communities in Europe, mainly from the perspective of oppression and exclusion.[23] Thus, there is a gap in the literature on the relation between the economy and minority existence with the exception of the focus of development studies on vulnerability.[24] Some sociologists have focused on the socio-economic exclusion of specific minorities, especially immigrants, whereas the economic empowerment of minorities has become the interest of political sociologists. Finally, while cultural studies exist in abundance in the field of anthropology,[25] the humanities lack studies on minorities, especially in the field of cultural production and minority literature. In short, the academic literature available in the area of minority studies has become somewhat unbalanced with a strong leaning towards history, law and international relations, while the social sciences have focused more on the processes of exclusion and inclusion rather than on the specific groups.

The overarching guiding method of this book falls within the inter-section between neo-institutionalism and ideas.[26] By neo-institutionalism, we mean the study of the impact of institutions upon individuals as well as with the inter-action between institutions and individuals. Institutions refer here broadly to patterns of political behaviour, informal conventions as well as formal structures, with specific attention paid to the way in which institutions embody values and power.[27] In short, the focus is on rules and conceptions, formal and informal, as well as dynamic (as opposed to static) and disaggregated (as opposed to holistic) conceptions of institutions and critical thinking about values and the contexts in which institutions exist and change. By ideas we mean concepts derived from the major ideologies that have fostered development in Europe during the modern era. Ideas are thus part of the large-scale historical change that influences institutions. This causal link is important, especially when studying minority issues where institutions have gone from not providing any interest in minority protection to grand conventions focusing particularly on minorities. While international actions were based on actual events, as in the case of the human rights regime after World War II or the European minority rights regime after 1989, the outcome was based on liberal ideals of individual rights to protection against violations committed by the state. A proper understanding of the state as an actor is thus the fundamental concept underpinning any analysis of minority issues in Europe. While we do not engage in analyses of statecraft, we analyse a number of sociological concepts relevant for statecraft and nation-building. Traditional conceptual analysis is, therefore, the foundation of our approach.

As indicated in the title of this book, we cover three main areas of minority studies. In Part I, we discuss minority issues in a historical context tracing first the early origins of minority governance up through the early 20th Century (Chapter 1) followed by a discussion of the developments in the second part of the 20th Century in terms of the intensified legal attention paid to the protection of individual members of minorities (Chapter 2). As noted, most of the traditional literature on minority studies emanates from the fields of history and international relations that we apply in these chapters. Next, we delve into a more detailed analysis of the international relations aspect of European politics and minority issues. We look at the intensified integration of the European Continent through the process of Europeanization and how this influences minority existence (Chapter 3). This chapters draws on alternative texts not traditionally part of minority studies. In Part II, we turn to the theoretical and conceptual aspects of understanding minority existence. Here, we put the main concepts involved in the understanding of minority issues under scrutiny. We ask how one might define culture, and whether ethnicity is different from culture *per se*? And what is the relation between minority membership and language (Chapter 4)? These differences in group definition and self-identification become manifested in the politics of most states since there is virtually no state in Europe that is not multicultural. This poses numerous challenges of how to accommodate group differences in societies that desire social unity (Chapter 5). Moreover, given the hyper-mobility which characterizes a globalizing world, the aspect of transnationalism as a social phenomenon with growing importance becomes relevant for the understanding of the 'fifth column' syndrome (Chapter 6). Here we draw on literature new to the field of minority studies which addresses identity and citizenship in new perspectives. The last focus of this Part analyses the ramifications of social change on the late modern life of minority existence (Chapter 7). What issues have become the 'hard' cases to accommodate and how do they influence co-existence in the public space? In Part II, we draw on literature from the fields of sociology, political science and political theory as well as international relations.

Part III turns to the policy aspect of minority protection. The neo-institutional approach is here applied against the conflict management and security regime that has developed in Europe since World War II (Chapter 8). Managing conflict involves law as well as institutions, and inter-agency relations are here of special importance. In the end, though, it comes down to how the individual state decides to structure its institutions for group participation (Chapter 9). How far will minority rights be implemented to ensure a democratic ethos that includes all groups and minorities? Moreover, the need for states to design specific policies which aim specifically at the inclusion of individuals through non-discrimination and positive measures becomes paramount (Chapter 10). Ending on a note of diversity management as the new paradigm for Europe is, therefore, not without reason.

The phenomenon of minorities in Europe is being redefined. From being a continent traditionally grappling with minority issues in terms of security and peace, Europe is a now forced to find justice for all through accommodation of diversity domestically. Granted, for centuries, Europe had to find ways to protect minorities against violations such as assimilation and persecution. However, in the 21st Century there is also a need to protect minorities against the discriminatory acts of fellow and new citizens. While conformity and uniformity remain the goals of many modern societies, diversity is a fact of life. We hope that this book will provide students with a set of tools with which they may begin to understand the fact of European diversity and how it relates to minority existence in the European context. For students who wish to proceed further, each chapter provides a guide to further reading.

Notes

1   See further, Tove H. Malloy, "National Minorities in the 21st Century Europe: new discourses, new narratives?" *ECMI Issue Brief*, No. 24 (ECMI, 2010).
2   Some might prefer to call this discourse, the integration discourse. In minority studies this invites confusion, as sociological integration is a common concept used in the understanding of minority accommodation. See further, Chapter 5.
3   Francesco Capotorti, "Study on the Rights of Persons Belonging to Ethnic, Religious and Linguistic Minorities", UN Doc. E/CN.4/Sub.2/384/Rev.1 and Jules Dechênes, "Proposal concerning a Definition of the term 'Minority'", UN Doc. E/CN.4/Sub.2/1985/31. See also Tove H. Malloy, *National Minority Rights in Europe* (Oxford University Press, 2005), Chapter 7.

4   For a good discussion see, Gaetano Pentassuglia, *Minorities in International Law* (Strasbourg: Council of Europe Publishing, 2002), Chapter III.

5   John Packer, "On the Definition of Minorities" in *The Protection of Ethnic and Linguistic Minorities in Europe*, eds. John Packer and Kristian Myntti (Åbo: Institute for Human Rights, 1995), pp. 23–65 as well as John Packer, 'Problems in Defining Minorities' in *Minority and Group Rights in the New Millennium*, eds. Deidre Fottrell and Bill Bowring (The Hague: Kluwer International Law, 1999), p. 252.

6   See for instance, the *UN Declaration on the Rights of Persons Belonging to National or Ethnic, Religious and Linguistic Minorities*, Art. 3(2), and the European Framework Convention for the Protection of National Minorities, Art. 3(1).

7   David March and Paul Furlong, "A Skin not a Sweater: Ontology and Epistemology in Political Science" in David Marsh and Gerry Stoker (eds.), *Theory and Methods in Political Science*, 2nd edition (Basingstoke: Palgrave Macmillian, 2002), pp. 17–41.

8   Inis L. Claude, *National Minorities: An International Problem* (Cambridge: Harvard University Press, 1955), p. 2; Jean A. Laponce, *The Protection of Minorities* (Berkeley: University of California Press, 1960), 6. See also in general, Carlile Aylmer Macartney, *National States and National Minorities* (London: Oxford University Press, 1934) and Tore Modeen, *The International Protection of Minorities in Europe* (Åbo: Åbo Akademi, 1969).

9   Arend Lijphart, "Self-Determination versus Pre-Determination of Ethnic Minorities in Power-Sharing Systems" in *The rights of Minority Cultures*, ed. Will Kymlicka, *The rights of Minority Cultures* (Oxford: Oxford University Press, 1995), pp. 275–288 at p. 275.

10 Will Kymlicka, *Politics in the Vernacular. Nationalism, Multiculturalism, and Citizenship* (Oxford: Oxford University Press, 2001), p. 54.

11 Jennifer Jackson Preece, *National Minorities and the European Nation-States System* (Oxford: Clarendon Press, 1998), p. 28.

12 Silvo Devetak uses the term in "Autonomy as One of the Means of Minorities' Protection. The Case of Slovenia" in *Ethnic Conflicts and Civil Society*, eds. Andreas Klinke, Ortwin Renn and Jean-Paul Lehners (Aldershot: Ashgate, 1997), pp. 99–115.

13 The concept autochthonous, if not well defined, could lead to discrimination. See "Constitution Watch" of Slovenia in *East European Constitutional Review* 102 (2001), pp. 41–44, reporting that the Constitutional Court of Slovenia has ruled the lack of an official definition a cause for concern, arbitrary and discriminatory.

14 Jackson Preece, op. cit., note 11.

15 Will Kymlicka, *Multicultural Citizenship. A Liberal Theory of Minority Rights* (Oxford: Clarendon Press, 1995), pp. 10–11.

16 *UN Convention* and *Protocol* relating to the Status of Refugees.

17 For a good discussion of defining immigrants according to their goals and status, see Alejandro Portes and Ruben G. Rumbaut, *A Portrait: Immigrant America*, 3rd edition (Berkeley: University of California Press, 2006), p. 19 ff.

18 Claude, op. cit., note 8; Laponce, op. cit., note 8; Jay A. Sigler, *Minority Rights: A Comparative Analysis* (Westport, Conn: Greenwood Press, 1982); Vernon Van Dyke, *Human Rights, Ethnicity, and Discrimination* (Westport, Conn: Greenwood Press, 1985); Will Kymlicka, *Multicultural Citizenship. A Liberal Theory of Minority Rights* (Oxford: Oxford University Press, 1995); Jackson Preece, op. cit., note 11; Eduardo Ruiz Vieytez, *The History of Legal Protection of Minorities in Europe, XVII–XX Centuries* (Derby: University of Derby, 1999); Kristin Henrard, *Devising an Adequate System of Minority Protection. Individual Human Rights, Minority Rights, and Self-Determination* (The Hague: Martinus Nijhoff Publishers, 2000).

19 Michael Keating, *State and Regional Nationalism: Territorial Politics and the European State* (London: Harvester-Wheatsheaf, 1988); Hurst Hannum, *Autonomy, Sovereignty, and Self-Determination: The Accommodation of Conflicting Rights*, 2nd edition (Philadelphia: University of Pennsylvania Press, 1996); Will Kymlicka, *Multicultural Citizenship. A Liberal Theory of Minority Rights* (Oxford: Oxford University Press, 1995); Michael Keating, *The New Regionalism in Western Europe. Territorial Restructuring and Political Change* (Cheltenham: Edward Elgar, 1998); Michael Keating, *Plurinational Democracy. Stateless Nations in a Post-Sovereignty Era* (Oxford: Oxford University Press, 2001); Will Kymlicka and Magda Opalski eds., *Can Liberal Pluralism be Ex-*

ported? Western Political Theory and Ethnic Relations in Eastern Europe (Oxford: Oxford University Press, 2001); Michael Keating and John McGarry eds., *Minority Nationalism and the Changing International Order* (Oxford: Oxford University Press, 2001); Tove H. Malloy, *National Minority Rights in Europe* (Oxford University Press, 2005).

20 For an overview of autonomy arrangements, see Hannum, op. cit., note 20.

21 Tove H. Malloy, "National Minority 'Regions' in the Enlarged European Union: Mobilizing for Third Level Politics?" *ECMI Working Paper* 24 (Flensburg: ECMI, 2005); Tove H. Malloy, "Forging Territorial Cohesion in Diversity: Are National Minorities Promoting Fourth-Level Integration?" in *The Protection of Minorities in the Wider Europe*, eds. Marc Weller, Denika Blacklock and Katherine Nobbs (Basingstoke: Palgrave Macmillan, 2008) pp. 54–91; Tove H. Malloy, "Creating New Spaces for Politics? The Role of National Minorities in Building Capacities of Cross-Border Regions" in *Regional and Federal Studies* 20 (2010), pp. 335–51.

22 Martin Klatt, *Fra modspil til medspil? Grænseoverskridende samarbejde i Sønderjylland/Schleswig 1945–2005* (Aabenraa: Institut for Grænseregionsforskning, University of Southern Denmark, 2006); Zoe Bray, *Boundaries and Identities in Bidasoa-Txingudi, on the Franco-Spanish frontier*, PhD-thesis, European University Institute, 2002.

23 Christian Joppke, *Immigration and the Nation-State: The United States, Germany, and Great Britain* (Oxford: Oxford University Press, 1999) and *Citizenship and Immigration* (Cambridge: Polity Press, 2010); Christian Joppke ed., *Challenge to the Nation-State: Immigration in Western Europe and the United States* (Oxford: Oxford University Press, 1998).

24 For a good exception see for instance, Keith Banting and Will Kymlicka, *Multiculturalism and the Welfare State. Recognition and Redistribution in Contemporary Democracies* (Oxford University Press, 2006).

25 The trend started with Clifford Geertz' seminal study, *The Interpretation of Cultures: Selected Essays* (New York: Basic, 1973).

26 Mark Blyth, "Institutions and Ideas" in Marsh and Stoker, op. cit., note 5, pp. 292–310.

27 Vivien Lowndes, "Institutionalism" in Marsh and Stoker, op. cit., note 5, pp. 90–108.

PART I

Chapter 1: European History of Minority Relations

Raul Cârstocea

Summary

The history of majority-minority relations in Europe from 1555 to 1945 exhibits the progressive emergence of mechanisms offering guarantees and varying degrees of protection to minority groups. Beginning with religious freedoms that can be traced back to the Late Middle Ages, extending to notions of civil and political rights in the context of the emergence of the modern, secular nation-state, and finally encompassing linguistic rights and a certain degree of cultural protection, the evolution of the rights of minority groups in Europe tells a story in which considerations pertaining to international peace and security gradually gave way to a liberal, rights-based understanding of politics, as well as illuminating the ensuing tensions between the two. As multinational empires gave way to nation-states and ethnicity or language replaced religion as the primary marker of identity, new political arrangements were designed to respond to these developments. Beyond the diversity of approaches to the treatment of religious or national minorities, the picture that emerges is one where significant modifications of international borders and political upheavals were consistently accompanied by changes in the status and degree of protection of minority groups. And this shows, in contrast to the linguistic connotation of the term 'minority', the centrality and importance of minority relations, and, ultimately, of minorities as such, however defined, to the very core of Europe's historical legacy.

Introduction

This chapter provides a succinct history of the diverse arrangements for the protection of minorities in Europe, from its earliest beginnings concerning guarantees of religious freedoms for minority groups to the establishment of an international minority regime after World War I and its eventual demise as a result of World War II. The history of the evolution of minority-majority relations and of the development of minority rights is meant to endow students with a historical perspective enabling them to understand that the contemporary minority rights regime is not an abstract creation occurring in a political vacuum, but the result of specific European historical processes that affected the ways in which minorities were conceptualized at different times in Europe's history and that progressively led to a higher degree of protection and eventually to the empowerment of minority groups, in spite of considerable setbacks and permanent re-negotiation. For purposes of brevity, the chapter follows an approach focusing on the most significant international accords and treaties that embedded changes in the status of minority groups, while also devoting attention to the political ideas and ideologies that influenced such changes. The primary assumption informing the presentation is that adopting a historical perspective to the evolution of minority rights allows us to see how all the important developments in international politics during the period under consideration were consistently accompanied by modifications in the status and degree of protection of minority groups. This aspect emphasizes the importance of studying minority-majority relations, as well as providing a historical context that permits assessing the relative importance, at different times, of the forces impacting upon their evolution. Students should consequently acquire an awareness of continuity and change in the history of the protection of minority groups over an extended timespan. The chapter is divided into five sections, covering respectively (I) the early beginnings of minority rights in the form of religious freedoms; (II) the emergence of nationalism and the increasing recognition of minority groups as national rather than religious; (III) the establishment of minority rights obligations as part of international treaties; (IV) the institutionalization of minority rights and their placement under the guarantee of an international organisation, the League of Nations; and (V) the functioning of the League of Nations, its limitations and demise.

Early beginnings: religious freedoms

As religion was the primary marker of social identity in Europe before the modern period, the history of minorities in the European space begins as a history of religious minorities rather than national ones, and the former can be said to have acted at least to some extent as a blueprint for arrangements concerning the latter. Dating back to ancient times, and involving significant persecutions of minority groups that were perceived as deviating from norms of behavior defined according to religious principles, religious minorities first came to be recognized and to some degree protected as such following the wars of religion between Christian and Muslim political entities over control of the Middle East, seen as the 'Holy Land' by both religions. One of the results of these conflicts was the regime of the capitulations which guaranteed to Christians in the Levant the right to appeal to the jurisdiction of their countries of origin, through the medium of consular courts. These were the result of bilateral negotiations between the states in question, were largely dependent on the good will of the Oriental sovereigns, and were often limited in scope, failing to prevent widespread discrimination and frequent persecutions.[1] Moreover, as with later provisions, these capitulations applied only to Christians who were subjects of certain states, and not to other religious minorities, such as the Jews.

A further important development in the history of religious minorities in Europe was introduced by the Ottoman Empire following the conquest of Constantinople (1453). Under the millet system, antedated by similar provisions in other Muslim states but fully established by sultan Muhammad II Fātih after 1453, the principle of religious tolerance was extended to non-Christian communities as well. As such, the main millets in the Ottoman Empire were the Greek Orthodox, Jewish, Armenian and Syrian Orthodox; smaller religious communities, such as the Catholics, Karaites, or Samaritans were also organized according to this system, and by the 19th century seventeen millets existed in the empire. Furthermore, rather than being limited to consular rights, the millet system provided for extensive autonomy for religious communities, which were given jurisdiction over education, social security, tax collection, health, religious affairs and family law matters.[2] While showing a degree of pluralism in the management of a multi-confessional empire, the millet system was however far from being based on a notion of the equality of all religions, but was rather predicated on the idea of the superiority of Islam over all other religions.

In Central and Western Europe, the Reformation challenged the previously undisputed position of Catholicism and made religious differences into an integral part of the European heritage. In its wake, wars of religion shook the very heart of Europe, and the new territorial arrangements that followed them saw a gradual but steady erosion of the dynastic empires and of the horizontal structure of feudal society, and the emergence of the modern international system of sovereign territorial states. At this time, the homogenizing principle within the emerging sovereign states was still religion and not nationality or ethnicity, as evidenced in the *cujus regio ejus religio* principle (translatable as 'whose realm, his religion'), explicitly mentioned for the first time in the Peace of Augsburg (1555). The Peace of Augsburg was a treaty signed by Charles V, Emperor of the Holy Roman Empire, and representatives of the Schmalkaldic League, an alliance of Lutheran princes, officially concluding the first major conflict between Catholics and Protestants. The aforementioned principle within the treaty allowed Lutheran and Catholic princes to choose the religion for the domains they controlled, thus providing for internal religious homogeneity within a principality, while allowing dissenting religious minorities to leave the territory with their possessions. However, the treaty was limited in its scope, recognizing an equal status to the Catholic faith only for Lutheranism (referred to in the treaty as 'the Augsburg confession') and not for the other Reformed confessions, such as Calvinism or Anabaptism. Furthermore, under the principle of *reservatum ecclesiasticum*, a prince-bishop who chose to convert to Lutheranism had to give up the territories he ruled.[3]

The Peace of Augsburg represented only a partial solution to the religious tensions in Europe, further exacerbated by the Counter-Reformation and the spread of Calvinism. The Cologne War of 1583–1588 exposed the weaknesses of the peace treaty, arising when a prince-archbishop of the city of Cologne converted to Calvinism. Against the background of the wars of religion fought between Catholics and Protestants ('Huguenots') in France (1562–1598) and the revolt of the seventeen protestant provinces in the Low Countries against the Counter-Reformation policies promoted by Phillip II of Spain (1568–1648), the mounting religious tensions in Europe culminated in the Thirty Years' War (1618–1648). The war pitched the Holy Roman Empire and its Catholic allies against Protestant states and their allies, including Catholic France (in an attempt to thwart the power of the Habsburgs and increase the influence of the Bourbon dynasty), the Christian Orthodox Zaporozhian Cossacks, and the Ottoman Empire. With a death-toll of almost 8,000,000 casualties including civilians, the war was one of the longest and most destructive conflicts in European history, and the first such conflict to involve most of the countries in Europe, making it the first war with a European dimension.[4]

The series of peace treaties signed between May and October 1648 in Osnabrück and Münster, generally referred to as the Peace of Westphalia (1648), marked the end of the Thirty Years' War. Widely considered by historians as a landmark signaling the beginning of the modern political order, in which sovereign states increasingly prevailed over dynastic empires as the main unit of international relations, the peace treaties included significant territorial adjustments and a general recognition of the exclusive sovereignty of a ruler over both people and territory. Yet more importantly for the history of minorities in Europe, the Peace of Westphalia also placed Calvinism on an equal footing with Catholicism and Lutheranism. At the same time, the provisions of the Treaty of Münster included the first explicit recognition of the rights of religious minorities within a state to freely practice their religion, in public at allotted times and in private at their will.[5] While the primary concern of the states involved in the conflict was at this point with maintaining international peace and stability and was not based on any conception of inalienable rights, the principle of religious tolerance established in the Peace of Westphalia (no longer involving population transfers but guarantees for a religious minority within a sovereign territory where the majority religion was of another denomination) represented a very important precedent for later developments in international law. Similar provisions were subsequently included in other treaties concluded at the end of the numerous conflicts that involved territorial adjustments in 17th and 18th Century Europe, such as the Treaty of Oliva (1660), the Treaty of Nijmegen (1678–1679), the Treaty of Ryswick (1697), the Treaty of Dresden (1745), the Treaty of Hubertusburg (1763), etc.[6]

The Enlightenment and the emergence of nationalism

In the 18th century, notions of political legitimacy based on the doctrine of the divine right of kings and entitlements from marriage, succession, purchase or conquest came under increasing attack from political philosophers, as they began to explore the normative relationship between the ruler and the ruled. Arguing for a political system that involved the consent of the governed, the Enlightenment challenged traditional views of legitimacy, introducing concepts of natural law and natural rights, popular sovereignty, political representation, and tolerance. These ideas found political expression with the American and French Revolutions, which squarely placed notions of the universal, inalienable rights of all citizens at the core of government. Despite limitations that restricted citizenship to propertied white males, thus excluding women, foreigners and men who were not property owners, as well as failing to tackle the issue of slavery, the declarations issued by the American and French revolutionaries were permeated by liberal democratic principles and consequently exerted considerable influence on the further development of rights-based liberal democracy.[7]

The French Revolution of 1789 extended these notions of natural rights from individuals to nations as well, with the Declaration of the Rights of Man and of the Citizen explicitly stating that 'the principle of all sovereignty resides essentially in the nation'.[8] The national idea, anticipated in the philosophy of the Enlightenment, subsequently gained increasing political weight in 19th century Europe as an alternative legitimizing principle challenging the former dynastic and religious allegiances, and represented the basis of a specifically modern political entity, the nation-state, whose existence was predicated on the congruence of the borders of the nation and the state. Paradoxically perhaps, notions of national self-determination were encouraged in certain parts of Europe by Napoleon in the context of his conquest, and, even when the French imperial ambitions were thwarted by the alliance of the other Great Powers, they found their expression in the numerous movements for national independence rising against the multinational empires of the 19th century. At the Congress of Vienna (1815), which marked the end of the Napoleonic Wars and was meant to prevent future hegemonic ambitions by a new balance of power system known as the Concert of Europe (representing a general framework for European politics until World War I and a predecessor of later international organizations such as the League of Nations and the United Nations), minority rights were recognized for the first time in international treaties as pertaining to national rather than religious groups.[9] Referring to the partition of Poland, the treaty stated that the Poles, who are respective subjects of Russia, Austria, and Prussia, shall obtain a representation, and National institutions, regulated according to the degree of political consideration, that each of the Governments to which they belong shall judge expedient and proper to grant them.[10] While no explicit guarantees or enforcement mechanisms were associated with these provisions, they would later be invoked by France and Great Britain in their protests against the actions of the Russian Empire. Furthermore, civil and political rights, and not only religious freedoms, were for the first time guaranteed for minority groups subject to territorial adjustments.

Throughout the 19th century, the granting of full civil and political rights to groups that increasingly identified themselves and mobilized along national lines is to be understood partly as an attempt of multinational empires to contain the rising tide of nationalism that would eventually lead to their collapse. The civic notion of the nation that had been one of the driving forces of the American and French Revolutions was however hardly suitable for the significant ethnic groups in Central and Eastern Europe living in multinational empires where they were in a subordinate position to the dominant group, and where calls for independence from foreign rule were based on an alternative form of national affiliation, a shared ethnic culture.[11] Movements for independence consequently sprung up all over Central and Eastern Europe (and not only, as was the case with the revolution that led to the establishment of independent Belgium in 1830) at the beginning of the 19th century, culminating in 1848 with the wave of revolutions that came to be known also as the 'Spring of Nations'. The Revolutions of 1848, while politically unsuccessful and defeated by imperial forces in the space of one year, set however into motion forces that eventually led to the *Risorgimento* and the unification of Italy (proclaimed a Kingdom in 1861, completely unified in 1870), to the unification of Germany (completed in 1871), and to the *Ausgleich* of 1866 which entailed *de facto* full Hungarian autonomy within the redefined Dual Monarchy of Austria-Hungary. In addition, the revolutions gave further impetus to the national movements of Czechs, Slovaks, Poles, Ukrainians, Romanians, Croats, Serbs, and Slovenes within the Habsburg and Ottoman Empires, resulting in their achieving a higher degree of autonomy and political representation within the empires or, in the case of Romania, Serbia and Montenegro, to outright independence following the Russo-Turkish War of 1877–1878.[12] As such, just as nationalism had become the most important driving force in European politics during the course of the 19th century, so did the issue of national minorities come to the fore in the context of the emergence of new nation-states, just as it became increasingly clear on the one hand that the idea of an overlap between national and state boundaries was a practical impossibility, and on the other that the opposing drives towards assimilation and exclusion of minority groups were two of the potential negative consequences of the nationalist orientation within the realm of international politics.

The Congress of Berlin (1878) and the establishment of minority rights obligations

If previous treaties made reference to the rights of religious or national minorities as expressions of benevolence or voluntary recognition on behalf of the state within the borders of which minority groups were to be found, those agreed upon by the representatives of the Great Powers (which now included the recently unified Kingdom of Italy and the German Empire) at the Congress of Berlin (1878) were the first to stipulate minority rights obligations.[13] The Congress, convened at the end of the Russo-Turkish War of 1877–1878 under German leadership, dealt with the changed balance of power in the Balkans, in an attempt to account for the declining power of the Ottoman Empire and to contain the Russian gains and growing influence in the region. More importantly for the purpose of minority rights, the Congress addressed the issue of the independence of Romania, Serbia and Montenegro, the establishment of Bulgaria as an independent principality within the Ottoman Empire, as well as the territorial changes that ensued as a result. The recognition of these countries' independence (including Bulgaria) was conditioned by their granting of equal civil and political rights to the minority groups within their new borders and their acceptance of the principle of non-discrimination on the basis of religion. Articles 5, 27, 35, 44 and 62 of the Treaty of Berlin, dealing respectively with Bulgaria, Montenegro, Serbia, Romania and the Ottoman Empire, guaranteed that differences in religious affiliation would not constitute a reason for excluding any person from the enjoyment of full civil and political rights in these states.[14]

There were multiple inter-related reasons behind these stipulations, which are important to take note of also because they anticipate later developments implemented at the end of World War I. First of all, they denoted the increasing Great Power awareness that any redrawing of borders in Europe would not be able to accomplish in practice the ethnic homogeneity that the nation-state was predicated on, least of all in Eastern Europe, and that significant ethnic and religious minorities would be left within the borders of the new states. Second, they exemplified both a reinforced commitment to a liberal and decisively secular conception of rights and the express desire to ensure that what was perceived as the mistreatment of minority groups under Ottoman rule would not occur again in the newly independent states. As such, they were designed to guarantee what has been referred to as a 'standard of civilization' as a precondition for the recognition of the new states as full (but not quite equal) members of international society. This latter aspect points toward a third motivation behind the imposition of minority rights obligations, i.e. the perception of the new Eastern European states as 'backward' by comparison to the Great Powers, in need of tutelage in their adoption of modern, liberal principles of rule.[15]

This paternalistic approach to the obligations set out for the newly independent states reflected on the one hand a new, explicitly interventionist orientation in international politics, although the only such intervention that actually occurred—the postponing of recognition of Romania's independence until 1880 due to its refusal to emancipate the Jewish minority—did not prevent Romania's *de facto* disregard of its obligations through a procedural subterfuge.[16] The most significant weakness of the minority rights obligations imposed at the Congress of Berlin was in fact that no explicit enforcement mechanisms were associated with them, the provisions being merely placed formally under the guarantee of the Great Powers. This potential threat of foreign interference was nevertheless strongly resented by the new nation-states that had recently gained their independence from foreign rule, and came to represent a constant source of tension in the years leading up to World War I. On the other hand, the paternalistic imposition of such obligations and the notions of the inherent Eastern European backwardness or inferiority reflected some of the prevailing ideas in fin-de-siècle Europe, where notions of racial inequality were becoming widespread at this time. Consequently, a nationalist ideology that had been associated with liberal principles and political emancipation at the beginning of the 19th century was gradually becoming more exclusionary and aggressive, and the rise of modern, ideological anti-Semitism was symptomatic of this shift. In a period when Europe's empires were confronted with growing national movements at home, this was also the time of the 'scramble for Africa', when colonial policies inspired by pseudo-scientific racism and eugenic ideas anticipated outside Europe some of the horrors of the two world wars, of the 'new imperialism' that saw a proliferation of chauvinism and jingoism, and, in the clash of rival imperial powers, led directly to World War I.

At the same time that seemed to witness the zenith of nationalism in ever more extreme forms, socialism provided an internationalist challenge to the dominant ideology of the day. Socialist thinkers, originating mostly from the multinational empires of Austria-Hungary, Germany and Russia, were fully aware of the problems engendered by the aspirations for self-determination of the national minorities within the borders of empires, and put forth their own, alternative views regarding the resolution of national minority issues in interpretations that emphasised the importance of economic factors and departed from a liberal paradigm that focused on the one hand almost exclusively on the nation-state and on the other on the preservation of the existing international balance of power. As such, Vladimir Lenin took the principle of national self-determination to its radical conclusion, arguing in his debates with Austrian, Dutch, German, or Polish social democrats that its Marxist interpretation necessarily entails the right to secession of every oppressed nation, and thus dismissing all arguments about the questionable viability of small independent states. In Lenin's view, a radical form of self-determination represented the only possible premise to the international solidarity that the working class movement saw as its ultimate goal.[17] This view stood in contrast to the widely held 19th century conception (espoused not only by liberals such as John Stuart Mill, but also by Karl Marx and Friedrich Engels) that saw a distinction between the so-called 'great nations' (such as England, France, Germany, Italy, Poland, etc.), viewed as civilized creators of great culture, and lesser nationalities, who were seen as 'primitive' and 'incapable' of cultural and political development (such as the Czechs, Slovaks, Croats, Basques, etc.), and consequently supplied the legitimizing principle for the assimilation of the latter to the former.[18]

Yet another contrasting view, put forth by Otto Bauer and Karl Renner, prominent representatives of Austro-Marxism, was not aimed at a revolutionary revision of the existing state borders, but argued instead for a non-territorial form of national autonomy. Conferring a positive value on cultural diversity, and anticipating in many ways contemporary debates about multiculturalism, Bauer and Renner's views on non-territorial autonomy transcended the paradigm that predicated a dichotomy between majority and minority groups, proposing a notion of collective representation of national groups as a basis for reforming the Austro-Hungarian Empire.[19] Criticised at the time by more radical Marxists as arguing for the preservation of the status quo, such notions were indeed being contemplated by the Austro-Hungarian leadership before the outbreak of World War I, in what appeared at the time as a desperate attempt to reform a breakaway empire. Moreover, after passing unnoticed for a long time, the idea of non-territorial autonomy has been making a remarkable comeback in recent years as part of the effort to ensure representative governance in multinational societies.

World War I and its aftermath: the new international order and the Minority Treaties

All hopes for reform of the multinational empires were shattered with the shot that killed the Archduke Franz Ferdinand of Austria, the heir to the throne of Austria-Hungary, on 28 June 1914. It was not a mere accident that the shot was fired by Gavrilo Princip, a Bosnian Serb student who was a member of *Mlada Bosna* (Young Bosnia), a revolutionary nationalist movement militating for a union of the South Slavs and independence from Austria-Hungary.[20] A fragile balance of power that saw escalating tensions between the Great Powers as a result of colonialism eventually collapsed with the spark that lit up the Balkan 'tinderbox', where conflicts prompted by nationalism and territorial claims had already led to two Balkan Wars (1912 and 1913). The resulting conflict was more destructive than any the world had ever witnessed previously, spreading to Africa, Asia and the Pacific to become the first conflict in history that can be described as a global war. The scale and nature of warfare also differed significantly from previous conflicts, involving a general mobilization of people and resources that has led to its identification as 'total war'. With the number of casualties estimated to have been over 37 million, the war also saw large-scale atrocities committed against civilian populations, including cases of pogroms and ethnic cleansing, with the massacres of Armenians, Assyrians and Greeks by the Ottoman Empire being widely considered today as an outright campaign of genocide—although Turkey, the successor state to the Ottoman Empire, continues to this day to steadfastly deny the claim.[21]

The aftermath of the war involved the most far-reaching redrawing of borders in Europe's history. The European multinational empires (the Habsburg, German, Ottoman and Russian Empires) collapsed, their place on the map taken up by new nation-states (Poland, Czechoslovakia, Albania, Finland, Lithuania, Latvia, Estonia) or considerably enlarged ones (the Kingdom of Serbs, Croats and Slovenes, later Yugoslavia, Greece, and Romania), at the expense of considerable losses of territory and population for the successor states of the Central Powers (Austria, Hungary, Germany, Turkey, Bulgaria). Coupled with the impact of the Russian Revolution of 1917, which saw the establishment of the first totalitarian dictatorship in Europe, and of the short-lived communist revolutions in other countries (most notably Hungary and Germany), coordinated attempts were made by the victorious Allied powers to consolidate the new states so as to create a buffer zone between the Soviet Union and Germany. This was all the more important since the ensuing Civil War in the Soviet Union presented ramifications into inter-state conflicts (the Finnish Civil War of 1918, the wars in the Baltic States between 1918 and 1920, the Polish-Soviet War of 1919–1921) that threatened stability and peace on the continent.

The liberal idea of national self-determination put forth in United States President's Woodrow Wilson's famous 'Fourteen Points' address to the US Congress on 8 January 1918, which constituted the basis of the American approach to the peace process, proved impossible to apply in Central and Eastern Europe insofar as it aimed at the creation of ethnically homogeneous nation-states. The redrawing of borders could not be carried out according to a single principle; instead, multiple considerations—demographic patterns, socio-economic considerations, geographical features, notions of 'historic right', strategic and security concerns, etc.—were combined, and almost always to the detriment of the losing side, that of the Central Powers. Some ethnic groups (Ruthenians, Ukrainians, Byelorussians) did not obtain independent statehood. Others (Croats, Slovenes, Slovaks) found themselves in multi-national states in which they felt they were in a subordinate position vis-à-vis other groups (Serbs, Czechs). Former dominant groups (most notably Germans and Hungarians) were left as significant minorities within the borders of the newly created or expanded states; no longer enjoying their previously privileged position as imperial elites, they resented their new status among (mostly) Slavic populations they had long regarded as inferior. Consequently, rather than accomplishing anything resembling ethnic homogeneity, some of the new nation-states reproduced within their borders the same pattern of ethnic and cultural diversity that had been characteristic of the pre-war multinational empires. In Czechoslovakia, national minorities accounted for 35% of the population (of which 24% Germans), not counting the Slovaks (16% of the population) who were themselves dissatisfied with their situation in the new state and consistently attempted to obtain more autonomy.[22] In Poland, minorities constituted approximately 33% of the population, with 15% Ukrainians, 9% Jews, 5% Byelorussians, 2% Germans and 1% Lithuanians.[23] In Greater Romania (as the enlarged interwar state came to be known), the proportion of national minorities increased almost fourfold, from 7.9% before the war to 28.1%.[24] This situation showed the limits of the Wilsonian self-determination approach to the peace process, partly due to Wilson's unfamiliarity with the demographic pattern in Central and Eastern Europe, and brought to the fore the necessity of introducing additional mechanisms for the protection of national minority groups within the redrawn borders.[25]

As a result, the Paris Peace Conference, convened in 1919, was informed by multiple considerations aimed at achieving a viable political solution that would prevent future destructive conflicts on the scale Europe had just witnessed. Several conflicting views of the peace treaty were put forth by the delegates of the Allied countries, the foremost of which was that between the peace of reconciliation articulated in Wilson's 'Fourteen Points' and the punitive peace that a majority of the public in Britain and France (as well as Belgium, Italy and Serbia), the countries that had borne the brunt of the war, asked for. In general terms, this dispute corresponded to the clash between a liberal rights-based conception of politics and the *Realpolitik* that had dominated 19th century international relations. All of these elements, from the idealist Wilsonian upholding of the principle of national self-determination for the countries in Central and Eastern Europe, through security concerns aimed to prevent the spread of communism and attempts to ensure that the successor states to the imperial Central Powers were considerably weakened so as to prevent future aggression, to genuine concern about the continuation of ethnic violence (particularly against the Jews) in certain areas, influenced the decision-making process and led to the establishment of the Committee for New States.[26] The purpose of the committee was to draft treaties for the protection of minorities in the new and enlarged states in Central and Eastern Europe.

This instance marked the first time in European history when Minority Treaties were drafted separately from peace agreements and explicitly acknowledged as such. Moreover, also for the first time, these were not to be guaranteed by individual Great Powers, but placed under the aegis of a newly created international organisation, the League of Nations. The establishment of the latter was called for in the last of Wilson's Fourteen Points and was aimed to act as the guarantor of the principle of national self-determination, providing "mutual guarantees of political independence and territorial integrity to great and small states alike."[27] The first Minority Treaty was the one signed with Poland, on the same day as the Treaty of Versailles, 28 June 1919. Its provisions, consisting of 12 articles, represented a framework for the other treaties: the Treaties of Saint-Germain-en-Laye (10 September 1919), signed respectively with Czechoslovakia and the Kingdom of Serbs, Croats and Slovenes; the Treaty of Paris (9 December 1919), signed with Romania; the Treaties of Sèvres (10 August 1920), signed respectively with Greece and Armenia.[28] Obligations regarding the protection of minorities were also included in the treaties whereby Albania, Estonia, Latvia and Lithuania joined the League of Nations. Finally, provisions regarding minority rights were also included in the Peace Treaties with some of the successor states of the Central Powers, respectively Austria (Saint-Germain-en-Laye, 10 September 1919), Bulgaria (Neuilly-sur-Seine, 27 November 1919), Hungary (Trianon, 4 June 1920), and Turkey (Lausanne, 24 July 1923).[29] Finland was exempt, as were France, Belgium, Denmark, Italy, and, most notably, defeated Germany.[30] This unequal application of the principle reflected the same outlook that had inspired the drafting of minority rights obligations at the Congress of Berlin, whereby the new states in Central and Eastern Europe were deemed intrinsically illiberal and 'inexperienced' in matters of government, although as Ignacy Jan Paderewski—the Polish Prime Minister and representative at the Peace Conference—noted, Greece antedated Italy, which possessed the status of 'Great Power', by 30 years.³¹ Consequently, the newly established or enlarged states in Central and Eastern Europe strongly resented the Minority Treaties, viewing them as an infringement of state sovereignty and decrying their status as second-class members of international society.

There were five general provisions in the Polish Minority Treaty which were consequently applied to all the states that entered such agreements. The first regarded the automatic acquisition of citizenship by a) persons habitually residing in the country's territory or possessing rights of residence there at the time when the treaty came into force and b) persons born in the territory of parents domiciled there at the time of their birth, even if they were not habitually resident there when the treaty came into force. This was coupled with the right to opt for a different citizenship, case in which the respective person would have to transfer to the territory of the state for which they opted within a period of 12 months. All persons who could not claim another citizenship automatically became citizens of the new state. The second provision entailed full and complete protection of life and liberty without distinction of birth, nationality, language, race or religion and the free exercise of any creed, religion or belief whose practices were not inconsistent with public order or public morals. The third guaranteed full equality before the law and the enjoyment of equal civil and political rights without distinction as to race, language or religion. According to the fourth provision, states could not restrict the use of any minority language in private intercourse, in commerce, in religion, in the press or in publications of any kind, or at public meetings, and facilities were to be provided for the use of minority languages before the courts. Furthermore, national minorities could set up at their own expense charitable, religious and social institutions, schools and other educational establishments, with the right to use their own language and to exercise their religion freely therein. Finally, the fifth provision stated that in towns and districts where there lived a considerable proportion of nationals belonging to racial, religious or linguistic minorities, these minorities were to be shall be assured an equitable share of public funds for educational, religious or charitable purposes.³² While the first article of the treaty entailed the recognition of these provisions as constituting fundamental laws, over which no other legal acts could prevail, the concluding article defined the stipulations as 'obligations of international concern [...] placed under the guarantee of the League of Nations'.³³ In addition to these general stipulations, special provisions (mostly entailing various measures concerning local autonomy and self-government) were included in the different treaties applying to the Jewish minorities in Poland, Romania, and Greece; the Muslim minorities in Yugoslavia, Greece, and Albania; the Szeklers and Saxons in Romania; the Ruthenians in Czechoslovakia; the Vlachs of Pindus in Greece; and the non-Greek (Russian, Serbian, Bulgarian) monastic communities of Mount Athos.[34]

On the one hand, these stipulations can be said to represent, at least in their intention, the high point of liberalism in the evolution of national minority rights. In addition to religious freedoms and civil and political rights, linguistic rights and a certain degree of cultural protection were guaranteed for the first time for minority groups. Moreover, at least formally, through the placing of these obligations under the guarantee of an international organisation, the minority treaties appeared to mark a decisive break from the balance of power considerations that had informed previous international arrangements concerning minority protection. The Minority Treaties, the first of their kind in history, thus represented an important step towards the protection of national minorities; for the first time, there was an official political recognition of the fact that nations were not necessarily homogeneous, and that the national minorities finding themselves in a foreign territory required additional guarantees for their well-being. An external, international body to foster the promotion of their rights was a much-welcomed creation. On the other hand, however, the practical implementation of the new minority rights regime, the procedural problems associated with its monitoring by the League of Nations, and an unequal application of the minority obligation that was reminiscent of the ones imposed on the Balkan states at the Congress of Berlin posed serious limitations to what appeared in principle as a very liberal international commitment.

The functioning of the League of Nations and its limitations

As already anticipated in the previous section, one of the most significant shortcomings of the Minority Treaties was that they were not seen as universally applicable, but were only designed for the 'new' states in Central and Eastern Europe. A Japanese proposal for global national and racial equality was thwarted by American, British and French opposition to what they perceived as a threat to their own colonial empires and to the segregation of African Americans in the United States.[35] The Western European powers, faced with growing dissension and rising national movements within their own borders or in the colonies (from Ireland, Wales, Scotland, Flanders, Alsace, Catalonia, and the Basque country to Egypt and India), were reluctant to apply at home the same principles they imposed on the successor states of the defeated empires in the name of liberal values. This led to the resentment of the treaty-bound states over arrangements seen as involving a paternalistic attitude, interference of Great Powers in the internal affairs of the state, and ultimately injustice and great power bias, involving a distinction between first class and second class countries. These were by and large the same complaints that had been expressed at the Congress of Berlin, reflecting the fact that the *Realpolitik* view of international relations was still structurally ingrained in the peace accord, despite its significant advancements in the direction of a more liberal view of politics.

Furthermore, the newly created League of Nations was crippled from its inception by the refusal to join of the United States, the very proponent of the organisation. Germany, the country with the largest number of nationals living outside its borders, was excluded from the League until 1925, and the Soviet Union did not join until 1934, by which time both Germany and Poland, the primary antagonists over minority issues in the League, had left it. The organisation was also rendered powerless by the lack of any enforcement mechanisms pertaining either to its role in monitoring the observance of minority rights obligations or to its collective security guarantee. As a result, these were left once again dependent on the goodwill and willingness to intervene of individual states; Britain and France's reluctance to intervene in such matters where their own national interests were not directly at stake meant that in practical terms the minority issues raised at the League of Nations often became the objects of dispute between the states involved in the matter, degenerating frequently into political struggles between revisionist states and those that aimed to preserve the status quo (e.g. Germany vs. Poland or Czechoslovakia, Poland vs. Lithuania, Hungary vs. Romania, Austria vs. Yugoslavia, Bulgaria vs. Greece, Greece vs. Turkey, etc.).[36] Consequently, instead of accomplishing its goal of promoting international cooperation, the League paradoxically generated more international enmity.

This problem was compounded by the irredentist or revisionist agenda of some of the former dominant groups in the pre-war multinational empires who found themselves in a subordinate position in the newly established or enlarged states (e.g. Germans in Poland and Czechoslovakia, Hungarians in Czechoslovakia and Romania). Often with the support of their kin-states, these groups used petitions to the League of Nations as part of the attempt to demonstrate the injustice of the peace terms or the ineffectiveness of minority guarantees, ultimately seeking to challenge the post-war settlement. These represented the bulk of the petitions put forth to the organisation, with those submitted by German minorities challenging Poland's observance of its national minority obligations making up 30% of the total received by the League.[37] Coupled with the separatist agendas of other national minorities (e.g. Croats in Yugoslavia, Slovaks in Czechoslovakia, Ukrainians in Poland), the revisionist claims supported by minority groups in the successor states constituted an important factor contributing to the destabilization of post-war European politics. Such claims were opposed by the counter-revisionist efforts undertaken by the beneficiaries of the peace treaty, leading to the creation of separate alliances (such as the Little Entente established by Czechoslovakia, Romania and Yugoslavia in 1920–1921, supported by France), which eventually proved ineffectual as well and only contributed to the proliferation of animosity between the revisionist states and those that sought to preserve the status quo.

The complex procedure according to which minority petitions could be put forth to the League of Nations and its subsequent amendments were also partly responsible for the ultimate failure of the organisation to ensure adequate protection of national minority rights. According to the final article of the Minority Treaties, responsibility for monitoring the implementation and observance of the Treaties lay with the Council of the League of Nations, with differences of opinion or disputes between a state and the Council being referred to the Permanent Court of International Justice (known also as the World Court). The Council was made up of four permanent members (Great Britain, France, Italy and Japan) and four non-permanent members that were elected by the Assembly of the League of Nations (which consisted of representatives of all the countries in the organisation) for a three-year term.[38] Although minority petitions could be sent to the League from any source, only individual Council members could place them on the agenda, which in practical terms meant that only states could take up the cause of national minority groups. A so-called 'Committee of Three', an ad hoc panel consisting of three members of the Council, decided whether a complaint should be brought to the attention of the Council; moreover, the state accused of breaching its minority obligations was allowed two months (a period extended to four months by a subsequent amendment) to formulate a response before this decision was made. Following the accused state's response, a decision could be made to bring the case to the Council, to dismiss it altogether, or to negotiate it secretly with the state so as to obtain a 'minimum number of concessions or reforms' that would resolve the issue.[39] The latter was by far the most frequent of the three possible outcomes, which, coupled with the fact that only cases that were brought to the attention of the Council or the Permanent Court of International Justice were made public, ensured that the entire procedure remained shrouded in secrecy. An amendment to the procedure passed in 1923 identified five conditions of receivability that had to be met by any petition submitted: 1) it must have had in view the protection of minorities in accordance with the treaties; 2) it could not be submitted in the form of a request for severance of the political relations between the minority in question and the state it was part of; 3) it could not originate from an anonymous or unauthenticated source; 4) it could not contain violent language; 5) it could not contain information or facts that had made the object of another recent petition.[40]

Several conclusions can be drawn from examining the procedural functioning of the League of Nations with regards to the petitions concerning the protection of minority rights. The procedure had a clear statist outlook, giving more weight to national sovereignty than to collective decision-making, and seeking to minimize the impact of complaints raised by non-state groups. It was essentially a conciliatory procedure, "designed to provide minimum enforcement of the treaties without inciting minorities or alienating their governments", on whose cooperation the system ultimately depended.[41] Thus, in its actual functioning, the League of Nations was eventually governed more by traditional, statist views of international relations than by the spirit of an international, collective commitment to the promotion of a rights-based understanding of politics. Coupled with other inadequacies (such as understaffing) which led to excessive delays in its procedure, this led some critics to characterize the League's policy as "directed more to protecting the states against their minorities than the minorities against oppression by the state."[42]

The result was that national minorities benefitted to different degrees from the treaties that aimed to guarantee their protection. Due to its statist bias, the system promoted mostly the demands of 'strong' minorities supported by kin-states, which, paradoxically, especially in the case of the former imperial elites of Austria-Hungary and Germany, were often precisely the groups that sought to undermine it. Minorities without a kin-state, such as Ruthenians, Vlachs, Byelorussians or Ukrainians were the ones least able to benefit from the minority rights regime, in spite of the special guarantees of cultural autonomy some of them had initially received. The Jewish minorities in the states bound by the treaties were somehow in an intermediary position, lacking a kin-state but having powerful links to international Jewish organizations and lobby groups that had considerable experience promoting their rights and militating against discrimination. These, however, proved ineffectual in the context of the rise of Nazism and extreme right-wing politics across interwar Europe, as did the League of Nations in preventing the proliferation of the international conflicts that eventually led to World War II.

Germany, the (largely self-interested) champion of minority rights during its membership in the League, left the organisation in October 1933, following Hitler's coming to power. Poland followed suit in September 1934, with Poles celebrating the end of "international servitude" by lighting bonfires throughout the country.[43] The system of international guarantees of minority rights collapsed under the pressure of the right-wing extremism sweeping across Europe, and the very notion of national minority rights was compromised as a result of World War II. The protection of the interests of ethnic Germans outside the country's borders had been the pretext Hitler invoked for the *Anschluss* with Austria and the annexation of the Sudeten region of Czechoslovakia, followed by the occupation of the remainder of the country after Slovakia declared its independence. Some ethnic Germans acted as a 'fifth column' of Nazi propaganda and formed diaspora national-socialist groups which, sponsored from Berlin, helped destabilize the countries of Central and Eastern Europe, from Austria and Czechoslovakia to Romania. Other national minorities supported the Nazis for the purpose of advancing their own independence agendas, eventually leading to the creation of the wartime republics of Slovakia and Croatia. Hungary also supported Nazi Germany in exchange for territories that had previously been part of Czechoslovakia and Romania. On the other hand, World War II, the most destructive conflict in human history, also saw the destruction of the Jews in the ultimate atrocity perpetrated against a national minority group on European soil, the Holocaust, together with the systematic extermination of the Roma by the Nazis and other Axis countries (Croatia, Slovakia, Hungary and Romania), the mass murder of Serbs by the Croatian Ustaša and that of the Poles by the Soviet Union.

The aftermath of the war saw the establishment of a universal human rights regime, under the aegis of another international organisation, the United Nations. Compromised by the association of certain national minorities with Nazi crimes, by their destabilizing role in interwar European politics, and by the perceived failure of the League of Nations to guarantee peace and stability in Europe, national minority rights lost their independent status after World War II.[44] As a result, they were included among human rights provisions, which emphasized the rights of individuals rather than those of groups. Thus, the Universal Declaration of Human Rights (1948) contains no reference to the rights of ethnic or national groups; instead, it mentions a list of individual rights which, while generally applicable, were deemed sufficient to cover the protection of members of ethnic groups as well. While little changed in this respect during the Cold War, national minority rights were to resurface following the collapse of communism as a result of the ensuing territorial changes, as well as of the re-emergence of ethnic conflict in the former Soviet Union and Yugoslavia. In spite of its ultimate failure, many of the principles of the post-World War I minority rights regime and its guarantee by the League of Nations were to be adapted to the post-1989 situation. The contemporary developments in the evolution of minority rights and the current regime for the protection of national minorities will constitute the subject of the next chapters.

Key points

- International agreements for the protection of minority groups are not to be understood as static regimes, but according to a processual paradigm that sees them as constantly developing over time as a result of shifts in the perception of politics and international relations.
- Historically, political upheavals and the most significant modifications of international borders were consistently accompanied by changes in the status and degree of protection of minority groups.
- With religion antedating nationality as the primary marker of social identity, the earliest guarantees for the protection of minority groups emerged in the form of religious freedoms—as with the millet system in the Ottoman Empire or the progressively more extensive rights granted to religious minorities in Western Europe following the Reformation.
- The emergence of nationalism and of notions of popular sovereignty led to the increasing recognition of minority groups as national rather than religious and their protection as such.
- While initially the protection of minorities was voluntary, dependent on the goodwill of the sovereign in a given territory, the end of the 19th century witnessed the establishment of minority rights obligations as a precondition for the international recognition of newly established nation-states, as a liberal, rights-based understanding of politics became gradually more influential.

- At the end of World War I, a minority rights regime was institutionally established for the first time in the form of a collective international commitment to upholding the guarantee of such rights and placed under the aegis of an international organisation, the League of Nations, with specific procedural rules guiding its operation.
- The first international regime for the protection of minorities collapsed due to its shortcomings and the persistence of a view of international relations that gave more weight to national sovereignty than effective international monitoring and sanctions, as well as due to the rise of exclusionary, extremist right-wing ideologies, being replaced at the end of World War II by a human rights regime.
- Each successive phase in the evolution of minority-majority relations was significantly influenced by the preceding one(s), often manifest in the form of a resistance to change in the name of preserving the status quo.

Further reading

CAMERON, EUAN. *The European Reformation*. Oxford: Clarendon Press, 1991.
CHARTIER, ROGER. *The Cultural Origins of the French Revolution*. Durham and London: Duke University Press, 1991.
DAVIES, NORMAN. *Europe: A History*. London: Pimlico, 1997.
DZOKIC, DEJAN. *Yugoslavism: Histories of a Failed Idea, 1918–1992*. London: Hurst & Co., 2003.
FINK, CAROLE. *Defending the Rights of Others: The Great Powers, the Jews, and International Minority Protection, 1878–1938*. Cambridge: Cambridge University Press, 2004.
FISCHER-GALAȚI, STEPHEN. "Nationalism and Kaisertreue". *Slavic Review* 22(1963), pp. 31–36.
GELLNER, ERNEST. *Nations and Nationalism*. Ithaca: Cornell University Press, 1983.
HILBERG, RAUL. *The Destruction of the European Jews*. 3rd ed. New Haven and London: Yale University Press, 2003.
HUTCHINSON, JOHN, and ANTHONY D. SMITH, eds. *Nationalism*. Oxford: Oxford University Press, 1994.
JELAVICH, BARBARA. *History of the Balkans*. Cambridge: Cambridge University Press, 1983.
MACARTNEY, CARLILE A., and ALAN W. PALMER. *Independent Eastern Europe*. London: Macmillan, 1962.
MACARTNEY, CARLILE A. *National States and National Minorities*. London: Oxford University Press, 1934.
SCHMITT, BERNADOTTE E. "The Peace Treaties of 1919–1920". *Proceedings of the American Philosophical Society* 104 (1960), pp. 101–110.

SLEZKINE, YURI. *Arctic Mirrors: Russia and the Small People of the North*. Ithaca: Cornell University Press, 1994.
SUGAR, PETER F. "The Nature of the Non-Germanic Societies under Habsburg Rule". *Slavic Review* 22 (1963), pp. 1–30.
TAYLOR, ALAN J. P. *The Struggle for Mastery in Europe: 1848–1918*. Oxford: Clarendon Press, 1954.
WALTERS, FRANCIS P. *A History of the League of Nations*. London: Oxford University Press, 1960.
WEDGWOOD, CICELY V. *The Thirty Years War*. London and New York: Methuen, 1981.

Notes

1   Helmer Rosting, "Protection of Minorities by the League of Nations", *The American Journal of International Law* 17 (1923), p. 642.
2   Stanford J. Shaw, "The Dynamics of Ottoman Society and Administration", in *History of the Ottoman Empire and Modern Turkey*, Vol. 1 (Cambridge: Cambridge University Press, 1976), pp. 112–168, here: 163–165 ; Muhidin Mulalić, "Multiculturalism and EU Enlargement: The Case of Turkey and Bosnia-Herzegovina" in *The Islamic World and the West: Managing Religious and Cultural Identities in the Age of Globalisation*, ed. Christoph Marcinkowski (Berlin: LIT and the Asia-Europe Institute, 2009), pp. 112–115.
3   "Forum: The Politics of Religion: The Peace of Augsburg 1555. A Roundtable Discussion Between Thomas A. Brady, Euan Cameron and Henry Cohn", *German History* 24 (2006), pp. 85–105.
4   The *Thirty Years' War: A Documentary History*, ed. Tryntje Helfferich (Indianapolis: Hackett Publishing Company, 2009), pp. ix–xxi.
5   *Treaty of Westphalia (1648)*, The Avalon Project, Yale Law School, Lillian Goldman Law Library, accessed July 10, 2013, http://avalon.law.yale.edu/17th_century/westphal.asp.
6   Jennifer Jackson Preece, "Minority Rights in Europe: From Westphalia to Helsinki", *Review of International Studies* 23(1997), pp. 75–92 (p. 77); Rosting, op.cit., note 1, p. 643.
7   Alfred Cobban, *The Nation-State and National Self-Determination* (London: Collins, 1969), p. 5.
8   *Declaration of the Rights of Man and of the Citizen (1789)*, accessed July 10, http://www.constitution.org/fr/fr_drm.htm.
9   Jennifer Jackson Preece, *National Minorities and the European Nation-States System* (Oxford: Clarendon Press, 1998), p. 60.
10 *Final Act of the Congress of Vienna/General Treaty (1815)*, accessed July 10, 2013, http://www.dipublico.com.ar/english/final-act-of-the-congress-of-viennageneral-treaty-1815/.
11 Hans Kohn, "Western and Eastern Nationalisms" in *Nationalism*, ed. John Hutchinson and Anthony D. Smith (Oxford: Oxford University Press, 1994), pp. 164–165.
12 *The Revolutions in Europe, 1848–1849: From Reform to Reaction*, ed. Robert J.W. Evans and Hartmut Pogge von Strandmann (Oxford: Oxford University Press, 2000), pp. 1–26.
13 Preece, op. cit., note 9, p. 62.
14 Rosting, op. cit., note 1, p. 645.
15 This was not the first instance where such minority obligations were imposed on newly established states in Europe, being anticipated by the London Protocol of 1830 which recognized the independence of Greece from the Ottoman Empire. However, the scope and the general applicability of the provisions far exceeded those stipulated in any previous treaties. Preece, op. cit., note 9, p. 64.
16 Raul Cârstocea, "Uneasy Twins? The Entangled Histories of Jewish Emancipation and Anti-Semitism in Romania and Hungary, 1866–1913", *Slovo* 21 (2009), pp. 74–76.

17 Vladimir I. Lenin, "The Revolutionary Proletariat and the Right of Nations to Self-Determination" in *Collected Works* 21 (1974), pp. 407–414, accessed July 10, 2013, http://www.marxists.org/archive/lenin/works/1914/self-det/ch01.htm.
18 Will Kymlicka, *Multicultural Citizenship* (Oxford: Clarendon Press, 1995), pp. 53, 69–70.
19 Ephraim J. Nimni, "Introduction for the English-Reading Audience" in *The Question of Nationalities and Social Democracy*, Otto Bauer (Minneapolis and London: University of Minnesota Press, 2000), xviii–xix ; See also Otto Bauer, "National Autonomy" (same volume), pp. 259–308.
20 Wayne S. Vucinich, "Mlada Bosna and the First World War" in *The Habsburg Empire in the First World War*, ed. Robert A. Kann, Bela Kiraly, and Paula S. Fichtner (New York: Columbia University Press, 1977), pp. 45–69.
21 Dominik J. Schaller and Jürgen Zimmerer, "Late Ottoman Genocides: The Dissolution of the Ottoman Empire and Young Turkish Populations and Extermination Policies – Introduction", *Journal of Genocide Research* 10 (2008), pp. 7–14.
22 Preece, op. cit., note 9, p. 68.
23 Norman Davies, *Heart of Europe: The Past in Poland's Present* (Oxford: Oxford University Press, 2001), p. 103.
24 Keith Hitchins, *Rumania: 1866–1947* (Oxford: Clarendon Press, 1994), p. 164.
25 Woodrow Wilson acknowledged the idealistic nature of the self-determination principle upon his return to the United States, stating in an address to the US Senate: "When I gave utterance to those words, I said them without the knowledge that nationalities existed … you cannot appreciate the anxieties that I have experienced as a result of the millions of people having their hopes raised", quoted in Alan Sharp, *The Versailles Settlement: Peacemaking in Paris* (Basingstoke: Macmillan Education, 1991), p. 156.
26 Carole Fink, "The Paris Peace Conference and the Question of Minority Rights", *Peace and Change* 21 (1996), pp. 276–279.
27 World War I Document Archive, *President Wilson's Fourteen Points (1918)*, accessed July 10, 2013, http://wwi.lib.byu.edu/index.php/President_Wilson's_Fourteen_Points.
28 Rosting, op.cit., note 1, pp. 647–648.
29 Preece, op. cit., note 9, pp. 73–74.
30 Fink, op.cit., note 26, p. 82.
31 Ibid, p. 281.
32 One of the problems with this formulation was that it did not specify what exactly constituted a "considerable proportion", leaving the matter to the discretion of the states that signed the treaties.
33 Treaty of Peace with Poland [Polish Minorities Treaty], Versailles, 28 June 1919, accessed July 10, 2013, http://www.macalester.edu/courses/intl245/docs/treaty_poland.pdf.
34 Preece, op. cit., note 9, p. 76.
35 Carole Fink, "The League of Nations and the Minorities Question", *World Affairs* 157 (1995), p. 198.
36 Preece, op. cit., note 9, p. 83.
37 Jacob Robinson, *Were the Minority Treaties a Failure?* (New York: Institute of Jewish Affairs, 1943), p. 252.
38 Frederick S. Northedge, *The League of Nations: Its Life and Times, 1920–1946* (Leicester: Leicester University Press, 1986), pp. 42–48.
39 Fink, op.cit., note 35, p. 200.
40 Preece, op. cit., note 9, p. 81.
41 Fink, op.cit., note 35, p. 200.
42 Cobban, op.cit., note 7, p. 37.
43 Fink, op.cit., note 26, p. 284.
44 Preece, op. cit., note 9, p. 84.

Chapter 2: European International Law

Tove H. Malloy

Summary

Since its founding in 1949, the Council of Europe has been the foremost promoter of human rights in Europe, and it has complemented this success by also acting as the moral leader on national minority rights. This is not to imply that the Council of Europe has been is successful in achieving human rights protection across the board; but that as a facilitator of democracy and the rule of law, the Council of Europe has been able to claim a number of successes since 1949. Nor is the statement above given to imply that the Council of Europe has been a moral pioneer on national minority protection; that distinction must be given to the OSCE. The European Union (EU) became a leading voice in the discourse on national minority protection in the mid-1990s by advocating national minority protection in the new democracies in Europe, i.e. within states seeking accession to and membership of the EU. Within the Union, the EU has adopted two directives on non-discrimination social rights as well as equality rights in employment relating to minorities.

Introduction

As noted in the previous chapter, it would be another almost three quarters of a century before the strong approach to minority protection adopted by the League of Nations again gained currency in European politics. Minority protection was not entirely forgotten in the interim period, but there was not enough backing among international organizations and national governments to seek the formation of a minority rights regime. While the United Nations (UN) continued examining the issues even during and after the drafting of the Universal Declaration of Human Rights (UDHR),[1] it was only in 1966 that a minority protection clause found its way into a UN instrument, the International Covenant on the Civil and Political Rights (ICCPR).[2] See our discussion in Chapter 8. At the European level, which will be the focus of this chapter, several efforts were made, and the ground work for the post-1990 momentum in this domain was laid by the Council of Europe. It is, however, important to note that when referring to the regime of European international law, there is no exclusion of UN provisions. UN treaty mechanisms are global and therefore also have relevance for minority protection in Europe.

This chapter will focus on the strictly regional approach to legal minority protection established in Europe after World War II. This includes a section on the Council of Europe as well as a section on the European Union (EU). Non-legal approaches to minority protection in Europe will be discussed in Chapter 3 with regard to the emerging EU approach to minority protection through programmes, and in Chapter 8 with regard to the security approach developed by the Organization for Security and Co-operation in Europe (OSCE).

Distinguishing between the normative approach and the political approach is important. Whereas the normative approach, meaning promoting legally binding provisions to which states and governments wishing to protect minorities can become party, is usually monitored and thus ensured some degree of accountability, the political approach, intending to provide for states and governments the opportunity to pledge good intentions about protecting minorities, may also allow for wriggling and bargaining among states as well as opt-ins and opt-outs of certain agreements and arrangements. With this taken into consideration, it should be noted that most normative initiatives take starting point in a political process.

The Council of Europe

Two conventions adopted by the Council of Europe have a direct bearing on the rights of 'national' minorities, namely the European Convention for the Protection of Human Rights and Fundamental Freedoms (ECHR) and the Framework Convention for the Protection of National Minorities (FCNM). Three other Council of Europe instruments support national minority protection, namely the European Charter for Regional or Minority Languages (ECRML), the European Charter of Local Self-Government, and the European Outline Convention on Transfrontier Co-operation (hereafter the Outline Convention). While these have a more indirect bearing on the protection of members of national minorities, insofar as they are not standard setting instruments, they are nevertheless important in order to begin drawing a full picture of the Council of Europe's efforts in this field.

As an organization supporting intergovernmental and parliamentary co-operation and created to help secure democracy in Europe to ensure that the totalitarianisms of World War II would not recur, the Council of Europe upon constituting itself adopted the core statutory principles of pluralist democracy, respect for human rights, and the rule of law. A major aim of the Council of Europe was to prevent the recurrence of the gross violations of human rights such as those which occurred at the hands of the fascist regimes. Today, each member state of the Council of Europe must not only embrace these principles, they must also sign and ratify the ECHR, as this Convention is considered a constitutive document of the Council of Europe.

The European Convention for the Protection of Human Rights and Fundamental Freedoms

Adopted in 1950, the ECHR is the strongest legal document of its kind in Europe and arguably in the world.[3] It is widely held that it is also the human rights document which can claim the greatest success at the global level. It does not provide minority rights *per se* but sets out an agenda of rights that interfaces with the essential concerns of minorities. These include the right to existence, to pluralism, to self-definition, to non-discrimination, to human dignity, to issues of human identity, including issues pertaining to private life, to the freedom of expression, to the freedom of religion, and to the right to participation.

The relevant article for minorities is Article 14, a non-discrimination clause. This article is also the main reason why there have been many cases relating to minority issues brought before the European Court of Human Rights in Strasbourg. Article 14 holds:

The enjoyment of the rights and freedoms set forth in this Convention shall be secured without discrimination on any ground such as sex, race, colour, language, religion, political or other opinion, national or social origin, association with a national minority, property, birth or other status.[4]

Technically, this article does not stand alone but must be claimed together with one of the other articles of the Convention. Thus, minorities who claim to suffer discrimination must relate the reason for the discrimination they are claiming to suffer to one of the other freedoms, for instance to the freedom of expression. Cases can be submitted to the Court only after the complaint has reached and been tried by the highest level court in a member state, and even then, a case must be deemed eligible for review. These are technical aspects which might seem to make it difficult for minorities to bring cases to the Court. Nonetheless, in its life span so far, the Court has adjudicated more than 100 cases related to issues of minority rights.

The reference to a 'national minority' in Article 14 of the ECHR was unique in the global context of rights of that time. Neither the United Nations' Charter, the UDHR nor the American Convention on Human Rights makes any mention of a minority. During the early years of the UN, there were serious discussions which took place to include minority rights in the UDHR in light of the atrocities committed during World War II as well as following the Nuremberg trials. However, this was vetoed by not only the then US Representative to the UN, Eleanor Roosevelt, who argued that individual human rights were adequate to protect also minorities, but also by some Eastern European member states' representatives who feared another League of Nations regime imposed on them.[5]

At this time In Europe, a different scenario unfolded. During the early discussions of the drafting of the ECHR, the then Danish Representative, Herrmod Lannung, was very much motivated by the existence of the Danish minority in Schleswig and thus wished to promote a minority rights approach. In fact, Lannung argued that while fundamental human rights were important,

it is necessary to extend, supplement and elaborate human rights in order that national minorities may secure the right to a free national life and protection against persecution and encroachment on account of their national convictions, aspirations and activities.[6]

Furthermore, according to Lannung, "the minority question was of general European interest and the neglect of the minority question could lead to serious disputes among the member states of the Council of Europe."[7] Lannung eventually proposed a text which held that "national minorities should be assured a free life with a free enjoyment of their own cultural development."[8] This text was not, however, adopted by the drafters of the ECHR. The drafting of the ECHR went through a number of different revisions, and Lannung continued his pressure, but eventually he had to accept the reference in Article 14 to "association with a national minority." In fact, a number of committee members felt that it was taking the issue too far while others together with Lannung would like to have seen a more inclusive article.[9]

Following the adoption of the ECHR, experts and observers on national minority rights continued to lament the lack of stronger *national* minority protection in the Convention. As a consequence, a committee was established to examine the possibility of writing a protocol to the Convention explicitly addressing national minority rights. Thus, in 1961 the committee proposed a text on national minority rights; which was not, however, adopted. In 1973, another group of Council of Europe experts issued a report stating that from a strictly legal point of view there was no need for additional provisions on national minorities. Therefore, nothing effectively happened until the dramatic changes in global politics forced reconsideration of the question in 1989, including the upheavals in Eastern Europe and the Balkans. This time it was clear that an instrument specifically addressing national minority protection was the way forward.

The post-1989 preparatory work of the Council of Europe on expanding national minority protection was undertaken in the early 1990s by the Parliamentary Assembly which issued a number of recommendations to political decision makers, the Committee of Ministers, including one recommendation (Recommendation 1201) suggesting the wording for an additional protocol to the ECHR.[10] While this protocol was not adopted, it has retained a reasonably strong standing in European minority politics as it has became one of the documents that new member states acceding to the Council of Europe were obliged to include in bilateral treaties negotiated between neighbouring states.[11] Particularly sensitive in this sense was the inclusion of a clause on autonomy into this document.[12] However, a number of new member states felt that obliging them to accept this clause while not imposing it on existing member states was hypocritical. Some new member states simply refused to include a clause on autonomy in bilateral treaties.[13] With regard to a protocol to the ECHR, it is worth noting that even though the Committee of Ministers decided at one point to draft a protocol on national minorities, such a protocol has never been adopted. Instead, an alternative route was taken.

Protocol 12

In 2000, a protocol expanding the rights of Article 14 was adopted by the Committee of Ministers and is now in force.[14] Protocol 12 requires the states party to the Convention to take positive measures, where necessary, to ensure that discrimination on the grounds mentioned in Article 14 does not happen. However, a number of countries have not yet signed this Protocol. The Protocol is considered controversial because it requires governments to take positive action to prevent discrimination. This is in contrast to the original aim of Article 14 which simply referred to the prohibition of discrimination.

The Framework Convention for the Protection of National Minorities

The breakthrough on *national* minority rights finally came in 1993 during the World Summit on Human Rights in Vienna, when the member states of the Council of Europe met informally on the side line of this global summit. During their separate meeting, the members of the Council of Europe decided to draft a convention specifying the principles to which member states would be willing to commit themselves in order to assure the protection of national minorities. The rationale for this decision was that national minorities should be protected and respected so that they would be able to contribute to stability and peace, and that it was a challenge for Europe to assure the protection of the rights of persons belonging to national minorities within the rule of law, respecting territorial integrity and the national sovereignty of states.

On the basis of this, the member states of the Council of Europe declared that

States should be willing to create the conditions necessary for person belonging to national minorities to develop their culture, while preserving their religion, traditions and customs. These persons must be able to use their language, both in private and in public and should be able to use it under certain conditions in their relations with the public authorities.[15]

These were the observations which eventually formed the substance of the FCNM. Within a period of just over one year, the FCNM was drafted and presented to the governments of member states (as well as non-member states) for signature in February 1995. It is important to note that the Council of Europe decided at that point also to invite non-members to sign the instrument, the reason being that a number of new states were vying to become members. The Convention entered into force in February 1998, and has been signed by 43 and ratified by 39 states.[16]

The FCNM is the first ever legally binding multilateral instrument devoted to the protection of national minorities *per se*.[17] The fact that it is legally binding is significant but should not be overestimated. As the title indicates, it is a 'framework' document which means that it sets out principles which states having ratified the FCNM must translate into domestic law as best as possible.

Without going into details about the FCNM, it should be noted that the provisions covered by the FCNM include non-discrimination, positive measures of cultural rights, freedoms similar to those in the ECHR, education and language rights, provisions on participation in public life and cross-border relations. Finally, the FCNM also places certain duties on members of national minorities to respect the majority and the law of the state in which they reside.

Since the FCNM does not independently grant rights to members of national minorities but puts obligations on states to create these rights, there is no system of submitting petitions to a court, such as is the case with the ECHR. Instead, the FCNM provides for a monitoring system that requires states to submit reports to the Council of Europe according to a certain schedule and outline. These state reports are evaluated by a committee of experts, the Advisory Committee (AC), designated to scrutinize these reports and to make recommendations to the members of the Committee of Ministers who pass on the recommendations to member state governments. The effectiveness of this type of self-reporting has been questioned by experts and observers, and in so far as it is the governments that write the reports upon which they will be evaluated, it seems rather prone to tactics of whitewashing. This situation has, however, been mitigated by a number of developments since the FCNM has entered into force.

First of all, one of the first actions of the AC was to suggest that a system of 'shadow' reports was put in place whereby non-governmental organizations are invited to submit reports following the same system as do state reports. This was accepted by the Committee of Ministers and shadow reports have begun to arrive in Strasbourg, albeit at a slower than optimal rate because the NGOs that prepare such reports either do not exist, or are ill-equipped to do so in a timely and proper fashion. Secondly, the AC has been very pro-active in its work with the reports. Realizing that the reports were not always representative of the actual situations on the ground, the AC has asked for more precise input, including input from national minorities themselves. The AC has also begun dialogue with member states' governments, and a system of country visits has been initiated.[18] The AC is, therefore, today to be commended for having effectively initiated a system of dialogue with member states governments in addition to the reporting system set out by the FCNM.

All things considered, the question is has the FCNM been effective? Opinions vary on this, and it is still too early to come to an informed conclusion. In general, legal practitioners are very critical about the effect of the instrument,[19] whereas political observers are considerably more optimistic.[20] Members of the latter group consider the FCNM to be one of the most important texts of the Council of Europe and believe it is destined to carry much of the burden of putting into effect national minority rights in the European space. This is notwithstanding the fact that a number of member states of the Council of Europe still have not signed and ratified the instrument and do not plan to do so in the foreseeable future.[21] The actual impact of the instrument in domestic litigation has recently been researched, and not surprisingly, the reference to the FCNM is greater in the new member states than in the old.[22] However, results are too few to create a reliable picture. Of course, even though the FCNM is cast as a framework text, it is legally binding and its language of international obligations is clear. There is a consensus among legal scholars that it goes beyond the ECHR in moral commitments on national minorities and perhaps even in effectiveness insofar, that it actively puts national minority rights on the agendas of member states governments as well as gives civil society the possibility to mobilize on the issue. The fact that it does not have a regular claim mechanism so that people can may submit a complaint to a court has been countered by the argument that the reporting system as well as the dialogue system initiated by the AC may in fact be more efficient in addressing structural problems related to national minority issues. This is because court cases only relate to one person or to a single national minority whereas the AC's work relates to the overall well-being of national minorities. This is an important factor in those countries where there are many national minorities, such as for example Romania.

On language rights, the FCNM has, however, yielded praise. It has been argued that the provisions on language rights in the FCNM have contributed greatly to the enhancement of the cultural rights of national minorities and some even argue that these provisions could be interpreted as creating functional cultural autonomy for national minorities if implemented.[23] While this latter argument is perhaps debatable, the FCNM has in some instances had the effect that its sister document, the ECRML has not.

A Definition?

On one aspect in particular, the FCNM has been heavily criticized. Like most other international human rights instruments which address national minority issues, the FCNM does not contain a definition of a national minority. In the context of European international law only a proposal for a European Convention for the Protection of Minorities drafted by the Venice Commission[24] in 1990 included a definition. That instrument was never adopted. During the preparatory discussions to the FCNM it was argued that national minorities differ so much from state to state that they defy definition. The drafters consequently settled for what they called a pragmatic approach and opted to start the drafting without embarking on a prior discussion of a definition.

The problem of a lack of a definition in the FCNM survived into the post-adoption period when the member states were asked to sign the instrument. Upon signing many states opted to attach declarations to the signature even though the instrument does not provision for signees to make declarations. Virtually all declarations made to the FCNM deal with the lack of a definition of a national minority in the instrument whereas the one made by Malta holds that there are no national minorities within the state. The arguments in the declarations basically come in two forms, those that define the recognized national minorities within the territory of the respective state and those that set out the criteria for determining which groups would qualify as national minorities within the respective state. What is interesting is not that these declarations are so concerned with the definition of a national minority or the lack thereof; that was to be expected. Rather, it is the intensity with which the states pay attention to *who* qualifies as a national minority within their territory and, in particular, who does *not*. By enumerating the national minorities that are eligible under the FCNM, some states automatically deny rights under the FCNM to other national minorities within their territory. The same effect could happen subsequent to the second category of declarations which put forth a test that the national minorities within a certain territory must pass to qualify.

The practice of states as evidenced in the declarations to the FCNM shows in general a curiously divided group of member states. Firstly, states with more or less territorially defined national minorities, such as Croatia, Romania, Spain, Portugal and the United Kingdom did not make declarations to the FCNM. Switzerland made a declaration essentially extending protection to internal minorities, or 'minorities within minorities' within each canton. Estonia, on the other hand, made a declaration excluding the Russian-speaking minorities by declaring that the FCNM only pertains to citizens of Estonia. This is unfortunate as many of the Russian-speakers in Estonia have not as yet received legal citizenship due to the fact that the citizenship law of Estonia requires mastery of the Estonian language as a prerequisite for receiving legal citizenship. A major part of the Russian-speakers do not yet speak Estonian. This is why the OSCE's High Commissioner on National Minorities (HCNM) has been communicating with the Estonian government to bring this legislation in line with European norms.²⁵ Other states, such as Slovenia and Macedonia, have followed their constitutional practice and enumerated the recognized national minorities living in their territories. Sweden and Denmark, not providing constitutional recognition as such to any national minority, have also enumerated the national minorities to be protected under the FCNM. However, while Sweden has included the Sami indigenous peoples, Denmark has chosen to exclude the indigenous community of Greenlanders living in both Greenland and Denmark.

The problem of a definition also affected the work of the AC as it was often met by arguments that minorities not covered by the FCNM should not be discussed. This has been mitigated by the AC which has taken a pragmatic approach to the issue, and in fact has begun to expand the circle of minorities eligible under the FCNM by softly seeking to address the non-included minorities with governments. In this sense, the AC follows the practice of the UN's Human Rights Committee. Therefore, international legal instruments operate not with a definition by law but a definition by fact.

The approach of working with a definition by fact becomes a problem however when the facts are not recorded, such as when statistics are not differentiating national minority membership through census taking or other modes of data collection. This is a problem in many countries in Europe either because governments are unaware of the importance of collecting such data or are unwilling. The interpretation of a number of constitutions in Europe prohibits data collection on the basis of racial and ethnic characteristics. Moreover, members of national minorities often mistrust the ability of governments to maintain the confidentiality of data collected on the basis of ethnic classification and fear that such information will be used to their detriment and result in negative stereotyping. Thus, there is an apparent need to identify legal lacuna which unfairly bar the collection of data on national minority membership and to identify strategies for collecting data which are consistent with privacy standards so as to overcome objections to this practice. It is furthermore important that the quality of the data collected is of such a standard that the national minorities included in these statistics feel that their identities are fairly represented. This includes a periodical review of categories.

The European Charter for Regional or Minority Languages

The ECRML was adopted and opened for signature in 1992, three years before the FCNM but did not enter into force until 1998, the same year as the

FCNM.²⁶ The ECRML does not provision rights, but rather seeks to ensure the protection of regional and minority languages with the rationale that a multilingual Europe is a richer Europe, and that languages that are under threat of dying out should be protected and promoted. The ECRML is therefore very much a cultural instrument, or one might argue a 'multicultural' instrument one might argue.

The ECRML does not provide examples of regional and minority languages eligible for protection but it does define regional and minority languages as traditional languages used by groups that are numerical numerically smaller than the majority population, who speak a language different from the official language of the state, whose language is not a dialect of the official language or a language of migrants, or is used as the mode of expression in certain geographical areas, or is used by members of these groups residing dispersed among the majority population. As the overall purpose of the ECRML is to promote the use of these languages in public as well as in private life, it is therefore clear that protecting immigrant languages in public use is not considered eligible under this Charter. For national minorities, however, the ECRML does hold paramount force as most national minority languages are both regional and different from the official language of the state.

The ECRML is complex in the way it is constructed. It is founded on a range of basic principles that states must agree to, among others the recognition of languages as an expression of cultural wealth, respect for the regions of the protected languages and the prohibition against redistricting with a view to separate language groups, the need for positive action to protect the languages, guarantee of teaching and study of the protected languages, introduction to non-speakers of the languages, allowing minority language groups to interrelate, the elimination of discrimination on the basis of minority languages, the promotion of respect between minority groups speaking different languages, and the establishment of bodies representing the interests of language minorities concerned. The ECRML therefore elaborates how states should implement these principles in the areas of education, relations with judicial, administrative authorities and public service authorities, the media, in economic and social life, and during trans-frontier exchanges. However, it allows for ratifying states to specify the languages within their territories that are eligible or not eligible for protection. The ECRML is monitored in much the same way as the FCNM although the ECRML provides for a few extra prerogatives of the committee undertaking the monitoring. These include on-the-spot visits to the regions without prior invitation by the government of the member state, and a report on implementation progress to the Parliamentary Assembly every second year.

Even though the ECRML does not confer rights *per se*, it is still held that it has taken an important place in the corpus of European standards on minority rights. It is a cultural diversity instrument which is not insignificant in the current political climate of the EU trying to bring "united in diversity" through closer integration.[27] It has furthermore been argued that the ECRML has positive synergy with both the ECHR and the FCNM.[28] Specifically, in comparison to the FCNM, the ECRML has presented governments with an avenue that is less demanding and yet allows for governments to achieve some objectives on minority rights. On the other hand, some governments may feel that the complex requirements of the ECRML may entail serious and sustained work on the part of the central administrations.[29] A major criticism from experts has been the fact that the ECRML does not protect the languages of immigrant groups and in an age of globalization and extensive migration this is seen as a major flaw.

At this point, it may be instructive to step back a few years in the history of the Council of Europe as the ECRML was conceived as an idea already in 1988 when the then Conference of Local and Regional Authorities of Europe—a standing conference which has since become the Congress of Local and Regional Authorities of Europe on par with the Parliamentary Assembly— conducted a survey of minority and regional languages and found that certain languages where at risk of becoming extinct.

The Congress of Local and Regional Authorities

The Congress of Local and Regional Authorities and its predecessor are an integral factor in the discussion of minority conventions and the Council of Europe. The Congress, which began as a standing conference in 1957, is today a full-fledged body of the Council of Europe. It derives its mandate both from the statutes of the Council of Europe and the European Charter of Local Self-Government. The latter gives the Congress the right to monitor local and regional democracy. In addition, the Congress concerns itself greatly with the implementation of the European Outline Convention.

The European Charter of Local Self-Government

The European Charter of Local Self-Government is a little known convention in European politics, often neglected by the minority discourse.[30] It was opened for signature in 1985 and entered into force in 1988. It endorses the basic principles of local democracy, including the principle of subsidiarity. And it maintains that local self-government is one of the cornerstones of a pluralist democracy, and that elected local representatives must have the right to manage a substantial portion of public affairs in their constituency. The Congress sees the Charter of Local Self-Government as a complementary instrument to the Council of Europe's other minority instruments, and as an important tool for national minority protection.

The Charter of Local Self-Government allows the Congress to monitor local democracy country-by-country, and the Congress prepares reports to that effect. In addition to the country reports, the Congress issues recommendations to the Committee of Ministers of the Council of Europe, in the same manner as the Parliamentary Assembly. These recommendations are based on committee work regarding thematic issues. The Congress has been particularly outspoken about the importance of local autonomy for national minorities and the value of including national minority representatives in the system of subsidiarity. It has also been a promoter of the participation of foreigners in public life at the local level.

More significantly, the Congress has been working now for many years on a draft European Charter of Regional Self-Government to be approved by the Committee of Ministers.[31] This is a convention which stresses the importance of regionalization in Europe and the relevance of regional authorities in the implementation of the principle of subsidiarity. However, it would seem that the political climate for sub-state level self-government may no longer be as open as it was in the 1980s when the Charter of Local Self-Government was adopted. The proposed Charter of Regional Self-Government remains stalled in the Council of Europe and it is not at all clear that it will ever be adopted.

The European Outline Convention on Transfrontier Co-operation

The Outline Convention was adopted in 1980 and with the aim to encourage and facilitate the conclusion of cross-border agreements between local and regional authorities within the scope of their respective powers.[32] Such agreements may cover regional development, environmental protection, the improvement of public services, etc., and the setting up of trans-frontier associations or consortia of local authorities. To allow for variations in the legal and constitutional systems within the Council of Europe's member states, the Outline Convention sets out a range of model agreements to enable both local and regional authorities as well as central governments to place trans-frontier co-operation in the context best suited to their needs. Under the Outline Convention, member states undertake to seek ways of eliminating obstacles to trans-frontier co-operation, and to grant to authorities engaging in international co-operation the facilities they would enjoy in a purely national context.

The Outline Convention gave birth to the so-called Euro-regions, of which there are today more than seventy. The Outline Convention has had special impetus for national minority issues after 1989 when the new democracies in Central and Eastern Europe were seeking membership of the Council of Europe and other European organizations. One of the conditions for these states to become members of the Council of Europe was namely to negotiate trans-frontier agreements with neighbours, in particularly with regard to national minority issues.[33] Consequently, the Council of Europe was asked to give advice to the new governments in these states. In 1998, a protocol to the Outline Convention was adopted to facilitate partnerships between Euro-regions in the democratized member states and 'new' Euro-regions in the new member states. The rationale for these partnerships is primarily that of knowledge transfer.

It is important to note that throughout its work—be it monitoring local democracy or encouraging trans-frontier relations—the Congress continues to stress the fact that these areas of concern are vital to the protection and promotion of national minority life. The Congress makes it very clear that it finds the principle of subsidiarity an important aspect of national minority protection and has adopted several recommendations to that effect.[34] It now also works closely with its sister organization in the EU, the Committee of the Regions, to promote the principle of subsidiarity as a tool also for national minority protection.

The question is how effective the Congress has been in its work with these Conventions? According to experts, the Congress has become an essential driving force in the progress made by the Council of Europe in the area of national minority protection.[35] It has been pro-active in making one of its main goals that of national minority protection, and it has taken up some of the most innovative initiatives within Europe in the field of standard-setting on national minority protection. It has furthermore been argued that the Congress has been instrumental in defining the principle of subsidiarity, and it has at times been willing to address issues that were not protected by international treaties. The Congress has also been instrumental in identifying state practices which violated the principle of local government. Last but not least, the Congress has been lauded for looking East as well as West in its monitoring of states practices. This means that the Congress has had the courage to monitor and criticize western European countries for their lack of attention to local democracy and national minorities. Indeed, the Congress is known to keep an eye on the western states that have decided to reform their sub-state divisions.

The European Union

While Chapter 3 will examine the EU's political approach in depth, a brief discussion of the EU's emerging approach with regard to the legal protection of minorities and the relationship between the EU and the Council of Europe will put the minority rights picture in Europe into context. Unlike the Council of Europe, which has been the frontrunner and foremost promoter of human rights and national minority rights in Europe since World War II, the then European Communities, now the EU, on the other hand, did not begin to include human rights in policy-making until the mid-1980s, and it only enshrined the respect for human rights in the 1991 Maastricht Treaty. Throughout this time, the EU has essentially been referring to the Council of Europe as the 'caretaker' of human rights promotion and monitoring. In fact, the EU has been accused of addressing both human rights and minority rights by proxy.[36] The EU discourse in the 1990s became strong on national minority rights protection but this was meant purely for an external audience, i.e. the aspiring member states. Hence, the so-called Copenhagen Criteria which were adopted by the European Council at Copenhagen in 1993 were very precise as to the conditions that the applicant states would have to fulfil, and these included in no uncertain terms the protection of national minorities. While the Copenhagen Criteria had no legal binding force, the forerunner to these eventually created a legally binding instrument related to the protection of minorities.

The Stability Pact

The Stability Pact, known also as the Baladur Plan, began its life as an EU foreign and security policy strategy and was eventually adopted by the representatives of the fifty-two member states of the OSCE in March 1995. It concerned six Central and Eastern European states (Bulgaria, the Czech Republic, Hungary, Poland, Romania and Slovakia) and the three Baltic States. The Pact should not be confused with the 1999 Stability Pact for South Eastern Europe.[37] The 1995 Stability Pact consisted of a Declaration and a list of agreements and arrangements which the participating states decided to include, agreements concluded between member states of the EU and the then nine candidate states, as well as agreements concluded by these states with other states.[38] Initially, it paid special attention to national minority issues, but this was later watered down as the focus on security and stability became stronger.[39] Inasmuch as the Stability Pact was primarily a security instrument and based on an increased awareness that preventive diplomacy deserved more attention in the area of national minority problems, it was not an instrument that awards rights as such.

However, whereas the Stability Pact was not legally binding, the bilateral treaties that it encouraged and those that were adopted together with the Stability Pact are legally binding.[40] Thus, it encouraged the conclusion of bilateral agreements and of trans-frontier co-operation rather than of multilateral co-operation alone following the tenets of the FCNM's Article 18.[41] This was meant to increase the level of co-operation between states as bilateral treaties are expected to settle conflicting issues through negotiation, and the Stability Pact has in fact given rise to a plethora of bilateral treaties.[42] But insofar as the document only pertained to the new democracies and states in Central and Eastern Europe as well as the Baltics, it was problematic as to both the scope and standards that it conveyed. It has been argued that the asymmetric character of the Stability Pact provided for double standards.[43] The likelihood that the Stability Pact will go down in history the same way as the Minorities Treaties of 1919 did is, therefore, apparent. Any future research on the effectiveness of the bilateral treaties would be able to assess this.

The Amsterdam Treaty and the Equality Directives

Internally, the EU pursued minority protection through the social protection path. This so-called Social Agenda began in 1997 when the EU included in the Amsterdam Treaty for the first time an article prohibiting discrimination within the Union on the basis of ethnic origin.[44] This article has since given rise to two important directives prohibiting discrimination as well as subsequent programmes working to eliminate discrimination against ethnic minorities. The first directive, the so-called Race Directive, or "Council Directive 2000/43/EC of 29 June 2000 implementing the principle of equal treatment between persons irrespective of racial or ethnic origin" prohibits discrimination against members of minorities on the basis of racial or ethnic belonging.[45] The second directive, the so-called Equal Employment Directive, or "Council Directive 2000/78/EC of 27 November 2000 establishing a general framework for equal treatment in employment and occupation" supports the first directive in aiming at equal treatment in the employment sector.[46] Most of the programmes designed to eliminate discrimination address inequality and exclusion in the socio-economic sphere of minority life, and there may no doubt that the programmes are also aimed at immigrant communities across the EU. Most notable are programmes adopted as part of the extensive programming within the Social Agenda for the EU.

The Charter on Fundamental Rights

Other minorities became part of the EU's non-discrimination package in 2000 when the European Council meeting at Nice adopted the Charter of Fundamental Rights of the European Union (hereafter the Charter).[47] With the entering into force of the (reformed) Lisbon Treaty in 2009, the Charter became legally binding on member states. Article 21 is the non-discrimination article which refers to minorities as follows:

Any discrimination based on any ground such as sex, race, colour, ethnic or social origin, genetic features, language, religion or belief, political or any other opinion, membership of a national minority, property, birth, disability, age or sexual orientation shall be prohibited.[48]

The Charter also gave the European Commission the possibility to press on with several initiatives on monitoring and implementing human rights. With the establishment in 2002 of an EU Network of Independent Experts on Fundamental Rights, a network of highly esteemed human rights experts from each member state set up by the European Commission upon request by the Parliament, monitoring of the situation of fundamental rights in the member states on the basis of the Charter began. The Network compiled an annual report on the status of fundamental rights in the Union until 2006. In its report for 2003, the Network specifically interpreted Article 21 of the Charter in a positive manner.[49] The Network suggested that for Article 21 to have any meaning and outcome with regard to national minorities, it might be necessary to adopt certain positive measures. Moreover, the report suggested that EU initiatives on the rights of minorities involve more than a purely legal approach. The report recommended that there be a requirement of consultation, even participation, of representatives of minorities in EU initiatives on minorities. Since the establishment of the Fundamental Rights Agency (FRA) in 2007, there have not been reports issued by the Network. Systematic monitoring within the EU therefore no longer takes place as the mandate of the FRA does not hold such a prerogative. It is important to note that generally the Charter did not bring any new rights to the citizens of the EU; it mainly brought the rights from the various treaties and other documents together under one roof.

The reference to minorities was largely due to the work of the European Parliament which has been very active on behalf of minorities over the years. The Parliament has issued recommendations arguing for more rights of citizens numerous time, including the rights of members of ethnic, linguistic and national minorities. In fact, the first time the Parliament recommended to the Council of Ministers and the Commission to expand the rights of minorities was in 1981.[50] Specifically, with regard to the Charter, the Parliament issued a number of recommendations and called on the EU to expand its standards with provisions included in both the FCNM and the ECRML.

The (reformed) Lisbon Treaty

Whether the decision-makers of the EU had listened to the Parliament is not clear, but the first version of the Lisbon Treaty that included the Constitution for Europe and which was adopted in October 2004 did include a reference to the "respect for the rights of persons belonging to minorities" in its core article on Union values.[51] This inclusion of a reference to minority rights was considered an important victory. The Constitution was not ratified due to popular opposition in France and The Netherlands, but the sentence was retained in the reformed (second version) Lisbon Treaty ratified in 2009.

There are several explanations as to how the drafters of the Constitution came to agree on inserting this sentence. It happened in fact rather late in the drafting process. According to the Hungarian Government, it was the political pressure exerted by the Hungarian delegates to the drafting which ensured the inclusion of this sentence.[52] Another explanation is that the HCNM put pressure on the drafters to insert the sentence.[53] However, the EU has made it clear many times that the Council of Europe is the custodian of human rights and national minority rights in Europe, and for the EU to walk the exact same path would be unnecessary. The 2009 Lisbon Treaty also provisions that the EU will sign the ECHR and this process is now under way. This does not mean that the EU has chosen the best approach to human rights and minority rights protection. Many would argue that it should have its own system.

The European Approach

By way of conclusion, it would appear that there is a desire to work together and complement each other rather than step on each other's toes, possibly resulting in turf battles with regard to minority protection in Europe. To this effect, the Council of Europe and the EU have initiated closer co-operation between their two secretariats, and there is a clear sign that the two organizations co-ordinate on a number of issues related to human rights.[54] However, are standard setting and monitoring enough? Even if together they are creating a pan-European approach to minority protection, the difference between minorities and majorities remains. This is why perhaps the EU has the greatest promise in terms of erasing the difference. While nation states do not appear to be disintegrating, borders within the EU do. And therefore it becomes more difficult to determine who is a minority and who is a majority. Hence, where the Council of Europe is filling the function of promoting respect through standard setting, the EU may be filling the role of facilitator through programming. This is examined in the next chapter.

Key Points

This chapter has argued that:

- The Council of Europe has been the foremost promoter of minority rights in terms of standard setting, with specific attention given to national minorities,
- The Congress of Local and Regional Authorities in Europe has taken the lead in promoting local and regional democracy aimed at including minorities in decision-making,
- The EU is neither a moral leader nor a pioneer when it comes to national minority rights because it has influenced the discourse prima-

rily through declarations of intentions and conditionality imposed on candidate states,
- Following the Amsterdam Treaty (1997), the EU began internal standard setting through the adoption of the two equality directives (2000) and Article 21 of the Charter of Fundamental Rights,
- Due to the increased co-operation between the Council of Europe and the EU, the greater picture of a pan-European regime for standard setting in the area of minority protection includes both organizations,
- The effectiveness of the European approach spans from direct impact through the petition system under the ECHR to indirect impact through dialogue with governments as initiated by the AC on the FCNM as well as through the EU's norm diffusion power and internal directives.

Further reading

ÅKERMARK, ATHANASIA SPILIOPOULOU. *Justification of Minority Protection in International Law*. London: Kluwer International Law, 1997.

BLOED, ARIE and PIETER VAN DIJK. *Protection of Minority Rights through Bilateral Treaties*. The Hague: Kluwer Law International, 1999.

BRÖLMANN, C. et al., eds. *Peoples and Minorities in International Law*. Dordrecht: Martinus Nijhoff,1993.

CUMPER, PETER and STEVEN WHEATLEY, eds. *Minority Rights in the "New" Europe*. The Hague: Martinus Nijhoff, 1999.

DE VARENNES, FERNAND. *Language, Minorities and Human Rights*. The Hague: Martinus Nijhoff,1996.

FREEMAN, MICHAEL. *Human Rights. An Interdisciplinary Approach*. Cambridge: Polity Press, 2002.

GALBREATH, DAVID and JOANNE MCEVOY. *The European Minority Rights Regime. Towards a Theory of Regime Effectiveness*. Palgrave Macmillan, 2012.

GILBERT, GEOFF. "The Council of Europe and Minority Rights". *Human Rights Quarterly* 18 (1996), pp. 160–89.

JACKSON PREECE, JENNIFER. *Minority Rights. Between Diversity and Community*. Cambridge: Polity Press, 2005.

JACKSON PREECE, JENNIFER. *National Minorities and the European Nation-States System*. Oxford: Clarendon Press, 1998.

JONES, PETER. *Rights*. London: Macmillan Press, 1994.

KYMLICKA, WILL. *Multicultural Citizenship*. Oxford: Clarendon Press, 1995.

LANTSCHNER, EMMA. *Soft Jurisprudence im Minderheitenrecht: Standardsetzung und Konfliktbearbeitung durch Kontrollmechanismen Bi- und Multilateraler Instrumente.* Nomos, Baden-Baden, 2009.

MALLOY, TOVE H. *National Minority Rights in Europe.* Oxford: Oxford University Press, 2005.

PACKER, JOHN and KRISTIAN MYNTTI, eds. *The Protection of Ethnic and Linguistic Minorities in Europe.* Turku/Åbo: Åbo Akademi University, 1997.

PENTASSUGLIA, GAETANO. *Minorities in International Law.* Strasbourg: Council of Europe Publishing, 2002.

PHILLIPS, ALAN and ALLAN ROSAS, eds. *Universal Minority Rights.* Turku/Åbo and London: Åbo Akademi University Institute for Human Rights and Minority Rights Group (International), 1995.

THORNBERRY, PATRICK. *International Law and the Rights of Minorities.* Oxford: Clarendon Press, 1991.

VAN DYKE, V. *Human Rights. Ethnicity and Discrimination.* London: Greenwood Press, 1970.

Notes

1 Mark Mazower, "The Strange Triumph of Human Rights, 1933–1950", *The Historical Journal* 47(2004): pp. 379–98.

2 Article 27 of the ICCPR reads: "In those States in which ethnic, religious or linguistic minorities exist, persons belonging to such minorities shall not be denied the right, in community with the other members of their group, to enjoy their own culture, to profess and practise their own religion, or to use their own language." G.A. res. 2200A (XXI), 21 U.N. GAOR Supp. (No. 16) at 52, U.N. Doc. A/6316 (1966), 999 U.N.T.S. 171.

3 *Convention for the Protection of Human Rights and Fundamental Freedoms*, as amended by Protocols No. 11 and 14, European Treaty Series No. 5.

4 Ibid.

5 Mazower, op. cit., note 1.

6 Patrick Thornberry and Maria Amor Martin Estebanez, *Minority Rights in Europe* (Strasbourg: Council of Europe, 2004), p. 40.

7 Ibid.

8 Ibid.

9 Thornberry and Estebanez, op. cit., note 6, p. 41.

10 Article 11 of *Recommendation 1201 (1993) on an Additional Protocol on the Rights of National Minorities to the European Convention on Human Rights*, adopted by the Assembly on 1 February 1993, refers to local autonomy.

11 See also below regarding the *Outline Convention* and the *Stability Pact*.

12 See also Chapter 9 for a discussion of autonomy.

13 When negotiating a bilateral treaty on friendly relations with Hungary, Slovakia refused to insert reference to Recommendation 1201 due to the autonomy requirement in Article 11. See Kinga Gál, "Bilateral Agreements in Central and Eastern Europe: A New Inter-State Framework for Minority Protection?" *ECMI Working Papers* 4 (Flensburg: ECMI, 1999).

14 Protocol No. 12 to the *Convention for the Protection of Human Rights and Fundamental Freedoms*, European Treaty Series 177 of 4.11. 2000.

15 Explanatory Report to the FCNM, Section 5, accessed July 23, 2013, http://www.coe.int/t/dghl/monitoring/minorities/1_AtGlance/PDF_H(95)10_FCNM_ExplanReport_en.pdf.
16 As of July 23, 2013.
17 *Framework Convention for the Protection of National Minorities and Explanatory Report*, European Treaty Series No 157 open for signatures 1.2.1995.
18 See Tove H. Malloy and Ugo Caruso, *Minorities, their Rights, and the Monitoring of the European Framework Convention for the Protection of National Minorities* (Leiden: Brill Publishers, 2013).
19 Geoff Gilbert, "The Council of Europe and Minority Rights", *Human Rights Quarterly* 18 (1996), pp. 160–90.
20 Marc Weller, "Creating the Conditions necessary for the Effective Participation of Persons belonging to National Minorities: A critical evaluation of the first results of the monitoring of the Framework Convention for the Protection of National Minorities 1998–2003." Paper submitted to the Council of Europe's Conference marking the fifth anniversary of the FCNM, 30–31 October 2003.
21 The list of so-called "conscientious objectors" includes Andorra, Belgium, Iceland, Luxembourg, Monaco, France, Greece, and Turkey as per 25.7.2013.
22 Tove Malloy, Roberta Medda-Windischer, Emma Lantschner and Joseph Marko, "Indicators for Assessing the Impact of the Framework Convention for the Protection of National Minorities in its State Parties" (report presented during the Conference Enhancing the Impact of the Framework Convention, 9–10 October, 2008, accessed July 23, 2013, http://www.coe.int/t/dghl/monitoring/minorities/6_Resources/PDF_IAConf_Report_Bolzano_en_12nov08.pdf.
23 Thornberry and Estebanez, op. cit., note 6, p. 116.
24 The Venice Commission is a consultative body of the Council of Europe on matters of constitutional law and is composed of experts appointed by the governments of the member states. It began work in 1990 on opinions concerning among others constitutional reforms in Bulgaria, Poland and Romania, local self-government, and the federal and the regional state as well as the European Convention for the Protection of Minorities. See the Editor's note to 'European Commission for Democracy through Law: Proposal for a European Convention for the Protection of Minorities' in Human Rights Law Journal, 12 (1991), pp. 265–273.
25 See further Chapter 8.
26 *European Charter for Regional or Minority Languages*, European Treaty Series No. 148 open for signature 5.11.1992.
27 See, accessed July 23, 2013, http://europa.eu/about-eu/basic-information/symbols/motto/index_en.htm.
28 Kristin Henrard and Robert Dunbar (eds.), *Synergies in Minority Protection. European and International Law Perspectives* (Cambridge: Cambridge University Press, 2008).
29 Like the FCNM, the ECRML lacks signatures and ratifications from a number of countries, including Albania, Andorra, Azerbaijan, Belgium, Bulgaria, Estonia, France, Georgia, Greece, Iceland, Ireland, Italy, Latvia, Lithuania, Malta, Moldova, Monaco, Portugal, Russia, San Marino, FYROM, and Turkey as per 25.7.2013.
30 *European Charter of Local Self-Government*, European Treaty Series No. 122 open for signatures 15.10.1985.
31 *Draft European Charter of Regional Self-Government*, accessed July 23, 2013, http://groups.csail.mit.edu/mac/users/rauch/misc/regions/charter_self_government.html.
32 *European Outline Convention on Transfrontier Co-operation*. European Treaty Series 106 opened for signatures 21.5.1980.
33 These were the bilateral agreements that were to include reference to Recommendation 1201.
34 Recommendation 43 on "Territorial Autonomy and National Minorities" of 27 May 1998; Resolution 52 on "Federalism, regionalism, local autonomy and minorities" of 3 June 1997 and Recommendation 70 on "Local law/special status" of 23 November, 1999.
35 Thornberry and Estebanez, op. cit. note 6, chap. 10.
36 James Hughes and Gwendolyn Sasse, "Monitoring the Monitors: EU Enlargement Conditionality and Minority Protection in the CEECs", *Journal on Ethnopolitics and Minority Issues in Europe* 4 (2003), p. 1.

37 This was also an EU initiative with more than forty partners, which also ceased to exist but was a programme of implementation and has set out ambitious working tables for democratization, human rights, economic construction, security issues, military and defence, and justice and home affairs for the states of Albania, Bosnia-Herzegovina, Croatia, the Federal Republic of Yugoslavia and Macedonia, accessed July 23, 2013, http://www.stabilitypact.org.
38 See Gál, op.cit., note 13.
39 See Florence Benoît-Rohmer and Hilde Hardeman "The Pact on Stability in Europe" in *Helsinki Monitor* 4 (1994), pp. 38–51 at p. 41.
40 Benoît-Rohmer and Hardeman, op. cit., note 39, p. 49.
41 See Snezana Trifunovska, "The Issue(s) of Minorities in the European Peace and Security Context", *International Journal on Group Rights* 3 (1996), pp. 283–299.
42 See Arie Bloed and Pieter Van Dijk, Pieter, eds., *Protection of Minority Rights through Bilateral Treaties. The Case of Central and Eastern Europe* (The Hague: Kluwer Law International, 1999). See also Gál, op. cit., note 13.
43 Benoît-Rohmer and Hardeman, op. cit., note 39, p. 50.
44 Article 13 of the Amsterdam Treaty reads: "Without prejudice to the other provisions of this Treaty and within the limits of the powers conferred by it upon the Community, the Council, acting unanimously on a proposal from the Commission and after consulting the European Parliament, may take appropriate action to combat discrimination based on sex, racial or ethnic origin, religion or belief, disability, age or sexual orientation." Treaty of Amsterdam amending the Treaty of the European Union, the Treaties establishing the European Communities and certain related acts, signed on 2.10.1997, *Official Journal of the European Communities* C 340, 10 November 1997.
45 *Council Directive 2000/43/EC* of 29 June 2000 implementing the principle of equal treatment between persons irrespective of racial or ethnic origin, *Official Journal* L 180, 19/07/2000 P. 0022 – 0026.
46 *Council Directive 2000/78/EC* of 27 November 2000 establishing a general framework for equal treatment in employment and occupation, *Official Journal* L 303, 02/12/2000 P. 0016 – 0022.
47 *Charter of Fundamental Rights of the European Union (2000/C 364/01), Official Journal of the European Communities* C 364/1, 18.12.2000.
48 Art. 21 of Charter, ibid.
49 The reports, accessed July 23, 2013, http://cridho.uclouvain.be/en/eu_experts_network/.
50 *Resolution on a Community Charter of Regional Languages and Cultures and on a Charter of Rights of Ethnic Minorities* (Rapporteur: Arfe).
51 Article 2 reads: "The Union is founded on the values of respect for human dignity, freedom, democracy, equality, the rule of law and respect for human rights, including the rights of persons belonging to minorities. These values are common to the Member States in a society in which pluralism, non-discrimination, tolerance, justice, solidarity and equality between women and men prevail." *Treaty establishing a Constitution for Europe*, signed 29.10.2004, *Official Journal of the European Union*, C310/1, 16.12.2004.
52 Contribution submitted by Mr Peter Balazs and Mr Jozsef Szajer, members of the Convention, and Mr Neil MacCormick, Mr Peter Eckstein-Kovacs and Mr Istvan Szent-Ivanyi, alternate members, "Respect for minorities and the European constitutional structure" of 25 March 2003, CONV 639/03, CONTRIB 286, and letter from Hungary to the Italian Presidency of 13 October 2003 cited on the HTMN webpage, accessed July 23, 2013, http://www.hhrf.org/htmn/background/prop_eu.htm (no longer available). The representatives of Romania also made similar contributions.
53 See Krzysztof Drzewicki, "A Constitution for Europe: Enshrining minority rights", *OSCE Magazine*, March 2005, 19–21; Max van der Stoel, "Looking Back, Looking Forward: Reflections on Preventing Inter-Ethnic Conflict" in *Facing Ethnic Conflicts. Toward a New Realism*, eds. Andreas Wimmer, Richard J. Goldstone, Donald L. Horowitz, Ulrike Joras, and Conrad Schetter (Rowan and Littlefield Publishers, Lanham, 2004), pp. 113–119.
54 See for instance, *Agreement between the European Community and the Council of Europe on cooperation between the European Union Agency for Fundamental Rights and the Council of Europe, Official Journal* L 186, 15.7.2008, pp. 7–11.

Chapter 3: Europeanisation

Tamara Hoch Jovanovic

Summary

The concept of Europeanisation concerns the domestic effects of European integration processes. Thus, the perspective of Europeanisation is becoming useful in the aim to analyse the link between the European Union (EU) and minorities, specifically the effects on domestic minority rights as a consequence of EU-promoted rules, norms and governance structures. There are different avenues through which the EU can influence domestic minority rights, both directly and indirectly. This is seen in the EU enlargement processes and the EU neighbourhood policy which show how the EU matters directly as a source of change through external relations by pushing EU accession states and neighbouring countries to reform domestic minority rights systems. Indirectly, the EU can affect the domestic minority rights policies of existing member states through EU law and policy, but by also providing opportunities for minority groups to participate in EU policies. EU frameworks have, therefore, potential for fulfilling the protection, preservation and promotion of minority rights.

Introduction

Throughout the 1990s, the EU did not make any substantial contribution to the codification of minority rights in Europe as discussed in Chapter 2. Instead, the EU matters in a different way for domestic minority rights' policies, which differs from many traditional minority rights instruments and approaches. Most provisions and standards on the protection of minorities in Europe, since the early 1990s, were developed by the Council of Europe (CoE) and the Organization for Security and Cooperation in Europe (OSCE) and have seen different degrees of impact on domestic minority rights regimes. However, EU policy making and legal structures provide alternative means and measures which can contribute to the fulfilment on protection, preservation and promotion of minority groups and their activities. The EU's ability to affect domestic minority policy and minority groups does not emerge through clear legal standards or judicial mechanisms as is often assumed to be necessary by traditional minority rights paradigms.[1] Instead, the broader European integration environment provides a different setting for institutional interaction by for instance offering funding for minority-relevant activities or for the development of networking beyond national borders. Likewise, with broader Europeanisation of domestic policy and legal systems, minority groups are also affected by economic, political and legal changes stemming from EU politics and the reconstructed structures which encompass many societies. Similarly, whereas formal implications through the means of standard-setting are limited, the EU can help to fulfil a different role by activating and empowering national minority groups as partners and actors in policy implementation or as participants within the European-level polity. This chapter guides the reader through selected EU frameworks with a focus on how some EU-induced developments contribute to the protection, preservation and promotion of minority groups in Europe in the context of European integration. Different Europeanisation mechanisms are reviewed in order to show how the literature on Europeanisation approaches the processes of domestic change, within which changes in domestic minority rights can also be located. Finally the chapter reviews the gradual construction, or emergence, of a policy stance at the EU level.

The concept of Europeanisation

Europeanisation as a research agenda does not repeat existing notions from early European integration studies, such as why European integration takes place, or why states join the EU, nor does it address the creation of new powers for the EU. Such questions have been addressed by classic integration theories such as liberal intergovernmentalism and neo-functionalism, both concerned with grasping the essence of the European integration process itself and what is often termed as "history making decisions."[2] Instead, the study of Europeanisation emerged at a later stage of European integration, by providing a gateway to understand domestic consequences caused by established EU institutions, policies and legislation. By addressing questions of domestic consequences as caused by the EU, Europeanisation brings domestic and comparative politics into what had largely been an international relations-dominated field.[3] Similarly, it also elevates the study of the EU into the landscape of political science and governance studies as a way to understand domestic change caused through European Integration.

In this chapter, Europeanisation will be confined to a process by which the triad of domestic policy, polity and politics changes along the engagement with the EU.[4] However, domestic impact through engagement with the EU is not limited to existing EU member states only. Instead, Europeanisation processes can also extend beyond the group of EU member states, especially regarding candidates and applicant states, as in the nearest neighbourhood where there is no prospect of EU membership. In the context of EU enlargement, the Europeanisation literature has demonstrated the weight of EU-induced reform among official candidates for EU accession through conditionality.[5] Looking beyond existing EU member states is important in order for students to be able to understand how the EU can matter in a policy field such as that of minority rights, given that the EU acts across different levels. Even before EU-studies scholars began to depict the usage of the concept as a so-called domestic consequence barometer of European integration and EU politics, history studies invoked Europeanisation in reference to transnational cultural diffusion[6] or as an "exporting" concept of European values, social norms and authority.[7] As such, the literature does not limit Europeanisation to only a force of EU-ization. Many studies often invoke processes of domestic change and implications triggered through broader European-level norms and rules, making it applicable to other institutions as well. However, this chapter limits the concept to an explicit EU-related phenomenon given the aim to unpack what role the EU can play in domestic minority policy and on minority groups and through which means the EU is able to play such a role.

Europeanisation mechanisms

There is a myriad of ways through which the EU can matter in domestic politics and become an agent of change. A key distinction between different Europeanisation mechanisms is that of 'direct' versus 'indirect' direction, also known as vertical versus horizontal Europeanisation processes.[8] Direct or vertical mechanisms of change are often intentional and depart from a defined policy at the EU level. In vertical Europeanisation, a mechanism conforms to a process in which a policy transcends from the EU down to the domestic level. One common mechanism here is coercion or intentional mimetism, which aims at achieving convergence between the EU and the domestic level. Horizontal mechanisms of Europeanisation, on the other hand, view Europeanisation as a process where there is no pressure on the member states from the EU to conform to specific rules which have been defined in EU policy-making.

Instead, domestic adjustment takes place through processes of socialization or patterns of emulation, market correction or through idea diffusion and discourses. Similarly, horizontal Europeanisation can become activated through state-to-state interaction, whereas vertical mechanisms conform to a chain which runs down from the EU to the domestic level. Accordingly, when the EU and the domestic level are encountered, the EU can enforce vertical mechanisms through adaptational pressure and prescriptive models, whereas horizontal mechanisms contribute to an installation of a context where change is produced through processes of framing or market competition processes.

One of the most common and oldest mechanisms in the Europeanisation literature is the vast EU-produced legislative rules. Through legislative mechanisms, the EU often prescribes a specific institutional model or policy template that member states are expected to adopt and implement.[9] In those cases where the EU holds an exclusive competence in a given policy field, it is also able to legislate alone and adopt acts which are made binding upon national legislation.[10] Examples of exclusive competences are set out in Article 3(1) TFEU and cover areas such as customs union and monetary policy.[11] A common mechanism of legal harmonization over national law and policy is through coercion.

Another common mechanism by which the EU can affect the domestic setting is through instituting policies which are commonly referred to as policies of regulatory competition.[12] This concept is common to the context of the EU single market, which established an environment in which member states compete to gain advantages for domestic firms and multinationals.[13] A common consequence is that these policies of market regulation trigger a race between states and firms which consequently affect market standards at the domestic level.

Apart from the above legal and market oriented mechanisms of Europeanisation, it is also acknowledged that the EU can establish a context in which change is triggered through learning process across and between countries.[14] For instance, through regular, repeated, detailed discussion and comparison between member states' policy activities, a convergence of opinion between states regarding specific policy paradigms and agreements on which policy choices and models are most appropriate may be produced. Related to the learning process, regular interaction, cooperation and socialization can also produce behavioural effects, by triggering the emergence of new norms, ideas, beliefs and practices.[15] This tends to be more of a long-term process, given that socialization is largely centred on behavioural change among actors. Examples of outcomes are for instance a more cooperative spirit or altered expectations among domestic actors.

Apart from the above, there is also a common bottom-up mechanism embedded in Europeanisation research, namely member states' attempt to both export and import policy models.[16] In this context, Brussels, or any other policy-making arena, can serve an arena in which individual member states can attempt to spread their own standards to others.

A final mechanism of Europeanisation is the classic goodness of fit notion which has structured many Europeanisation studies so far. According to the goodness of fit model, domestic change is catalysed by the degree of fit or extent of compatibility between the EU and the domestic level on a given policy, legislation or other initiative. Whereas a good fit between the EU and the domestic level on a given policy issue is not expected to generate high pressure for domestic adaptation, and therefore also low domestic change, a low level of compatibility will create a misfit and an environment conducive to more pressure for domestic change.[17] This so-called classic model in Europeanisation research acknowledges the domestic setting as an important conditioning variable in the process of Europeanisation, including the role of intervening variables which intervene in the Europeanisation process either according to a rational choice pathway or through the socialization and internalization of new belief systems. The constructivist variant identifies norm entrepreneurs as central intervening variables. These are anticipated to act through the use of moral argumentation in order to persuade actors to redefine interests and identities, ultimately engaging them in processes of social learning.[18] The rationalist pathway on the other hand identifies veto-players as powerful coalitions that will help to facilitate change or assist governments to achieve change. Veto-players are normally concerned with a redistribution of resources and power dynamics.[19]

Finally, the Europeanisation research agenda identifies four possible outcomes of domestic change. These are known as inertia, absorption, transformation and retrenchment.[20] Inertia normally corresponds to lack of change, and implementation refers to a delay or a resistance to EU-induced change. Absorption, on the other hand, resembles minor change or adoption to EU rules or norms, constituting domestic change which does not replace existing paradigms or understandings in any fundamental way. The typology of transformation refers to the outcome in which most fundamental domestic change can be depicted, because this typology covers those processes which lead to a replacement of pre-existing patterns by producing substantial changes in domestic rules, institutions, beliefs and discourses. The final typology, retrenchment, resembles a rather paradoxical reaction, in that domestic policies become even less EU-like than what they were before encountering EU rules and norms.

Europeanisation and minority rights

A clear division may be placed between the two main perspectives on how Europeanisation impacts domestic minority rights through EU-induced rules and norms. First, an overly top-down and vertical form of Europeanisation is observed in the external relations of the EU. Through the application of EU conditionality towards accession and candidate states, reforms relating to domestic minority rights have become anchored in EU requirements on rule adoption in which reform in domestic minority rights are incorporated. Similarly, albeit to a much lesser extent, the protection of minority rights is integrated into the promotion of human rights across neighbourhood countries through partnership declarations under the framework of the European Neighbourhood Policy (ENP). In fact, the EU began to matter most for domestic minority policies in the context of external relations, and especially during the three recent EU enlargement rounds since 2004. However, there are numerous horizontal Europeanisation processes ensuing from EU law, policy and governance structures which have contributed to the proliferation of minority rights in EU member states. Such horizontal Europeanisation processes of change are often triggered through indirect means and measures without necessarily invoking tools on minority rights *per se*. Given that the EU still lacks clear minority competences and a uniform minority policy, the potentials for EU-induced change of domestic minority policies are usually explored across an indirect spectrum in which minority rights can be compensated through alternative EU policies and law. Below, two different Europeanisation processes in the context of minority rights will be explored.

EU Enlargement and Europeanisation

Membership requires that the candidate country has achieved stability of institutions guaranteeing democracy, the rule of law, human rights and respect for and protection of minorities, the existence of a functioning market economy as well as the capacity to cope with competitive pressure and market forces within the Union.[21]

The above statement taken from the Copenhagen Presidency Conclusions of 1993 marks an important turn in EU's approach and commitment to minority rights. A key commitment among the EU institutions on the protection of minority rights can be observed through the creation and imposition of certain conditions, i.e. conditionality, from 2004 until the present, that applicant states to the EU need to fulfil before they are granted full accession.[22] The package of conditions is known as the Copenhagen criteria. Within the political conditions of the Copenhagen criteria, a specific condition required the need to fulfil the "respect for and protection of minority rights", and to demonstrate "stability of institutions" in order to qualify for EU membership.[23] The implementation of the Copenhagen Criteria, including that of minority protection, was monitored by the European Commission through regular annual reports and by the European Council through Accession Partnerships' program[24] Accordingly, the monitoring of applicant states undertaken by the Commission commonly raised critiques and recommendations for reform, all the while highlighting that the lack of reform could bear negatively for a prospective EU member state's overall membership prospects. For instance, Slovakia's EU accession process was interrupted during the course of accession due to what was referred to by the Commission as poor domestic performance on minority issues.[25] As such, the process of conditionality regarding aspirant nations to EU accession began to be viewed as successfully able to transfer and integrate the most dynamic European norms and values into domestic systems, wherein external pressure from EU bodies became a powerful source for change. For example, new non-discrimination and minority rights legislation was introduced throughout Central and Eastern Europe during the period of time before many of these nations became full EU members.[26] It was also within this ambit that the clearest link between the EU and minorities was installed, through the Europeanisation of domestic minority-related laws and policies. To borrow Gwendolyn Sasse's words: "The actual democratic criteria were a breakthrough by inserting a minority speak within a normally less advanced minority entity (EU)."[27] Consequently, Europeanisation studies also mushroomed, by becoming further defined at the outset of the evaluation of the minority-related laws and policies of candidate nations, in which changes ranged across domestic legal and political constellations. In some cases the adoption of EU-recommended law resulted in a streamlining of domestic minority legislation, such as in the cases of Latvia and Estonia,[28] whereas in others the EU pressured nationalistic regimes to change their minority politics which was at that time not in-line with the EU understanding of minority rights, as was the case in Slovakia.[29] As such, the EU minority criteria gave impetus to cover a new dimension, or blind spot, in the ongoing efforts towards the Europeanisation of new policy fields. With this, the EU also joined the European minority rights regime, by contributing to the development of domestic policies in the area of minority rights protection through the instrument of conditionality.

Like much of the enlargement driven literature relating to processes of Europeanisation, theoretical explanations have ranged between rational versus constructivists' explanations. Each dimension distinguishes mechanisms by which states reshape domestic minority policies in response to the EU. The constructivists built their claims around the idea that the accession states would gradually change their preferences, absorbing EU values and principles into domestic structures.[30] One of the central claims here builds on the idea that actor behaviour changes through processes of imitation or argumentative persuasion, generating an ultimate status of an appropriate nature and acceptance of the values which were promoted through the conditionality.[31] According to the rational choice approach, on the other hand, EU conditionality was interpreted by national actors along the calculation of benefits and rewards that the final EU membership would bring. More specifically, the acceding countries choose to comply with the EU-induced rules in order to enhance their membership prospects, thus acting according to an incentive-driven logic, rather than the logic of persuasion or socialization as assumed by constructivists. In reality, joining the EU as a full member constituted one of the key foreign-policy goals of most Central and Eastern European states in states by the early 1990s.[32] Similarly, reforms of domestic minority policies and legal instruments were closely intertwined with ongoing democratic transitions across the accession landscape, in which democratic consolidation became advertised as a method to 'return to Europe'. Accordingly, analyses have also largely concluded that the impact of the EU in the accession countries which subsequently implemented the Copenhagen criteria came mainly as the result of the external incentives of accession conditionality rather than from social learning or lesson-drawing.[33] In other words, the willingness of a nation to align with EU structural demands as can be seen in the Copenhagen Criteria, for example, is directly related to whether or not that nation has been officially recognised as a candidate for full membership. However the conclusions drawn fail to explain what happens to the policy field once EU membership becomes a *de facto* certainty by neglecting what happens once processes of Europeanisation replaces notions of compliance, which themselves had been previously built upon notions of EU-driven conditionality and the close monitoring of progress during the stage before full accession. The question remains as to whether an incentivized structure of top-down control remains sustainable once those incentives cease to exist after a nation becomes a full EU member state.

Regarding the external Europeanisation referred to above, the EU confronted double standard accusations, as it possessed no similar rules and approaches to be applied internally. It has been argued that the promotion of minority standards is an external matter, but that the EU exempts from any similar undertaking in its internal *acquis*, and as such existing member states were exempted from the same demands on minority rights protection when compared to EU accession countries.[34] Double standard charges were further accentuated with passing of the Amsterdam Treaty of 1997, which amended (the former) Article 6 TEU by incorporating most of the values enshrined in the Copenhagen criteria; however, the Treaty was passed only after "disincorporating" the minority criterion from the founding values of the EU.[35] The double standard accusations were met by the Commission with the defence that the reason for why minority rights were left out of the EU treaty was that all the political criteria which were defined in the Copenhagen Criteria were already enshrined as constitutional principles, stating that (the former) Article 6 TEU already fully covered the protection of minorities.[36] However, an interesting development is noted from this time onwards in the minority-related EU discourse, for which the Copenhagen momentum should not be underestimated as having been an innovative starting point. For instance, the very incorporation of minority rights into the EU enlargement strategy signalled for the first time that the EU considers there to exist a distinction between individual human rights and minority rights, implying that the EU recognizes the need to ensure distinct minority rights protection approaches, resulting in the instigation of a new institutional and political fact.[37] As such, this not only provided a new avenue for minority protection across the Central and Eastern European countries, but this new reality also created another level of discourse among EU institutions and political actors who promoted the activation of such new principles for internal and domestic application. A few years later, the founding EU values were expanded to include the protection of minorities, as can be seen in Article 2 TEU (former Article 6 TEU), preceding heated debates within the EU and between member states.[38]

European Neighbourhood Policy, Europeanisation and minority rights

A second dimension linked to the EU's external relations and its policies relating to minorities is encompassed by the European Neighbourhood Policy (ENP). During the 1990s, the EU began to include minority rights within the human rights conditions that have become a standard element of the EU's bilateral trade association agreements with non-EU states.[39] The ENP resembles a more distant fashion of EU partnership to its immediate neighbourhood through bilateral treaties. The ENP differs from EU enlargement strategies in that it does not invoke any accession conditionality or transfer of the *acquis communitaire*, given that the final goal of the bi-lateral relationship in question is not expressed in terms of EU membership.[40] Instead, bi-lateral partnership and cooperation is fashioned upon specific 'Action Plans' which are drawn up between each partner country and the EU, with the overarching aim of achieving a deepening level of economic integration and political cooperation. Today, 16 countries are part of the ENP, stretching across the EU's southern and eastern borders.[41]

In principle, whereas each partnership agreement is unique in that it reflects the needs and capacities of each country, the EU also attaches a cross-cutting principle on the promotion of particular values throughout its neighbourhood policy. At the centre of such value promotion, the EU normally engages its partners in democratic development, stability, the rule of law and human rights. The respect for human rights is promoted in almost every bilateral agreement, and is subsequently made a 'condition' for cooperation and interaction, a principle similar to that of conditionality, applied during the EU enlargement process. Minority protection is included in several action plans, being embedded within the overall mutual commitment of common values and especially that of human rights. Some of the most prominent cases are, for example, the action plans between the EU and Ukraine, which clearly stipulates that "ensuring respect for rights of persons belonging to national minorities (based on legislation brought in line with 'European standards' and cooperation between government authorities and representatives of national minorities) is a priority."[42] The Action Plan with Moldova devotes even more attention to the protection of national minorities, wherein the EU promotes the necessity to ensure appropriate implementation of the CoE commitments.[43]

Similarly, regarding the Action Plan with Georgia, the EU reiterates that the respect of persons belonging to national minorities is an objective, and goes one step further by encouraging Georgia to sign and ratify CoE minority instruments.[44] By encouraging such objectives through partnerships, the EU aims at an approximation of the partners' legislation, norms and standards to those of the EU, as such aiming at an outward Europeanization in line to the achievement during the enlargement process. As such, the EU endeavours to integrate the neighbourhood into broader European-level norms and rules on minority rights.

Similar to the processes related to enlargement Europeanisation, the difference between incentive-driven versus socialization processes deserves attention. There is a difference in the arguments, given that the ability of the EU to generate change in its neighbourhood is strongly diminished when full EU membership is not an option.[45] The enlargement literature largely concludes that the fast pace of reform in EU accession states was underpinned by the EU membership prospect,[46] whereas the same intensity and degree of change in the neighbourhood is difficult to encourage through partnership frameworks which lack a membership prospect. Some scholars argue that little progress has taken place in the EU neighbourhood due to the lack of specificity of EU demands, the absence of a clear timetable for the implementation of the goals laid down in the Action Plans, and progress is especially curtailed due to the fact that the reform actions outlined are not binding.[47] The question that arises then, is whether or not the EU can matter as a source of change without offering the prospect of membership? In this regard, constructivist scholarship, drawing on premises of transnational diffusion, argues that socialization mechanisms are most likely to gain the upper-hand in those contexts where no EU membership is possible.[48] Accordingly, Europeanisation mechanisms in such contexts are predominantly of an indirect character, whereby the EU has been understood as a transnational socializing force,[49] one of value export,[50] and even one which triggers imitation practices and lesson-drawing in the neighbourhood, which is also known as emulation.[51]

The above shows how the dynamics of Europeanisation have been studied within the context of EU external relations. In the enlargement context, both the Europeanisation and minority studies literature repeatedly argue that the most powerful EU mechanisms which drove domestic reform on the protection of minority rights was EU conditionality which paved the way towards EU membership.[52] Thus, whereas the enlargement process remains endowed by a compliance-induced process of Europeanisation, in which the EU had the upper-hand through the promise of membership as a source for domestic change, the broader neighbourhood, rather, invokes according to the constructivist an Europeanisation process of transnational diffusion and socialization.

EU internal frameworks and minority rights

Currently, an internal EU minority policy is contested, given the fact that there is (still) no uniform EU minority policy for existing member states. However, this does not mean that no minority links exist between the *acquis communitaire* and minority rights. Links that could provide for a fulfilment of minority rights stretch across different policy areas, EU legislation and fundamental principles.

A major area of internal consensus on the meaning of minority protection at the EU level has emerged during the period of time between the Maastricht treaty and the Lisbon treaty. The Maastricht treaty entrenched fundamental rights while also introducing an explicit requirement on the respect for national and regional diversity. Similarly, the Maastricht treaty also established a political European Union by incorporating social policy aspects and the cultural diversity principle into what had previously been an overwhelmingly economic Union. For minority studies in general, this so-called "de-economisation of European integration" as marked by the Maastricht innovations, created the major link between EU-policy making and minority rights.[53] However, the Lisbon treaty has been much more ground-breaking, as it has officially introduced the word 'minority' for the first time within the *acquis communitaire*. Article 2 TEU states that the EU founding values include the respect for the rights of persons belonging to minorities.[54] The Lisbon treaty also made the Charter of Fundamental Rights (the Charter) legally binding, which makes a second explicit reference to a "national" minority in Article 21.[55] This article lists the grounds upon which discrimination is prohibited within the EU when implementing EU law, entailing for the first time in EU history that national minority belonging is a ground to be respected. Moreover, the Charter also reiterates the EU's commitment to the safeguarding of linguistic and cultural diversity.[56]

The above gradual, but salient, evolution of the protection of minority rights within EU frameworks has been summarized by Bruno De Witte as an "incipient EU minority rights policy constituted by specific (and often quite limited) activities in a number of different fields."[57] In other words, minority rights at the EU level have turned into a field with links across different policy fields and whose objectives are most often defined elsewhere. The following section reviews the EU's ability to generate effects pertaining to minority rights within the areas of protection, preservation and promotion.

The EU and the protection of minorities

Protection, being the end all of minority rights, corresponds to a solid basis within the field of human rights. However, minority rights, and the protection which these rights (intrinsically) entail, transcend the scope of individual human rights by demanding additional special rights in order to compensate for disadvantages linked to the circumstances of minorities and to establish factual equality between a majority (population) and a minority (population).[58] Many minority studies experts identify the necessity in the implementation of non-discrimination measures which incorporates clear legal implications towards public and private entities in case of breaches of minority rights.[59] As such, the protection dimension invokes the existence of legal regulation and the possibility to turn to a court if a minority right is breached. It is directly related to this concern that many international treaties and conventions on minority rights have been drafted. Although EU treaties have been (relatively) weak in providing protection for minority groups, the indirect provision of Article 13 TFEU referring to non-discrimination legislation includes the possibility for recognised minorities to have cases heard by the ECJ. Moreover, EU actors and institutions repeatedly reassert that the respect for human rights, the respect for minorities and the respect for human dignity are the founding principles of the EU, which is also a key for joining the Union and for remaining a member of it.[60]

A particularly important nexus in the European context which addresses minority rights and the protection these rights entail arises from EU non-discrimination legislation and EU human rights foundations. The former consists of a detailed EU secondary law with binding effects on domestic legislation of member states through the Race Equality Directive, designed to combat discrimination based on racial and ethnic origin. Moreover, the Charter, which became legally binding after the Lisbon Treaty came into force 1 December 2009, provides an additional level of protection through Article 21, by prohibiting discrimination on the ground of national minority membership.[61] Next to non-discrimination legislation, minority protection finds support in general EU human rights developments. Human rights are embedded in EU treaties as general advisory principles of any EU action and they provide solid ground for the ECJ to link human rights to other activities when member states act under EU law. Regarding the Lisbon Treaty, the "respect of rights of persons belonging to minorities" was added to the list of EU founding values in Article 2 TEU. This introduction was not accompanied by any legal standards *per se*, but the potential of it is yet to be realised in ECJ rulings of dispute cases between national minorities and the general implementation of EU law. However, Article 2 TEU is backed up by a sanctioning mechanism. Article 7 TEU provides for possible sanctions by stipulating that the Council may determine (based on proposals from the Commission and the European Parliament) if there is a case of a serious and persistent breach of the principles laid down in Article 2 TEU by a member state, for which sanctions can be undertaken against this member state.[62] Sanctions normally refer to the exclusion or suspension of voting rights in EU institutions. However, in order to avoid having to resort to such drastic measures, the human rights situations in member states are evaluated through annual reports prepared by a network of human rights experts.[63] The so-called Network of Independent Experts in Fundamental Rights was established by the Commission in 2002, with the principal task to review each member state's human rights performance, including the action (or inaction) of member states relating to minority rights. The network prepares annual reports, with a specific focus on compliance with human rights and teh Charter when implementing EU law. Similarly, the operation of this network is expected to enhance the EU's conflict prevention capabilities as envisaged by Article 7 TEU.[64]

The EU and the preservation of minority identities

Preservation is here understood as referring to those EU-induced measures and activities which stimulate the preservation of a distinct minority identity. Such efforts may be seen to be especially important when relating to the survival of the minority group as such and directly pertain to facilities designed to preserve the culture, language and identity characteristics of a minority community.

A major contribution to preservation of minority groups by EU frameworks stems from the diversity principle and EU culture policy, which emerged with the Maastricht Treaty and Article 128 TEC, today Article 167 TFEU. Symbolically, the EU acknowledged that culture is an important part of European integration, as none of its member states is culturally homogenous. Scholars also understand the diversity slogan as a potential route for the better accommodation of minorities within the EU.[65] However, this introduction marked a new endeavour by providing the EU with a competence on culture for the first time. The article asks the EU to contribute to the preservation and protection of the cultures of its member states, while respecting national and regional diversity.[66] It is of a non-binding nature wherein the EU is expected to supplement and complement member state activities in the field of culture, but by refraining from any measures of legal harmonization over domestic law and policy on cultural issues. Consequently, regulative instruments do not necessarily guarantee clear legal entitlements on cultural questions in EU member states. This relates to the reading of the treaty content which confers how the objectives of the culture policy should be implemented and met. Wordings such as 'support' and 'complement' regarding member state actions[67] are characteristic of EU cultural policy.[68] The objectives and provisions of EU culture policy grant the EU institutions a facilitating role, by stipulating the necessity of respecting, contributing and fostering the preservation of cultural and linguistic diversity as an integral part of EU action. A similar commitment is reaffirmed in the Charter on the respect of cultural, religious and linguistic diversity.

It should be noted that although no formal or binding mechanisms have yet been developed for the management of EU culture cultural policies, the EU can impose direct demands and pressure on their implementation and if necessary. For example, EU's role in the field of culture was reiterated in paragraph 4 of Article 167 TFEU, which states that the "Union shall take cultural aspects into account in its actions under the provisions of the Treaties, in particular in order to respect and to promote the diversity of its cultures."[69] This same endeavour became reaffirmed in Article 22 of the Charter, which repeated that the EU shall respect cultural, religious and linguistic diversity. Article 3 TEU also refers to cultural and linguistic diversity as an EU value which shall be respected and that the EU shall ensure that Europe's cultural heritage is safeguarded and enhanced.[70] Such mainstreaming commitment was also affirmed in a speech by Romano Prodi on the role of culture in the EU, when he stated that; "there is a greater sensitivity towards the many different identities that make up our continent. The objective of safeguarding diversity, particularly cultural and linguistic diversity, is a thread that now runs through all our policies."[71] Towards this end, the EU has increasingly become very clear that it views its own contribution to the flourishing of all cultures in Europe as an obligation.

The requirements described above, as set out in the EU treaties, have so far only been implemented through soft instruments such as periodical programs and budgetary schemes. The resources which the EU normally develops in order to implement some of its non-binding commitments, have been described as a combination of more hybrid models of EU involvement in specific policy fields.[72] As of yet, the programs Kaleidoscope, Ariane and Raphael ran until 1999, which then became replaced by the periodic program known as Culture 2000 Program, which ran from 2000–2006[73], while the current program is referred to as the Culture Program 2007–2013.[74] The programs can be characterised as putting effort towards the goal of seeing the full implementation of EU cultural policies within all member states so that the objectives set out in EU treaties many be (increasingly) fulfilled. However, objectives towards the preservation of cultural and linguistic diversity differ from one program to the next. For example, the current Culture Program 2007–2013 states the objectives of the promotion of transnational mobility of cultural players, the encouragement of the transnational circulation of cultural works, and the encouragement of intercultural dialogue within the EU.[75] Moreover, the rationale of the Culture Program 2007–2013 rests on the perceived benefits that cultural and linguistic cooperation can produce for the overall European integration process. The Commission also performs an active role in the field of culture with its introduction of the "European agenda for culture in a globalized world."[76]

The role that the EU has defined for itself in the area of culture and European cultural policy as envisaged by the EU treaties can be described as a mechanism with certain benefits for minority groups. The relevance for such activity at the supranational level can be depicted in the undertaking of new activities which aim at the support and the supplementation of domestic action in the area of cultural and linguistic diversity. Second, the principal support in this area is provided through the establishment of a budget. EU assistance in lessening financial burdens which directly relate to minority issues and which would not exist were the minority dimension not be present within a particular context, is integral to efforts of support and supplementation, usually accompanied by awareness and increased transnational interaction. One cultural program in particular, the Ariane Program,[77] considered a minority provision (*stricto sensu*), aimed not only at supporting the production of books relating to particular minority groups, but also to organise events related to cultural education surrounding particular minority groups, illustrating not only the desire on the part of the EU to preserve minority culture and heritage, but the desire to enhance and support the educational sector of minorities to ever greater extents.

Issues over minority languages were the first initiatives linked to minorities which were initially approached by EU institutions, especially by the European Parliament (EP). Today, EU language policy holds a weaker base in EU treaties than that of culture. Language as a *sui generis* EU policy area does not figure into EU treaties on its own. Instead language is integrated within other policy areas, especially upon EU cultural policies which often embed 'languages' into the broader area of European cultural heritage.[78] Several scholars have also understood that by defining EU culture policies, the EU automatically incorporated language as a defining principle.[79] As such, an EU language policy relates to the same clauses in the EU treaties as culture policy, largely defined by the commitments made by the EU to respect cultural and *linguistic* diversity and the stated objectives to safeguard and enhance such diversity in Europe as envisaged in Article 3 (3) TEU, 167 TFEU, and Article 22 Charter. Links between minority languages and EU frameworks can also be traced to EU education policy[80] in which the EU commits to supporting and supplementing member state action on vocational training.[81]

Although the issue of regional and minority languages is longstanding among EU institutions, this issue has also initially been a complicated one. The EP was the first institution to pay attention to minority languages, attempting to insert the issue in the European agenda. The initial activities culminated in a number of non-binding resolutions, in which the EP recommended a range of measures on how to increase support and promotion of regional and minority languages in the areas of culture, education, media, and public policy.[82] The resolutions were, however, never adopted due to a lack of support from the remaining EU institutions. Despite the lack of support to adopt the resolutions and to make them binding vis-à-vis the member states, they have served a catalyst for future developments, culminating in the set-up of numerous budgetary lines and in the establishment of an EP Intergroup for Traditional Minorities, National Communities and Languages. With this, the EP has also appeared as the most minority-friendly EU institution.[83]

Another complex issue has arisen during EU-led efforts to protect minority languages at the supranational level over how to interpret the phrase 'linguistic diversity', which appears, for example, in articles Article 3 (3) TEU and Article 22 of the Charter. This issue is complex because the question as to whether or not this phrase should be interpreted as a clause directly relevant for regional and minority languages.[84] However, despite the different readings of this phrase it has served as a yard-stick for the development of different institutional initiatives on the promotion of the use and respect of minority languages in the EU.[85] Nearly every EU institution has proceeded with a number of initiatives relating to the promotion of linguistic diversity, characterised by political support normally adopted in policy fields that lack clear legal principles. The most common tools are provided through an allocation of expenditure, programs and projects. The backbone of such initiatives revolves around the means to promote and support national and transnational projects, adding minority languages as an important factor within language development.

The European Council in support of the EP established a resolution on the promotion of linguistic diversity in 2002, disclosing that one of the encouragements which the Council makes in the member states is to preserve and enhance the linguistic diversity of the Union.[86] This resolution developed within the broader decision on the part of EU lawmakers to promote linguistic diversity and language learning which resulted, in part, in 2001 having been commemorated as the European Year of Languages. These two developments paved the way towards the creation of an Action Plan by the Commission to address new goals on language learning. Although the key ambitions of this initiative revolved around aims to promote language learning across the Union as a whole, it informed the member states that the linguistic situation is an important aspect of the Union, calling for the development of national action plans to meet the common goals. Although the above EU-level initiatives do not equal a full-fledged minority policy, they display a willingness on the part of the EU to promote regional and minority languages as an integral part of European common heritage.

This combination of institutional and economic readiness has informed further projects relating to promotion and research of minority languages. EBLUL and Mercator are examples of such initiatives which were established not only in order to promote minority languages through research and documentation, but also to establish a European based network for those active in this field. Although both operate without a clear legal basis at the EU level, they have contributed to an increased awareness of certain minority languages, documented information on the multiplicity of lesser used languages in EU member states and these initiatives have contributed to increased levels of cross-border networking.[87] Moreover, both the EBLUL and Mercator are largely upheld and promoted through the EP Intergroup for minorities. This EP Intergroup for minorities was established through a vote in December 2009 by a number of MEP's and is instilled with the function to promote the awareness of national and linguistic minority issues in Europe. Originally established in 1983, the present incarnation of the EP Intergroup for minorities continues the long tradition of the EP of using the cross party Intergroup as the forum to focus on and develop policy regarding the national and linguistic minority question.[88] A body like this can enable new mobilization efforts through pan-European approaches on national minority matters, maximize the scope of different EU resources available for minority groups, and keep the topic alive at the EU level. At the same time, the EP Intergroup for minorities also serves an important link to Brussels and as a channel for lobby activities for minority actors.

The Charter can also be considered to add an indirect legal basis which can be used by institutions to initiate further programs on the preservation of minority languages in the EU. The wording in Article 22 of the Charter reaffirms the role of 'linguistic diversity', adding new substance to both linguistic and cultural interpretations by the institutions and in particular the ECJ. This clause has already inspired the Commission to initiate further programs on regional and minority languages.[89]

Nearly each agenda and program presented above rests on a fixed budget, providing opportunities to apply for funding. It should not be underestimated, given that experts often argue that "money is by no means the 'be-all and end-all' of minority issues."[90] Thus, EU-level funding is clearly a new form of entering the discourses of accommodating the particular needs of national minority groups, especially where national funding is scarce on related matters.

The matter of the usage of minority languages within the EU has landed in front of the ECJ on a number of occasions. In fact, such a matter also corresponds to the only minority-related issue which has been tried by the ECJ and in which the ECJ has taken a clear stance in favour of minority language use. There are in particular two cases in which the ECJ has ruled in favour of linguistic minority groups, namely the Mutsch[91] and Bickel and Franz cases.[92] Basically, these two ECJ rulings provided a legal precedent on the right to use a minority language in criminal proceedings in another EU member state, although this right is limited to those languages that are given official status within the EU.

The EU and the promotion of minorities

Minority groups, their activities and cultures can also be promoted through processes of social and economic integration. EU regional development policy has not only facilitated access to resources in terms of funds for European regions, but it also allows for the development of new activities which can facilitate for minorities' political and societal participation. The politics of regional integration can ascertain the role and visibility of minority groups in minority-inhabited regions. As the EU provides new means and principles for socio-economic integration through its regional development policy, it is also likely to contribute to the promotion of minority activities, their identities and cultures. Several scholars conclude that EU regional policy has an impact on the standing of national minorities[93], despite the fact that the EU treaty content on regional policy does not relate to minorities *per se*.[94] There is in particular an uncountable element attached to the importance of new opportunities for not only political participation, but also societal participation for minorities in European regions.[95]

Possibilities for the promotion of minority groups and their identities in their regions can be anchored in practical consequences stemming from EU regional development policy and the economic assistance attached to this policy domain in Articles 174–178 of the TFEU.[96] EU regional development policies are implemented through periodical initiatives and funded through budgetary schemes. At the bulk of the regional policy is also the idea that regional policy does not necessarily need to run through the logic of the centralized state, instead it incorporates subsequent levels for implementation and management of regional questions. Basically, when contrasted to exclusive national control over regional matters and distribution of funds, many arrangements emanating from European-induced programs on local or territorial cooperation require that certain decision-making mechanisms are facilitated and handed down to regional levels.[97] This is relevant for minority groups living in fixed regions. Some of the minority relevant gains which emerge with EU-induced regional policy are especially reflected in the support which can be used to promote minorities to engage in regional development and to manage some regional questions on their own. Consequently, this also speaks of a promotion of cultural traits within minority-inhabited regions. Research has shown how minorities can become active participants in EU-initiated programs, such as those that aim at economic development in border regions.[98] Similarly, changes in minority-inhabited regions in the direction of more autonomous practices have been linked to EU regional policy and structural strategies.[99] As such, a thorough effort on the part of EU institutions on the regulation of regional development policies can provide support to activities that stimulate promotion of minority groups by informing new forms of mobilization among sub-national groups. EU policy regional stems from early ideas on introducing measures that can help "reduce disparities between the levels of development of various regions."[100] It is also this idea to provide subsidies for poorer and outskirt regions which scholars consider one of the key advantages for minority groups belonging to the EU.[101] With periodical enlargement rounds and problems relating to the growth in regional disparities across all EU member states, the scope of regional policy became an even greater concern to the EU. This culminated not only in a shift in regional policy, but it also contributed to a systematic division between numerous EU funds concerned with specific regional sectors and objectives. It is in line with this evolution and specification of the funding opportunities, that the EU marks relevant approaches which can be used by minority groups to not only develop own regions according to own needs, but also to promote their identities and cultures once engaging in development strategies.

The legal basis and authority that the EU holds in the area of regional development is well established within EU treaties. Article 3 TEU declares that the EU shall 'promote territorial cohesion' among the member states as one of the key objectives of the Union. This objective is furnished with a regulative basis and a list of objectives for the fulfilment of EU regional policy, the form of governance to be used and a financial scheme for its implementation. Article 174 TFEU specifies that the EU has the competence to strengthen the economic and social cohesion of the EU, with particular attention given to 'reducing disparities between the levels of development of the various regions and the backwardness of the least favoured regions'. In general, the policy aims at making regions more equal, which may positively affect minorities living in poorer or outskirt regions. Article 175 TEU states that member states shall conduct their economic policies in coordination with one another in order to attain the aim at reducing regional disparities. Similarly, the formulation and implementation of EU policies and actions, including the implementation of the internal market, shall take into account the objectives set out in Article 174 and shall contribute to their achievement. This general policy objective is funded through Structural Funds, the European Agricultural Guidance and Guarantee Fund, the Guidance Section; European Social Fund, the European Regional Development Fund, the European Investment Bank and the other existing financial instruments. Nearly a third of the entire EU budget is provided on a periodical basis directly related to the achievement of certain regional policy objectives. The chief aims of the overall funding can be sorted into: 1) promoting the development and structural adjustment of regions whose development is lagging behind: 2) encouraging economic and social conversion of areas facing structural difficulties: 3) and the modernisation of policies and systems of education, training and employment.[102]

The aim to attain economic and social cohesion within the EU relates to the importance in connecting European regions and stimulating interregional cooperation, whereas for instance the European Social Fund supports action in the areas of economic inclusion, social inclusion and integration of disadvantaged people. Similarly, by focusing specifically on the reduction of imbalances between regions, the ERDF finances the objectives of territorial cooperation for which it has established the Interreg initiative with a particular focus on fostering interregional cooperation. The Interreg constitutes primarily cross-border, transnational and inter-regional cooperation, with a particular emphasis on the integration of remote European regions. Although the Interreg does not make any explicit reference to minorities, it does highlight some content which could be relevant for historical minorities living in fixed regions. For example, cross-border and transnational cooperation can help to supply minorities with cultural contacts and material goods from their kin-state, supporting the promotion of their cultural traits. Similarly, by backing up the right to participation in the management of regional affairs and the right to engage in cross-border and transnational cooperation, initiatives like the Interreg also help to activate and promote minority group participation.

Another initiative which links EU regional policy and the promotion of minority groups and their activities is rooted in the EU's attempts to standardize cross-border cooperation by providing it with a legal basis. In 2006, the EU created the European Grouping of Territorial Cooperation (EGTC) with the aim to facilitate and to promote horizontally-spread territorial cooperation among European regions.[103] Based on Article 175 TFEU, cross-border, transnational and interregional cooperation is provided a legal basis with the EGTC.[104] With the aim to strengthen European social and economic cohesion, the EGTC supports the reduction of barriers to territorial cooperation. Likewise, this legal framework with a basis in the treaties of the EU also encourages development of horizontal cooperation by incorporating regional and local authorities into the process, bringing the policy implementation process beyond the scope of state-level actors. Some scholars have argued that instruments like the EGTC are relevant for minority-inhabited regions, and especially for minorities living in border regions.[105] However, by carrying several unintentional effects, such instruments can also enhance minority participation in regional and cross-border affairs, for example as observed in the German and

Danish border region where regional policy has warranted attention on increased minority participation in not only regional matters, but also in minority politics.[106] Through changes in territorial structures, the many processes of EU policy making contribute to the establishment of new spaces and platforms for networking and interaction among actors other than state and governmental officials and as such, provides an important insight of how minority activity can be promoted through EU policies.

Human rights & minority protection (*protection*)	EU Culture- and language diversity (*preservation*)	EU Cohesion policy (*promotion*)
Article 2 TEU: *human dignity, freedom, democracy, equality, rule of law, human rights and minority rights*	Article 167 TFEU: *culture policy*	Article 174 – 178 TFEU: *EU Cohesion policy; regional development*
Article 10 & 19 TFEU: *non-discrimination & the Race Directive 2000*	Article 165 TFEU: *Education & linguistic diversity*	*European Grouping of Territorial Cooperation (EGTC): Article 175 TFEU*
Article 21 Charter: *Non-discrimination (national minority)*	Article 3 TEU: *Respect for cultural & linguistic diversity & safeguard of cultural heritage*	*Subsidiarity principle: Article 5 TEU* *Structural Funds: EDRF & ESF*
Article 6 & 7 TEU: *Guarantee and remedy* ECJ: *Case Law* FRA: *Information base; reporting systems; transparency* *Institutional synergy European human rights law (CoE): ECHR; ECtHR; FCNM; ECRML* *EP & Commission Human rights annual reports*	Article 22 Charter: *cultural, religious & linguistic diversity* *Periodical initiatives: Culture 2000; Culture 2007–2013* *Ad hoc projects, ex: European Year of Languages 2001* *EP resolutions: safeguard of minority languages* *Independent bodies: Mercator (Commission); (former EBLUL)*	*'3 Objective' programme: Convergence; regional competitiveness; territorial cooperation* *Periodical initiatives, ex: Interreg, Eurorreg, Leader* *Committee of Regions*

Tab. 1

Key points

- EU policy making and law does not exclude minority rights, even if it lacks a clear minority policy vis-à-vis the member states. The overview of its frameworks according to the tool-kit of protection, preservation and promotion, incorporates not only several links to minority rights, but also enables studies on Europeanisation and minority rights,
- The Europeanisation of minority rights in countries that are approaching EU membership often takes a direct and vertical direction, largely at the outset of formal compliance mechanisms. However the external projection of EU rules and norms throughout the broader EU neighbourhood relates much closer to the literature on diffusion given the lack of membership prospects,
- With regard to Europeanisation processes within existing member states, (in many instances) the EU can have a greater impact through the use of more indirect tools and in a horizontal fashion along a variety of policies and institutional initiatives,
- The protection of minorities finds support in EU commitments to human rights, secondary legislation on the prohibition of discrimination on grounds such as ethnic, racial and belonging to national minority, and the use of litigation strategies to the ECJ,
- The preservation of minority identities and their languages is supported through the EU's many commitments to cultural and linguistic diversity,
- The promotion of minorities and minority-related activities can be facilitated through EU regional development policies, and in particular through the objectives which serve to promote regional effectiveness and interregional cooperation and their consequences on minority participation.

Further reading

AHMED, TAWHIDA. *The Impact of EU law on Minority Rights*. Oxford: Hart Publishing, 2011.

ARIAS, AIMEE KANNER and MEHMET GURSES. "The complexities of minority rights in the European Union". *The International Journal of Human Rights* 16, 2012.

LADRECH, ROBERT. *Europeanization and National Politics*. Basingstoke: Palgrave, 2010.

MALLOY, TOVE H. "Creating Spaces for Politics? The Role of National Minorities in Building Capacity of Cross-border Regions". *Regional and Federal Studies* 20 (2010), pp. 295–314.

MALLOY, TOVE H. "National Minorities in the 21st Century Europe: new discourses, new narratives?", *ECMI Issue Brief* 24. Flensburg: European Centre for Minority Issues, 2010.

SCHIMMELFENNING, FRANK and ULRICH SEDELMEIER. *The Europeanization of Central and Eastern Europe*. Ithaca: Cornell University Press, 2005.

SCHIMMELFENNING, FRANK. "Europeanization beyond Europe". *Living Review in European Governance* 7, 2012.

TOGGENBURG, GABRIEL, ed. *Minority Protection and the Enlarged European Union: The Way Forward*. Budapest: Local Government and Public Service Reform Initiative, 2004.

TOPIDI, KYRIAKI. *EU Law, Minorities and Enlargement*. Antwerp: Intersentia, 2010.

Notes

1 Ahmed Tawhida, *The Impact of EU Law on Minority Rights* (Oxford: Hart Publishing, 2011).
2 James Caporaso, "Towards a Normal Science of Regional Integration", *Journal of European Public Policy* 6 (1996), pp. 160–164; Andrew Moravcik, *The Choice for Europe: Social Purpose and State Power from Rome to Maastricht* (Ithaca: Cornell University Press, 1998).
3 Klaus Goetz and Simon Hix, *Europeanised Politics? European Integration and National Political Systems* (London: Frank Cass, 2000).
4 Robert Ladrech, *Europeanization and National Politics* (Basingstoke: Palgrave, 2010).
5 Frank Schimmelfenning and Ulrich Sedelmeier, *The Europeanization of Central and Eastern Europe* (Ithaca: Cornell University Press, 2005).
6 Yasemin Nuhoglu Soysal, *Limits of citizenship: Migrants and post-national membership in Europe* (Chicago: University of Chicago Press, 1994).
7 John Kohout, "On Potacka's Philosophy on History", *Filosoficky Casopis* 47 (1999), pp. 97–103.
8 Claudio M. Radaelli, "The Europeanization of Public Policy", in *The Politics of Europeanization*, eds. Kevin Featherstone and Claudio Radaelli (Oxford: Oxford University Press, 2003, pp. 27–56.
9 Christoph Knill and Dirk Lehmkuhl, "The national impact of European Union regulatory policy: Three Europeanization mechanisms", *European Journal of Political Research* 41 (2002), pp. 255–280.
10 Paul Craig and Grainne de Burca, *EU Law: Text, Cases, and Materials* (Oxford: OUP, 2011).
11 Article 3 (1) TFEU establishes the areas in which the Union shall have exclusive competence: customs union; the establishing of the competition rules necessary for the functioning of the internal market; monetary policy for the Member States whose currency is Euro; the conservation of marine biological resources under the common fisheries policy; common commercial policy. Par. 2 states that the Union shall have exclusive competence for the conclusion of international agreements.
12 Radaelli, op.cit., note 8, p. 40–44.
13 Ibid.
14 Knill and Lehmkuhl, op.cit., note 9.
15 James G. March and Johan P. Olsen, *Rediscovering Institutions: The Organization Basis of Politics* (New York: The Free Press, 1989).
16 Claudio M. Radaelli and Romain Pasquier, "Conceptual Issues" in *Europeanization: New Research Agendas*, eds. Paolo Graziano and Maarten P. Vink (Basingstoke: Pallgrave Macmillan 2007).

17 Tanja A. Börzel and Thomas Risse, "Conceptualizing the Domestic Impact of Europe", in *The Politics of Europeanization*, eds. Kevin Featherstone and Claudio Radaelli (Oxford: Oxford University Press, 2003, pp. 57–80; Maria Green Cowles et al. Transforming Europe: Europeanization and Domestic Change (London: Cornell University Press, 2001).
18 Jeffrey T. Checkel, "The Europeanization of Citizenship?" in *Transforming Europe*, Ibid, pp. 180–197.
19 Börzel, and Risse, op. cit., note 17.
20 Radaelli, op. cit., note 8.
21 European Council in Copenhagen, 21–22 June, 1993.
22 Gabriel N. Toggenburg, ed. *Minority Protection and the Enlarged European Union: The Way Forward* (Budapest: Local Government and Public Service Initiative, 2004), pp. 5–8.
23 Gwendolyn Sasse, "Minority Rights and EU enlargement: Normative overstretch or effective conditionality?" in *Minority Protection and the Enlarged European Union*, Ibid, pp. 59–81.
24 Frank Hoffmeister, "Monitoring Minority Rights in the Enlarged European Union", in *Minority Protection and the Enlarged European Union*, op.cit. note 22, pp. 93–94.
25 Sasse, op. cit., note 23.
26 Rachel Guglielmo, " Human Rights in the Accession Process: Roma and Muslims in an Enlarged EU", in *Minority Protection and the Enlarged European Union*, op. cit note 22, p. 37.
27 Sasse, op. cit., note 23.
28 Hoffmeister, op. cit., note 24.
29 Zsuzsa Csergo, Beyond Ethnic Division: Majority-Minority Debate about the Post-Communist State in Romania and Slovakia. *East European Politics and Societies* 16 (2002), pp. 1–28.
30 March and Olsen, op. cit., note 15.
31 Paul J. DiMaggio and Walter W. Powell, *The New Institutionalism in Organizational Analysis* (Chicago: Chicago University Press, 1991).
32 Hans-Jürgen Grabbe, *The EU's Transformative Power: Europeanisation through Conditionality in Central and Eastern Europe* (Basingstoke: Palgrave, 2005).
33 Schimmelfennig and Sedelmeier, op. cit., note 5.
34 Sasse, op. cit., note 23.
35 "The Copenhagen European Council stated that 'membership requires that the candidate country has achieved stability of institutions guaranteeing democracy, the rule of law, human rights, and the respect for and protection of minorities'. Article 6 of the Amsterdam Treaty enshrines the constitutional principles that 'The Union is founded on the principles of liberty, democracy, respect of human rights and fundamental freedoms and the rule of law.'"
36 European Commission: *Composite Paper – Reports on progress towards accession by each of the candidate countries* 1999.
37 Sasse, op. cit., note 23, p. 79.
38 Ibid, p. 80.
39 Gabriel N. Toggenburg, "A Rough Orientation through a Delicate Relationship: The European Union's Endeavours for its Minorities", *European Integration Online Papers* 4 (2000).
40 The Lisbon Treaty commits the EU to 'development of special relationship with neighbouring countries aiming to establish an area of prosperity and good neighbourliness, founded on the values of the Union and characterized by close and peaceful relations based on cooperation'. For that purpose, the EU may conclude specific agreements with the countries concerned', Article 8 TEU.
41 The *ENP framework* is proposed to 16 closest neighbours of the EU; Algeria, Armenia, Azerbaijan, Belarus, Egypt, Georgia, Israel, Jordan, Lebanon, Libya, Moldova, Morocco, Palestine, Syria, Tunisia and Ukraine. The ENP is not yet fully activated in all 16 countries, given that Action Plans are yet to be activated in Algeria, Belarus, Libya and Syria.
42 *EU-Ukraine Action Plan*, 2008.
43 *EU-Moldova Action Plan*, 2004.
44 *EU-Georgia Action Plan*, 2005.

45 Frank Schimmelfennig, "Europeanization beyond Europe", *Living Review in European Governance* 7 (2012).
46 Guido Schwellnus, "The Adoption of Non discrimination and Minority Protection Rules in Romania, Hungary, and Poland", in *The Europeanization of Central and Eastern Europe*, eds. Frank Schimmelfennig and Ulrich Sedelmeier (Cornell University Press, 2005).
47 Gwendolyn Sasse and Claire Gordon, *The European Neighbourhood Policy* (Bozen: EURAC Research, 2008), p. 25
48 Tanja Börzel and Thomas Risse, "From Europeanisation to Diffusion: Introduction", *West European Politics* 35 (2012), pp. 1–19.
49 Schimmelfennig, op. cit., note 45.
50 Ian Manners, "Normative Power Europe: a Contradiction in Terms?" *Journal of Common Market Studies* 40 (2002), pp. 235–258.
51 Thomas Diez et al. "The European Union and Border Conflicts: The Transformative Power of Integration" *International Organization* 60 (2006), pp. 563–593.
52 Ulrich Sedelmeier, "Europeanization" in Erik Jones et al (eds.), *The Oxford Handbook of the European Union*, (Oxford: Oxford University Press, 2012).
53 Toggenburg, op. cit., note 39, p. 2.
54 Article 2, TEU: 'The Union is founded on the values of respect for human dignity, freedom, democracy, equality, the rule of law and respect for human rights, *including the rights of persons belonging to minorities*. These values are common to the Member States in a society in which pluralism, non-discrimination, tolerance, justice, solidarity and equality between women and men prevail'. (Emphasis added).
55 Article 21, Charter: 'Any discrimination based on any ground such as sex, race, colour, ethnic or social origin, genetic features, language, religion or belief, political or any other opinion, membership of a national minority, property, birth, disability, age or sexual orientation shall be prohibited'. (emphasis added).
56 Article 22, Charter: ‚The Union shall respect cultural, religious and linguistic diversity'.
57 Bruno DeWitte, "The Constitutional Resources for an EU Minority Protection Policy", in *Minority Protection and the Enlarged European Union*, op. cit. note 22, p. 122.
58 Kristian Henrard, "Ever-increasing synergy towards a stronger Level of Minority Protection between Minority-specific and Non-Minority-Specific Instruments", in *European Yearbook of Minority Issues* 3, eds. EURAC and ECMI (Martinus Nijhoff Publishers: Leiden, 2003).
59 Gudmundur Alfredsson, "A Frame with an Incomplete Painting", *International Journal on Minority and Group Rights* 7 (2000), pp. 291–304.
60 Romano Prodi, A Union of minorities seminar on Europe – Against anti-Semitism, For a Union of Diversity. Brussels, 19 February 2004, accessed August 8, 2013, http://europa.eu/rapid/press-release_SPEECH-04-85_en.htm.
61 Article 19 TFEU: 'Without prejudice to the other provisions of the Treaties and within the limits of the powers conferred by them upon the Union, the Council, acting unanimously in accordance with a special legislative procedure and after obtaining the consent of the European Parliament, may take appropriate action to combat discrimination based on sex, racial or ethnic origin, religion or belief, disability, age or sexual orientation; *Council Directive 2000/43*, 29 June, implementing the principle of equal treatment between persons irrespective of racial or ethnic origin, OJ 2000 L 180/22; Article 21, Charter: 'Any discrimination based on any ground such as sex, race, colour, ethnic or social origin, genetic features, language, religion or belief, political or any other opinion, membership of a national minority, property, birth, disability, age or sexual orientation shall be prohibited.'
62 Article 7 TEU: ‚On a reasoned proposal by one third of the Member States, by the European Parliament or by the European Commission, the Council, acting by a majority of four fifths of its members after obtaining the consent of the European Parliament, may determine that there is a clear risk of a serious breach by a Member State of the values referred to in Article 2. Before making such a determination, the Council shall hear the Member State in question and may address recommendations to it, acting in accordance with the same procedure.
63 Officially known as the Network of Independent Experts in Fundamental Rights, as created by the Commission in 2002.

64 Guglielmo, op. cit., note 26, p. 41.
65 Toggenburg, op. cit., note 22, p. 10–11.
66 Article 167 TFEU' The Union shall contribute to the flowering of the cultures of the Member States, while respecting their national and regional diversity and at the same time bringing the common cultural heritage to the fore'.
67 Article 167 (2) TFEU 'Action by the Union shall be aimed at encouraging cooperation between Member States and, if necessary, supporting and supplementing their action.'
68 In relation to areas such as employment, social policy, education, cultural policy and regional protection, the EU should, according to the Treaty provisions, support and complement the member states actions in relation to the field in question.
69 Article 167 (4) TFEU.
70 Article 3 (3) TEU 'It shall respect its rich cultural and linguistic diversity, and shall ensure that Europe's cultural heritage is safeguarded and enhanced.'
71 Romano Prodi, The Impact of the reforms and enlargement on the islands regions, The reasons for island status. *Convention of the Association of Industry of the Province of Sassari*. Sassari, 24 January 2003, accessed August 8, 2013, http://europa.eu/rapid/pressReleasesAction.do?reference=SPEECH/03/28&format=HTML&aged=1&language=EN&guiLanguage=en.
72 Tove H. Malloy, "National Minorities in the 21st Century Europe: new discourses, new narratives?" *ECMI Issue Brief* 24 (2010). Flensburg: European Centre for Minority Issues.
73 Decision No 508/2000/EC.
74 Decision 1855/2006/EC.
75 European Commission, Progress Report, Culture 2007–2003, p. 8.
76 Communication from the Commission to the European Parliament, the Council, the European Economic and Social Committee and the Committee of the Regions on a European agenda for culture in a globalizing world; COM(2007) 242.
77 2085/97/EC.
78 Kyriaki Topidi, *EU Law, Minorities and Enlargement* (Antwerp: Intersentia), p. 103
79 Melissa Kronenthal, *From Rhetoric to Reality? A Critical Assessment of EU Minority Language Policy and Practice*, Mercator Working Paper 13 (Barcelona: CIEMEN, 2003)
80 Article 165 (2) TFEU 'developing the European dimension in education, particularly through the teaching and dissemination of the languages of the Member States; Article 166 TFEU: The Union shall implement a vocational training policy which shall support and supplement the action of the Member States, while fully respecting the responsibility of the Member States for the content and organisation of vocational training.'
81 Dónall Ó Riagáin, " The lesser used languages of Europe & their participation in the programmes of the European Union, " (Contribution to the Europa Diversa Expert Meeting: *Linguistic proposals for the future of Europe*, Barcelona, May 31 – June 1, 2002).
82 Kronenthal, op. cit., note 79.
83 Toggenburg, op. cit., note 22, p. 6.
84 *EU Law, Minorities, and Enlargement*, op. cit note 78, p. 103
85 De Witte, op. cit., note 57, pp. 121–122.
86 *Council Resolution 14/02/2002*.
87 Riagáin, op. cit., note 81.
88 Kinga Gál and Davyth Hicks, "The European Parliament Intergroup for Traditional Minorities, National Communities and Languages, 2009–2014", *Europäische Journal für Minderheitsfragen* 3–4 (2010), pp. 236-250.
89 Riagáin, op. cit., note 81.
90 Amato Giuliano and Judy Batt, " Minority Rights and EU Enlargement to the East", *European University, RSC Policy Paper No 98* (1998).
91 ECJ 137/84, Mutsch, 1985.

92 ECJ 137/84, Mutsch, 1985.
93 Tove H. Malloy, "Creating Spaces for Politics? The Role of National Minorities in Building Capacity of Cross-border Regions", *Regional and Federal Studies* 20 (2010), pp. 295–314; John McGarry and Michael Keating, *European Integration and the Nationalities Question* (London and New York: Routledge, 2006).
94 Dia Anagnostou and Ann Triandafyllidou, *Regions, minorities and European policies: A state of art report on the Turkish Muslims of Western Thrace, Greece* (Athens: ELIAMEP, 2007).
95 McGarry and Keating, op. cit., note 93, p. 9–10.
96 See Title XVIII, 174–178 TFEU on Economic, Social and Territorial Cohesion.
97 Batt and Amato, op. cit., note 90.
98 Tove H. Malloy et al, *Competence Analysis: National Minorities as a Standortfaktor in the German-Danish Border Region – Working with each other, for each other* (EURAC: Bolzano, 2007, pp. 26–27)
99 Anagnostou and Triandafyllidou, op. cit., note 90.
100 Article 174 TFEU: 'the Union shall aim at reducing disparities between the levels of development of the various regions and the backwardness of the least favoured regions.'
101 McGarry and Keating, op. cit., note 93.
102 Evangelia Psychogiopolou, "Minorities and the EU: Human Rights, Regional Development and Beyond", *EU Policy Paper prepared for the EUROREG*, Sixth Framework Programme: Citizens and Governance in Knowledge Based Society (2006).
103 See *Regulation (EC) 1082/2006* of the European Parliament and of the Council.
104 Article 1 (2) EGTC 'The objective of an EGTC shall be to facilitate and promote cross-border, transnational and/or interregional cooperation, hereinafter referred to as 'territorial cooperation', between its members as set out in Article 3(1), with the exclusive aim of strengthening economic and social cohesion. '
105 Jens Woelk, Francesco Palermo and Josef Marko, *Tolerance Through Law. Self-Governance and Group Rights in South Tyrol.* (Leiden: Martinus Nijhoff Publishers, 2007); Klatt, M and Jørgen Kühl, "National Minorities and Cross-border Cooperation between Hungary and Croatia. A Case-Study of Baranya/Hungary and Osiječko–baranjska County/Croatia", in *European Yearbook of Minority Issues* 6, eds. EURAC and ECMI (Leiden: Brill, 2008), pp. 193–210.
106 Tove H. Malloy, Minority Rights and the Dynamics of Europeanisation: Convergence in the Regional Governance of the Danish-German Border Region on What One Preaches, the Other Practices, in *Minority Politics within the Europe of Regions* (Cluj and Napoca: The Romanian Institute for Research on National Minorities/Sapientia Hungarian University of Transylvania, 2011), pp. 37–59.

PART II

Chapter 4: Ethnicity, Culture and Language: Individuals and Groups

Federica Prina

Summary

Ethnicity, culture and language are complex, multi-faceted concepts. They contribute to the identity of persons belonging to both the majority and minorities. When minorities call for recognition, they tend to call for their cultures and languages to be recognised and valued. Differing cultures, languages, and traditions may cause frictions between groups if they are not carefully managed; minority policies should ideally guarantee cultural pluralism while also seeking to integrate minority groups within the wider society. The notions of ethnicity, culture and language, and their significance for individuals and groups, will be analysed from a political science perspective in the European context, also incorporating into the discussions references to international norms protecting and promoting cultural and linguistic pluralism.

Introduction

Moving from the regime of protecting and promoting minorities, Part II will turn to the conceptual aspect of minority existence. Thus, this Chapter introduces the reader to the notions of ethnicity, culture and language. It links culture and language as identity markers to 'the group' (treated primarily as a minority group within the state), and the way members of the group experience them. It provides an overview of the relations between the state and minority groups, and between individual members of the group. It then examines the cultural and linguistic rights of groups and individuals, along with the responsibilities of states to actively promote minority languages and cultures. The chapter is divided into six sections. First, the chapter will provide an overview of notions of ethnicity, culture and language. Second, it will consider the relations between the state (and the majority) vis-à-vis minority groups, with reference to their recognition. Third, it will address the internal heterogeneity of groups, in light of the differences between its individual members, and the importance of individual choice. Fourth, the chapter will discuss the protection of languages and cultures as linguistic and cultural rights, with reference to the distinction between individual and collective rights. Fifth, it will outline the significance of the positive responsibilities of states to actively promote cultural and linguistic diversity. Finally, some considerations will be made on intra-group and inter-group dynamics with regard to dialogue and participation.

Ethnicity, Culture and Language

As noted in the Introduction, there is currently no universally accepted definition of 'minority'. As Thornberry puts it, in international law "there seems to be only general agreement that there is no generally agreed definition of 'minority.'"[1] Even without an agreed definition, minority rights concerns have existed for centuries, and have been the subject of international agreements, treaties and declarations. These instruments have delineated a minority's core features, although their exact meanings (and the responsibilities of states vis-à-vis minorities) have been the subject of debate and varied interpretations. Initial concepts (with the 1648 Treaty of Westphalia) focused on tolerance vis-à-vis minority faiths. Following the First World War, with the League of Nations, this was extended to encompass elements of ethnicity and language. Indeed, in the absence of a definition of minority, the qualifying adjectives 'ethnic' and 'linguistic', alongside 'religious', are repeated in UN documents. For example, these adjectives can be found in Article 27 of the International Covenant on Civil and Political Rights,[2] which stipulates:

In those States in which ethnic, religious *or* linguistic *minorities exist, persons belonging to such minorities shall not be denied the right, in community with the other members of their group, to enjoy their own culture, to profess and practise their own religion, or to use their own language.* [emphasis added]

These expression are further included, *inter alia*, in the title of the UN Declaration on the Rights of Persons Belonging to National or Ethnic, Religious and Linguistic Minorities.[3] Yet, no definitions of the corresponding noun forms (ethnicity, language or religion) have been agreed upon. These adjectives themselves tend to lose meaning in the absence of the definition of the respective noun; Packer thus argues: "to say that something is 'green' is not very helpful if one has no idea to what it applies."[4] This section attempts to unpack the concepts of ethnicity, culture and language.

Ethnicity

As is the case with the expression 'minority', there is no universal consensus on the meaning of 'ethnicity'. In the Oxford English Dictionary "ethnic" emerges as a multi-faceted term: it includes "having a common national or cultural tradition",—"denoting origin by birth or descent rather than nationality"; and "relating to race or culture."[5] Hence ethnic may denote culture, tradition and race: an ethnic group is a cultural entity with or without physical characteristics. It means that ethnic is broader than 'racial', as well as 'national', as it encompasses both. It was the broadest term available during the drafting of Article 27, which opts for the use of "ethnic" over "race", so as to also incorporate cultural traits.[6] In fact, the specific protection of race (rather than ethnicity) would implicitly legitimise supremacist doctrines and policies.[7] One should not confuse 'ethnicity' with 'ethnic characteristics'. While the latter includes religion, physical traits and language, ethnicity is a social category.[8] People who coexist in the same territory for prolonged periods of time tend to develop common ways of life, and come to share the same characteristics.[9] Political communities have been created on the basis of ethnic characteristics such as language, which serve as unifying factors.

There are distinctions between 'primordialism' and 'instrumentalism' in their approach to ethnicity. Primordialism is grounded on a belief in fixed ethnic ties that create social structures; according to primordialists, there is continuity between modern and past ethnic groups, which have maintained throughout history basic (primordial) characteristics linked to kinship and biological traits. Primordialists thus differ from the modernists,[10] as the latter locate the formation of nations and nationalism within modernity itself, and the creation of the nation-state. Instrumentalists believe that ethnicity is instrumental in the sense that it is devised and employed as part of a strategy to gain specific goals such as power or status. Identities thus created are not fixed but mutable, moulding around changing political circumstances.

Another distinction exists between 'constructivism' and 'essentialism' in the approach to ethnicity and identity. Constructivists see ethnic identities as 'constructed', and the product of evolving circumstances and social action. For example, Max Weber saw ethnicity as a social construct, based on a subjective perception of 'community' (*Gemeinschaft*); the belief in *Gemeinschaft* was seen by Weber to be at the basis of the existence of the group. Essentialists, instead, see a well-defined, fixed essence, in the shape of specific characteristics, in groups, which do not evolve with societal change.

Culture

There are numerous definitions of culture. Geertz, an anthropologist, takes the following position: "Believing with Max Weber, that man is an animal suspended in webs of significance he himself has spun, I take culture to be those webs."[11] Parekh stresses the importance of meanings that people attach to their experiences. He sees culture as: "The beliefs or views human beings form about the meaning and significance of human life and its activities and relationships [that] shape the practices in terms of which they structure and regulate their individual and collective lives."[12] A similar approach is followed by Reidel, who offers the following definition: "A set of shared meanings, norms, and practices that form a comprehensive world view that serves to unite a group and contribute to the identity of its members."[13] Stavenhagen sees culture as a "coherent self-contained system of values and symbols."[14] Meanwhile, UNESCO provides a very broad definition of culture, as "The totality of ways by which men create a design for living. It is the process of communication between men; it is the essence of being human."[15] Hence, culture can encompass meanings and interpretations (of one's experiences), a world view, and a system of values and symbols. Reidel adds that shared meanings and practices are unifying factors in a group and contribute to its members' identity.[16]

Culture is further contained in the expression "multiculturalism"—which has itself been seen to signify the "equal recognition of cultures."[17] In its common usage, multiculturalism has acquired 'ethnic', more than strictly cultural, connotations. In Western Europe, it has often been linked to policies vis-à-vis Muslim minorities—communities religiously and ethnically distinct from the majority population in addition to following distinct cultural practices. In *Multiculturalism without Culture*, Phillips warned against the abundance of stereotypes in the perceptions of non-Western cultures—with assumptions that actions by persons belonging to (non-Western) minorities tend to be dictated, in a quasi-deterministic fashion, by one's cultural and ethnic background.[18]

Language

Language has been defined as "the method of human communication, either spoken or written, consisting of the use of words in an agreed way."[19] Language is the means through which the members of a group communicate; yet language is not only functional: it also is a highly prominent group identity marker[20]—for three reasons. First, language is at the heart of the expression of a group's identity.[21] Each language is distinctive, embodying the way of life and history of a particular group. Martin Estebanez writes, "linguistic communication [is] possibly the most intangible and at the same time fundamental of [...] spaces [for the development of a group's identity], as language permeates almost every aspect of minority identity."[22] Second, language encompasses all social spheres: the choice of language in the media, the public sector, employment, parliament and the courts has social repercussions, with a potential for linguistic discrimination. Third, language is a symbol of power. In the development of states, the dominant group's language tends to crystallise and consolidate as the dominant language.[23] As Hannum puts it, the failure to grant linguistic rights has been "the hallmark of the repression of minorities."[24] In opposition to the dominant group, minorities use their languages to assert their independence and cultural uniqueness.

The use by national minorities of languages differing from the majority's can lead to societal friction.[25] The existence of numerous language policies and language laws in the world demonstrates a pressing need, in many regions, to manage these issues through agreements that contain tensions and inequalities.[26] Indeed, language has taken up a political significance. The link between language and ethnic identity means that language can come to symbolise the essence and the unity of the group.[27] Indeed, ethnic groups have based their political claims on ethnic characteristics such as language and culture, which contribute to the formation of a collective identity.[28] One can then talk about 'politics of nationalism'. An illustration of this is provided by the Former Yugoslavia, where there was a multiplication of languages (Croatian, Serbian and Bosnian) from what was one treated as one language (Serbo-Croatian). Political claims as separate nations have then been constructed around claims of possessing distinct languages.[29] It led to the politicisation of language issues, which became embroiled in political battles.

The State, Society and its Groups

The international regime is built around states. In many cases, these have been conceived as 'nation-states'—or possessing boundaries where ethnicity and state coincide. However, at the sub-state level a multitude of groups can also be found. For the purposes of this chapter, we treat 'group' primarily in the sense of a 'minority' within a state. Within a state that is conceived as a nation-state, a minority group is effectively considered an anomaly, and a menace to unity.[30] Yet as the cultural pluralism of states becomes increasingly apparent, states seek solutions to guarantee stability and peaceful coexistence. One cannot say that diversity is a new phenomenon; however, the increasingly fast pace of human migration patterns lead to frequent movement of members of different groups, while the media and new technologies allow people to cultivate different aspects of their identities. For example, in the case of migrants, the media—particularly new media—offers new opportunities to maintain a connection with the country of origin—or that of one's parents'—as well as integrating in the country of residence. The ethno-cultural homogeneity of the 'nation-state' increasingly appears a myth; one should, therefore, speak of the national state rather than the 'nation-state'.

Perceptions of the Group

What do we mean by a 'group'? Is it the sum of its parts? Or do individuals taken collectively generate a separate, overarching entity? According to Taylor, the group is more than the sum of its parts.[31] The interaction of members of a group creates a new entity through the exchange of shared meanings that is more than the sum of its individual members. According to this view, the group *per se* is a separate unit of analysis.[32]

In conceptualising the group, a clear distinction exists between the 'communitarian' and 'liberal' approaches. The communitarian view is that we cannot perceive ourselves away from our allegiances to our community. Thus, communitarianism stresses the bond between the individual and the group: an individual is viewed as the product of the community, and of its values and beliefs—firmly rejecting the perception of human beings as atomistic individuals. Instead the liberal view is that we form our own perceptions without being restricted by the cultural values of our community. One may also differentiate between two types of groups: as a political community constructed as a "community of putative *descent*", or as "a community of putative *consent*" [emphasis added].³³ In the first case the group is imagined in relation to blood ties (even when such blood relations are simply a myth). Putative consent, instead, is "imagined as a bond of law or promise."³⁴ This distinction is closely linked to that between ethnic and civic forms of nationalism.³⁵

Recognition

In practice, the lack of a definition of 'minority' means that states can decide what a minority is. In the case of the Framework Convention for the Protection of National Minorities (FCNM)³⁶, ratifying states have provided lists of their national minorities in their periodic reports to the Advisory Committee on the FCNM. However, some groups are not recognised as national minorities, despite calls for recognition.³⁷ Taylor argues that the non-recognition of minorities and of their distinctiveness has harmful consequences:

*Non-recognition or misrecognition can inflict harm, can be a form of oppression imprisoning someone in a false, distorted, and reduced mode of being [...] misrecognition shows not just a lack of due respect. It can inflict a grievous wound, saddling its victims with a crippling self-hatred. Due recognition is not just a courtesy we owe people. It is a vital human need.*³⁸

The absence of official recognition results in a lack of measures by the state to preserve minority languages and cultures. In turn, this can develop into a 'loss of a community', which is seen by Arendt as "[s]omething much more fundamental than freedom and justice", and "the calamity which has befallen ever-increasing numbers of people."³⁹ With minority languages disappearing at a fast pace, a person can find oneself being the last speaker of his/her language.

Tensions ensue from the non-recognition of the value and dignity of minorities, and from the dominance of one group over another. Cultural dominance can be expressed by imposing a particular language on minority groups: in these cases, language becomes the "emblem of that dominance."⁴⁰ The loss of control over one's cultural expression (for example when witnessing the impending death of one's language) can lead to a sense of alienation.⁴¹ Even when minorities do not display an interest in their language and culture, these attributes remain identity markers; while dormant, they have the potential to resurface. It leads to the multiculturalists' argument that the accommodation of minorities can pre-empt the escalation of tensions. Indeed, the impetus for the promulgation of the FCNM came from the 1990s armed conflict in the Balkans.[42] The post of the OSCE High Commissioner on National Minorities was established in 1992 specifically to seek an early resolution of ethnic tensions.

Despite this, policies for the accommodation of minorities, and multiculturalism itself, have been criticised for consolidating the separation of societies' various groups. The different treatment of members of the majority and of minorities, foreseen in multiculturalist approaches to diversity, has been linked to inequality.[43] These critiques are in turn linked to the vision of a multiculturalism that creates a series of mono-cultures living one alongside another—each in a segregated neighbourhood with minimal interaction with either the majority or other minorities.[44] Yet minority rights policies do not forcefully imply fragmentation, or instability and antagonism between groups. Ideals of unity *and* the accommodation of minorities are not mutually exclusive. Rather, it is the societal marginalisation of particular groups that can lead to radicalisation. Attempts to transcend difference, with the (unrealistic) objective of creating a colour- and difference-blind society, is not a viable option. The rejection of difference results in the failure to assess minorities' special needs and potential discrimination—undercutting opportunities for the formulation of adequate minority policies. Different ethnicities may feel a common loyalty towards their state, as in the commonly-cited example of Switzerland, with its multi-layered identity: the canton, the cultural/linguistic group, and the overarching Swiss identity.[45] Indeed, Guibernau argues that the adoption of a "cosmopolitan attitude", as an overarching identity, does not necessitate renouncing one's national identity. It simply requires adding another layer—a "cosmopolitan layer"—to it.[46] Multiple loyalties lead to "a balance between cohesion, equality, and difference."[47]

The Group and its Members

Minorities, as the expression itself suggests, are commonly understood in relation to the majority. It reinforces the view of the minority as culturally monolithic and in opposition to the majority, which is seldom the case. Groups do have characteristics that distinguish them from the wider society, but groups also display a degree of internal diversity.

A Group's Internal Diversity

The assumption of homogeneity within a group implies an "essentialist" and "reified" understanding of culture.[48] Numerous authors have criticised the reductionist model that stresses internal homogeneity, together with a clear-cut separateness from other groups.[49] There has been criticism of the notion of each culture as "separate, bounded and internally uniform"[50] and of a "package picture of cultures."[51] These concepts are closely connected to what Brubaker, in *Ethnicity without Groups*, calls "groupism",—the tendency to take discrete, sharply differentiated, internally homogeneous and externally bounded groups as basic constituents of social life, chief protagonists of social conflict, and fundamental units of social analysis.[52] This approach ignores the nuances and the multiple facets of a group and its dynamic, ever-changing character. It can also reflect an assumption of minorities as static, when compared with the dynamism of dominant cultures.[53] Thus, Brubaker has pointed to the imposition from above of social categories such as nationhood, which are "institutionalised, discursively articulated [and …] embedded in culturally powerful and symbolically resonant myths, memories and narratives." One should thus consider "the ways in which [those who are] categorised appropriate, internalise, subvert, evade, or transform the categories that are imposed on them."[54]

Individuals within the Group

The above tells us that individual members of a group are different. They relate to the group in different ways: persons belonging to a group experience events at the same time, and these experiences intersect, but they can well be experienced differently by different group members. Individual members have various forms of identification with their group(s). Thus, Jackson-Preece refers to an "inherent tension in human affairs between competing desires for freedom and belonging […] Freedom requires autonomy of action; belonging requires coordination […] Freedom creates diversity; belonging creates uniformity."[55]

Is the group always good for individuals? It has been argued that leaving a group (through emigration or religious conversion) can sometimes give rise to feelings of liberation.[56] Yet this implies that the individual has experienced limited freedom as a member of the group. Instead, an individual ought to be free to choose his/her cultural allegiance—meaning that an individual is not 'trapped' in a given social role. One should be able to preserve, but also reinterpret and leave a cultural group.[57] As noted, the liberal view places an emphasis on individual freedoms rather than the group. At the same time, Taylor and Kymlicka see a continuum between the individual and the group.[58] They argue that moral autonomy comes from self-understanding, which, in turn, is developed through interaction with others; thus, cultural membership is necessary for autonomy. The individual may be part of a group, but s/he can re-interpret its customs and values. Moreover, according to Phillips, essentialist perceptions of culture, by which persons are defined principally by their culture, ought to be avoided.[59] This means doing away with generalisations over what constitutes supposed 'universal values' or, for example, what might be considered to be quintessential 'Muslim values'—and rather accept the freedom of each individual to determine her/his cultural values, his/her identity, or a combination of identities.

The emphasis is, then, on human agency. Clearly one of the choices available to persons belonging to minorities is to join others in advancing their rights as a group. Similarly, the minority rights system makes it a matter of choice whether or not a person ought to be treated as a member of a minority.[60] Voluntary assimilation is an option; and when a person opts to remain, wholly or partially, culturally distinct from the majority, this does not preclude, but rather should be accompanied by, the opportunity for wider social integration. 'Collective action' should be understood in this context: as coordinated, concerted action, without necessarily being approached in the same manner by all members of a group. The protection of tradition should not come at the cost of individual choice—not only for the importance of individual freedom, but also to enable to group to evolve via the evolution of its members and preventing it from becoming frozen through the reification of culture.[61] The dynamics between the individual and the group mean that group members may well be in large part shaped by the group's culture, but individual members also contribute to shaping the group by continuously reinterpreting it.[62]

From Ethnic Characteristics to Rights

The attributes of culture are intrinsically bound up with identity.[63] An alternative expression to cultural rights may be the "right to identity"—i.e. the right of minorities to control their cultural destiny.[64] It includes the enjoyment of those rights that enable a minority group to express its identity through the free practice of its distinct cultural traditions, the use of its language, and/or the practice of its religion. In turn, the expression of an individual's social and cultural identity is inextricably linked to his/her dignity.[65] Human dignity is the ultimate objective of human rights—of which minority rights constitutes an essential component.

Group Rights versus Individual Rights

Minorities are groups of individuals, but are their rights to be treated as collective or individual rights? A distinction in approach is found between 'individualists' and 'collectivists'. Individualists see the primacy of the individual over the community, rejecting the view that groups *per se* may have rights.[66] Thus, the community may be important for the well-being of individuals, but the individuals themselves exercise the choice as to whether or not to be part of it. Collectivists view a community as having specific interests and rights as a community, which need to be balanced against individual rights.[67] Sanders, for example argues that individual rights are not enough to protect cultural rights: the community also needs to be protected.[68]

Overall, the human rights law system is based upon an individualistic framework of human rights. Packer summarises this position "while the existence of human beings and states are 'axiomatic' in international law, the existence of human *groups* is problematic. Conceptually, international law struggles with the definitions of actors beyond the 'State'" [italics added].[69] Indeed, over the years, an Anglo-American concept of minority rights has become predominant—one based primarily on non-discrimination and equality before the law.[70] As a result, there has also been a focus on individual rather than group rights. Thus, the European Convention on Human Rights[71] does not contain provisions specifically for the protection of minorities. The process of judicial review is activated when one or more person(s) claiming to have been the victim(s) of a specific human rights violation submit a case to the European Court.[72] In Article 27 ICCPR,[73] as well as in the FCNM, the expression used is 'persons belonging to ... minorities', rather than 'national minorities' *per se*, or 'peoples'. At the same time, Article 27 adds that these persons shall not be denied the right to enjoy one's culture, practice one's religion or speak one's language "in community with the other members of their group."[74] The provision, then, incorporates a collective element. This group dimension was added because "individuals do not exist shorn of cultural, linguistic or religious peculiarities; they do not exist *in abstracto*."[75] Similarly, the enjoyment of culture, the practice of religion and the use of language tend to take place with other members of a group, as well as being acts that solidify the group's unity. In particular, a language has to be understood by the various members of a group in order to enable communication between them.

Peter Jones differentiates between collective and corporate conceptions of group rights. In the first case, the right is held jointly by the members of the group (albeit not by any one single individual). The corporate approach, instead, provides a moral standing to the group as such. The rejection of group rights normally relates to 'corporate' rights:

[I]f we conceive group rights as corporate rights, then we cannot represent them as human rights; but if we conceive them as collective rights, then we can represent some group rights either as human rights or as closely akin to human rights… Corporate rights cannot be human rights because they are rights held by corporate entities rather than by human beings.[76]

Group rights are rights of groups *qua* groups. They include: self-determination (Article 1 of the 1946 UN Charter); special rights given to indigenous peoples (land rights, and other rights—such as special hunting or fishing rights—that enable indigenous peoples to preserve their traditional way of life); special representation (participatory rights); self-government; and special regimes (exemptions from jurisdictions). An example of exemption from jurisdiction is the system of self-governance of indigenous peoples in Canada and the US: Native Americans have argued that they should be exempt from judicial review from the Supreme Court, as it would entail their social norms being reviewed by judges from a different cultural tradition, and therefore potentially subject to cultural bias. Some Native Americans have thus argued that they should be directly accountable to international human rights tribunals.[77] The rationale is that Native American self-government upholds universal human rights, albeit through different (non-Western) procedures more aligned to the cultural traditions and way of life of the indigenous peoples in question.

Group-differentiated Rights

A tug of war between group rights and individual rights is often assumed. Yet the two sets of rights are not necessarily in antagonism with one another, when individual freedom is assured. Reidel argues that, in fact, cultural groups can be best protected by approaching cultural rights chiefly as individual rights—indeed, she says, it is the individual members of groups who are the "gatekeepers" to the protection of culture, balancing the latter with individual interests.[78] Kymlicka contends that the debate as to whether collective rights have priority over individual rights (or vice versa)—or whether certain rights (such as language rights) are individual or group rights—is sterile. He argues that what matters is the notion of justice, which may be realised only when different groups are afforded different rights in order to accommodate their differing needs.[79] He calls these "group-differentiated rights." In his view, liberal theory is not incompatible with the granting of specific rights to certain groups, although this might at first sight appear counter-intuitive. Indeed, group-differentiated rights are in line with the (liberal) principles of justice and equality.[80] The purpose of special rights afforded to certain groups is to ensure that all groups benefit from real, rather than formal, equality. These measures are meant to reduce the group's vulnerability, which often originates from past injustices. Kymlicka identifies three kinds of group-differentiated rights: special representation; self-government (guaranteeing autonomy in spheres of interest to the minority, such as education and language programmes); and poly-ethnic rights (protecting religious and cultural practices).[81]

Kymlicka further draws a distinction between 'external protections' (protection of the minority group from the wider society) and 'internal restrictions' (protection of the individual from the group). The latter relates to the concern that groups may oppress their own members, for example by preserving rigid gender roles within patriarchal groups, which may lead to practices such as forced marriages or female genital mutilation. On the one hand, there are at times instances of group leaders seeking to control other members. On the other, practice shows that most of the demands for group-specific rights by minorities in Western democracies have been for external protection, in order to contain assimilatory tendencies emanating from the wider society.[82] The aim, then, is to reduce the vulnerability of minority groups vis-à-vis the majority, rather than increasing the power of members of a minority vis-à-vis other members. Most liberal democracies have sought to reach a balance between external protections and internal restrictions, by promoting minority cultures but outlawing illiberal practices that can harm vulnerable members of minority groups.[83] Indeed, the minority rights system is located within the human rights framework, not in conflict with it. The FCNM Explanatory Report specifies that it does not endorse practices "contrary to national law and international [human rights] standards."[84] Similarly, the UN Human Rights Committee's General Comment No. 28 on Equality of Rights between Men and Women clarifies that Article 27 of the ICCPR never justifies gender inequality.[85] According to Kymlicka, the expression "collective rights" is deficient as it is too broad, and thereby unable to differentiate between external protections and internal restrictions.[86] Similarly, one may argue that, rather than attempting to draw a clear distinction between group and individual rights, one should look for ways of balancing the two.[87]

Protection and Promotion of Cultural and Linguistic Pluralism

This section analyses some of the complexities in the protection and promotion of minority cultures, in relation to positive responsibilities of states—and the debate as to whether specific minority rights are a necessary addition to the international human rights system to meet the needs of minority groups.

Positive Measures: Overcoming 'Benign Neglect'

Cultural rights are not restricted to minorities. They are incorporated in general human rights international conventions and declarations, such as the 1948 Universal Declaration of Human Rights, the ICCPR, and the International Covenant on Economic, Social and Cultural Rights (ICESCR).[88] As such, all human beings should enjoy cultural rights. Thus, closely connected to the debate on individual versus collective rights is the debate as to whether the general human rights system, on its own, is sufficient to protect the rights of minorities, or whether special policies benefiting these groups should be adopted (in the shape of the group-differentiated rights referred to above). The adoption of the FCNM—and of the European Charter for Regional or Minority Languages,[89] which protects languages—indicates a propensity towards the second position. Yet some scholars argue that the rights of minorities can be protected via the existing human rights system, and that culture can be protected through, for example, the right to freedom of expression and association.[90]

De Varennes argues that linguistic rights amount to fundamental human rights, rather than belonging to a special category of rights;[91] thus, for example, everyone charged with, and being tried for, a criminal offence holds the basic right of receiving the cost-free assistance of an interpreter if s/he cannot understand or speak the language used in court.[92] This right cannot be divorced from the fundamental right to a fair trial. It has, however, been pointed out that the active promotion of minority languages requires special language policies.[93] Cultural and linguistic diversity can disappear when not actively promoted. In particular, 'language death' is a widespread phenomenon. The overwhelming majority of languages are spoken by minuscule populations: 96% of the world population speak 4% of languages.[94] Speakers of lesser-used languages tend to be linguistically assimilated by larger groups.

Why should we care? Musschenga argues that cultures should be preserved for their "intrinsic value."[95] The significance of language is highlighted by Crystal: he contends that all people, not only persons belonging to linguistic minorities, should be concerned when a language dies.[96] Krauss argues that "just as the extinction of any animal species diminished our world, so does the extinction of any language."[97] Similarly, Mithum writes, "the loss of languages is tragic precisely because they are not interchangeable, precisely because they represent the distillation of the thoughts and communication of a people over their entire history."[98] If language death is a loss for everybody, it is even more so for the group whose language it is. Language encompasses a group's history and as such incorporates its particular perspectives on life.[99]

Although general human rights mechanisms do benefit minorities as well as the majority, they are not sufficient to satisfy the specific needs of minority groups.[100] Human rights law is silent on issues that are crucial to minorities, such as representation in parliament or the language in which education is available. Moreover, universal human rights do not incorporate considerations specifically on the preservation of ethnic and cultural traits, and effectively downplay their significance.[101] In countries without mechanisms for minority protection, decision-making on matters affecting minorities continues to be effectively controlled by the majority.[102] Thus, cultural rights are included in minority rights documents. For example, Article 5(1) FCNM states:

The Parties undertake to promote the conditions necessary for persons belonging to national minorities to maintain and develop their culture, and to preserve the essential elements of their identity, namely their religion, language, traditions and cultural heritage.

The minority rights regime imposes a positive obligation on states to promote minority rights—not only the negative responsibility to refrain from interference with the expression of a group's identity, in a form of 'benign neglect'. Some documents, such as the UN Convention on the Elimination of All Forms of Racial Discrimination (CERD)[103] and the FCNM, provide for the establishment of "special measures' to advance minorities" rights, implying that benign neglect is insufficient to guarantee the rights of minorities. Affirmative action in support of minorities is widely recognised as non-discriminatory and acting to elevate a minority to genuine equality with the majority.[104] While special measures are needed to preserve minority groups, both minority policies and general human rights law can benefit minorities. The right to undergo a trial in a language one understands is certainly a fundamental human right; additionally, cases have been considered by the European Court of Human Rights on various issues of concern to minorities.[105] Alongside this, a state can adopt promotional measures to revitalise regional or minority languages.[106]

Limitations to Minority Protection

Despite the positive obligations of states vis-à-vis minorities, the minority rights system has some limitations. First, some countries, such as France, refrain from recognising any minorities, and from ratifying documents such as the FCNM. Second, some documents for the protection of minorities are non-binding[107] while others include several "escape clauses."[108] In the case of the FCNM, these include expressions such as "when required" and "[States] shall *endeavour* to ensure, as *far as possible* and *within the framework* of their education systems ..." [italics added].[109] Such careful wording is linked to concerns of states of losing their sovereignty at the hands of minority groups and supranational institutions (the Council of Europe, the European Union and the United Nations). Overall, states have tended to focus primarily on negative obligations (non-discrimination, non-interference), rather than positive ones (proactive promotion of minority cultures and languages). In particular, Article 27 of the ICCPR is worded negatively (persons belonging to minorities "shall *not* be denied the right..." [italics added])—the only case of this type of formulation in the entire treaty.

Third, international documents on minority rights are flexible but also vague. Given the different circumstances of each minority, binding and non-binding international instruments alike leave much to the member states' discretion in devising measures to accommodate their minorities. Yet this is a double-edged sword: on the one hand, it allows the flexibility required to develop tailor-made policies for each group.[110] On the other, international (and often domestic) legislation on minority rights remain vague, with only a sketch of the states' minimum obligations, rather than precise guidelines. Flexibility can thus lead to vague and half-hearted minority policies.

Fourth, some limitations are created by numbers. While minorities are numerically smaller than majorities, the minority group needs to have a big enough membership to justify measures to preserve such distinctiveness.[111] In Canada, for example, the right to be educated in French is activated in regions where numbers warrant.[112] Similarly, the European Charter for Regional or Minority Languages (ECRML) states that specific measures are to be applied when the number of users of a regional or minority language "justifies" the measure,[113] or when "the number is considered sufficient."[114] Finally, groups are treated differently whether there are national (old) minorities, with a traditional presence in a state, or new minorities. States that have ratified the FCNM and ECRML are under no obligation to actively promote the cultures and languages of immigrants.

Intra-group and inter-group dynamics

If one accepts that cultural and linguistic pluralism has an intrinsic value, minority cultures and languages should be appreciated by the majority as well as by minorities. When the majority is exposed to minority cultures and languages, for example through minority language classes in school, new intra-group dynamics develop. International law is clear that states are to promote forms of "inter-cultural dialogue"[115] between various groups. Dialogue is multi-directional: between groups (inter-group), and also within a single group (intra-group). Dialogue can enhance mutual understanding between members of different groups—whereas the absence of dialogue tends to fuel prejudice and intolerance. Inter-group dialogue further includes negotiations between members of the majority and of minority groups on mechanisms for their peaceful coexistence in a society that is cohesive but also culturally diverse. In these discussions, it is helpful to think of these groups as "co-nations": the term implies equality in status and dignity for all ethnic groups, rather than distinguishing between dominant and non-dominant ethnicities.[116]

When engaging in dialogue, state officials need to further consider that, as noted, groups are heterogeneous and membership fluid. Moreover, an individual's identity is not shaped solely by his/her ethnic background, but by gender, age, profession, level of education, and political affiliation. Given these multiple layers of identity there should, at least, be an attempt by the majority population to formulate strategies to deal with such diversity, by widening the potential for participation, enabling different segments of the minority population to become involved.[117] While minority groups should be allowed to develop a "group-oriented dimension" through the right of association,[118] a group's internal differences should also be recognised, through a system of representation that allows a wider range of voices to receive attention during consultation. The expectation, within and outside the group, of general consent, can lead to a stultified debate, in which group members are pressured to agree rather than expressing their genuine beliefs. It is only through open dialogue, in which no voice is marginalized, that solutions can be negotiated for the peaceful and harmonious coexistence of individuals and groups. In the next chapter, we examine issues related to coexistence of ethnic groups.

Key Points

- The protection of minority cultures and languages, and of persons belonging to ethnic, religious or linguistic minorities, has been incorporated into international human rights documents. However, exact definitions of 'ethnicity', 'culture' and 'language' have still not been universally agreed upon,
- There are various theories as to whether the individual should have primacy over the group, or *vice versa* (as seen in debates between liberals and communitarians, and between individualists and collectivists). The liberal approach acknowledges the importance of the community for individuals, but places an emphasis on human agency and individual choice,
- Not only are societies heterogeneous, but so are also minority groups themselves. Groups are formed by individuals with different views and characteristics, even if they are united by a common language, culture or religion. Identities are complex, fluid and often multi-layered; individuals continuously renegotiate their relationship with the group,
- The international human rights system is designed around the protection of the individual, rather than the group. However, some rights can also be claimed and enjoyed collectively by minority groups, and individual and group rights can coexist fulfilling different functions,
- In order to preserve minority cultures and languages, minority groups need states to implement measures for their active promotion (group-differentiated rights). The preservation of cultural pluralism

should be sought in recognition of the 'intrinsic value' of all cultures and languages,
- Measures for the promotion of minority rights, such as affirmative action, create what may seem like privileges for specific groups. However, there is a broad-ranging consensus that such policies are necessary for the institution of substantive (rather than formal) equality. These policies are needed to place minority (disadvantaged) groups on an equal footing with the majority,
- Multiculturalism and minority policies have been criticised for preventing minorities from integrating into the wider society, consolidating group differences and fragmentation. However, far from wishing to ossify minority groups, minority rights are a complex and fluid combination of integration and diversity,
- Inter-cultural dialogue (both intra-group and inter-group) plays a crucial role in facilitating mutual understanding and tolerance, as well as participation in decision-making processes by both members of minorities and of the majority.

Further reading

ALSTON, PHILIP, ed. *People's Rights*. Oxford: Oxford University Press, 2001.

BRUBAKER, ROGERS. "Ethnicity, Race and Nationalism", *Annual Review of Sociology* 35 (2009), pp. 21–42.

FISHMAN, JOSHUA. *Language and Ethnicity in Minority Sociolinguistic Perspective*. Clevedon, Avon: Multilingual Matters, 1989.

FOTTRELL, DEIRDRE, and BILL BOWRING, eds. *Minority and Group Rights in the New Millennium*. The Hague: Martinus Nijhoff Publishers, 1999.

GLAZER, NATHAN. "Individual Rights against Group Rights", in *The Rights of Minority Cultures*, edited by HUTCHINGSON, JOHN, and ANTHONY D. SMITH. Ethnicity. Oxford: Oxford University Press, 1996.

JONES, PETER, ed. *Group Rights*. Farnham: Ashgate, 2009.

JONES, PETER. "Group Rights and Group Oppression", *Journal of Political Philosophy* 7 (1999), pp. 353–377.

WILL KYMLICKA. *Multicultural Citizenship: A Liberal Theory of Minority Rights*. Oxford: Clarendon Press, 1995.

Notes

1 Patrick Thornberry, *International Law and the Rights of Minorities* (Oxford: Clarendon, 1991), p. 164.
2 *International Covenant on Civil and Political Rights*, 999 U.N.T.S. 171, adopted 16 December 1966, entered into force 23 March 1976.
3 Adopted on 18 December 1992, GA Res 47/135.
4 John Packer, "On the Definition of Minorities", in *The Protection of Ethnic and Linguistic Minorities in Europe*, eds. John Packer and Kristian Myntti (Turku: Abo Akademi University, 1993), p. 57.
5 *The Concise Oxford Dictionary of Current English*, 9th edition. Oxford: Clarendon Press, 1995.
6 Thornberry, op. cit. note 232, pp. 160–1.
7 Philip Vuciri Ramaga, "The Bases of Minority Identity", Human Rights Quarterly 14 (1992), pp. 409–428, p. 413.
8 Jennifer Jackson-Preece, *Minority Rights: Between Diversity and Community* (Malden: Polity, 2005), pp. 136–137.
9 Ibid., p. 139.
10 Such as Ernest Gellner and Benedict Anderson. See Ernest Gellner, *Nations and Nationalism*. 2nd ed. (Malden: Blackwell Publishing, 2006); and Benedict Anderson, *Imagined Communities: Reflections on the Origin and Spread of Nationalism* (London: Verso, 1991).
11 Clifford Geertz, *The Interpretation of Cultures* (New York: Basic Books, 1973), p. 5.
12 Bhikhu Parekh, *Rethinking Multiculturalism: Cultural Diversity and Political Theory* (Cambridge, MA: Palgrave McMillen, 2000), p. 142.
13 Laura Reidel, "What are Cultural Rights? Protecting Groups with Individual Rights", *Journal of Human Rights* 9 (2010), pp. 65–80, p. 66.
14 Rodolfo Stavenhagen, "Cultural Rights and Universal Human Rights", in *Economic, Social and Cultural Rights. A Textbook*, eds. Asbjørn Eide, Catarina Krause and Allan Rosas (Dordrecht: Martinus Nijhoff Publishers, 1995), p. 66.
15 1970 *Statement on Cultural Rights as Human Rights* by the United Nations Education Scientific, and Cultural Organization.
16 Reidel, op. cit., note 244, p. 66.
17 Paul Kelly, "Introduction. Between Culture and Equality", in *Multiculturalism Reconsidered*, ed. Paul Kelly (Cambridge: Polity, 2002), p. 5.
18 Anne Phillips, *Multiculturalism without Culture* (Princeton: Princeton University Press, 2007)
19 *The Concise Oxford Dictionary*, op. cit. note 236.
20 Together with a third identity marker (religion), language and culture overlap and are intertwined. For example, the script of a particular language can also be considered part of its culture. Ramaga op. cit., note 238, p. 427.
21 See, for example, David Crystal, *Language Death* (Cambridge: Cambridge University Press, 2000).
22 Martin Estebanez, M.A. "Council of Europe Policies Concerning the Protection of Linguistic Minorities and the Justiciability of Minority Rights", in *Minorities, Peoples and Self-Determination*, eds. Nazila Ghanea and Alexandra Xanthaki (Leiden: Martinus Nijhoff Publishers, 2005), p. 269.
23 According to Anderson, this process occurred through the development of the printing press. Anderson, op. cit., note 241.
24 Hurst Hannum, "Contemporary Developments in the International Protection of the Rights of Minorities", *Notre Dame Law Review* 66(1991), pp. 1431–1460, p. 1441.
25 Tove H. Malloy, *National Minority Rights in Europe* (Oxford: Oxford University Press, 2005), p. 35.
26 Joseph-G Turi, "Typology of Language Legislation", in *Linguistic Human Rights: Overcoming Language Discrimination*, ed. Tove Skutnabb-Kangas (Berlin: Mouton de Gruyter, 1994).

27 Jackson-Preece, op. cit., note 239, p. 110.
28 Ibid., pp. 137-8.
29 Vanessa Pupavac, "Politics and Language Rights: A Case Study of Language Politics in Croatia", in *Minority Languages in Europe*, eds. Gabrielle Hogan-Brun and Stefan Wolff (Basingstoke: Palgrave MacMillan, 2003), pp. 138-154. Also see Dubravko Škiljan, "From Croato-Serbian to Croatian: Croatian Linguistic Identity", *Multilingua* 19 (2000), pp. 3-20.
30 Jennifer Jackson Preece, *National Minorities and the European Nation-States System* (Oxford: Clarendon Press, 1998).
31 Charles Taylor, *Philosophical Arguments* (Cambridge, MA: Harvard University Press, 1995), p. 189.
32 Ibid.
33 Jackson-Preece, op. cit., note 239, p. 138.
34 Ibid., pp. 138-9.
35 The traditional distinction between ethnic and civic forms of nationalism comes from Kohn's seminal work (Hans Kohn, *The Ideal of Nationalism. A Study in its Origins and Background*. New York, Collier Books, 1944). One should note, however, that the distinction between 'civic' and 'ethnic' nationalism is not always clear-cut: there is some blurring and overlapping between the two. See Rogers Brubaker, "The Manichean Myth: Rethinking the Distinction between 'Civic' and 'Ethnic'", in *Nation and National Identity. The European Experience in Perspective*, eds. Hanspeter Kriesi et al., (Zurich: Ruegger, 1999).
36 *Framework Convention for the Protection of National Minorities*, ETS No. 157, adopted 1 February 1995, entered in force 1 February 1998.
37 For example, Poland has not recognised the Silesians or their language. See Tomasz Kamusella, "Poland and the Silesians: Minority Rights à la Carte?" *Journal on Ethnopolitics and Minority Issues in Europe* 11(2012), pp. 42-74.
38 Charles Taylor, "The Politics of Recognition", in *Multiculturalism: Examining the Politics of Recognition*, ed. Amy Gutman (Princeton: Princeton University Press, 1994), pp. 25-6.
39 Hannah Arendt, *The Origins of Totalitarianism* (New York: World Publishing, 1972), pp. 296-7.
40 Crystal, op. cit., note 252, p. 77.
41 Ibid., p. 78.
42 The Preamble to the FCNM states that "the upheavals of European history have shown that the protection of national minorities is essential to stability, democratic security and peace in this continent". Recommendation 1134 (1990) of the Parliamentary Assembly of the Council of Europe qualifies minority rights as "an essential factor for peace, justice, stability and democracy". PACE Recommendation 1134 (1990) "On the Rights of Minorities", 1 October 1990.
43 Brian Barry, Culture and Equality: An Egalitarian Critique of Multiculturalism (Cambridge: Polity, 2001).
44 Rumy Hasan, *Multiculturalism: Some Inconvenient Truths* (London: Politico's, 2010), pp. 11-13.
45 Kurt R. Spillman, "Ethnic Coexistence and Cooperation in Switzerland", in *Ethnic Conflicts and Civil Society: Proposals for a New Era in Eastern Europe*, eds. Andreas Klinke, Ortwin Renn and Jean-Paul Lehners (Aldershot: Ashgate, 1997), p. 203; p. 211.
46 Montserrat Guibernau, *The Identity of Nations* (Cambridge: Polity, 2007), p. 195.
47 Alexandra Xanthaki, "Multiculturalism and International Law: Discussing Universal Standards", *Human Rights Quarterly* 32(2010), pp. 21-48, p. 24.
48 Phillips, op. cit., note 249, pp. 8-9
49 Seyla Benhabib, *The Claims of Culture: Equality and Diversity in the Global Era* (Princeton: Princeton University Press, 2002), p. 4; James Tully, *Strange Multiplicity: Constitutionalism in an Age of Diversity* (Cambridge: Cambridge University Press, 1995), p. 10.
50 Ibid., (Tully), p. 10.
51 Uma Narayan, "Undoing the 'Package Picture' of Cultures", *Signs* 25 (2000), pp. 1083-1086.
52 Rogers Brubaker, "Ethnicity without Groups", *European Journal of Sociology* 43 (2002), pp. 163-189, p. 164.

53 Albert W. Musschenga, "Intrinsic Value as a Reason for the Preservation of Minority Cultures", *Ethical Theory and Moral Practice* 1(1998), pp. 201–225, p. 206.

54 Rogers Brubaker, Margit Feischmidt, Jon Fox and Liana Grancea, *Nationalist Politics and Everyday Ethnicity in a Transylvanian Town* (Princeton: Princeton University Press, 2006), p. 10.

55 Jackson-Preece, op. cit., note 239, pp. 5–6.

56 Michael Hartney, "Some Confusions Concerning Collective Rights", in *The Rights of Minority Cultures*, ed. Will Kymlicka (Oxford: Oxford University Press, 1995), p. 72.

57 Reidel, op. cit., note 244, p. 66.

58 Taylor, op. cit., note 269; Will Kymlicka, *Multicultural Citizenship: A Liberal Theory of Minority Rights* (Oxford: Clarendon Press, 1995).

59 Phillips, op. cit., note 249.

60 *The Explanatory Report on the Framework Convention for the Protection of National Minorities* states that Article 5(2) FCNM "does not prohibit voluntary assimilation" (§45). Jackson-Preece notes: "We cannot choose our ethnicity but we can choose to suppress or express it in our social relations". Jackson-Preece, op. cit., note 239, p. 161.

61 Reidel, op. cit., note 244.

62 Ibid., p. 75.

63 See for example, Wolf Mannens, "The International Status of Cultural Rights for National Minorities", in *Minority Rights in the 'New' Europe*, eds. Peter Cumper and Steven Wheatley (The Hague: Martinus Nijhoff Publishers, 1999), p. 186. See also Article 1(1) of the *UN Declaration on the Rights of Persons Belonging to National or Ethnic, Religious and Linguistic Minorities*: States shall protect the existence and the national or ethnic, cultural, religious and linguistic identity of minorities within their respective territories and shall encourage conditions for the promotion of that identity [italics added].

64 Thornberry, op. cit., note 1, pp. 141–2; Gaetano Pentassuglia, *Minorities in International Law: An Introductory Study* (Strasbourg: Council of Europe, 2003), p. 133.

65 John Packer, "Problems in Defining Minorities", in *Minority and Group Rights in the New Millenium*, eds. Deirdre Fottrell and Bill Bowring (The Hague: Martinus Nijhoff Publishers, 1999), p. 247.

66 Kymlicka, op. cit., note 289. Donnelly, for example, argues that only human beings can have human rights. Jack Donnelly, *Universal Human Rights in Theory and Practice*, 2nd ed. (Ithaca: Cornell University Press, 2003), p. 25.

67 Kymlicka, op. cit., note 289, p. 47.

68 Douglas Sanders, "Collective Rights", *Human Rights Quarterly* 13 (1991), pp. 368–386.

69 Packer, op. cit., note 235, p. 23.

70 See, for example, Miriam J. Aukerman, "Definitions and Justifications. Minority and Indigenous Rights in a Central/East European Context" *Human Rights Quarterly* 22 (2000), p. 1022.

71 *Convention for the Protection of Human Rights and Fundamental Freedoms*, ETS No. 005, 4 November 1950, entered into force 3 November 1953.

72 A Council of Europe member state can also submit a case against another state, but it has occurred very seldom.

73 The ICCPR also envisages a system of individual complaints.

74 Similarly, Article 3(2) of the FCNM states that the rights contained in the treaty may be enjoyed by persons belonging to national minorities 'individually as well as in community with others'.

75 Thornberry, op. cit., note 232, p. 12.

76 Peter Jones, "Human Rights, Group Rights, and Peoples' Rights", *Human Rights Quarterly* 21 (1999), pp. 80–107, p. 88.

77 Kymlicka, op. cit., note 289, pp. 39–40.

78 Reidel, op. cit., note 244, p. 66.

79 Kymlicka, op. cit., note 289, p. 47.

80 Ibid., p. 34.

81 For example, these rights can include exemptions from specific dress codes when these are in conflict with religious traditions. Ibid., p. 38.
82 Ibid.,p. 42
83 Ibid.
84 Explanatory Report, op. cit., note 291, §44 (explanatory note on Article 5(1) FCNM, on the preservation of traditions of national minorities).
85 On the basis of the decision of the UN Human Rights Committee in *Sandra Lovelace v. Canada*, Communication No. 24/1997, Views of 30 July 1981.
86 Kymlicka, op. cit., note 289, p. 45.
87 Reidel, op. cit., note 244, p. 73.
88 993 U.N.T.S. 3, adopted on 16 December 1966, entered into force 3 January 1976.
89 *European Charter for Regional or Minority Languages*, ETS No. 148, adopted 5 November 1992, entered into force 1 March 1998.
90 Chandran Kukathas, "Are There Any Cultural Rights?" in *The Rights of Minority Cultures*, ed. Will Kymlicka (Oxford: Oxford University Press, 1995) p. 73.
91 Fernand De Varennes, "Language Rights as an Integral Part of Human Rights", *International Journal on Multicultural Societies* 3(2001), pp. 15–25.
92 Article 6(3)(e)of the *European Convention on Human Rights*. Similarly, pursuant to Article 5 of the European Convention: 'Everyone who is arrested shall be informed promptly, *in a language which he understands*, of the reasons for his arrest and the charge against him.' [emphasis added].
93 See, for example, François Grin, *Language Policy Evaluation and the European Charter for Regional or Minority Languages* (Basingstoke: Palgrave Macmillan, 2003).
94 As reported in Crystal, op. cit., note 252, p. 29.
95 Musschenga, op. cit., note 284.
96 Crystal, op. cit., note 252.
97 Michael Krauss, "The World's Languages in Crisis", *Language* 68 (1992), pp. 4–10, p. 8.
98 Marianne Mithum, "The Significance of Diversity in Language Endangerment" in *Endangered Languages: Language Loss and Community Response*, eds. Lenore A. Grenoble and Lindsay J. Whaley (Cambridge: Cambridge University Press, 1998), p. 189.
99 Crystal, op. cit., note 252, p. 35.
100 Malloy, op. cit., note 256.
101 Jackson-Preece, op. cit., note 239, p. 174.
102 Will Kymlicka, Multicultural Odysseys: Navigating the New International Politics of Diversity (Oxford: Oxford University Press, 2007), pp. 4–5.
103 Adopted and opened for signature and ratification by General Assembly resolution 2106 (XX) of 21 December 1965, entered into force on 4 January 1969.
104 Article 1(4) of the *UN International Convention on the Elimination of All Forms of Racial Discrimination (ICERD)*, states that: Special measures taken for the sole purpose of *securing adequate advancement* of certain racial or ethnic groups or individuals requiring such protection as may be necessary in order to ensure such groups or individuals equal enjoyment or exercise of human rights and fundamental freedoms *shall not be deemed racial discrimination* […] [italics added]. Similar provisions are found in Article 4(3) FCNM and its Explanatory Report; and Article 7(2) of the European Charter for Regional or Minority Languages.
105 For example, see Roberta Medda-Windischer, "The European Convention on Human Rights and Language Rights: Is the Glass Half Empty or Half Full?" In EURAC and ECMI (eds.) *European Yearbook of Minority Issues* 7 (2008/9) (Leiden: Brill, 2010), pp. 95–121.
106 It should also be noted the right to free interpretation for a person undergoing a trial for a criminal offence applies to all languages, while promotional measures relate to 'regional or minority languages' in the sense of Article 1 of the *European Charter for Regional or Minority Languages*.
107 Such as the *UN Declaration on the Rights of Persons Belonging to National or Ethnic, Religious and Linguistic Minorities, and documents of the Organisation for Security and Cooperation in Europe** (OSCE).

108 Jelena Pejic, "Minority Rights in International Law", *Human Rights Quarterly* 19 (1997), pp. 666–685, p. 677.
109 Article 14 of the *FCNM*.
110 Kymlicka, op. cit., note 333, p. 61.
111 Geoff Gilbert, "The Council of Europe and Minority Rights", *Human Rights Quarterly* 18(1996), pp. 160–189, op. cit., note 15, p. 167.
112 Kymlicka, op. cit., note 289, p. 45.
113 See, for example, Articles 8(2) and 9(1).
114 See, for example, Article 8(1)(a)(3).
115 See Article 6(1) of the FCNM.
116 Malloy, op. cit., note 256, p. 38.
117 See, for example, Anne Phillips, *Democracy and Difference* (Cambridge: Polity, 2002), p. 21.
118 Joseph Marko, Effective Participation of National Minorities. A Comment on Conceptual, Legal and Empirical Problems (Strasbourg: Council of Europe, 2006), p. 4.

Chapter 5: Conflict and Unity

Hanna Vasilevich

Summary

Although Europe is a diverse society where minorities and majorities coexist, the question remains as to how Europe will decide to address and benefit from this diversity. There is no unanimous approach to policies on ethnic diversity accommodation, and history has shown that the approaches are as diverse as the contexts. Some minorities have the backing of a kin-state, while others may have to fend for themselves in ongoing mediation with policy-makers. The strategies for management of ethnic diversity run the gamut from methods of genocide, ethnic cleansing/forced mass-population transfers, partition and/or secession (self-determination), assimilation or integration to hegemonic control, arbitration, cantonisation or federalisation, as well as consociationalism or power-sharing.

Introduction

As concluded in the previous chapter, a multiethnic composition of populations poses certain challenges for states, where both majorities and minorities must deal with issues such as political representation, self-determination, the public use of language, and other policy dilemmas. Thus, each state faces the challenge of how to find a balance between the preservation of national unity and the protection and promotion of cultural diversity. Despite the choices made by the individual state, the European minority framework promotes a respectful attitude towards ethnic groups residing within the territory of the state.[1] At the same time, the state exercises its authority and legitimacy over the territory and population in order to maintain the stability of its political system. Historically, in order to homogenize populations, states and governments implemented different types of policies regarding their minorities. These policies "were based on the assumption that ethnic fragmentation was to be overcome by the assimilation of smaller groups into the larger nation."[2] The gravest forms of such policies are genocide or mass expulsion. Other forms are assimilatory policies which are based on the forced adoption of customs, traditions, language, and religion typical to the ethnic majority; it is not an uncommon practice to deny or refuse to grant minorities their political rights, segregate them, or to implement discriminatory economic measures.[3] Other examples of behavior on the part of states illustrate different approaches towards minorities. These are characterised by maintaining policies aimed at avoiding potential conflicts between the country's majority and minority groups. To this end, the states of residence and kin-states may sign bilateral treaties on good neighborliness, mutual respect, and protection of the minorities residing on their territory. The introduction of such a system has led to the creation of the modern multilateral system, which began with the League of Nations, and which underlines the need for and importance of the protection of minorities.[4]

The current system of minority protection was developed after the end of the Cold War. Considering that "ethno-cultural conflicts have become the most common source of political violence in the world,"[5] and that "minority rights cannot be subsumed under the category of human rights,"[6] this chapter will take a closer look at the issues of conflict and unity. It will introduce the notions of ethnic conflict and unity with respect to minorities and discuss the existing forms of ethnic conflict regulation, with a special emphasis on the trilateral relationship between the minority/state of residence/kin-state. Minority demands will be analyzed and special attention given to methods aimed at eliminating and managing differences.

Defining conflict and unity

In the attempt to homogenize and nationalize heterogeneous societies, states have tried to emphasize their authority and legitimacy over the territory and population in order to maintain stability and their political system's efficiency. However, the notion of identity is a contested one, since the identity of a group is more than simply the sum of the identities of its individual members. Anthony Smith defines ethnic community, or *ethnie*, as "a named human population with a myth of common ancestry, shared memories, and cultural elements; a link with a historic territory or homeland, and a measure of solidarity."[7] He specifies six elements that form the collective identity of the group:

1. The name of the group,
2. The belief or myth of common ancestry,
3. Historical memories,
4. Shared culture,

5. The attachment to a specific territory, and
6. The element of solidarity.[8]

Donald Horowitz emphasises the inclusiveness of the conception of ethnicity, as it "embraces differences identified by color, language, religion, or some other attribute of common origin," and is also based "on the contextual and in some ways accidental determination of attributes of difference."[9] He explains this contextual character of determination:

Group A speaks a language different from that of Group B, so language becomes the indicator in this relationship. But if, instead of Group B, the environment contained only Groups A and C, then religion or color or place of origin might differentiate the groups. In a typical multigroup environment, moreover, different attributes are invoked for differing group interactions.[10]

Thus, the identity of an ethnic group is a result of the collective efforts of members to define their own group through the prism of solidarity vis-à-vis the existence of the 'Other', who plays a facilitating role in this process. In other words, "the 'Other' is a crucial symbol in the definition of who 'we' are— our identity… [as] the construction of the 'Other' is about both the perception and fear of difference."[11] It is thus common to emphasize the relative and dialectical character of group identity, which is determined by social interactions and activities that determine borders between 'them' and 'us.' Such division, according to Michael Billig, is necessary, as "nationalism does not provide a single way of talking about the world."[12] This shows that "ethnicity is thus not an inherent, 'natural' trait or 'essential' property of people(s) or territories, but a structural code with the political function of exclusion or inclusion."[13]

The perception of 'us' and 'them' also implies a mode of judgement, in that everything related to 'us' is seen as the standard by default, and any variation or distinctiveness typical of 'them' is seen as a factor of difference. Such a division between 'us' and 'them' has two dimensions. On the one hand, it is impossible to acknowledge oneself as a part of 'us' without the existence of 'them.' On the other hand, that which is meant by the term 'them' performs the role of a consolidating factor for 'us' (see also our discussion in Chapter 7). According to Billig, "'we' can accuse 'them' in threatening 'us', [which threatens] the idea of nationhood', thus damning 'them' 'we' can claim to speak for all of 'us',"[14] which serves as a consolidating motto. This 'us' adheres to a particular territory, since this geographical area represents the homeland where 'our' culture is being cultivated. In other words, the culture itself is attached to a certain territory that is the territory of 'our' homeland.

As discussed in Chapter 4, the existence of a border along ethnic lines implies that social interactions may be determined through inclusion or exclusion on the basis of an 'us-them' dichotomy. Accordingly, belonging to 'us' infers a contribution to the maintenance of a collective identity that is shared by all the members of the group applying the identification marker 'us'. This sense of collective identity forms the image and perception of the group in the eyes of others, those falling under the category of 'them.' This image of the group has definite criteria that are common for the particular group and thus distinguish it from other groups with similar characteristics, implying the social construct of the collective identity of the group. National identity, one of the numerous forms of collective identity, can also be measured through the dichotomy of 'us-them' when the former is being determined through the latter.[15]

National minorities, however ethnically, religiously, or linguistically different from the rest of the population, are potentially considered to be 'Others' or 'them' by the majority. While describing the ideology of nationalism, Joseph Marko shows the structural code for this exclusion in the form of an equation:

| Identity = equality = inclusion, or |
| Difference = inequality = exclusion. |

Tab. 2: **Structural code for exclusion** (Source: Joseph Marko, "The Law and Politics of Diversity Management: A Neo-institutional Approach", in EURAC and ECMI (eds.), *European Yearbook of Minority Issues* 6 (Leiden: Brill, 2008), pp. 251–79 at p. 270.)

Depending on the policies pursued by the state of residence, some minorities express solidarity with and loyalty to their state of residence, while others express hostility that may lead to conflicts. Those excluded from the majority and seen as different may become hostile to the rest of the population, while also becoming a source of resentment for the majority due to their differences (see further our discussion in Chapter 7). Loyalty and solidarity can play a consolidating role in bringing all actors to a situation of understanding and mutual respect. However, for the minority group to feel solidarity with the majority, state support is needed. Said support can be expressed through, for example, the official recognition of their language by allowing them to be taught and to receive at least part of their education in their native tongue, as well as allowing said minorities the possibility of addressing state authorities in their native language, including through the use of interpreters. At the same time, attempts towards the homogenization of minority groups could lead to non-violent or violent ethnically-driven conflict.

Ethnic conflict refers to "one particular form of social conflict, namely that in which the goals of at least one conflict party are defined in (exclusively) ethnic terms and in which the primary fault line of confrontation is one of ethnic distinctions."[16] Conflict on the grounds of ethnicity is "a world-wide phenomenon"[17] and "a persistent feature of modernity" that has been brought to the fore of international relations, as "the last few years have brought seismic changes in the relations between several ethnic communities around the world."[18] The 20th Century, with all its tragedies, wars, and shifts of borders, has left Europe with a number of conflicts that have determined, and still do determine, the interethnic relations on the continent. Despite high expectations after the collapse of the communist regimes and the end of the Cold War, the number of ethnic conflicts "show[s] no sign of abating."[19] Horowitz notes "the concept of ethnicity means that ethnic conflict is one phenomenon and not several… [as it] takes different courses, depending on whether relationships between groups are ranked or unranked and on how groups are distributed in relation to territory and state institutions."[20] Such conflicts may be classified as either group-state conflicts (ethnic group vs. state institutions) or inter-ethnic conflicts (different ethnic groups within the state, including majority and minority/ies).[21] These two categories could jointly characterize a conflict, and ethnic conflicts could also take on an international dimension, provided that the kin-state of the minority in question becomes involved.[22]

Michael Brown stresses that ethnic conflicts can be understood through the security concerns of the involved ethnic groups. Two prerequisites determine this. Either the groups involved reside in close proximity to each other, or "national, regional, and international authorities must be too weak to keep groups from fighting and too weak to ensure the security of individual groups."[23] Thus, ethnic conflict can be attributed to security issues, which in turn means that any ethnic-driven conflict is a threat to the social integrity of the state[24] and thus to one of the main goals of the state—that of unity within its territory.[25] The necessity for unity is one of the crucial elements in the formation and development of nation-states in the homogenization of heterogeneous identities within its borders, and it is unity that "keeps alive the idea of a national identity."[26] Thus, unity here refers to top-down policies and practices conducted by the state and its institutions aimed at homogenization, i.e. "a state-led policy aimed at cultural standardization and the overlap between state and culture." [27]

Referring to minorities, Stefan Wolff emphasizes the conflicting doctrines of ethno-nationalism that are central in relations between the state of residence and minority,[28] as "the political function of 'nationalism' as an ideology… [is] to 'camouflage'… normative decisions in the social construction of political 'unity.'"[29] Wolff also highlights the potential threat inherent in the relations between state of residence and its minority/ies, a threat which is usually connected to the minorities' "attempts to preserve, express and develop their respective ethnic identities."[30]

Minority demands

The notion of minority as such refers to the numerical inferiority of an ethnic group when compared to the most populous ethnic group within a particular country. However, as noted in the Introduction of this volume, there is no universally agreed-upon definition for the term 'minority', and the term varies both in scientific literature and legislation. A state divided along the 'us-them' dichotomy, but which seeks to accommodate both majority and minority demands, may experience several scenarios regarding inter-group relations. These are outlined by Joseph Marko in Table 3:

	Equality	Inequality
Unity	Integration	Assimilation
Diversity	Autonomy	Separation

Tab. 3: **Scenarios for the inter-group relations** (Source: Joseph Marko, "The Law and Politics of Diversity Management: A Neo-institutional Approach", in EURAC and ECMI (eds.), *European Yearbook of Minority Issues* 6 (Leiden: Brill, 2008), p. 271.)

At the same time, within the context of the relations between a minority and its states of residence, Danspeckgruber defines five scenarios of minority-majority relations in cases where a minority may attempt to achieve a greater level of autonomy within a nation-state:

1. Secession, followed by independent statehood with the creation of a new state with its own territory, new borders, and international recognition,
2. Secession followed by accession to a kin-state, which does not create a new state, but changes the borders between the original state

of residence and the kin-state, as the seceded territory will be incorporated into its kin-state,

3. Partition and partial secession, followed by either independent statehood or accession to another state affects the borders as well and involves a third party—the kin-state,
4. Continuation of the status quo, which would in some instances not be a viable solution and might lead to the intensification of tensions and possible conflict, but in some cases is seen as a method to avoid conflict,
5. Self-governance plus regional integration is the scenario that avoids altercation and helps establish regional stability. This scenario is also seen as one with more freedom and autonomy than enjoyed before, but which keeps existing borders in place and, via an increase and broadening of authority exercised by minorities, will "minimize instability and challenges to regional peace."[31]

The reaction of authorities to minority demands and the policies they pursue may result in different paths of development of inter-ethnic relations within a particular society. Marko names two preconditions for the maintenance of equality among ethnic groups, namely the recognition of diversity as well as the institutionalization of some level of autonomy for the minority group.[32] Table 4 illustrates the possible developments of the situation in an interethnic society, depending on the existence of the preconditions mentioned above:

Non ↑	Re-cognition		Non ↑
↓ Assimilation	↓ Integration ↓ Representation	↓ Autonomy ↓ Individual Cultural Territorial	↓ Separation ↓ Segregation Ethnic Cleansing Secession

Tab. 4: **Possible developments of the situation within an interethnic society** (Source: Joseph Marko, "The Law and Politics of Diversity Management: A Neo-institutional Approach", in EURAC and ECMI (eds.), *European Yearbook of Minority Issues* 6 (Leiden: Brill, 2008), p. 272.)

Marko notes, therefore, that the politics of autonomy and integration pursued by the state "have to be kept in a careful 'dynamic equilibrium', as there is a constant danger of assimilation or ghettoization of ethnic groups."[33]

Minority demands and interstate relations

In his theoretical framework dealing with the relational triangle between "national minorities, nationalizing states, and external national homelands,"[34] Rogers Brubaker also stresses the constant imbalance between the "nationalizing policies" of the state of residence, which national minorities view as an attempt to assimilate them in such a way that they would lose part, or all, of their cultural heritage.[35] Thus, they mobilize against such policies with possible external support from their kin-state, which may make demands on the part of the minority for minority identities to be preserved through the recognition of cultural rights. Thus, the relationship between a nationalizing state and an external national homeland may be oppositional, due to the aforementioned nature of national politics (often, but not always, assimilative) that govern a national minority's situation. Despite criticisms,[36] Brubaker focuses on a triangular perspective of minority/state of residence/kin-state relationships.

The at times uneasy relationship between the kin-state and the state of residence has also been noted by Francesco Palermo, who argues that "the treatment of national minorities in inter-State relations reveals a latent but fundamental contradiction,"[37] as it is generally the responsibility of the state of residence to protect minorities who live on its territory. However, minorities often enjoy policies of their kin-states, i.e. "states whose majority population shares ethnic or cultural characteristics with the minority population of another State."[38] Consequently, "the majority of States have in place some constitutional provision, ordinary legislation, administrative practices or policy that promotes specific groups residing abroad based on ethno-national considerations."[39] Such legal provisions and policies have been adopted in some European countries, including Denmark, Hungary, Romania, Poland, Russia, Greece, and Slovakia. In some cases, the preferential treatment goes as far as granting ethnic kin-members living abroad full citizenship of the kin-state. This is the case with Hungary, Romania, and Russia (granting Russian citizenship to the residents of Abkhazia, Southern Ossetia, Transnistria, Estonia, and Latvia).

The adoption of kin-state legislation and policies may lead to the preferential treatment of minorities by their kin-states. This may not be met with an explicitly positive reaction from the state of residence.[40] Thus, there should be certain self-imposed limits to the scope of such laws, as per the Venice Commission. In the Commission's view, "the preferential treatment can be justified in the genuine pursuit of the aim of maintaining cultural links with the kin-state."[41] Preferential treatment should not contradict the principles of equality and non-discrimination, and it should concern a purely cultural and social dimension. Hence, minority-related domestic law on the part of kin-states may be justified to the extent that such legislation does not have extra-territorial effect. In other words, the kin-state's preferential treatment of ethnic kin with foreign citizenship while they are living in the kin-state must not have negative consequences.

At the same time, "even if the domestic act of the kin-state includes measures with extraterritorial effects, its proper implementation directly requires the co-operation of the home state."[42] Gabor Kardos summarizes the scope of legislation and the principles behind such legislation. The kin-state should recognise the primary role to be played by the home state and the international community in minority issues; it should adhere to international human rights mechanisms and procedures of international bodies; it should favour bilateralism; and in the case of unilateral legislation, concentrate on culture and avoid extra-territorial effects.[43] This is often backed by the existence of numerous bilateral agreements that regulate the status of minorities on both sides of the border. Hence, the existence of minority-related legislation in the kin-states, combined with the bilateral agreements and domestic legislation of the states of residence may provide minorities with additional protection and opportunities to maintain and develop their culture and education.

The existence of minority-related bilateral treaties is an important part of inter-state relations. This complements the fact that minority issues in general often play an important role in the relations between states. At the same time, "there is surprisingly little in terms of established international law in this respect."[44] The Bolzano/Bozen Recommendations on National Minorities in Inter-State Relations produced by the OSCE High Commissioner on National Minorities is one attempt to "offer guidance to States and minorities on how to properly deal with this sensitive issue by bringing some clarity as to the international standards applicable in cases involving national minorities in inter-State relations."[45] One of the main ideas embodied in the Bolzano/Bozen Recommendations is the fact that

minorities may not and ideally should not, be the cause of conflict. On the contrary, minority communities that 'transcend' State frontiers often serve as a bridge between states, contributing to prosperity and friendly relations, and fostering a culture of pluralism and tolerance, particularly in the border regions.[46]

Thus, the Bolzano/Bozen Recommendations are aimed at channeling kin-state activism towards the maintenance of stable cooperation and good relations between the countries involved.[47]

At this point, it is important to underscore the difference between minorities with kin-states and those without kin-states. The former may enjoy additional opportunities to maintain and develop their culture and education by virtue of the existence of domestic laws of the state of residence, combined with the bilateral agreements and the legislation of the kin-states. In Brubaker's terms, those who do not have a kin-state lack an external homeland (i.e. kin-state) and are thus isolated vis-à-vis nationalizing policies of the state or residence. As a result, the minorities do not have the external advocate for their interests that minorities belonging to a kin-state do—especially if that kin-state is a neighboring country. The scope of action for such minorities is therefore limited by the domestic legislation of the states of residence, and as such, the opportunities to preserve, develop and maintain their language and culture are narrowed in comparison. The Roma communities in various European countries may serve as an example of a minority without a kin-state. On the one hand, they are recognized as a national/ethnic minority in many states. On the other hand, they do not have a kin-state that could serve as a centre for the coordination, protection, and promotion of various Roma communities throughout Europe. As a result, the Roma population in Europe is fully subject to the differing domestic policies pursued by states in which Roma communities reside.

Forms of ethnic conflict regulation

This part of the Chapter deals with ethnic conflict regulation. McGarry and O'Leary refer to a taxonomy that is empirically based.[48] They have identified eight macro-levels of ethnic conflict regulation:

Methods aiming at eliminating minority differences:
- Genocide,
- Ethnic cleansing/forced mass-population transfers,
- Partition and/or secession (self-determination),
- Assimilation and/or integration.

Methods aiming at managing minority differences:
- Hegemonic control,
- Arbitration (third party intervention),
- Cantonisation and/or federalisation,
- Consociationalism or power-sharing.⁴⁹

Methods aiming at eliminating minority differences

McGarry and O'Leary distinguish four forms that are aimed at eliminating differences in ethnically diverse societies. These are genocide, ethnic cleansing/forced mass-population transfers, partition and/or secession (self-determination), and assimilation/integration. It should be noted that Will Kymlicka has noted that these methods include forms characteristic of events that have occurred in various parts of in the world, and some of them, due to their cruel inhuman nature (genocide being the prime example), are not part of the contemporary theories of minority rights and democratic citizenship.⁵⁰ For this reason, the typology should be seen only as an analytical tool that assists in understanding the complex issues of minority differences in culturally diverse societies, not as a tool that suggests exclusively viable and legal options for diversity management.

Genocide

Acts of genocide, arguably the worst crime against humanity, are the most terminal form of difference elimination. Considering that the existence of minorities is a matter of fact, the international minority-related legal norms ensure minorities the "right to existence."⁵¹ The term genocide was first coined by Raphael Lemkin as:

*a coordinated plan of different actions aiming at the destruction of essential foundations of the life of national groups, with the aim of annihilating the groups themselves. The objectives of such a plan would be disintegration of the political and social institutions, of culture, language, national feelings, religion, and the economic existence of national groups, and the destruction of the personal security, liberty, health, dignity, and even the lives of the individuals belonging to such groups. Genocide is directed against the national group as an entity, and the actions involved are directed against individuals, not in their individual capacity, but as members of the national group.*⁵²

Later, in the UN 1948 Genocide Convention, the definition of genocide was solidified and acquired independent importance as a specific crime. This Convention defined genocide through a descriptive listing of the "acts committed with intent to destroy, in whole or in part, a national, ethnical, racial or religious group," including:

- Killing members of the group,
- Causing serious bodily or mental harm to members of the group,
- Deliberately inflicting on the group conditions of life calculated to bring about its physical destruction in whole or in part,
- Imposing measures intended to prevent births within the group,
- Forcibly transferring children of the group to another group.[53]

The use of the term 'genocide' may cause controversy in its evaluation. Accordingly, in some cases there could be significant controversies predominantly over the use of the term 'genocide' when discussing certain historical events. The most notable case is that of the massive efforts towards the forced deportation of more than one million Armenians by the Turks. The Armenian side interprets these events as falling under the category of genocide. This view has received significant international recognition in many countries of the world, which have officially recognized the atrocities committed by the Turks against the Armenians as genocide. The Turkish side, however, opposes this interpretation. It claims that these events were "a part of the war," arguing that "there was no systematic attempt to destroy the Christian Armenian people."[54] The differences in interpretation of these events have posed one of the main obstacles in maintaining bilateral relations between Armenia and Turkey.[55]

Forced mass-population transfer/ethnic cleansing

Another grave form of the elimination of differences is the forced mass-population transfer of a minority, which is also referred to as 'ethnic cleansing.' While forced mass-population transfers have occurred previously in history, the term 'ethnic cleansing' is relatively new. Schabas refers to the Security Council Commission of Experts on violations of humanitarian law during the wars on the territory of former Yugoslavia, whose description of ethnic cleansing refers to "rendering an area ethnically homogenous by using force or intimidation to remove persons of given groups from the area".[56] He further lists the types of activities defined by the Commission as characteristic of ethnic cleansing. They are:

murder, torture, arbitrary arrest and detention, extrajudicial executions, sexual assault, confinement of civilian population in ghetto areas, forcible removal, displacement and deportation of civilian population, deliberate military attacks or threats of attacks on civilians and civilian areas, and wanton destruction of property.[57]

Tadeusz Mazowiecki, a former Special Rapporteur of the Commission on Human Rights, equates ethnic cleansing with "a systematic purge of the civilian population with a view to forcing it to abandon the territories in which it lives."[58] Thus, the notion of ethnic cleansing has its roots in the events connected to the period of collapse of the former Yugoslavia. The breakup of the country produced a number of examples of what may be interpreted as ethnic cleansing when an ethnic group has tried to secure its dominance over a certain territory.[59] At the same time, ethnic cleansing and forced mass-population should be distinguished from population exchanges, which are "the transfers which accompany agreed secessions or partitions, such as those between Greece and Turkey after the end of the First World War."[60]

Partition and secession (self-determination)

Partition, unlike genocide and forced mass population transfer, respects the right of an ethnic group to self-determination and thus describes a situation when a previously united political entity is divided into a number of smaller political entities that receive recognition. This form of ethnic conflict regulation is typical of large political entities that are undergoing processes of disintegration linked to growing nationalist sentiments (i.e. the desire for self-determination) and interethnic tensions.

McGarry and O'Leary use the terms partition, self-determination, and secession as different yet interchangeable forms, arguing that partition could be a solution to settle ethnic conflicts among ethnic communities that do not wish to live within one multiethnic state together.[61] They see the issue of self-determination as a principle behind partition. The major focus of self-determination lies within four questions: "Who are the people? What is the relevant territorial unit in which they should exercise self-determination? What constitutes a majority? And does secession produce a domino effect in which ethnic minorities within seceding territories seek self-determination for themselves?"[62] McGarry and O'Leary consider the principle of self-determination an easy issue to deal with only when a group of people represents a majority within a certain region and expresses that they belong to an ethnic group differing from that of the state's majority. It is rare that partition solves the issue and becomes an optimal win-win solution for all actors. Exemplary cases of optimal secession are few: Norway's secession from Sweden, Slovenia's from Yugoslavia, Iceland's from Denmark, and the quite recent secession of Montenegro from the state union with Serbia. When minorities are left behind, such was the case in Northern Ireland and Kashmir after the partition of Ireland and India, there is potential for actual conflict, often times violent and long-running.[63]

If and when this method is ever successful, partition resolves national and ethnic conflict via the principle of divorce.[64] McGarry and O'Leary identify three different ways by which partition may be enacted: (1) by external imposition—for example as a result of the allied division of the Ottoman Empire and Austro-Hungary after World War I, and the example of the partition of Germany after World War II; (2) by the agreement of the divorcing parties—i.e. the 1993 Czechoslovakia partition and the 1991 USSR dissolution, and (3) by the core of the relevant state—such as in the case of the UK's decision on Ireland's secession between 1920–25.[65] Though self-determination in the form of founding a sovereign independent state may serve as an avenue for a minority to escape discrimination and oppression, for some it may be seen as way towards political and economic freedom or the only possibility of protecting and preserving their own culture and traditions from disappearance.[66] However, the question of founding a new sovereign state may potentially be explosive, as "nationality and ethnicity …create zero-sum conflict and therefore provide ideal material for political entrepreneurs interested in creating or dividing political constituencies."[67]

Integration versus Assimilation

McGarry and O'Leary unite the two notions of 'integration' and 'assimilation' into a single method of macro-political conflict regulation. They refer to both integration and assimilation as an attempt by the state to regulate ethnic conflict through the means of embracing a new transcendent identity over the categories of population in question.[68] The distinction between these two notions is explained by McGarry and O'Leary in that "integration is aimed at creation of a common civic, national or patriotic identity, while assimilation has a goal to maintain a common ethnic identity though the merging of differences into a single melting pot."[69] The essence of assimilation is that "ethnic groups have to give up their different cultural and/or political behaviour in order to be treated equally."[70] Within the scenarios of inter-group relations outlined by Joseph Marko and described above, assimilation occurs if the policies aimed at political unity are being conducted by a state with a concerted effort being made—especially by those in positions of power—to negate the minorities, or the 'Other.'[71] Affected by assimilation policies and processes that are meant to essentially negate their culture and identity, the members of a minority may gradually switch from using their own cultural markers, such as language, culture, and traditions, and slowly begin to embrace those of the ethnic majority.

Assimilation policies may be conducted at various levels, starting from school education onwards, and, depending on the society they are applied in, such policies may be formulated and designed to pursue the goal of either merging various identities into an identity that has already been established, or merging such identities into what may be considered a newly formed, or a newly emerging, identity.[72] The most profound example of the first model is seen in today's modern France.[73] Thus, in the French model, "the school was the central tool of assimilation into French culture and could not tolerate ethnic self-expression."[74] Examples of the second model come from the former USSR and Yugoslavia.[75] According to Kymlicka and Norman, the current trend shows that assimilation is not favored by Western political theorists working within this sphere, who mostly "focus on one or more of the last three methods for managing differences from the above taxonomy; namely, territorial autonomy (e.g. federalism), non-territorial power-sharing (e.g. consociationalism), or multicultural integration."[76]

Assimilation is also addressed in the pan-European framework for the rights of minorities. While any attempt at non-voluntary assimilation of the persons belonging to minorities is widely condemned, the voluntary assimilation of persons belonging to minorities is proclaimed as being acceptable according to common liberal democratic (i.e. Western) rules and norms.[77] Nevertheless, "scholarly views put forward on Article 27 of the ICCPR refer to the prohibition of all forms of integration and assimilation pressure."[78]

With regard to integration policies, McGarry and O'Leary emphasize that policy-makers

favour reducing the differences between ethnic communities, ensuring that the children of the (potentially rival) ethnic communities go to the same schools, socializing them in the same language and conventions, encouraging public and private housing policies which prevent ethnic segrega-

tion, and ensuring that the work-place is ethnically integrated through outlawing discrimination.[79]

However, Kymlicka and Norman emphasize the particular necessity of differentiating between efforts of assimilation and efforts of "multicultural integration."[80] Both of these practices foresee the maintenance of "a new transcendent identity" built on either citizenship or equal membership in the state, as well as the integration of people from various ethnic kin into common political and social institutions. The difference is that of approach. The essence of multicultural integration is that it refers to a policy framework that "does not have the intent or expectation of eliminating other cultural differences between subgroups in the state" and "accepts that ethnocultural identities matter to citizens, will endure over time, and must be recognized and accommodated within these common institutions."[81] In pursuing such practices, the state hopes that its "citizens from different backgrounds can all recognize themselves, and feel at home, within such institutions."[82]

Integration has also become one of the top priorities of the OSCE High Commissioner on National Minorities (HCNM) in assisting the OSCE member states in accommodating diversity in their multiethnic societies. One method of accommodation is "maintaining constructive interaction and a 'common sense of belonging' in society by all persons, regardless of their ethnic, cultural linguistic or religious backgrounds" for the purpose of achieving long-term stability and prosperity, as well as to avoid potential tensions in the society in question by means of instituting integration policies managed in a sustainable manner.[83] These commitments resulted in the publication of the Ljubljana Guidelines on Integration of Diverse Societies in 2012.[84] Integration is understood in the Guidelines as "a dynamic, multi-actor process of mutual engagement that facilitates effective participation by all members of a diverse society in the economic, political, social and cultural life, and fosters a shared and inclusive sense of belonging at national and local levels."[85] Based on an inclusive approach and active participation, the Ljubljana Guidelines promote the idea of "integration of multi-ethnic societies rather than integration of a minority group into a particular society."[86] As a result, instead of being a method aimed at eliminating differences, integration becomes a mechanism that contributes to the maintenance of multiethnic societies based on an inclusive approach, equal opportunities, and the active participation of all groups in the society for the sake of long-term stability and prosperity. For more on the HCNM's Recommendations, see the discussion in Chapter 8.

Methods aiming at managing minority differences
Hegemonic control
There are several approaches appropriate for the accommodation of minorities. The first one can essentially be described as hegemonic control, which refers to a system where "the ruling class does not attempt to eliminate or merge the identities of minority groups, but is merely content to make any "overtly violent ethnic contest for state power either 'unthinkable' or 'unworkable' on the part of the subordinated communities."[87] This form of accommodation is typical of imperial or authoritarian societies; however, the hegemonic model can also be utilized in formally established democracies that protect rights such as equality and minority freedoms.[88] Historical examples of hegemonic control may vary from cases where minorities dominated formally democratic institutions (South Africa, Rhodesia, Kosovo, Fiji), to cases where a majority rule system has been implemented in a liberal democracy (Northern Ireland).[89] In the latter, hegemonic control can occur by majority rule in a situation

where there are two or more deeply established ethnic communities, and where the members of these communities do not agree on the basic institutions and policies the regime should pursue, or where the relevant ethnic communities are not internally fragmented on key policy preferences in ways which cross-cut each other…[90]

Therefore, as McGarry and O'Leary summarize, the existence of the majoritarian system of liberal democratic government cannot provide a fully-fledged guarantee of the rights and liberties of ethnic minorities.[91] As Kymlicka and Norman note, this method has gained no sympathy among current scholars—not because this form is unachievable—but because of the obvious injustice of its nature and its clear incompatibility with the fundamental principles of democratic societies.[92]

Arbitration
Arbitration is the method least recognized by scholars in the regulation and management of ethnic conflict and has mostly been dealt with in such academic fields as peace studies and international relations. According to McGarry and O'Leary, arbitration is applicable to situations in bi- or multi-ethnic states.[93] Arbitration in settlements of interethnic conflict is defined as "the intervention of a 'neutral', bi-partisan or multi-partisan authority."[94] Arbitra-

tion should also be distinguished from mediation. The latter implies that a third party is present to assist the parties of a conflict in reaching a compromise and to facilitate their finding an appropriate solution that will settle the conflict in question. The former places a third-party in a different position, as the third party's primary duty is to make decisions on the relevant conflict-related matters.[95]

There are some criteria that provide classification for arbitration. Arbitration may be pursued in two dimensions—the political and legal dimensions. Political arbitration encompasses certain parliamentary and extra-parliamentary measures, including informal meetings and gatherings, ad hoc commissions, ombudspersons, or formalized mediation procedures. Legal arbitration, on the other hand, relates more to the various types of courts and commissions that prepare recommendations of an advisory and binding character aimed at the adjustment and settlement of conflict.[96] Moreover, arbitration can be internal and external. In cases of internal arbitration, the arbiter's duties are usually performed by someone who is not a member of the ethnic communities involved in the conflict. Another criterion that is highly relevant is that the parties of the conflict view the arbiter as a legitimate authority in the conflict, and that both parties, whatever the outcome, will respect their decision. McGarry and O'Leary provide examples of such personalities, who in different multiethnic societies managed to perform the duties of an arbiter, mentioning, among others, Josip Broz Tito of Yugoslavia, Mahatma Gandhi of India, or Julius Nyerere of Tanzania.[97] In cases of external arbitration, the conflict is not likely to be settled within the existing domestic political system. In such cases, a single external agent or state, a bi-partisan authority, or a multi-partisan authority may perform the role of external arbiter.[98]

A multi-partisan arbitration process is referred to as co-operative internationalization, which requires the involvement of an international organization.[99] Some examples of such involvement could be the peacemaking and peacekeeping operations of the UN in Cyprus, the Middle East, or Africa.[100] The bi-partisan arbitration process falls within Brubaker's triadic nexus as described previously in this chapter, as it involves two states that express a high level of interest in a region due to the existence of a minority there. Such a process of arbitration can result in "an agreement by a state which maintains sovereignty over the relevant region to consult with another interested state over how that region's government is conducted, and grant the external government a role as a guardian of an ethnic minority within the relevant region."[101]

Examples of minority-related conflicts which have been successfully settled through such processes of arbitration include the Åland Islands (Finland and Sweden), South Tyrol (Italy and Austria), or Northern Ireland (the UK and the Republic of Ireland).[102] As Bauböck writes, Brubaker's conclusion implies that this triadic nexus, due to its structure, may potentially induce conflict escalation; however, the outcome is largely dependent on the contingent factors of social and political agency.[103] On the one hand, the actors in the examples of bi-partisan arbitration given above in every case recognized the legitimate rights of the kin-states to safeguard their ethnic kin within the neighboring state, but on the other hand, these examples may also serve as warnings of why minorities should not become the center of potential escalations of tensions in inter-state (international) relations. They are also examples of how fears, myths, and memories should not become decisive factors in relations within the triangle of 'minority-host state-kin-state.'[104]

Cantonisation and federalisation

According to McGarry and O'Leary, the cantonisation and the federalisation of methods of conflict regulation are fully applicable within the framework and norms of liberal democracies.[105] Cantonisation refers to the "regional management of ethnic diversities…[when] the relevant multi-ethnic state is subjected to a micro-partition in which political power is devolved to (conceivably very small) political units, each of which enjoys mini-sovereignty."[106] This is the Swiss model.[107] At the same time, this must not be confused with administrative decentralization, as "it is built upon the recognition of ethnic difference and allows for asymmetrical relations between cantons and the central government."[108] Within the classification of McGarry and O'Leary, apart from the Swiss model of cantonisation, a prime example of European efforts and processes of cantonisation can be seen in Bosnia and Herzegovina and its particular internal structure that serves the purpose of preventing bloody conflict among its constituent peoples,[109] the Bosniaks, the Croats, and the Serbs.[110] McGarry and O'Leary outline the following characteristics of a federal model, noting that such a model features:

- The separation of powers or concurrent powers in certain domains between central and provincial governments,

- Codified and written constitutional provisions securing status of subunits,
- The consent of federal units in case of constitutional changes or amendments; and bicameral legislation.[111]

They further define three approaches to the design of federal subunits:

- Federalism as nation building, when borders of a subunit are designed in a way to impede minorities from becoming the majority in these units,
- Cosmopolitan federalism, which considers nationalism and accommodating minorities while drawing subunits' borders,
- Multinational nationalism, which designs the boundaries of the subunits so that cultures of at least two ethnic groups find institutionalised forms of expression and protection on a durable basis.[112]

Lijphart defines ethnic federalism as a "special form of segmented autonomy."[113] He further states that this territorial form of autonomy implies a federal arrangement that contains the following elements:

- Geographic concentration of the segments of plural society,
- The boundaries of the subunits of the federation must follow segmental boundaries in the most precise way,
- High homogeneity of the federation's subunits, as far as its segmental composition is concerned.[114]

Carl Friedrich has formulated the attractiveness of federalisation as due to its "territorially diversified values, interests and beliefs overarched by joint values and beliefs."[115] The federal model may ensure a durable and reliable solution for those countries that face or may potentially experience secessionist problems. In relation to minorities, if they are regionally concentrated, the federal subunits may be established in such a way that, within its borders, the minority constitutes a majority. This can provide such a minority an extensive capacity for self-governance and secure their ability to enjoy independence in decision-making in certain areas without the concern that the majority could simply outvote them.[116]

In Europe, there are various examples of the federal organization of states, which are mainly based on economic and regional or territorial grounds.[117] In

Germany and Austria, federalism as such does not contain any ethnic-based criteria.[118] Thus, in today's Germany, the role of federalism "acquires new substance in the form of regional responsibilities such as the protection of monuments and historical sites, the preservation of architectural traditions, and the promotion of regional culture."[119] As for Austria, "the absence of territorially based ethno-linguistic heterogeneity that generates broad centralizing pressures" is the defining feature of federalism.[120] Thus, Austria resembles a unitary state and the country is described as "a federation without federalism."[121] In Spain, the country ensures collective autonomy for the Basque Country and Catalonia,[122] and this "federalising minority group recognition has played a vital part in ensuring that country's relatively smooth transition from authoritarian to democratic rule."[123] Though the organization of Italy as a federal state may be questionable, the federal unit Alto Adige/Trentino (South Tyrol) enjoys administrative autonomy on the basis of language diversity,[124] similar to the rationale for the federal organisations of Switzerland and Belgium, which are based on the ethno-linguistic grounds.[125]

Federalism may serve as one of the forms for territorial autonomy,[126] defined as:

an arrangement aimed at granting a certain degree of self-identification to a group that differs from the majority of the population of the state, and yet constitutes the majority in a specific region. Autonomy involves a division of powers between the central authorities and the autonomous entity.[127]

Territorial autonomy should be distinguished from non-territorial autonomy as referring to "an autonomous unity defined in 'personal' terms."[128] It applies to "a particular (ethnic) group"[129] and is also defined as 'personal autonomy', i.e. an autonomy which "applies to all members of a certain group within the state, irrespective of their place of residence… to preserve and promote the religious, linguistic, and cultural character of the group through institutions established by itself."[130] The defining feature of territorial autonomy is that it refers to an entity clearly defined in terms of territory. Moreover, the autonomous status of the territory may not depend on "whether the individuals living on this territory belong to one or another ethnic group".[131] Its scope may vary from administrative autonomy to full self-government.[132] Administrative autonomy usually refers to arrangements in the sphere of executive powers within a centralized domestic legislative framework.[133] Full self-government also implies that a subunit, subject to domestic national law, is entitled to pass its own legislation and to possess significant powers not only in the judiciary sector, but in the administrative and executive functions within the territory as well. The term "full self-governance" in this context does not extend to the areas of national defense policies or foreign affairs, nor does it extend to monetary or general economic policies.[134]

Consociationalism
Consociationalism, also known as consociation or power sharing, may function as a method of inter-ethnic conflict prevention. It largely resembles federalism, but contains some additional characteristics that are derived from the principle of power sharing. Consociationalism represents a system that consists of various elements where each element possesses a high level of collective autonomy in its internal ability to self-govern and is represented at the highest level of the decision-making process of a given state.[135] The main principles of consociationalism are essentially the recognition and acceptance of ethnic diversity, referring to a person or group being able to enjoy all of the benefits of equality such as the securization of the rights, opportunities and freedoms of all ethnic communities concerned, as well as the creation of various political and social institutions. It is seen as "a group-based approach centered on co-operation between political elites as the major mechanism to manage dispute" in which "ethnic differences have to be taken as a given, recognized, and made integral in the institutional design."[136] In addition to the development of a proportional electoral system in which the main groups of the society are sufficiently represented, Lijphart identifies four additional institutional arrangements necessary to implement a consociationalist model:

- Community autonomy—also referred as 'segmental autonomy'- self-governance in the places of geographic concentration of ethnic group/minority,
- Minority or mutual veto powers for protection of essential issues that affects the ethnic group's vital interests,
- Grand coalition government with major political parties representing all major segments in a divided society, and
- Proportional representation in public administration, employment, and expenditure.[137]

Among the most common examples of the consociational model are Belgium and Switzerland. Bosnia and Herzegovina are also a consociational model that is not, however, considered successful, because the practical implementation of this model has experienced that "the problem in the multi co-nation consociationalism established ... is primarily material rather than ethical."[138]

In spite of a number of failures of "delicate consociational compromise"[139] in Cyprus, Lebanon, and Northern Ireland, consociationalism is considered a much better alternative to the other possible negative outcomes discussed in the previous sub-sections, especially in cases of the escalation of violent conflict, resulting in bloody secession, genocide, etc., as it is focused on the self-governance of the ethnic community/minority.[140] Being a potentially highly unstable system, due to its functioning in a multi-ethnic and heterogeneous society, the consociational model requires a number of conditions to ensure its functionality and a high probability of long-term success. These conditions are summarized by McGarry and O'Leary as:

- The ethnic communities concerned do not have to strive to achieve the goal of integration or assimilate the other community into their own in a short- or medium-term perspective,
- The ethnic communities concerned have to be in possession of political leaders that belong to the successive generations involved into the conflict settlement and committed to the preserving the consociational system,
- The political leaders of an ethnic community have to possess internal autonomy, which provides the capacity for reaching compromises and not being blamed for treason.[141]

Considering the highly demanding requirements, consociationalism has its supporters as well as its critics. Opponents of consociationalism, such as Horowitz, argue that the arrangements offered by consociationalists are "morally unacceptable and practically prone to collapse."[142] McGarry and O'Leary recognize the weaknesses of the system, concluding that "consociationalism may only be applicable in moderately rather than deeply divided societies."[143]

Summing up the methods available for ethnic conflict regulation, it must be emphasized that of the eight models that form McGarry and O'Leary's taxonomy, three of them are absolutely non-applicable and constitute crimes against humanity, i.e. genocide, ethnic cleansing, and forced mass-population transfers. The other five methods of this taxonomy incorporate both positive and negative tools, and their successful application in any one specific case is highly dependent on any number of wide-ranging factors. Nevertheless, none of these remaining five methods is considered the most ideal solution for the adjustment and settlement of ethnic conflict.

Key points

- Europe is characterized by the diversity of its societies, as the existence of various ethnic, linguistic, or religious minorities is a given. However, the continent faces the dilemma of how to address and benefit from this diversity.
- There is no unanimous approach to policies on ethnic diversity, as the groups towards which these policies are applied and the societies that apply these policies are all unique.
- In terms of minorities, one of the key factors affecting them is whether or not they have their own kin-state. The existence of a kin-state seems to provide a minority with an additional impetus to preserve, maintain, and develop its own culture. Moreover, the existence of a kin-state provides a minority with the possibility of receiving additional legal protection beyond that which is provided by the state of residence.
- Minorities without a kin-state are more vulnerable, since their rights are dependent upon the country of residence's domestic legislation and obligations under international multilateral treaties.
- Historical developments in Europe show different approaches towards managing diversity. States have maintained their own attitudes on this matter, which can roughly be summarized as a split between those aimed at eliminating diversity and those aimed at managing it.
- Among the methods aimed at eliminating minority differences, it is possible to define the methods as genocide, ethnic cleansing/forced mass-population transfers, partition and/or secession (self-determination), assimilation and/or integration.
- Ethnic conflict regulations that are aimed at managing diversity include hegemonic control, arbitration, cantonisation and/or federalisation, consociationalism or power sharing.
- Integration is seen by the HCNM OSCE as a tool for the maintenance of multiethnic societies, which provides inclusive treatment and equal opportunities for members of all groups as well as the promotion of the active participation of minorities in society in order to ensure long-term stability and prosperity in that country.

Further reading

BROWN, MICHAEL E., *Nationalisms and Ethnics Conflicts*. Cambridge, Mass.: MIT Press, 2001.
CORDELL, KARL and WOLFF STEFAN. *Ethnic Conflict: Causes, Consequences, and Responses*. Cambridge: Polity, 2009.
DANERO IGLESIAS, JULIEN et al., eds. *New Nation-States and National Minorities*. Colchester: ECPR Press, 2013.
DEUTSCHER, IRWIN and LINDA LINDSEY. *Preventing Ethnic Conflict: Successful Crossnational Strategies*. Lanham: Lexington Books, 2005.
FINLAY, ANDREW. *Governing Ethnic Conflict: Consociation, Identity and the Price of Peace*. London: Routledge, 2011.
ROSS, MARC HOWARD. *Cultural Contestation in Ethnic Conflict*. Cambridge: Cambridge University Press, 2007.
TARR, GEORGE ALAN, ROBERT FORREST WILLIAMS, and JOSEPH MARKO, eds. *Federalism, Subnational Constitutions, and Minority Rights*. Santa Barbara: Greenwood Publishing Group, 2004.
WELLER, MARC and KATHERINE NOBBS, eds. *Political Participation of Minorities*. Oxford: Oxford University Press, 2010.
WIMMER, ANDREAS. *Nationalist Exclusion and Ethnic Conflict: Shadows of Modernity*. Cambridge: Cambridge University Press, 2002.
WOLFF, STEFAN. *Ethnic Conflict: a Global Perspective*. Oxford: Oxford University Press, 2007.

Notes

1. One of the examples is minority rights aimed at protection of existence, protection and promotion of identity and participation in political life, and protection from discrimination and persecution.
2. Carmen Kettley, "Power-sharing and ethnic conflict: The consociational-integrative dichotomy and beyond", in European Yearbook of Minority Issues, eds. EURAC and ECMI (Leiden: Brill, 2003), pp. 247–67 at p. 253.
3. Will Kymlicka, *Multicultural Citizenship: A Liberal Theory of Minority Rights* (Oxford: Oxford University Press, 1995), p. 2.
4. Ibid.
5. Ibid., p. 1.
6. Ibid., p. 4.
7. Anthony D. Smith, "The Ethnic Sources of Nationalism", in *Ethnic Conflict and International Security*, ed. Michael E. Brown (Princeton: Princeton University Press, 1993), pp. 27–41 at pp. 28–9.
8. Ibid., pp. 29–30.
9. Donald L. Horowitz, *Ethnic Groups in Conflict*, 2nd ed. (Berkeley: University of California Press, 2000), p. 41.
10. Ibid., 41–2.

11 Simon Clarke, "Culture and Identity", in *The SAGE Handbook of Cultural Analysis*, eds. Tony Benett and John Frow (London: SAGE Publications, 2008), pp. 510–28 at p. 519.
12 Michael Billig, *Banal Nationalism* (London: SAGE Publications, 1995), p. 86.
13 Joseph Marko, "The Law and Politics of Diversity Management: A Neo-institutional Approach," in European Yearbook of Minority Issues 6 (2008), pp. 251–79 at p. 270.
14 Billig, op.cit., note 12, p. 87.
15 Ibid., p. 127.
16 Stefan Wolff, *Disputed Territories: the Transnational Dynamics of Ethnic Conflict Settlement* (New York: Berghahn Books, 2003), p. 8. Here Wolff links this definition to a broader definition of the notion of 'conflict' provided in his book, which is referred to as "a situation of social tension in which two or more actors who interact with each other pursue incompatible goals, are aware of this incompatibility, and claim to be justified in the pursuit of their particular course of action to realize their goals".
17 Horowitz, op.cit., note 9, p. 3.
18 John McGarry, and Brendan O'Leary, *The Politics of Ethnic Conflict Regulation: Case Studies of Protracted Ethnic Conflicts* (London: Routledge 1997), ch. 1 at p. 1.
19 Kymlicka, op. cit., note 3, p.1.
20 Horowitz, op.cit., note 9, p. 53.
21 Stefan Wolff, and Marc Weller, *Autonomy, Self-governance and Conflict Resolution: Innovative Approaches to Institutional Design in Divided Societies* (London: Routledge, 2008), ch. 1 at p. 8.
22 Ibid.
23 Michael E. Brown, *Ethnic Conflict and International Security* (Princeton: Princeton University Press, 1993), ch. 1 at p. 6.
24 Wolff and Weller, op.cit., note 21, p. 8.
25 Billig, op.cit., note 12, p. 130.
26 Ziporah G. Glass, "Building toward 'Nation-ness' in the Vine: A Postcolonial Critique of John 15.1–8." In *John and Postcolonialism: Travel, Space, and Power*, eds. Musa W. Dube Shomanah and Jeffrey Staley (London: Continuum – Sheffield Academic Press, 2002), pp. 153–169 at p. 155.
27 Daniele Conversi, "Cultural Homogenization, Ethnic Cleansing and Genocide," in *The International Studies Encyclopedia*, ed. Robert A. Denemark (Oxford and Boston: Wiley-Blackwell, 2010) pp. 719–42 at p. 720.
28 Wolff, Disputed Territories, 7.
29 Marko, op.cit., note 13, p. 270.
30 Wolff, op.cit., note 16, p. 6.
31 Ibid., pp. 28–30.
32 Marko, op.cit., note 13, p., p. 272.
33 Ibid.
34 Here the nationalizing state is a state of residence, the external national homeland is a kin-state.
35 Rogers Brubaker, "National Minorities, Nationalizing States, and External National Homelands in the New Europe," *Daedalus* 124 (1995), pp. 107–132 at p. 107.
36 See for instance: David J. Smith, "Framing the national question in central and eastern Europe: a quadratic nexus?" *Global Review of Ethnopolitics* 2 (2002), pp. 3–16; Michele E. Commercio, *Russian Minority Politics in Post-Soviet Latvia and Kyrgyzstan: the Transformative Power of Informal Networks* (Philadelphia: University of Pennsylvania Press, 2010).
37 Francesco Palermo, "National Minorities in Inter-State Relations: Filling the Legal Vacuum?" in *National Minorities in Inter-State Relations*, eds. Francesco Palermo and Natalie Sabanadze (Leiden and Boston: Martinus Nijhoff Publishers: OSCE, 2011), pp. 3–27 at p. 3.
38 Ibid., p. 5.
39 Ibid.,p. 3.

40 Gabor Kardos, "Role for the Kin-States?" in *Beyond Sovereignty: From Status Law to Transnational Citizenship?, ed.* Osamu Ieda (Hokkaido: Slavic Research Center, 2006), pp. 127–137 at pp. 134–5.
41 Cited by: Gabor Kardos, Ibid., p. 135.
42 Ibid., pp. 135–6.
43 Ibid., pp. 136–7.
44 Palermo, op. cit., note 37, p. 3.
45 Ibid., p. 4.
46 Ibid., p. 16.
47 Ibid., p. 20.
48 McGarry and O'Leary, op.cit., note 18, pp. 4–5.
49 Ibid., p. 4.
50 Will Kymlicka, and Wayne Norman, *Citizenship in Diverse Societies* (Oxford: Oxford University Press, 2000), ch. 1 at pp. 12–3.
51 Gaetano Pentassuglia, *Minorities in International Law: An Introductory Study* (Strasbourg: Council of Europe, 2002), p. 79.
52 Ibid.
53 *UN Convention on the Prevention and Punishment of the Crime of Genocide*, adopted 9 December 1948, accessed July 6, 2013, http://www.hrweb.org/legal/genocide.html.
54 Turkey protests Sweden Armenia 'genocide' vote, BBC News, March 11, 2010, accessed July 6, 2013, http://news.bbc.co.uk/2/hi/8563483.stm.
55 For more information, refer to: Ronald Grigor, Suny et al. eds., *A Question of Genocide: Armenians and Turks at the End of the Ottoman Empire* (Oxford: Oxford University Press, 2011).
56 William A. Schabas, "Ethnic Cleansing and Genocide: Similarities and Distinctions", in *European Yearbook of Minority Issues* 3 (2005), pp. 109–28 at p. 113.
57 Ibid.
58 Ibid.
59 For more details about these endeavors, refer to: Cathie Carmichael, *Ethnic Cleansing in the Balkans: Nationalism and the Destruction of Tradition* (London: Routledge, 2002) or Michael Mann, *The Dark Side of Democracy: Explaining Ethnic Cleansing* (Cambridge: Cambridge University Press, 2005).
60 McGarry and O'Leary, op.cit., note 18, p. 9.
61 Ibid., p. 11.
62 Ibid., p. 12.
63 Ibid.
64 John McGarry, and Brendan O'Leary, "The Political Regulations of National and Ethnic Conflict in Parliamentary Affairs," in *A Journal of Comparative Politics* 47 (1994), pp. 94–115 at p. 99.
65 Ibid., p. 99.
66 Ibid., p. 100.
67 Ibid., p. 101.
68 McGarry and O'Leary, op.cit., note 18, pp. 16–7.
69 Ibid., p. 17.
70 Marko, op.cit., note 13, p. 271.
71 Ibid., pp. 270–271.
72 McGarry and O'Leary, op.cit., note 18, p. 17.
73 Ibid.
74 Bhikhu Parekh, *Rethinking Multiculturalism: Cultural Diversity and Political Theory* (Cambridge, Mass.: Harvard University Press), p. 250.

75 Ibid.
76 Kymlicka and Norman, op.cit., note 50, p. 15.
77 Merja Pentikäinen, *Creating an Integrated Society and Recognising Differences: The Role and Limits of Human Rights, with Special Reference to Europe* (Rovaniemi: Lapland University Press, 2008), p. 329.
78 Ibid., p. 107.
79 McGarry and O'Leary, op.cit., note 18, p. 17.
80 Kymlicka and Norman, op.cit., note 50, p. 14.
81 Ibid.
82 Ibid., 14.
83 Press Release: OSCE High Commissioner on National Minorities launches guidelines on integration of diverse societies, issued 7 November 2012, accessed July 6, 2013, http://www.osce.org/hcnm/96929.
84 *Ljubljana Guidelines on Integration of Diverse Societies*, pp. 4–5, accessed July 6, 2013, http://www.osce.org/hcnm/96883.
85 Ibid., p. 3.
86 Ibid., p. 4.
87 Ibid., p. 13.
88 McGarry and O'Leary, op.cit., note 18, pp. 23–4.
89 Ibid., pp. 24–25.
90 Ibid., p. 25.
91 Ibid.
92 Kymlicka and Norman, op.cit., note 50, p. 13.
93 McGarry and O'Leary, op.cit., note 18, p. 27.
94 Ibid.
95 Ibid.
96 Ulrich Schneckener, "Models of Ethnic Conflict Regulation: the Politics of Recognition," in *Managing and Settling Ethnic Conflicts: Perspectives on Successes and Failures in Europe, Africa and Asia*, eds. Ulrich Schneckener and Stefan Wolff (London: Hurst & Co. Publishers, 2004), pp. 18–39 at p. 30.
97 McGarry and O'Leary, op.cit., note 18, pp. 28–9.
98 Ibid., p. 29.
99 Ibid.
100 Ibid.
101 Ibid., p. 30.
102 Ibid.
103 Rainer Bauböck, "Political Community beyond the Sovereign State: Supranational Federalism and Transnational Minorities," in *Conceiving Cosmopolitanism: theory, context and practice*, eds. Steven Vertovec and Robin Cohen (Oxford: Oxford University Press, 2002), pp. 110-136 at p. 131.
104 Rogers Brubaker, Nationalism Reframed: Nationhood and the National Question in the New Europe (Cambridge: Cambridge University Press, 1995), pp. 75-6.
105 McGarry and O'Leary, op.cit., note 18, p. 30.
106 Ibid., pp. 30–31.
107 Ibid., p. 31.
108 Ibid.
109 See: *Constitution of Bosnia and Herzegovina (preamble)*, Constitutional Court of Bosnia and Herzegovina , accessed July 6, 2013, http://www.ccbh.ba/eng/p_stream.php?kat=518 .

110 McGarry and O'Leary, op.cit., note 18, p. 31.

111 Ibid., p. 33.

112 Summarized in: Liam D. Anderson, *Federal Solutions to Ethnic Problems: Accommodating Diversity*, (London: Routledge, 2013), p. 4, on the basis of: John McGarry, and Brendan O'Leary, "Federation as a Method of Ethnic Conflict Resolution," in *From Power-Sharing to Democracy: Post-Conflict Institutions in Ethnically Divided Societies*, ed. Sidney John Roderick Noel (Toronto: McGill-Queens University Press, 2005), pp. 263–96 at pp. 269–72.

113 Anderson, op.cit., note 112, p. 14.

114 Ibid.

115 Cited by: Tinatin Khidasheli, "Federalism and Consociationalism: Perspectives for Georgian State Reform," in *Federal Practice. Exploring Alternatives for Georgia and Abkhazia*, eds. Bruno Coppieters et al. (Brussels: VUB University Press, 2000), pp. 195–202 at p. 197.

116 Kymlicka, op.cit., note 3, pp. 27–8.

117 Tove H. Malloy, *National Minority Rights in Europe* (Oxford: Oxford University Press, 2009), p. 42.

118 Ibid.

119 *Federalism and Self-government*, accessed July 6, 2013, http://www.collasius.org/DEUTSCHLAND/4-HTML/03-foeder-e.html .

120 Jan Erk, *Explaining Federalism: State, Society and Congruence in Austria, Belgium, Canada, Germany and Switzerland* (London: Routledge, 2008), p. 18.

121 Ibid., pp. 17–8.

122 Malloy, op.cit., note 117, p. 42.

123 Smith, Graham, "Sustainable Federalism, Democratization, and Distributive Justice," in *Citizenship in Diverse Societies*, eds. Will Kymlicka and Wayne Norman (Oxford: Oxford University Press, 2000), pp. 345–65 at p. 346.

124 Malloy, op.cit., note 117, p. 42.

125 Ibid.

126 Kymlicka and Norman, op.cit., note 50, p. 15, p. 26.

127 Ruth Lapidoth, *Autonomy: Flexible Solutions to Ethnic Conflicts* (Washington: US Institute of Peace Press, 1997), pp. 74–5.

128 Wolff and Weller, op.cit., note 21, p. 15.

129 Ibid.

130 Lapidoth, op.cit., note 127, p. 75.

131 Wolff and Weller, op.cit., note 21, p. 13.

132 Ibid.

133 Ibid., pp. 13–14.

134 Ibid.

135 Malloy, op.cit., note 117, p. 178.

136 Roberto Belloni, "Peacebuilding and Consociational Electoral Engineering in Bosnia and Herzegovina," *International Peacekeeping* 11 (2004), pp. 334–53 at p. 336.

137 Arend Lijphart, *Democracy in Plural Societies* (New Haven and London: Yale University Press), p. 25; McGarry and O'Leary, op.cit., note 18, p. 35; Belloni, op.cit., note 136, p. 336.

138 Malloy, op. cit., note 117, p. 183.

139 McGarry and O'Leary, op.cit., note 18, p. 36.

140 Ibid., p. 37.

141 Ibid., pp. 36–7.

142 Wolff, Stefan "Conflict Resolution Between Power Sharing and Power Dividing, or Beyond?" *Political Studies Review* 5 (2007), pp. 377–393 at p. 377.

143 McGarry and O'Leary, op.cit., note 18, p. 37.

Chapter 6: Transnationalism

Zora Popova

Summary

Although the social sciences concept of transnationalism was coined in the second half of the 20th Century by scholars interested in migration issues, key problems of the transnational agenda were outlined decades earlier. The emblematic article of Randolph Bourne "Transnational America" published in 1916, discussing the failure of America as a melting-pot, the challenges of assimilation of immigrants into another culture, and the connection between a person and their "spiritual country" as a basis for their sense of nationality, outlines the perspective relevant for contemporary minority studies.[1] Various definitions of transnationalism and connotations have relevance for key concepts, such as identity, citizenship, multiple loyalties and diaspora. This specific discourse is thus applicable to minority issues, including the wide-spread conception that Roma are transnational actors which is challenged by the discourse.

Introduction

There are two different perspectives for studying and analyzing minority issues, which delineate different problematic fields with their specific questions and approaches. The perspective that dominates the scientific discourse is the macro perspective, which we have discussed in Part I. Adopting a top-down approach to minorities and their concerns, scholars focus on provisions and regulations within the frameworks of national and international legislation, on their implementation by governments and public bodies, and on institutional relations between authorities and institutions representing minority communities. Within this field, research interest is usually directed towards exploring the political and civil processes at the level of both the national state and international levels, as well as towards analyzing the varieties of patterns in majority–minority relations. Protection of minority rights, implementation of minority rights, minority agenda, diversity, tolerance, integration, and empowerment are among the key concepts regularly used to articulate minority issues. The macro-perspective is interested in the minorities as collective bodies and socio-political actors, as well as in the dynamics between the states and the groups. And although acknowledging that these minority groups are quasi-stable formations (considering the fact that belonging to a minority community is a right granted to the individuals and not an obligation), the top-down approach often ignores the internal community dynamics and their possible impact on macro-structures in general.

These specific internal community dynamics and the relations among the individual members of a minority community, as well as relations between minorities and the majority, are object of analysis for the micro approach to minority issues, which we discuss in Part II. The bottom-up approach, non-dominant in the scientific research, examines factors that either enable or impede people to act as members of a minority, such as the norms and values, or the dichotomy between the individual and collective rights. The focus here falls on daily practices and on the acts of citizenship, on the identity perception and life choices, on community social capital, as well as on the ownership and practicing of minority rights. Among the key concepts used when minority issues are looked at, though the micro-perspective are identity, belonging, individual choice, norms and values, networks, active citizenship, and ownership of rights. Although interested predominantly in the socio-cultural processes at the level of the individuals and their relations with the different collective bodies (e.g. own minority community and/or majority society), the scholars working in this field still cannot ignore such macro-frameworks since they shape and regulate the socio-political frameworks that have a direct impact on the life of the individual, as discussed in Chapter 5.

Introducing these two different approaches towards studying and analyzing minority issues is important in order to clarify the difference between the notions of "international" and "transnational", especially when used to describe phenomena and processes from this particular field of research.[2] Projecting the two concepts in light of the above outlined discourse, it becomes apparent that the notion 'inter-national' encompasses the idea of relations between spaces that are delineated by borders and between agents that belong to those spaces. The concept has very strong structural and political connotations. At the same time, transnational infers the idea of diminished importance of borders, of processes and phenomena that occur regardless of the political borders of states. The concept challenges the existing structures and systems and focuses on dynamics, processes and phenomena that occur, not because but in spite of borders, the key agent of which is not the state but the individual.

Understanding the processes and phenomena at the micro-level and the impact on technology and globalisation on dynamics within and among individuals and communities are among the key issues that could become clearer when addressed through the perspective of transnationalism. The current Chapter will look at how this 'transnational discourse' can advance minority research by taking into account the impact that global developments have on minority dynamics. To begin, however, it is important to outline the concept and the parameters of this particular field of study.

Brief History of the Concept

Although first used in the beginning of the 20th Century, the notion of transnationalism was coined decades later in debates among migration scholars. Between 1980s and 1990s, scholars were focused on the phenomenon of transnationalism as such, projected as a mechanism used to resist processes of assimilation. During the second 'wave'—between the mid-1990s and the first decade of the 21st Century—the focus of scholars fell mainly on problems with the conceptualisation and measurement of transnationalism, again with regard to migration processes and communities. In the context of globalisation, scholars[3] began exploring the connection between transnationalism and broader developments in religious, economic and cultural border-crossing linkages and emerging structures.[4] During this second period, the discussions on transnational migration projected against the observed changes of the time-space perceptions and the attempts to address the issues in a systematic way, resulted in the proliferation of transnational terminology (e.g. transnational communities, transnational social fields, transnational social formations and transnational social spaces). According to Thomas Faist, this shift of the concept became dominant for migration research in the 1990s, replacing the notions of multiculturalism, minorities and cultural pluralism.[5]

The differences between the approaches to transnationalism can also be accounted for by disciplinary divides. While anthropologists and ethnologists are interested in transnational kinship systems[6] and ethnicity-based affiliations, sociologists would rather explore "translocal" communities and immigrant entrepreneurship.[7] Political scientists focus on issues of membership in multiple states[8] as well as on political activities involving emigration country governments, migrants and nationalist movements.[9] Scholars are also divided on the issue of whether transnationalism is a new process or whether it is just a new concept that refers to phenomena known at least since the end of the 19th Century. Some theorists claim that it should be considered a specific model of ethnic community formation resulting from the failed attempts of the settlement society to incorporate immigrant communities and the reduced but still existing possibilities for cross-border relations. Others insist that transnationalism stems from the increased intensity, extensity and velocity of border-crossing exchanges that occurred after the 1970s.[10] Jackson, Crang and Dwyer also point out that the interactions denoted by the term transnationalism are not new phenomena.[11] Furthermore, Al-Ali and Koser question whether the replacement of the notion of international migration with "transnational migration" has been indeed grounded on any new developments.[12] Theorists argue that in fact a theory of transnationalism is still missing,[13] and that the various typologies and descriptions have been used as tools for studying border-crossing ties and linkages which result in transnationalism being addressed as a historically and contingent phenomenon. The lack of not only a distinct approach but also distinct views towards examined social patterns, often addressed equally well by the older paradigms of race relations, ethnic identity, and change, therefore, challenges the need for delineating the study of transnationalism as a specific scientific field.

However, Faist claims that transnationalism can be approached from the perspective of the mechanisms through which it works. Leaving the micro level aside, Faist is interested in the intermediate mechanisms that can help understand the interactions of transnational social formations (e.g. forms of exchange, reciprocity, solidarity and control), and in the master mechanisms that enable the study of the development and impact of transnational spaces on systems, politics and polity as well as migrant incorporation. This, in his view, is a precondition to project the transnational ties and linkages on broader theories of space, time and society. Taking into account the dynamics between social integration (i.e. politics focused on the incorporation of the immigrants as transnational actors in the system) and system integration (i.e. polity as the inter-linkage of parts into the a social system as a whole), Faist suggests that a third stage in the development of transnationalism as a field of research and analysis is slowly coming forward. Introducing systemic aspects of transnationalization, such discussions need to go beyond the "fashionable terms 'deterritorialization' and 'resistance' of migrants to nationalist ideologies to include problems of statehood in the fields of territoriality, sovereignty and legitimacy."[14] When considering transnational ties in the light of the polity (the order of political systems), membership/citizenship are the key issues that are coming to the fore. At the same time, transnational spaces need to be approached as systems *per se* regardless of whether they form societies in the most strict sense of the term or not.

Definitions of Transnationalism

Defining transnationalism is a challenge not only because misleading implications are often ascribed to the concept by researchers that are not directly involved in the field, but also because there is a number of issues on which even scholars working on the topic cannot reach a common understanding. According to Vertovec, transnationalism should not be addressed as a new theoretical approach since it "inherently builds upon a number of preceding ones", such as the Chicago School of Sociology and the Manchester School of Anthropology.[15] Furthermore, the notion has become over-used to describe too-wide a range of phenomena "from specific migrant communities to all migrants, to every ethnic diaspora, to all travellers and tourists."[16] Recognising that transnational patterns can take many forms in socio-cultural, economic and political arenas and each of those can be explored from a broad or narrow perspective as well as in connection to the intensity of the exchanges and communication, Vertovec emphasises that transnationalism should not be approached as a single theory but rather through the establishment of a typology of transnationalisms and the conditions that affect them. Departing from this standpoint, the definitions of transnationalism presented below have been grouped according to the core issues upon which they build.

Interaction and Networks

According to the Oxford English Dictionary, transnational relations refer to regular cross-border interactions of predominantly non-state actors that have an impact on politics across borders—such as nongovernmental organizations (NGOs), multinational corporations (MNCs), religious actors, terrorists, criminal actors, and diasporas and ethnic actors.[17] As a field of study, transnationalism explores the social and cultural consequences of globalization on societies and relations among communities and individuals, paying special attention to migration and hybrid identities. The concerns of the early transnational relations debates during the 1970s, which focused on the juxtaposition of society versus states, are still shaping research on transnational actors. Focusing on the movement of goods, people, and ideas across national boundaries which have challenged the strict distinction among nations, Kaplan and Grewal look at transnationalism from the perspective of the connections between people and their daily lives "here and there."[18] They point to the impact that actions and cultures have on people in diverse places. Itzigsohn and Cabral refer to transnationalism as a web of linkages that affects every aspect of the lives of people in their places of residence, emphasizing the social interactions and exchanges that transcend the political and geographical boundaries of a single nation.[19] Vertovec argues that transnationalism, understood in terms of long-distance community networks, preceded even the nation itself. Within the core of the concept as approached today is the specific nature of the links between people and institutions—these intensified relationships across space function in real time and regardless of the presence of the international borders.[20]

According to Portes, the contacts and activities across national borders of expatriate community members do not constitute a new field for scientific investigation *per se*. It is the intensity of exchanges, the new modes of transacting and the multiplication of activities within the core of such new phenomena is referred to as transnationalism. Transnational activities are hence those that take place

on a recurrent basis across national borders and that require a regular and significant commitment of time by participants. Such activities may be conducted by relatively powerful actors, such as representatives of national governments and multinational corporations, or may be initiated by more modest individuals, such as immigrants and their home country kin and relations. These activities are not limited to economic enterprises, but include political, cultural and religious initiatives as well.[21]

Similarly to Portes, Glick Schiller also views transnationalism as consisting of regular social contacts that enable economic, political, and cultural activities and exchanges.[22]

Identities and De-territorialisation

Transnational communities and the people who consider themselves a part of these communities represent an intrinsic aspect of transnationalism. Members of such communities possess identities based primarily on the attachment to a 'homeland' or home culture, and not necessarily to a specific geographic territory. These rather virtual ties transcend space and time and are arguably more powerful than those connecting people with territories. The notion of a transnational community puts the emphasis on human agency: not only the existence of but furthermore the flourishing of such groups is a result of cross-border activities, which link individuals, families and local communities. The increase in number of transnational communities in the age of globalisation has had a direct impact on many longstanding means of signifying differences founded upon territoriality and on the mechanisms for controlling those. Transnational communities represent a powerful challenge to the traditional ideas of nation-state belonging.[23] Increase in mobility, growth of temporary, cyclical and recurring patterns of human migration, cheap and easy travel have altered the understanding of migration as a single act of transfer from one state to another.

Transnational communities do not necessarily refer only to migrants, as cross-border groups with common cultural, sporting, political or other interests might also consider themselves a community. However, in practical terms, groups arising from migrations are the most significant type, and most research on transnational communities refers to these groups. Clearly, migrants have always lived in more than one setting, maintaining links with a real or imagined community located in the state of origin. What has changed in recent decades is the context of globalisation that facilitates the construction of social relations transcending national borders. The increase in mobility and the development of communication has contributed to such relations and has created a transnational space of economic, cultural and political participation.[24] According to Rouse, migrants maintain involvement in only one space, while transnationals have "dual lives"—both within the host community and within their communities of origin, maintaining economic, social, religious, and organisational relationships that span borders;[25] furthermore, they are claimed by more than one state.[26] As Lee and Francis point out, transnational relationships, and connections occur across boundaries.[27] Reflecting on the transnational perspective, scholars emphasise that it, in fact, does not decrease the importance of categories such as global, local, or nation-state, but that it demands that we take into consideration how notions that are often taken for granted such as citizenship and identity may change when they are constituted across space.[28]

Focussing on de-territorialization as a result of the cultural implications of transnational capital, the anthropologist Arjun Appadurai has developed a set of notions to reflect the emerging spaces: ethnoscapes, mediascapes, technoscapes, finacescapes and ideoscapes. In his view, what is most important among these post-territorial "scapes" are what are referred to as ethnoscapes, because they have a direct impact on currently observed societal changes and affect both domestic and international politics. Appadurai addresses these spaces in terms of social relationships and social practices.[29] The members of these de-territorialised communities, bounded together on the basis of shared and maintained cultural values and social practices, are prone to develop "double identities" based on their dual membership of and participation in both the settlement community—as immigrants—and in the home nation community—as diaspora.[30] Such dual political double political participation and membership (sometimes based on cultural affiliation rather than legal status) is possible because in the age of globalisation the state governs individuals based on their citizenship, as opposed to location,[31] and hence national law and policy can have a direct impact on the lives of people beyond of a particular sovereign state.[32] In contrast to the few examples of immigrant communities that have managed to preserve their cultural identity in pre-globalisation times (e.g. the Italians in San Francisco and New York, the Mexicans in California), the development of this dual identity makes transnationals in principle more resilient to assimilation in the traditional sense.[33]

Technology and Globalisation

A number of scholars—e.g. Portes, Vertovec, Itzigsohn, Glick Schiller, address transnationalism as a social, economic, political and cultural phenomenon closely connected with technological progress and the processes and forces of globalisation.[34] Guarnizo and Smith's definition of transnationalism clearly emphasises the connection between globalisation and transnationalism.[35] According to their view, transnationalism refers to the globalization of capitalism and the repositioning of states, nations, class, gender and ethno-racial formations within this global restructuring; decolonialization, the universalization of human rights, and the rise of cross-national institutional networks are examples of the transnational dimensions of global political transformation. The complexity of the transformation occurring alongside the movement through space as a result of intensified cultural inter-connectedness and mobility across geographical locations and political borders is the essence of what is meant by "trans".[36] Transnationalism enables, therefore, the understanding of "the cultural specificities of global processes, tracing the multiplicity of the uses and conceptions of 'culture.'"[37] According to Portes, the specific feature of transnationalism is the high volume of exchanges on a daily basis through the diverse media.[38] Vertovec emphasises that this possibility for communication and cultural exchange not only allows for the maintenance of certain cultural identities, but also integrates diverse cultures in a type of "cultural hybridity."[39] This enhanced connectivity produces, in fact, the new type of groups, identities, and nationalisms.[40] The new communication technology that enables the real time exchange of ideas, news, images, behavioural models as well as new transportation technology, is at the core of transnationalism as a concept and as a life-style.[41] The challenge, however, is to identify and examine simultaneous processes and their intersections at the horizontal and vertical, at the national, the subnational, and the transnational levels, but also to understand the spatial expansion of social networks from below, which facilitate the reproduction of migration, business practices, cultural beliefs, and political agency.[42]

Key Approaches to Transnationalism

The fact that the term transnationalism is built from two words, which are quite commonly used, leaves many people with the false impression that the concept is understandable. The definitions presented above outline some of the specific connotations attached to the notion as used by the social sciences, although they do not fully lift away the vagueness. Furthermore, the variety of approaches used by scholars to address and examine transnationalism contributes to the complexity of the field. Vertovec understands transnationalism as a complex phenomenon that performs within a number of dimensions.[43] Approached as social morphology, it refers to the social transformations that span across borders, which are a direct result of the functioning of networks, enabled by new technology. These networks, however, can be either positive or negative (violent and/or illegal). According to Vertovec, this perspective provides a clearer view of ethnic diasporas today and the triadic relationship between those groups, the host and the home state. While the diasporas from the past can be viewed as imagined communities with regard to the homeland,[44] the current technological development has enabled them to become an active part of the nationhood. Such real but non-physical connections justify that current transnational communities are approached as "dispersed diasporas."[45]

Furthermore, transnationalism is a type of consciousness that maintains the collective memory. In contrast to the traditional, the current diaspora consciousness accumulating and integrating new experience, decentres the attachments and builds not only dual but rather multiple identities. Transnationals are hence people, who are 'home-away-from-home', and who can be linked to more than one home and nation. As Anderson points out, in the pre-technology age, the shared past and common consciousness was the key factor for the formation of imagined communities.[46] In the age of cyberspace, however, people form communities based on their connections to networks and not necessarily to a territory. Finally, new technology and global media, enabling the flow of communication between spaces, establishes transnationalism as a mode of cultural reproduction with a special impact on the emergence of hybrid cultural phenomena and, eventually, of new ethnicities.[47]

Analysing the community dynamics through the economic activities of their members, transnationalism can be explored as an avenue of capital—not only through the organisation and the functioning of transnational companies (the major institutional form of transnational practises through the globe-spanning structures of networks), but also through direct capital flows. According to estimates, the average annual flow of immigrant money by the end of the 20th Century had reached 75 billion USD.[48] This has pushed governments to develop policies aimed at reincorporation of transnationals. Portes emphasises that although the origin of many current transnational communities might be economic, transnational activities are cumulative and subsequently encompass political, social and cultural pursuits.

Vertovec approaches transnationalism also as a political engagement that reveals new dialectics of global and local anew, not necessarily compatible with the national politics. In his view, transnational political activities have become possible due to technological progress, which has enabled the mobilization of political support membership and participation, regardless of distances and the physical national borders.[49] By changing the relationship between people and space and by creating 'social fields' that connect and position actors in more than one nation (both as a location and as a membership), transnationalism in fact contributes to the (re-)construction of place. The concept has contributed to the connotation of locality with a structure of feeling and with the ideology of a community, pushing aside the traditional references to territory. According to Vertovec, this growing disjuncture between territory, subjectivity and collective social movement and the steady erosion of their relationship[50] has lead to the formation of what Appadurai calls "trans localities."[51] Finally, with regard to transnational agents, Vertovec points out the differences between the two types of actors—the institutions (such as the transnational social movement organizations or the international NGOs) and the diasporas. The transnational institutions seek to change the status quo on a variety of levels. The focus of their work are usually issues that are not connected to any specific state, but that can be related to all of them—such as environmental issues, human rights, women rights, peace, and self-determination issues. While the institutions, through their concerns and work, create a common (universal, global) supra-national platform, the diasporas, on the other hand, because of their maintained and intensive engagement with the homeland (for example, through the opening of regional party offices) constitute "deterritorialised nation states."[52] Transnationalism, hence, can help us understand not only the formation and the maintenance of communities today, but also of the observed changes and dynamics within such communities.

The confusion with regard to the understanding of the concept of transnationalism can also be attributed to the fact that the existing literature on the subject tends to mix the various levels at which transnationalism performs (e.g. the individual level with the networks of social relations, the level of the community, and the level of broader institutionalised structures such as local and national governments) exploring issues from the individual achievements to institutional initiatives.[53] Identifying the individual and their networks as the proper unit of analysis, Portes looks at grass-root transnational activities as developed in reaction to policies, politics or socio-economic conditions and affirms the idea that transnationalism emerges at the state level only when governments realise that they can benefit from expatriate communities and try to channel their homeland involvement.[54] Departing from this stand-point, the approach that Portes adopts to analyse transnationalism focuses on the heterogeneous set of its activities defined by the area and the level of institutionalisation. Portes' typology of activities distinguishes between economic, political and socio-cultural transnationalism.[55] The mobilisation of contacts across borders in search of suppliers, capital and markets are at the core of transnational economic initiatives, which can also be analyzed through the historical perspective. Political transnationalism, according to Portes, refers to the activities of communities, political parties and governments that are driven by the desires of the respective actors to achieve political power and influence in either the host or home country. The socio-cultural transnational activities, however, aim at the reinforcement of national identity abroad, in the maintenance of sense of community and in the growth of the feeling of pride in diversity (for example, enhanced by cultural events—e.g. festivals, music, sport, celebration of national holidays abroad, and goods).[56] The difference between the activities within each of those three areas can be accounted for by referencing the differences in the levels of institutionalisation. The activities performed by individuals and their networks are of a low level of institutionalisation. Although sharing similar features, they differ in character from the highly institutionalised transnational initiates and are conducted by multinational corporations and states. In the literature on transnationalism, these differences are often referred to as transnationalism "from below" and "from above."[57] The table below presents a systematic overview of the Portes' typology.

		Sector		
		Economic	Political	Socio-cultural
Level of institutionalisation	Low	Informal cross-country traders Small businesses created by returned immigrants in home country Long-distance circular labour migration	Home town civic committees created by immigrants Alliances of immigrant committee with home country political associations Fund raisers for home country electoral candidates	Amateur cross-country sport matches Folk music groups making presentations in immigrant centres Priests from home town visit and organize their parishioners abroad
	High	Multinational investments in Third World countries Development for tourist market of locations abroad Agencies of home country banks in immigrant centres	Consular officials and representatives of national political parties abroad Dual nationality granted by home country governments Immigrants elected to home country legislatures	International expositions of national arts Home country major artists perform abroad Regular cultural events organized by foreign embassies

Tab. 5: **Systematic overview of the Portes' typology** (Source: Portes, Alejandro, Luis E. Guarnizo and Patricia Landolt, "The study of transnationalism: pitfalls and promise of an emergent research field", *Ethnic and Racial Studies* 22 (1999), pp. 217–237, here: p. 222.)

Historically, transnationalism can be seen as having emerged from the economic activities of diaspora elites (e.g. the Venice Republic), and the political references were mainly made towards the 'native lands under foreign control'.[58] In the 20th Century, however, the logic of capital expansion (local labour—global goods) has had a direct impact on the development of the new frameworks of the transnational perspective. Portes also emphasises that although today transnational activities differ between areas and the level of institutionalisation, they are interlinked and are dependent on factors such as the regularity of contact, routine and the mass involvement of actors. To create these networks across space, transnationalism needs access to infrastructure such as technology and communications.[59]

Similarly to Portes, Faist is also interested in the institutionalisation of social and symbolic ties that bind people and communities across national borders. However, the focus of his approach does not include transnational activities as such, but rather favours the types of transnational spaces that the activated ties constitute. According to Faist, transnational social formations are "sustained ties of persons, networks and organizations across the borders of multiple nation-states, ranging from weakly to strongly institutionalized forms."[60] Faist conceptualises, therefore, the dimensions of the trans-boundary social capital in two ways: in terms of the time-space compression of ties and in terms of the organisation of ties.[61]

When addressing the perspective of time-space compression, Faist analyses their extensity (in the three aspects: the location of activities, the actors involved and the fields covered) and their intensity (in density of ties and in speed of transactions).[62] With regard to the linkage patterns in networks, organisations and communities, the focus falls on infrastructure (modes of transportation and communication, informal norms and procedures), regulations (law, state policies—formal norms and procedures, hierarchies and patterns of authority) and institutionalisation (transnational spaces with varying degrees of institutionalisation), as presented in the table below. Faist defines the category of transnational spaces with a low degree of formalised networks as diffusion—contact fields for the exchange of goods, capital, information, ideas and practices.[63] These transactions do not require close and sustained contact between the people involved and often contacts are made in an ad hoc fashion (at the market place or tourist sites) or can lead to a diffusion of social or cultural practices across borders.

Degree of formalisation	
Low: Networks	High: Institutions
Diffusion: Fields for the exchange of goods, capital, persons, information, ideas and practices	Small kinship groups: Households, families
Issue networks: Networks of business people, epistemic networks, advocacy networks	Communities and organisations: Religious groups, enterprises

Tab. 6: **Degree of formalisation** (Source: Faist, Thomas, "The Transnational Turn in Migration Research: Perspectives for the Study of Politics and Polity", in Maja Povrzanovicǎ Frykman (ed.), *Transnational Spaces: Disciplinary Perspectives*, (Malmö: IMER, Malmö University, 2004), p. 7.)

The binding principle within transnational kinship groups is the reciprocity in exchanges, which is the basis of equivalence as a social norm. The relations between members of transnational kinship groups are highly formalised and the sense of belonging to a common homeland is strong—even among members that live apart or work abroad. According to Faist, a typical example of such relationship types can be considered "transnational families, who conceive themselves as both an economic unit and unit of solidarity and who keep, besides the main house, a kind of shadow household in another country."[64] Remittance of household or family members from country of immigration to country of emigration is also a typical activity in within this social space.[65]

The issue networks (also referred to as transnational circuits) function on the basis of the mutual obligations and expectations of the actors. They are defined as a set of individual or collective actors (from individual families to sovereign states) and the relations that connect them. Although these networks are characterised by a rather homogeneous set of ties, there is no formal membership status as within the organisations. The exchange of information and services within the issue networks is driven by a common goal. Advocacy networks (focused on human rights), business, science, and environmental protection networks are some of the examples of such types of transnational spaces that can be regarded as being direct outcomes of instrumental activity.[66] Faist points out that among the examples here, the networks emerging among third-countries migrants who have already or are in the process of migrating to the European Union (EU) should also be considered.[67]

Transnational communities and organisations are the transnational spaces with the highest degree of deeply institutionalized ties and relations, imbued with a potentially long life-span.[68] The primary resource in the ties of transnational communities is solidarity, stemming from the shared ideas, beliefs, and symbols, which are eventually expressed in some sort of collective identity.[69] Geographic proximity is not a factor for the establishment and maintenance of transnational communities where the dense and continuous set of social and symbolic ties with a high emotional and moral charge are the basis for social cohesion. Examples of such transnational communities include not only transboundary religious groups and churches, but also diasporas. Regardless of the factors and events behind the territorial dispersion of the groups of people who, in the past, were a part of a geographically determined (national) community, diaspora members have a common memory of the homeland which is not only shared between members but may become an intrinsic element in the development of a vision, which would see the creation of a new land.[70]

Transnational organisations are commonly characterised by not only a high degree of formal control and the undertaking of considerable effort on the part of actors to coordinate social and symbolic ties, but also by a form of a bureaucratic rule and administrative instrumentation. In the views of Faist, an early type of transnational organisation developed out of issue networks, such as the Red Cross, Amnesty International and Greenpeace.[71] At the same time, this transnational space also contains and includes para-state associations such as the ethno-nationalist PKK (Partiya Karkaren Kurdistan) aiming at achieving territorial political autonomy. According to Waldinger and Fitzgerald, the intensification of worldwide communications, of mobility and of exchanges has negatively impacted the understanding that nation state and society converge.[72] Transnationalism in their view projects the new ways of conceptualising the connections between here and there, between source and destination, between host and home societies. The activated networks spanning the geographically remote spaces generate a multiplicity of imagined communities. Organised along different and often conflicting principles and extending loyalties beyond the place of origin, ethnic or national group, those imagined communities illustrate the root meaning of transnationalism.[73]

Communities are shaped not only by their members, but also by states and politics conducted within their borders.[74] Since states seek to control movement across territorial borders, the conditions that either enable of or impede the freedom of movement need to be taken into account when examining cross-border activities in light of transnationalism. From the perspective that states also regulate national membership, the important aspect to be taken into account is the variability in of the degree of institutionalisation of possessed by internal and external state boundaries, as well as the intensity by through which states police them.[75] The third aspect that needs to be considered when examining transnational communities is the particular loyalties (group, national, political) of members with social identities shaped by their connections to two or more states. Surely, the scope of the loyalties (multiple versus exclusive) also depends on the relationships among states (e.g. on international politics). Waldinger and Fitzgerald emphasise that the use, form and mobilisation of connections, which link the spaces and create a transnational realm, are subjected to multiple political constraints. At the same time, this approach affirms that transnational reality is a particular discourse and represents real and existing space that non-state actors create across and beyond ethnic/national/political/state borders, which, although possessing its own frameworks and logic of existence, can be directly affected by factors and developments at the national and international levels.

Transnationalism and Minority Issues

Outlining the transnational discourse, conceptualised and developed as a new research area and perspective in the 1990s and focusing on migrants as important social agents,[76] a controversial issue emerges. Transnationalism, as approached by theorists, examines phenomena and processes that occur within a wider (global) framework which expands beyond territorial space and spans geographic locations and communities regardless of the physical or historical distance. At the same time, as it was stated earlier in this Chapter, transnationalism also enables scholars to examine minority issues from below. The controversy is elusive. Adopting a transnational approach to minority issues requires that problems are addressed not at the institutional framework level (national, international, political, economic, social, legislative, normative, etc.), but at the level of relations between people and their networks. By focusing on the underlying dynamics and factors that span spaces and time-lines, transnationalism brings agency squarely into focus. With regard to the minority issues, the transnationalist approach contributes to the understanding of societal changes at communal and individual levels and lends insight during the assessment of their impact on macro-frameworks.

The point of intersection between transnationalism and minority issues is undoubtedly the diaspora—a term originating from the Greek language referring to the dispersal of a population through colonisation.[77] Though it may be a classical concept, the term has undergone dramatic changes and has become a rather politicised notion, often used by nationalist groups or governments in connection with agendas of nation-state-building or mobilisation of support from the diaspora members, of kinstate protection for minorities, the encouragement of financial investments or the promotion of political loyalty among economically successful expatriates.[78]

Building upon the original connotations of the concept, referring to the historical experience of particular groups (e.g. Jews and Armenians) and extending later to religious minorities in Europe, in the 1970s the applications and interpretations of the concept inflated. On the basis of their dominant characteristics, these can be summed up in the following three categories:

- Causes of migration or dispersal (historic—Jews, newer—trade diasporas, labour migration diasporas),
- Cross-border experiences of homeland with destination (return to a real, imagined or even non-territorial homeland); dense and continuous linkages across borders; experience of all mobile persons as "transnation."[79] The fact that the imagined homeland can be a non-territorial one, such as the Islamic *umma*, highlights that even within a historical perspective the term diaspora may refer to ethnic and even to religious groups or communities,[80]
- Incorporation or integration of migrants and/or minorities into the "host country"[81] (while older notions emphasise the cultural (political, economic) distinctiveness of a particular diaspora making and maintaining boundaries vis-à-vis the majority group(s), the contemporary notions exhibit a more inclusive character, accepting such concepts as "cultural hybridity."[82]

Approaching diaspora-related issues from a transnational perspective, the interest shifts from structural communal problems to the processes that transcend international borders which address abstract social phenomena. Diasporas can themselves be regarded as transnational spaces, but this is not by default. They are transnational as far as they constitute a realm of dynamic exchanges through the relatively stable, lasting and dense sets of ties, networks and organisations reaching beyond and across the borders of sovereign national states.[83] The grassroots activity of the community members and their networks are, when taken together, the driving engine of the processes.[84]

The diaspora and the transnational perspective both share similar features but they should not be taken as inter-replaceable concepts and approaches. Among the similarities that Faist points out is the fact that both of the terms are "extremely elastic" and concerned with sustained cross-border ties (including regions of origin, destination, and ties to regions of residence).[85] Both approaches examine the relations between communities and homeland, as well as issues of incorporation of persons into the settlement community, discussing the link between integration and cross-border engagement.[86] Despite such similarities, the perspectives incorporate significant differences. While diaspora literature investigates the cultural distinctiveness of groups, posing questions on the link between the cultural autonomy of minority groups and integration, transnational studies look more extensively into migrant incorporation and transnational practices.

The terms transnationalism and diaspora differ by the nature and scope of groups to which they refer. Diaspora relates most often to religious, ethnic and national groups and communities, while transnationalism addresses all sorts of social formations and phenomena, such as networks of businesspersons and social movements. In its postmodern conceptualisation diaspora relates to a form of transnational organisation spanning a specific country of origin and a set of settlement countries. The term transnational community, however, encompasses a range of phenomena, including cross-border village communities or borderland communities. "Thus, transnational communities encompass diasporas, but not all transnational communities are diasporas."[87] The other difference lies in the approaches to the understanding of identity and mobility. Diaspora studies usually focus on aspects of collective identity, while transnationalism explores identity through cross-border mobility. A diaspora is often regarded as being essentially the product of a traumatic or pragmatic dispersal, resulting in the emergence of a collective identity connected to a homeland or to a nation-building projects of so-called stateless diasporas;[88] however, when the reason for the dispersal is external (e.g. borders migrating over people) the focus fall on common identity—despite dispersal.[89] From a transnational perspective, collective identities are a product of either hybridity or cultural translations, in which mobile persons are involved as a result of their cross-border mobility and their involvement in the exchange of ideas and goods.[90]

Finally, it is the long-term horizon that distinguishes diasporas from transmigration and from transnational communities.[91] While time is a significant factor in the formation and maintenance of diasporas, often referred to as formations reaching across generations (e.g. Jewish, Armenian, Palestinian diaspora), transnational analysts are usually interested in more recent and contemporary migrant flows and not in historical continuity. Instead of stretching the term diaspora beyond its limits, Faist argues that it is better to "speak of a transnationalized and segmented cultural space characterized by syncretist identities, populated by sundry ethnic, political, religious and subcultural groups."[92] The major resources to bridge networks and groups across borders are local assets, such as various forms of social capital. This enables transmigrants not only to "think transnationally and act locally" but also to "think locally and act transnationally" and to "think transnationally and act transnationally."[93] Although developed within the field of migration research, Faist's approach to segmented cultural spaces, characterised by a significant dichotomy between cultural expressions and identity in the public realm, on the one hand, and in the private sphere, on the other, can be easily transferred to the field of minority issues. The table below, revealing the responses of immigrants and refugees to opportunities in the receiving and sending countries, is easily transferable and applicable for the assessment of minority-related processes and dynamics.[94]

Responses of immigrants and refugees according the dimensions of insertion	Adaptation in the Receiving Nation-State	Segregation in the Receiving Nation-State	Border-Crossing Expansion of Social Space
Economic	socio-economic integration by adaptation to autochthonous population	ethnic niches and enclaves; "middleman minorities" (groups specializing in trade and concentrating in the petite bourgeoisie) and/or socio-economic marginalization in the labour markets	transnational reciprocity and transnational circuits (high degree of transnational exchange, trade and traffic)
Political	citizenship (citizenship of one nation-state)	political autonomy in receiving country	transnational solidarity; multicultural citizenship; dual citizenship
Cultural	cultural assimilation (acculturation)	cultural segregation (collective identities transferred from sending country)	transnational community (syncretist collective identities)

Tab. 7: **Responses of Immigrants and Refugees to Opportunities in the Receiving and Sending Countries** (Source: Faist, Thomas, "International Migration and Transnational Social Spaces: Their Evolution, Significance and Future Prospects", in *InIIS-Arbeitspapiere* 9/98; Bremen: Institut für Interkulturelle und Internationale Studien, Universität Bremen, 1998, p. 4, Figure 1.)

Another issue of importance for minority studies, deriving from the comparative analysis of diasporic and transnational communities, relates to processes that have a direct impact on national states. Stefaan Verhulst points out that flows of information, communication, linkages and the increasing effectiveness of non-state actors and their networks increasingly challenge the role of identities and contributes to their de-territorialisation of both identities and public spheres.[95] Verhulst supports the idea of Arnold Toynbee, presented in 1961, that world-wide diasporas, rather than local national states, are most likely the "wave of the future."[96] The transnational approach to identity and the related dynamics within the context of current global developments provides interesting insights for the field of minority studies.[97] Focusing on the intensified linkages between individuals and their networks can help us understand why contemporary transnational communities should be regarded as real, rather than imagined. As distance is no longer a factor that impedes or enables contacts contact among people and institutions, the reasons for weak ties or the lack of effectiveness of networks should not be sought in the physical remoteness of actors.

Ong's approach to transnationalism, understood as "cultural specificities of global processes", points out the possibility to study and evaluate diversity through the examination of common processes and shared practices and to account for the weight of a variety of cultural aspects.[98] Within the new sociopolitical condition, the newly emerging types of identities (e.g. Vertovec presents nine case studies on transnational identities) are closely connected to the constitution of new types of citizenship: transnational, multiple identities,[99] flexible,[100] post-national,[101] diasporic,[102] or transnational[103] frameworks of citizenship. Understanding the dual-life models of transnationals and their impact on both home and host communities can foster the development of new platforms, policies and legislative frameworks regulating lives of national minorities as well.[104] In the 21st Century, multiple-citizenship cannot be regarded as an exception to the rule. Overlapping membership in political communities is hence a projection of this new identity/citizenship/membership paradigm.

The transnationalist perspective enables not only that minority issues are addressed at a grass-root level, but also that evolution of supra-national processes and their impact on the macro-framework that regulates the lives and rights of minorities is better understood. As Anderson and Hamilton suggest, the transnational approach could provide alternative solutions to ethnic and nationalistic conflicts.[105] According to their view, when (national) conflicts are rooted in geography, a way-out should be sought in alternative non-territorial solutions, which "cross the borders of states and of nations, combining transnational representative democracy with non-territorial forms of political participation."[106]

Are Roma Transnational?

The question to conclude with is whether Roma should be regarded as transnational or not. The answer to this question depends on the scope of using 'Roma' as a unit of analysis. If we focus singularly upon the Roma labour immigrants who are building new lives in foreign settlement societies, while maintaining their households back in home countries, the answer is that on this notion a Roma should be considered transnational. However, if by Roma we are referring to the various Roma communities that represent a part of minority groups in many European countries, the answer is that these are not transnational communities. Roma, as a European minority lack ties among individuals from different spaces, networks, and exchanges that are the core factors which characterise transnational communities as described above. The fact that the Roma live in a number of different European states should be seen as intrinsic as to why they have been denoted with an international status, but this should not be extended to Roma labour migrants, as this by no means implies a complementary transnational status in line with the frameworks of the term explored in this Chapter.

Key Points

When exploring the field of transnationalism, it becomes apparent that this exciting new area of research reveals a perspective that offers new dimensions for analysis while also demonstrates and puts forth new problematic conclusions to be further studied in minority research. To summarise, the transnational approach contributes to the understanding of:

- Contemporary diaspora dynamics,
- Current developments with regard to the formation of multiple identities
- The evolution of multiple loyalties

- The development of models of multiple membership (across national polities) and the establishment of multiple citizenship as a norm and not as an exception to the rule
- The impact of technology and processes of globalisation on the political, economic, social, and cultural development of communities—from the opening of traditional groups to the establishment of new (hybrid) communities through intensified networks-activity
- The hybridization of cultures
- The importance of networks and grass-root (linking) processes
- The shift of locality from a determinant of social roles and behaviour to the point of reference
- The evolving mechanisms (dual life models) that challenge assimilation patterns
- The possibilities for finding alternative solutions to territorial/national issues—e.g. through non-territorial autonomy, multiple citizenship schemes
- The need for new policies and frameworks to regulate such processes
- The need for rethinking of traditional paradigms and concepts with regard to identity, community, majority-minority relations and national/community loyalties
- The existence of institutions beyond the international level
- The need for the proper identification of new players and factors, both at grass-roots and meta levels, that determine and regulate political, economic, social and cultural processes.

This list outlines only a few of the aspects that transnationalism can bring forward within minority studies.

Further Reading

BAUBÖCK, RAINER and THOMAS FAIST, eds. *Diaspora and Transnationalism—Concepts, Theories and Methods*, IMISCOE Research – Amsterdam University Press, 2010.

FAIST, THOMAS. "Diversity – a new mode of incorporation?", in *Ethnic and Racial Studies* 32, 2009.

KENNEDY, PAUL and VICTOR ROUDOMETOF. *Communities Across Borders under Globalising Conditions: New Immigrants and Transnational Cultures, Institute of Social and Cultural Anthropology* (ISCA) at the University of Oxford—Working paper WPTC-01-17, 2001.

MITCHELL, KATHARYNE. "Transnational Discourse: Bringing Geography Back In", in *Transnational Discourse: Bringing Geography Back In. Antipode* 29, 1997.
POVRZANOVICÀ, MAJA FRYKMAN, ed. *Transnational Spaces: Disciplinary Perspectives.* Malmö University, IMER, Malmö, 2004.
SAFRAN, WILLIAM. "Diasporas in modern societies: Myths of homeland and return", in *Diaspora* 1 (1991), pp. 83–99.

Notes

1   Randolph Bourne, "Trans-national America", in *Atlantic Monthly* 118 (July 1916), pp. 86–97.
2   Looking at the definitions provided by the Oxford English Dictionary and Merriam Webster Dictionary, the concepts seem as if overlapping with international referring to something "existing, occurring, or carried on between nations; agreed on by all or many nations; used by people of many nations" and transnational, understood as "extending or operating across national boundaries, " Oxford English Dictionary online (accessed 12 May, 2013) http://oxforddictionaries.com; Merriam Webster Dictionary online, accessed 12 May, 2013, http://www.merriam-webster.com/.
3   Steven Vertovec and Robin Cohen, eds., "Migration, Diasporas and Transnationalism." (London: Edward Elgar,1999).
4   Thomas Faist, "The Transnational Turn in Migration Research: Perspectives for the Study of Politics and Polity"; in *Transnational Spaces: Disciplinary Perspectives*, ed. Maja Povrzanovicà Frykman (Malmö University: IMER, Malmö, 2004), p. 12.
5   Ibid.
6   Nyberg Sørensen, Nina and Karen Fog Olwig, eds., *Work and Migration: Life and Livelihoods in a Globalizing World (Transnationalism).* (London: Routledge, 2002); Maja Povrzanovicà Frykman, "Transnational Perspective" in *Ethnology: From 'Ethnic' To 'Diasporic' Communities" in Transnational Spaces: Disciplinary Perspectives*, ed. Maja Povrzanovicà Frykman (Malmö University: IMER, Malmö, 2004), pp. 77–101.
7   Alejandro Portes, Luis E. Guarnizo and Patricia Landolt, "The study of transnationalism: pitfalls and promise of an emergent research field" *Ethnic and Racial Studies* 22 (1999), accessed 16 June 2013, http://www.tandfonline.com/doi/pdf/10.1080/014198799329468.
8   Rainer Bauböck, "Recombinant citizenship" in *Inclusions and Exclusions in European societies*, Martin Kohli and Alison Woodward, eds. (London: Routledge, 2001); Rainer Baubock, "Transnational Citizenship: Membership and Rights" in *International Migration* (Aldershot: Edward Elgar, 1994).
9   Robert Smith, "Reflections on Migration, the State and the Construction, Durability and Newness of Transnational Life", in *Migration and Transnational Social Spaces*, ed. Ludger Pries (Aldersot: Ashgate,1999), p. 187–219; Eva Østergaard-Nielsen, "Transnational political practices and the receiving state: Turks and Kurds in Germany and the Netherlands", *Global Networks* 1 (2001), p. 261–281.
10 Faist, op.cit., note 4, p. 13.
11 Peter Jackson, Philip Crang, and Claire Dwyer, *Transnational Spaces* (London: Routledge, 2004).
12 Nadje Al-Ali and Khalid Koser, eds. *New Approaches to Migration: Transnationalism and Transformations of Home*, (London: Routledge, 2002).
13 Faist, op.cit. note 4; Paul Kennedy and Victoria Roudometof, *Communities Across Borders under Globalising Conditions: New Immigrants and Transnational Cultures* (Institute of Social and Cultural Anthropology (ISCA) at the University of Oxford – Working paper WPTC-01-17, 2001), accessed 15 June, 2013, http://www.transcomm.ox.ac.uk/working%20papers/WPTC-01-17%20Kennedy.pdf.
14 Faist, op.cit. note 4, p. 15.

15 Steven Vertovec, "Transnationalism and identity", *Journal of Ethnic and Migration Studies* Vol. 27 (2001), p. 576, accessed June, 2013, http://www.ub.unimaas.nl/ucm/e-readers/HUM2018/Vertovec.pdf.
16 Ibid.
17 Peter Hägel, "Transnational Actors", *Oxford English Dictionary*, accessed 14 May, 2013, http://www.oxfordbibliographies.com/view/document/obo-9780199743292/obo-9780199743292-0016.xml#obo-9780199743292-0016-div2-1.
18 Inderpal Grewal, and Caren Kaplan, eds. *Introduction to Women's Studies: Gender in a Transnational World* (New York: MacGraw Hill, 2002).
19 Jose Itzigsohn, Carlos Dore Cabral, Esther Hernández Medina and Obed Vázquez, "Mapping Dominican Transnationalism: Narrow and Broad Transnational Practices", *Ethnic and Racial Studies* 22 (1999), pp. 316–339.
20 Steven Vertovec, "Conceiving and researching transnationalism", *Ethnic and Racial Studies* 22 (1999), pp. 447–462, accessed 15 June, 2013, http://www.transcomm.ox.ac.uk/working%20papers/conceiving.PDF.
21 Alejandro Portes, "Conclusion: towards a new world – the origins and effects of transnational activities", *Ethnic and Racial Studies* 22 (1999), pp. 463–477.
22 Nina Glick Schiller, Linda Basch and Cristina Szanton Blanc, "From Immigrant to Transmigrant: Theorizing Transnational Migration", *Anthropological Quarterly* 68 (1995), pp. 48–63.
23 Manuel Castells, "End of Millennium" in *The Information Age: Economy, Society and Culture* III. 2nd ed., (Cambridge and Oxford: Blackwell, 2000).
24 Riva Kastoryano, "Settlement, transnational communities and citizenship", *International Social Science Journal* 52 (2000), pp. 307–312.
25 Roger Rouse, "Mexican migration and the social space of postmodernism", in Jackson, Crang and Dwyer, op. cit note 11, p. 28
26 Nina Glick Schiller, "Transmigrants and nation-states: Something old and something new in the U.S. immigrant experience" in *The handbook of international migration: The American experience*, ed. Charles Hirschman, Philip Kasinitz and Josh DeWind, pp. 94–119 (New York: Russell Sage Foundation, 1999); Al-Ali and Koser, op.cit. note 12.
27 Helen Lee and Steve Tupai Francis, eds. *Definitions of Transnationalism in Migration and Transnationalism: Pacific Perspective – Pacific Transnationalism conference*, La Trobe University in Melbourne, Australia, November, 2006), accessed June, 2013, http://epress.anu.edu.au/migration/mobile_devices/index.html.
28 Sanjeev Khagram and Peggy Levitt, "Constructing Transnational Studies" in *The Transnational Studies Reader*, eds. Peggy Levitt and Sanjeev Khagram (London: Routledge, 2008).
29 Arjun Appadurai, "Disjuncture and Difference in the Global Cultural Economy" in *Global Culture*, ed. Mike Featherstone (London: Sage, 1990), pp. 295–310.
30 Portes, op.cit.,note 21; Robin Cohen, *Global Diasporas; An Introduction* (London: UCL Press, 1997).
31 Christian Joppke and Ewa Morawska, *Towards Assimilation and Citizenship. Immigrants in Liberal Nation-States*. (Basingstoke: Palgrave Macmillan, 2003); Christian Joppke, "Beyond National Models: Civic Integration Policies for Immigrants in Western Europe", 30 *Western European Politics* (2007), pp. 1–22.
32 Glick Schiller, Basch and Szanton-Blanc, op.cit., note 22.
33 Vertovec, op.cit., note 20.
34 Steven Vertovec, *Transnationalism – Key Ideas* (London: Routledge, 2009).
35 Luis E. Guarnizo and Michael Peter Smith, "The Locations of Transnationalism" in *Transnationalism from Below*, Comparative Urban and Community Research, Michael Peter Smith and Luis E. Guarnizo eds. (New Brunswick, New Jersey, 1998).
36 Aihwa Ong, *Flexible Citizenship: The Cultural Logic of Transnationality* (Durham, NC: Duke University Press, 1999).
37 Ibid.
38 Portes, Guarnizo and Landolt, op.cit note 7.

39 Vertovec, op.cit. note 20.
40 Inderpal Grewal, *Transnational America*: Feminisms, Diasporas, Neoliberalisms" in Transnational America 22–23 (2005).
41 Guarnizo and Smith, op. cit. note 35.
42 Ibid, p. 24.
43 Vertovec, op.cit., note 20.
44 Benedict Anderson, *Imagined Communities: Reflections on the Origins and Spread of Nationalism* (London: Verso, 1983).
45 Vertovec, op.cit., note 20.
46 Anderson, op. cit., note 44.
47 Stuart Hall, "Old and New Identities, Old and New Ethnicities" in *Culture, Globalization and the World-System: Contemporary Conditions for the representation of identity*, ed. Anthony D. King (Houndmills, Macmillan, 1991).
48 Luis E. Guarnizo, Alejandro Portes and William Haller, "Assimilation and Transnationalism: Determinants of Transnational Political Action among Contemporary Migrants" in *American Journal of Sociology* 108 (2003), pp. 1211–1248; accessed 14 June, 2013, http://hcd.ucdavis.edu/faculty/webpages/guarnizo/AssimTrans.pdf.
49 Vertovec, op.cit. (1999), note 20, p. 10.
50 Ibid, p. 13.
51 Arjun Appadurai, "The Production of Locality" in *Counterworks: Managing the Diversity of Knowledge*, ed. Richard Fardon (London: Routledge, 1995).
52 Vertovec, op.cit. (1999), note 20.
53 Portes, Guarnizo and Landolt, op.cit., (1999), note 7, p. 220.
54 Ibid.
55 Ibid, p. 221.
56 Portes Guarnizo and Landolt, op.cit. (1999), note 7.
57 Luis E. Guarnizo, "The emergence of a transnational social formation and the mirage of return migration among Dominican transmigrants", *Identities* 4 (1997), pp. 281–322.
58 Portes, Guarnizo and Landolt, op.cit., note 7, p. 225.
59 Ibid, p. 224.
60 Thomas Faist, T, *Transnationalization in International Migration: Implications for the Study of Citizenship and Culture*; WPTC-99-08; (Institute for Intercultural and International Studies (InIIS), University of Bremen (1999), p. 2, accessed May 2013, http://www.transcomm.ox.ac.uk/working%20papers/faist.pdf.
61 Ibid, p. 4.
62 Ibid, pp. 5–6.
63 Ibid, p. 8.
64 Ibid.
65 Faist, op.cit., note 60, p. 8.
66 Faist, op.cit., note 4, p. 8.
67 Ibid, p. 9.
68 Ibid.
69 Faist, op.cit. note 60, p. 8.
70 Faist, op.cit. note 4, p. 10.
71 Ibid.
72 Roger Waldinger and David Fitzgerald, "Transnationalism in Question", *American Journal of Sociology* 109 (2004), p. 1177; accessed 12 June, 2013, http://www.sscnet.ucla.edu/soc/faculty/waldinger/pdf/B7.pdf.

73 Ibid, p. 1178.
74 Ibid.
75 Ibid.
76 Schiller, Basch and Szanton-Blanc, op.cit, note 22.
77 Stefaan Verhulst, "Diasporic and Transnational Communication: Technologies, Policies and Regulations", *The Public* 6 (1999), accessed 12 June, 2013, http://Javnost-Thepublic.Org/Article/Pdf/1999/1/2/.
78 Thomas Faist, "Diaspora and Transnationalism: What kind of dance partners", in *Diaspora and Transnationalism: Concepts, Theories and Methods*, eds. Rainer Bauböck and Thomas Faist (Amsterdam: Amsterdam University Press, 2010), p. 10.
79 Arjun Appadurai, *Modernity at Large: Cultural Dimensions of Globalization* (Minneapolis: University of Minnesota Press,1996).
80 Faist, op.cit., note 78, pp. 12–13.
81 Ibid.
82 Ibid.
83 Ibid, p. 14.
84 Within the social sciences, transnationalism regards non-state actors as agents of change: diasporas exist in a triangular socio-cultural relationship with the host society and the homeland. This is the main point of distinction between transnational relations in within the political science sub-discipline of international relations and the concept of transnationalism that focus on non-state actors (Portes, op.cit., note 21.)
85 Faist, op.cit. (2010), note 78.
86 Thomas Faist, "Diversity – a new mode of incorporation?' in *Ethnic and Racial Studies* 32 (2009).
87 Ibid, p. 21.
88 Kathrin Kissau and Uwe Hunger "The Internet as a Means of Studying Transnationalism and Diasporas", in *Diaspora and Transnationalism*, op. cit. note 78.
89 Myra A. Waterbury, "Bridging the Divide: Towards a Comparative Framework for Understanding Kin-State and Migrant-Sending Diaspora Politics" in *Diaspora and Transnationalism*, op. cit. note 78.
90 Faist, op.cit. note 78, p. 21.
91 Russell King and Anastasia Christou, "Diaspora, Migration and Transnationalism: Insights From the Study of Second-Generation 'Returnees'", *Diaspora and Transnationalism*, op. cit. note 78.
92 Thomas Faist, T., "International Migration and Transnational Social Spaces: Their Evolution, Significance and Future Prospects" in *InIIS-Arbeitspapier* 9/98; (Institut für Interkulturelle und Internationale Studien, Universität Bremen, 1998), p. 31.
93 Ibid, pp. 32–33.
94 Ibid, p. 4, Figure 1.
95 Verhulst, op. cit, note 77, p. 33.
96 Ibid, p. 32.
97 Vertovec, op. cit., note 20.
98 Ong, op.cit., note 36, p. 4.
99 Steven Vertovec, "Introduction", in *Migration and Social Cohesion*, ed.. Steven Vertovec, Aldershot: Edward Elgar (1999); Steven Vertovec, "Minority associations, networks and public policies: re-assessing relationships" *Journal of Ethnic and Migration Studies* 25 (1999), pp. 21–42.
100 Ong, op.cit., note 36.
101 Yasemin Nuhoglu Soysal, *The Limits of Citizenship: Migrants and Postnational Membership in Europe* (Chicago: University of Chicago Press, 1994).
102 Michel S. Laguerre, *Diasporic Citizenship: Haitian Americans in Transnational America* (London: Macmillan, 1998).

103 Rainer Bauböck, *Transnational Citizenship: Membership and Rights in International Migration* (Aldershot: Edward Elgar, 1994)

104 Vertovec, op. cit., note 20, p. 575.

105 Anderson, J. and D. Hamilton, *National Conflict, Transnationalism and Democracy: Crossing borders in Ireland*; conference paper presented at Nationalisms and Identities in a Globalized World, (17–22 August 1998), accessed 12 May, 2013, http://www.nuim.ie/staff/dpringle/igu_wpm/anderson.pdf.

106 Ibid, p. 1.

Chapter 7: Late Modernity

Tove H. Malloy

Summary

The influence of late modern societal changes on minority existence has created a number of controversial developments in the way societies govern diversity and cope with difference. These social changes have occurred to some extent as a result of external global forces inducing hyper-mobility resulting in increasingly diverse societies. These external forces may be regional, such as the phenomenon of Europeanization, or global, as in the case of globalization and North-South relations. Human inter-action comes under pressure to cope with alterity and difference when the meeting of multiple cultures in the altered public space engenders new scenarios of self-identification. Minorities often get caught in the middle of this process which at times promotes xenophobia and racism. This in turn puts a greater demand on our understanding of culture and groups, and requires new analytical tools and approaches, such as constructivism and critical thinking. The balancing of different views of culture, including relativist and universalist views of minority cultures, as well as the management of cultural diversity, has come into public debate while at the same time as numerous cases have shown us that the complexity of cultural meetings in the public sphere is very difficult to manage, let alone legislate. This has ramifications for how Europeans approach and understand minority existence in late modern Europe.

Introduction

As discussed in the previous chapter, minority studies are forging new frontiers within the social sciences. Like transnationalism, the reality of late modernity requires students to question traditional assumptions. Our world today looks more uncertain than ever before. At the end of the last century, scholars gloomily spoke of the end of the 'nation-state'[1] and the 'end of history'.[2] Others warn us that we were in fact witnessing the end of ideology, and that global politics was now a matter of culture; cultures against cultures in a 'clash of civilizations'.[3] These were sweeping statements about a world that was becoming much more inter-connected and perhaps inter-dependent for good and for bad. Cosmopolitans say it is good; particularists say it is bad. Often cosmopolitans are elitists who favour open economic markets, whereas particularists represent non-dominant groups without a voice of power. We had already been warned that we were transitioning to a new paradigm called the "risk society"[4] signified by the word 'change'. Social change is a phenomenon that makes many people insecure. And insecure people feel better when they can prophesize gloom rather than boom. The fact of the matter is, we do not know how insecure our world has become but as scholars we are dedicated to exploring it.

Minority issues in Europe are, as noted in Chapter 1, a product of the modern era, and they have by and large been approached through the prevailing thought frame of modernism. Thus, minority existence has been interpreted in the light of modernity and post-medieval security structures as well as the power relations of the national state developed after the Peace of Westphalia (1648). With the events of late modernity, the integration of Europe, mass communication and hyper-mobility, minorities have encountered new power structures and new social settings. This requires new modes of analysis to understand minority existence in the 21st Century. This Chapter will discuss minority issues with reference to the forces and events of late modernity, such as Europeanization, globalization and North-South politics. This will be pursued through the lens of academic debates about narratives and discourses guided by conceptual analysis.

By discourse we do not mean a debate or a discussion, nor a chain-of-texts or articulations of opinions. A discourse is a space where forces of power vie for hegemonic positions in the formation of a polity that aims to govern certain aspects of human life. This is of course crudely put. More correctly, experts would state that a discourse is neither an organizing centre nor is it a structure. A discourse does not promote meaning; it informs social interaction. It does not prescribe cognitive action; it influences it.[5] The identity of a discourse is constructed through political struggles and is also transformed through political struggles. In fact, discourse identities compete for hegemonic position through political struggles. Moreover, a discourse does not presuppose order; it is defined by the presence of conflict or divergent opinions. Thus, the hegemonic identity or position of a discourse changes when it is confronted with conflicts or divergent views it cannot bring under control. It follows that discourses are relational, and their identities are formed through differentiation from other discourses. In a way, discourse identities compete for space on the political horizon by articulating concrete positions within a realm of non-fixed activity. Hence, discourses and their identities become fixed through the relationship with other discourses which together constitute a totality called a discursive formation.

Narrative is a word borrowed from the science of history or historiography. Essentially it is a method of storytelling which chronologically organizes a single coherent story. Usually it is descriptive rather than analytical; it is concerned with people not abstract circumstances, and it deals with the particular and specific rather than the collective and statistical.[6] Historiographers would like to think that narrative is a tool exclusive to their discipline which has been cultivated by historians of eminence, such as Thucydides, Gibbon and Macaulay. This method gave way in the 20th Century to a hegemonic force of 'new historians' who favoured a method of quantitative detail and cause-and-effect analysis. The science of history thus became influenced by a methodology informed by the natural sciences, i.e. positivism. This changed in the 1960s and 1970s when new historians began returning to the method of storytelling because they wanted to discover "what was going on inside people's heads in the past, and what it was like to live in the past, questions which inevitably lead back to the use of narrative."[7] In short, historians of the narrative tradition rebelled against the reliance on positivistic methods based on quantitative and cause-and-effect analysis.

The aim of the Chapter is to provide a critical political view of minority issues that are set in the reality of late modern societal relations. The Chapter will first offer definitions of the core concepts (Sections 1, 2 and 3) followed by a discussion of the two most debated minority views in late modernity (Section 4).

Late Modernity

The idea of modernity concerns the interpretation of the present time in light of historical reinterpretation.[8] It refers to the confluence of the cultural, social, and political currents in modern society. The term signals a tension within modern society between its various dynamics and suggests a process by which society constantly renews itself. The word 'modern' comes from the Latin word *modus*, meaning now, but the term 'modernity' has a stronger meaning, suggesting the possibility of a new beginning based on human autonomy and the consciousness of the legitimacy of the present time.[9] The roots of the notion of modernity point to a certain time period. The Oxford Dictionary of Sociology defines modernity as a term used to characterize the stage in the history of social relations, which dates roughly from the end of 18th Century to the present, characterized by the democratic and industrial revolutions.[10] This definition indicates that the features of modernity differ from social organization which characterized life before the 18th Century. However, modernity is not only contrasted with its predecessor, but also increasingly with its successor. Some theorists have argued that there has not been a fundamental shift, and that instead, current changes indicate a radical intensification of the characteristics embedded within modernity, with the life altering consequences of these changes reaching all aspects of everyday life.[11] Most notable has been Jürgen Habermas's argument that the Enlightenment paradigm of reason may be outdated but not dead; rather, it needs to be updated in light of the social realities of late modern society.[12] This line of reasoning is followed by Anthony Giddens, Ulrich Beck and Zygmunt Bauman who have suggested that we live in late or high modernity.

Giddens argues that "high" or "late" modernity is a post traditional order characterised by a developed institutional reflexivity.[13] The globalising tendencies of modern institutions are accompanied by a transformation of day-to-day social life having profound implications for individual activities. The self becomes a reflexive project, sustained through a revisable narrative of self-identity. The reflexive project of the self thus is a form of control or mastery which parallels the overall orientation of modern institutions towards, what Giddens calls, "colonising the future."[14] Yet reflexivity also helps promote tendencies which place that orientation radically in question—and which provide the substance of a new political agenda for late modernity.

Reflexive identity is also the focus of Ulrich Beck's theory of the risk society.[15] Arguing that by the latter part of the 20th Century individualism deepened its hold on the western imagination with people becoming better educated and the technological-information revolutions no longer required unskilled and uneducated work forces but just the opposite, the emergence of a highly educated information society which displaced the older manual worker society of the previous period took place.[16] Instead of a high value being placed on long term loyalty to the corporate institutions and structures of the 20th Century, these new classes of people within the information society reflected back on their relationships with these institutions and concluded that they no longer needed to make them primary focus of their lives in order to maximize their own individual self-development. Hence, what began to emerge in the late 20th Century was a radical shift in the focus of meaning in western societies from a culture where meaning and identity were grounded in loyalty to institutions and structures to one in which meaning and identity are grounded in the self as the primary agent of meaning. Almost overnight, the institutions and structures of the 20th Century quickly entered a place where their legitimacy was questioned and most loyalty to them removed.

A slightly different account of late modernity is found in Zygmunt Bauman's theory of liquid modernity.[17] Bauman examines how we have moved away from a "heavy" and "solid", hardware-focused modernity to a "light" and "liquid" software-based state of modernity. Previously, Bauman argues, people were immersed in "solid societies" that produced the norms by which people lived. People could structure their lives by being members of their society and could measure their success by measuring themselves against their society's norms. Modernity's emphasis on the individual has resulted in the destruction of these norms all in the name of giving freedom and self-determination to the individual. However, this freedom and self-determination is in many ways an illusion. Society may have restricted an individual but arguably it enabled the individual by supplying the support and infrastructure for them to live their lives. Now individuals must construct themselves without support, including constructing the measures that allow them to assess the meaning and success of their lives. In this way, it can be said that they are bound by their own freedom. Moreover, the loss of inter-dependency is enabled by technologies that are not dependent on proximity. Long lasting relationships and societies are built by people who have to find ways to live together and face the exigencies of their physical and economic environments. Both traditional technology and the dependence on territory are diminished and the technologically and economically enabled can move from one opportunity to another and are not tied to the economic fortunes of any one particular territory. Those tied to a territory are fated to experience booms and busts with no long lasting support from society. The result is a society of individuals who are tied only to themselves and only to the present.

In the following, we will examine the relationship between minority existence and this new world of reflexive individuals seeking to make sense of the social change that is brought on by external forces of change. We begin by defining these external forces.

External Forces and Social Change

The relations between external forces and social change often have greater influence on minorities than on the members of the majority, especially if members of minorities do not have the social and human capital to build capabilities that help avert negative influence. This Section examines the three main forces that affect social change.

Europeanization

As discussed in Chapter 3, Europeanization usually refers to the moral, political and economic power of the developed countries of the European Continent and their influence on the remainder—and less developed—countries of the Continent in terms of values and norms, especially democratic values. It is thus more than EU integration, which is however seen as a primary outcome of these forces. Some scholars would argue that there is an Orientalism present in the forces of Europeanization, while most see the EU dimension as the dominating force. Robert Ladrech argued in 1994 that Europeanization is an 'incremental process reorienting the direction and shape of politics to the degree that European Community political and economic dynamics become part of the organizational logic of national politics and policy-making' thus starting a trend that focused primarily on the forces of integration through the formation of the European Union.[18] This focus also seems to dominate Tanja Börzel's 1999 argument that Europeanization entails "a process by which domestic policy areas become increasingly subject to European policy-making."[19] And this was continued by Risse, Cowles and Caporaso in 2001, when they argue that

the emergence and development at the European level of distinct structures of governance, that is, of political, legal and social institutions associated with political problem solving that formalizes interactions among the actors, and of policy networks specializing in the creation of authoritative European rules.[20]

In sum, the EU seems to be the force of Europeanization in most scholars' view. Thus, Adrienne Héritier argues *the process of influence deriving from European decisions and impacting member states' policies and political and administrative structures. It comprises the following elements: the European decisions, the processes triggered by these decisions as well as the impacts of these processes on national policies, decision processes and institutional structures.*[21]

Claudio Radaelli begins to provide a more expansive view of Europeanization by including aspects of external relations. Thus, Radaelli holds that Europeanization refers to

processes of (a) construction (b) diffusion and (c) institutionalization of formal and informal rules, procedures, policy paradigms, styles, 'ways of doing things' and shared beliefs and norms which are first defined and consolidated in the making of EU decisions and then incorporated in the logic of domestic discourse, identities, political structures and public policies.[22]

An inherent assumption in these definitions is that in question are only EU member states. However, the EU's special role in Europeanization processes has also been seen as a force articulating global politics. In his theory about the EU's normative power, Ian Manners defines this as the way "it changes the norms, standards and prescriptions of world politics away from bounded expectations of state-centricity."[23] These are the norms generally acknowledged within the United Nations system as universally applicable. In other words, Europeanization has a power that goes beyond the borders of the EU.

The forces of the EU's Europeanization processes have had an important impact on the existence of minorities. It is now common knowledge that the EU's enlargement policies required new member states to adopt minority protection legislation. As noted in Chapter 3, the European Council, the EU's highest political decision forum, adopted the so-called Copenhagen Criteria in 1993. These Criteria were guidelines for the next and biggest enlargement wave which included ten Eastern European countries in 2004. These criteria included specific requirements on minority protection of minorities with citizenship in the accession countries by which governments would have to comply in order to become eligible for membership. Although not all countries that became members in 2004 actually complied entirely with the requirements, it is an example of the forces behind Europeanization that benefited minorities.

Globalization

Globalization, on the other hand, has had a much more mixed impact on the lives of members of minorities. While globalization as a concept shares some of the forces assigned to Europeanization, including the Orientalist force of the transfer of ideas and ideals from the developed to the developing world, it is often seen in a much more expedient light because Europeanization has by and large been linked to development through democratization and with positive results to speak for it. Globalization is usually linked to the necessity of financial and economic transnational exchange, and for this reason it makes more sense to speak of global politics rather than globalization. Moreover, there is much less empirical data showing that a process of globalization is in fact taking place. David Held et al. argue that globalization can usefully be conceived as a process (or set of processes) which embodies a transformation in the spatial organization of social relations and transactions, generating transcontinental or interregional flows and networks of activity, interaction and power.[24] They characterize globalization by four types of change.

The first type of change relating to the characteristics of globalization involves a stretching of social, political and economic activities across political frontiers, regions and continents. Secondly, such processes of change suggest the intensification, or the growing magnitude, of the inter-connectedness and flows of trade, investment, finance, migration, culture, etc. Thirdly, the growing extensity and intensity of global interconnectedness can be linked to a speeding up of global interactions and processes, as the evolution of worldwide systems of transport and communication increases the velocity of the diffusion of ideas, goods, information, capital, and people. Fourthly, the growing extensity, intensity and velocity of global interactions can be associated with their deepening impact such that the effects of distant events can be highly significant elsewhere and even the most local developments may come to have enormous global consequences. In this sense, the boundaries between domestic matters and global affairs can become increasingly blurred. Held et al. therefore view globalization as the widening, intensifying, speeding up, and growing potential for impact of world-wide inter-connectedness. By conceiving of globalization in this way, it becomes possible to map empirically patterns of world-wide links and relations across all key domains of human activity, from the military to the cultural realm.

Culture and globalization are the spheres where minority issues have become the focus of fierce debates and debacles. Intensified cultural exchanges as a result of open borders and hyper-mobility have increased the diversity of most societies. Notwithstanding that cultural diversity has a potential of strengthening our societies, it has nevertheless been cast in a rather negative light in global politics, as discussed below. One argument is that it has had a devastating social impact on the most vulnerable groups in the underdeveloped world. This factor has been related to the so-called North-South divide.

North-South Politics

The North-South divide refers to the gap in development between countries of the North, such as Western Europe and the United States of America as well as Canada and Japan, whereas the South represents countries in Africa, Latin America and Asia. The debate on the development gap was first started by a commission of statesmen lead by the German Chancellor Willy Brandt. In a 1980 report, the commission highlighted the failure of the world economic system to provide social and economic equality for humanity.[25] Arguing that the economic trends needed to be reversed, and that solutions and strategies needed to be urgently implemented, the Commission warned that growing income disparity of the Northern and Southern states, would lead to financial and economic instability as well as the growing problem of poverty. They further argued that there is a mutual interest for developed and developing countries to deal with the disparity in order for humanity to survive the "immense risks threatening mankind." They believed that co-operation was the tool to create change and facilitate worldwide growth and development. To enforce one national model of development onto another was deemed unnecessary. The report made recommendations in a number of areas of concern, including poverty, health, housing, equality, migration, the environment, disarmament, trade and energy. Above all, the report was an appeal to all world leaders and people from every strata of life to participate in the shaping of a common future for the world.

In the three decades after 1980, much has been done to overcome the gap. International organizations, such as the World Bank and the International Monetary Fund as well as key UN agencies, such as the United Nations Development Program, have worked with both sides of the development gap to improve the situation. But results have been mixed. The inability to overcome many problems has created a flow of migrants from the South to the North. Not only economic inequality but also violent conflicts in both Africa and Asia have pushed destitute groups towards the European Continent. The insecurity and unwillingness of European countries to welcome the destitute has created a new environment of antagonism in the public sphere. Xenophobia, Islamophobia, and a general hostility towards foreigners have become the order of the day in many European societies, as discussed below. And unlike the minority rights regime adopted by European governments for members of minorities holding citizenship, there does not exist a comprehensive minority protection scheme for so-called third country nationals. At best, governments have been willing to adopt certain anti-discrimination measures but this is a negative measure that does not require governments to be pro-active in order to overcome discrimination. We discuss Europe's approach to anti-discrimination more detailed in Chapter 10. The confrontation between different cultures is blamed for many of the ills of late modernity. In the next Section, we discuss some of the ontological processes of minority existence in diverse societies.

Ontological Diversity

Ontology is a philosophical concept that refers to the nature of being, of existence, of reality. It is usually analysed through categorization and conceptual understanding. In this Section, we discuss aspects of diversity that have emerged in late modernity as problematic realities in societal relations. Basically, understanding cultural exchanges in diverse societies is a question of understanding how individuals and groups handle alterity, or otherness. The social processes of forming individual and group/minority identities influence the way in which we meet with otherness in the public sphere.

Identity and difference

When politics become xenophobic and hostile in culturally diverse societies it is likely that there is a negative self-identification of identities in play. Negative self-identification can manifest itself as antagonism. Antagonism usually emanates from the impossibility to deal with alterity. William Connolly explains alterity as the otherness which is related to the process of linking identity to difference.[26] Difference is intrinsically linked to personal identity, in that identity is established in relation to a series of differences. Without difference, personal identity cannot exist. Simultaneously, within the process of personal self-identification, identity is fixed into a permanent form often thought to be the only true identity. In order to protect and maintain personal identity, differences may become converted into otherness. This conversion happens through a process of negation. Identity is thus a slippery, insecure experience, dependent on its ability to define difference it will counter, resist, overturn or subvert definitions of difference in order to eventually negate the difference. Identity stands in complex, political relation to the differences it seeks to fix. It is an endless play of definition, counter-definition, and countering of counter-definitions. Contingency of identity is, therefore, a stable part of identity itself.

However, identity formation contingent on the self's definition of the 'Other' makes for a troubled relationship with ethics. To act ethically may mean to call some comforts of identity into question.[27] To be ethical is thus to put one's identity at risk. Hence, to be ethical one has to interrogate one's essential self and seek to go beyond toleration and show respect. In doing so one enters the space of the nexus between identity and difference. The implication is that a reassessment of one's true identity may be required. To avoid this seemingly unpleasant process, many believe that morality is defined by the identity they already confess. To ensure ethical behaviour in social integration processes, identity has therefore to be de-essentialized through the incorporation of contingency rather than the negation of difference.

Moreover, ethical behaviour also has to be fostered at the collective level. This is particularly complex in divided societies. Connolly explains that personal identity and collective identity are connected through the channel of freedom.[28] People must be able to believe that state institutions carry with them sufficient efficacy to promote the collective ends we prize. Thus one's self-identification as a free individual is bound with a common belief in the capacity of the state to promote publicly defined purposes. Similarly, if one knows that one's choices and judgements matter in the public realm, this sense of awareness also informs the orientation one takes to a variety of other social roles. Thus, when circumstances are favourable, the personal-collective identity relationship is one of loyalty. When they are unfavourable, they degenerate into either disaffection with the state or a nationalism in which the tribulations of history are attributed to an evil otherness which must therefore be neutralized.

Serious threats to freedom can grow out of these ideological links between personal and collective identity.[29] First, the logics of collective identity may organize the idealisms and egoisms of its legitimate members into a collective egoism. And collective egoism becomes more intense whenever it is faced with internal or external affronts to its self-assurance. Second, in believing that one's identity or the collective identity of one's group is the best and only true identity for the group, the function of converting difference into otherness sets in. Collective dogmatization thus occurs when the group is confronted by disruptive contingencies. This is often what happens when collective dogmatization constructs minorities as objects of resentment to protect its own collective identity. Such resentment often turns into a generalized, existential resentment formed by people or groups unwilling to explore necessary injustices in their own political ideals.[30] These injustices are usually undeserved; often they cannot be eliminated. But what is alarming is that if these injustices are not recognized by the individual or the group unknowingly afflicting them on others, they conceal the fact that they foster a feeling of existential resentment in the person unwilling to take the steps to self-scrutinize. In other words, from the base of a political ideal, which is not fully analyzed and scrutinized, can emanate, without wilful intent, a "politics of resentment" that legitimizes injustices.[31] They are, therefore, rewarded by those of the in-group who harbour the same resentment.

As threats are perceived as real, they become the energy for the dogmatization of identity. This can have severe ramifications within divided societies. In the effort to realise a vision of a unified citizenry, nation and sovereignty based on a majority identity, there is a likelihood that the educational elites of marginalised groups emerge as radicalized minority elites.[32] However, as Andreas Wimmer explains, an integration process where the contingencies of personal identity are taken into consideration, ethnic closure can be avoided, and collective identity can be redefined. In the process of redefinition, possibilities of respect may come to play thus resulting in a more democratic integration process. Such a system depends in turn on the successful politics that helps us to see our identities as ambiguous and contestable and contested. If successful, Connolly argues that social integration may appear as an "exciting engagement with difference, the challenge of the Other, the disruption of certainties, the recognition of ambiguities within one's self as well as one's differences with others."[33] Indeed, it has been argued that a robust social integration strategy neither evades nor confirms difference.[34] An ethics that confirms difference while avoiding negation of the Other is more likely to foster social integration within deeply divided societies.

Culture and 'groupism'

The processes of collective dogmatization and resentment are often fed by people's misinformed understanding of the notion of culture. Culture is immensely complex to define, as discussed in Chapter 5. Here we focus on constructivist approaches to culture. As a social phenomenon, which means that it is fundamentally constructed by human beings and thus constantly changing, Roger Ballard defines it very succinctly, when he argues that "cultural systems are not God-given: rather they are always and everywhere the creation of their users. As a result they are never fixed and static, but are constantly being rejigged, reinterpreted and indeed reinvented by their users."[35] In this respect, cultural processes are a mark of human creativity where new ideas, new perceptions and new inventions—as well as new fashions—are created. Because culture is transmitted through learning, we as individuals are 'coded' to carry certain cultural values just as we are coded to speak certain languages. This means that just as we can learn several languages, we can also learn the practices of several cultures.

The constructivist view has convincingly been argued by Anne Phillips who holds that culture is often represented as a falsely homogenising reification which exaggerates the internal unity of cultures, solidifies differences that are more fluid, and makes people from other cultures seem more exotic and distinct than they really are.[36] On this view, culture is not a liberator but a straitjacket forcing members of such cultural groups into a regime of authenticity, denying them the chance to cross cultural borders, borrow cultural influences and to define and redefine themselves.[37] In other words, as opposed to the homogenizing view of culture, the fluidity of culture renders boundaries between cultures highly permeable, and it is almost impossible to identify individuals by discrete cultural tags. This is the type of analysis which brings Rogers Brubaker to argue that this fluidity has ramifications for how we assess groups because there is a tendency to view ethnic groups as bounded and fundamental units of analysis while seeing them in a substantialist light.[38] The tendency to see ethnicity as "groupism" rather than a "relational, processual and dynamic phenomenon" prevents people from seeing group identity in terms of categories, schemas, encounters, identifications, languages, stories, institutions, organizations, networks, and events.[39] This impedes our understanding of ethnic affairs and ethnic studies.

One aspect of group life, which academics have discussed, is the phenomena of so-called illiberal practices founded on, or based on, cultural traditions of some minority groups. Such practices may be considered illiberal because they suppress the autonomy and free choice of the individual, and they often involve violating the freedoms of women and young girls. In late modernity these questionable practices have come to the fore through increased knowledge and exchange about other cultures. In Europe, the most controversial cultural customs are the idea of planned marriages, which are usually planned by senior male members of the family, honour killings, the application of Sharia law as well as the prohibition against sending young girls to kindergartens or schools and forcing them to wear a headscarf. Lately, the circumcision of small boys has also become controversial. In Africa, as well as in parts of the Western world, the tradition of circumcising young girls has drawn the greatest alarm. Female genital circumcision is banned in most Western countries; nevertheless, there are doctors in Europe and North America who perform the operation.[40] Lesser known traditions include wife beating as part of a husband's duty.[41] Society now regulates these issues by the human rights protection schemes and especially gender rights. Unfortunately, there is not a clear understanding among the general public of the impact of such cultural traditions on the victims and how to avoid such harm.

Academics discuss these issues in terms of a tension between cultural relativism and universalism. Basically, cultural relativism refers to the idea that culture holds the sole source of the validity of a moral right or rule, whereas cultural universalism would hold that culture is irrelevant to those rights or rules because they are universal.[42] The view of cultural relativism is considered somewhat nuanced in that there might be stronger and weaker versions of cultural relativism. The strongest notion of cultural relativism would consider the individual human being lower in importance than the group, and thus, in the question of the survival of the culture of the group, the individual may have to sacrifice. In the weak version of cultural relativism, the individual does hold some importance as a human being but the group still holds priority. Cultural universalism, on the other hand, is represented in the current international minority rights regime which seeks to protect the cultural rights of the individual, and where these are of a collective nature, such as language rights and freedom of association, they are nevertheless seen as individual rights. See also the discussion in Chapter 4.

Debates

With dogmatization and resentment at play within diverse societies, as well as difficulties in defining and understanding culture and group identity formation, it is not surprising that the public debates on minority issues can become confused. In the era of late modernity, we have seen both prominent academics and prominent leaders taking the lead in confusing the issues and thus contributing to disturbing the peace. This Section will assess the two most prominent arguments given in efforts to explain the social phenomena facing the world with regard to diversity. The first discussion focuses on the global sphere, while the second addresses issues at the domestic level.

'Clash of civilizations'

With the collapse of the bipolar world in the early 1990s, mobility across previously closed borders became possible. New markets and opportunities opened both for organizations and individuals. One could argue that the world became smaller because it became more connected. This inter-connectivity became further deepened through electronic media and the possibility to know what happens, when it happens. Exacerbated by the results of ineffective North-South politics, the migration from continent to continent became the road to survival and freedom for many individuals. In this scenario, cultures that had previously been confined to certain geographic areas now became embedded in new communities through migration, and cultures met cultures in the streets as well as in the boardrooms. This did not mean, however, that the whole world copied American or Argentinian society. Rather, in many countries, especially in Europe, this state of global connectivity created parallel societies where the cultural meeting in the public space took on an agnostic approach, often laced with xenophobic and Islamophobic undertones. In some cases the result is that cultures become more entrenched separately as the awareness of differences becomes negated; in other cases, it means new opportunities arise and cultural characteristics mingle and mix with each other rendering societies richer through diversity. One of the most authoritative arguments against a positive view of diversity was made by a prominent American scholar.

In 1993, Samuel Huntington published an article titled, "The Clash of Civilizations?" in which he took up the discussion of global diversity in light of the changing security environment and specifically the national interests of the United States.[43] To Huntington, there was no doubt, the meeting of civilizations, which he defined as cultures, after the opening up after the Cold War, was the next space for conflict in the late modern world. In fact, he would go as far as argue that the next world war would be between civilizations as opposed to national unit like states.[44] Huntington built his argument around a number of factors:

1. Over centuries differences among civilizations have generated the most prolonged and violent conflicts,
2. Interactions among different civilizations increase consciousness about differences thus invigorating animosities,
3. Modernization separates people from their local identity community and thus allows for the breeding of fundamentalism, especially among young educated people,
4. De-Westernization of elites in non-Western societies contributes to anti-Western sentiments,
5. Unlike ideological views, cultural characteristics cannot mutate and become hybrid, especially not where two religions meet each other,
6. Economic (bloc) regionalism will exacerbate the differences between civilizations.

In short, the world would be defined as an "us-them" paradigm.[45] It would be the West against the Rest. Ideology would give way to cultural views and customs. The 'end of ideology' would see a world of clashes both at the micro and macro levels. At the global level, the world would be divided along certain fault lines separating religions from one another. This would mean that states would fight for economic hegemony and power in international governance structures, while at the local level societies on the fault lines would experience conflicts about territory and populations. And in this scenario, bilateral conflicts would ensue due to kin-state politics and power grabs.

Some of the arguments by Huntington have become relevant due to developments after 11 September 2001, while one could argue that the onset of an economic crisis that defies any definition renders other of his arguments moot. However, the general approach is based on an archaic conception of the state and global politics and hardly relevant for minority issues in late modernity. Huntington overlooks entirely the mingling of cultures that started long before he wrote his article. The United States opened up for Asian immigration in 1975 after the fall of Saigon,[46] and many countries in Europe had opened their doors to immigration from the former colonies. This state of cultural diversity at the domestic level did not play an important role in Huntington's analysis. Moreover, the economic hegemony of the Western bloc was already becoming eroded by the emergence of the so-called 'tiger' economies in the East. Nevertheless, the phrase 'clash of civilizations' survives numerous critiques of Huntington's analysis and approach, many countering his lack of rigour and critical thinking in terms of the academic arguments.[47] It is used again and again in the rhetoric against ethnic minority groups exhibiting different cultural customs and traditions than mainstream society. It pitches the relativists against the universalists.

Multiculturalism is 'dead'

Another debate that is considered by many to be misleading and to have derailed the understanding of minority issues in late modernity is the debate on multiculturalism. Speaking to the youth wing of her party, the Christian Democratic Union, on 16 October 2010, the German Chancellor Angela Merkel declared that multiculturalism in Germany had "utterly failed."[48] This remark came at a time in Germany where the debate about multiculturalism had been stirred by the publication by a public figure and business man, Thilo Sarrazin, in which he argued that Muslims lower the intelligence of German society. Less than six months later, the newly elected Prime Minister of the United Kingdom (UK), David Cameron, joined the choir in a speech given to a security conference in Munich in which he argued that the "doctrine of state multiculturalism had encouraged different cultures to live separate lives."[49] This, according to Cameron, was a failure by mainstream society to encourage foreigners to belong. In short, two leading politicians in two European countries representing each a population of 60–80 million of which large portions are not indigenous throwing up their arms in despair. Notwithstanding that politicians play politics, the fact that they turn negative to a concept that actually defines a reality of European society, which has been factual for many centuries, is cause for concern.

The idea that multiculturalism had failed was not, however, invented by the leaders of Germany and the UK. In 2008, the Council of Europe's "White Paper on Intercultural Dialogue" from the Committee of Ministers began the trend.[50] And in 2009 the UNESCO "World Report on Cultural Diversity" followed suit.[51] The White Paper argued that multiculturalism had failed and that inter-culturalism should be the preferred model for Europe, whereas the UNESCO Report called for a post-multiculturalist alternative. These texts see inter-culturalism as the next generation of democratic frameworks for diversity. They hold that inter-culturalism and inter-cultural dialogue will overcome the limits of multiculturalism, and inter-culturalism will promote integration over 'balkanization', fractionalized societies and xenophobia. It is important to remember that these two organizations have traditionally been the standard bearers of multiculturalism. Thus, in discussing multiculturalism, it is, therefore, necessary to deconstruct the concept a bit.

There are several dimensions to multiculturalism that are usually and mistakenly jumbled into one, thus creating confusion. Multiculturalism has at least four dimensions.[52] First, 'multiculturalism-as-a-fact' is the sociological dimension which establishes that our societies are, for a fact, composed of culturally diverse groups—since the exodus from Palestine this has been the reality. Second, 'multiculturalism-as-ideology' refers to the human rights dimension of dignity which holds that multiculturalism promotes the freedom of the individual and the equality for all, while also offering the protection of cultural groups—since the League of Nations and the Minority Treaties this has been a European reality and since the adoption of the International Covenant on Civil and Political Rights in 1966 this has been a global reality. Third, 'multiculturalism-as-policy' is the democratic dimension ensuring that diversity management becomes institutionalized in the governing of modern societies—since 2000 this has been the approach in the EU. And fourth, 'multiculturalism-as-ethics' is the communication dimension which now is being recast as inter-culturalism and dialogue, but which includes more than a dialogue because it refers to the need to go beyond tolerance in order to show respect—since the emergence of religious tolerance in the philosophy of John Locke and others this has been the belief in Europe.

Academics have also joined the debate and some have been critical of multiculturalism in favour of inter-culturalism which they have defended through four arguments. First, they see inter-culturalism as co-existence+ ('co-existence-plus'), meaning enhanced co-existence, because it implies better communication.[53] Second, they believe that it synthesizes many groups into a common patchwork,[54] and third they argue that it promotes cohesion through mutual integration.[55] Finally, they see inter-culturalism as a critical approach to relativism because it allows for the separating religion and ethnicity.[56] However, lately, a correction to the academic debate has argued that inter-culturalism is no different than multiculturalism.[57] All the characteristics mentioned above—co-existence+, synthesis, cohesion, and critical approaches to relativism—are also part of multiculturalism. For instance, they argue that inter-cultural dialogue is not new to multiculturalism. People in multicultural societies have co-existed for years.[58] Communication is clearly a part of multiculturalism.

Therefore, Will Kymlicka has argued that the inter-culturalism discourse started by the Council of Europe and UNESCO is in fact nothing but rhetorical, political hype to show that governments want to take the attention away from the difficulties arising from multiculturalism by giving it a new name.[59] On this view, multiculturalism has been false credited on the wrong premises because social science research shows that the same governments that adopted the White Paper and the World Report have done nothing further to try to implement inter-culturalism instead of multiculturalism. Indeed, social science research shows that multicultural policies are in fact having an effect. Recent research on street planning in Amsterdam has shown that immigrant communities are in fact very active in communal meetings thus actively involved through inter-cultural dialogue.[60] And it is common knowledge that parliaments, media, public spaces and work places are becoming increasingly multicultural.

The primary losers in this debate are thus the most vulnerable members of minorities who are singled out as scapegoats in the public space while often left without a voice to explain their concerns. The key questions one might ask are why does xenophobia arise in diverse societies and how one might avoid situations in which xenophobia becomes a danger to members of minorities. The latter we discuss in this book in Part III. Here it suffices to note that the concept comes from the Greek words ξένος (xenos), meaning "stranger", "foreigner", and φόβος (phobos), meaning "fear".[61] According to Andreas Wimmer, xenophobic and racist views are not instrumental to a fight for scarce jobs or housing.[62] Neither is it appropriate to interpret such views as a result of a culture clash that is caused by migratory movements across countries and continents. They are not mere radicalizations of the discourse of exclusion and devaluation which political and administrative elites generate and institutionalize, for example, in immigration policies. Xenophobia and racism should be seen as appeals to the pact of solidarity into which state and society have entered in modern national states and which in times of intensified social conflicts seems fragile in the eyes of downwardly mobile groups. The xenophobic discourse serves not only to reassure identity when nationalistic self-images run into crisis but is also an element of a political struggle about who has the right to be cared for by the state and society: a fight for the collective goods of the modern state. In the next Section, we discuss how inclusiveness in the public space is often highjacked by the inflexibility of people as well as the inflexibility of political and legal systems.

Public Space Issues

Scholars have analysed the public sphere for centuries and sociologists took a new look at it in the 1960s when modern society began to change due to mass production, mass communication and mass movement. In his seminal work, *The Structural Transformation of the Public Sphere*, Jürgen Habermas argued that the public sphere of democracies is rather a field of competition among conflicting interests, in which organizations representing diverse constituencies negotiate and compromise among themselves and with government officials, while excluding the public from their proceedings. While public opinion is taken into account, it is not in the form of unrestricted public discussion. Its character and function are indicated rather by the terms in which it is addressed, public opinion research, publicity, public relations work, and so forth. The press and broadcast media serve less as organs of public information and debate than as technologies for managing consensus and promoting consumer culture. Thus, a re-feudalization of society happened when the boundaries between state and society blurred. State and society became involved in one another's spheres; the private sphere collapsed into itself. The key feature of the public sphere, the rational-critical debate was replaced by leisure.[63] Arguably, if Habermas was writing about the public sphere today, he might have a different view given the rise of social media and the opportunities for individuals to have a voice. But the power play in the public sphere is no less extensive and often manipulating, and at times with the result that the most vulnerable and weak are excluded from having a voice.

The importance of affording minorities the right to have a voice has been argued by James Tully in his theory of inter-cultural "multilogue".[64] Inter-cultural multilogue refers to the on-going negotiations that diverse groups in divided societies should have as part of the self-organization of their societies. It is a view of political and social ordering that views constitutionalism not as a fixed set of uniform rules but as a flexible entity that is constantly renegotiated to adjust to the on-going changes of modern society. Thus, Tully sees the constituting document of a society as a living document. An important aspect of this multilogue is that all groups in society are able to be heard in their own language in the broad sense of speech both semantically and instrumentally. Tully builds his theory upon three cornerstone concepts, or conventions, of inter-cultural multilogue, 'mutual recognition', 'consent' and 'continuity'. By mutual recognition Tully is referring to the principle of equality of self-governing groups as espoused by the treaty system that regulated the relations between the Aboriginal peoples of North America and the British Crown.[65] The second convention of trust, that of consent, is derived from the principle of *q.o.t.* in Roman law and later articulated by John Locke, or *quot omnes tangit ab omnibut comprobetur*, "what touches all should be agreed to by all."[66] The third convention of trust, continuity, refers to the principle of respect, meaning that the ways and customs of diverse groups and peoples are evidence of their free agreement and therefore the continuity of the group's culture in terms of norms, values and traditions should be respected.[67] According to Tully, these three conventions should be seen as preconditions for inter-cultural multi-logue. They constitute a duty to listen to the other side.

To be respected enough to have a voice in the public space thus includes the full spectrum of communication. In the late modern era of hyper-mobility and increased pluralism and diversity, this poses a number of challenges to the rules that organize the public space. A pluralistic approach to rule-making must take into account quite a number of aspects of diversity, including diverse opinions, customs, approaches and needs, to mention a few. In late modernity, the arguably most controversial public space issue has been the freedom to exhibit one's religion, both in terms of personal appearance and appearance as a group.

Religion and symbols

Headscarves and minarets are probably the two most debated religious symbols in Europe. Thus, one could argue that Islam is the most controversial religion, but that would be simplifying the approach; other traditional religions also promote the use of head coverings. Nevertheless, in Europe the debate has centred on persons of the Muslim faith. Religious garment and minarets both relate to minority existence in an increasing diverse Europe. With North-South politics induced migration, the fabric of populations in Europe has changed, and cultures and religions are becoming more visible in the human landscape. For many groups, religion has more than a spiritual function and thus it holds a vital place in people's daily lives. This has created a new 'meeting' in the public space of secularized Western societies, which fought hard for centuries for the right to separate religion from the state and thus from the interference of state religion in private life. The fact that this fight against a hegemonic religion did not fully succeed, and Western societies therefore still celebrate Christian holidays and customs publicly and with state sanction, remains a problem in an increasingly multicultural world. This has led to a degree of hypocrisy in how states adjudicate diversity.

Since 1989, when three young women attending public secondary school in Creil, France, were suspended for wearing Muslim headscarves during classes, the debate over religious garments in public spaces has been on-going. In connection to the 1989 case, the French supreme court, the *Conseil d'État*, ultimately ruled that religious symbols could be worn in public schools as long as they did not constitute an act of intimidation, provocation, proselytizing or propaganda, threaten health, security, the freedom of others or disturb order. In the 1990s and early 2000s, more than 100 female students were suspended or expelled from school for wearing headscarves. Many of these cases were annulled by the French courts. In 2004, the French Assembly adopted a new law on religious garment of ostentatious character used by a number of religions.[68] This law was confirmed by the *Conseil d'État* in 2007[69] and upheld by the European Court of Human Rights in 2008. The latter ruled that the right to freedom of religion has not been compromised.[70] Notwithstanding the strength of secularism in the French value system and the legal technicalities involved therein, the public debates that surrounded the issue were not very helpful in shedding light on the matter.

Some academics have, however, attempted to make sense of the issue. Anna Galeotti has addressed the issue in terms of toleration in her book *Toleration as Recognition* in which she argues that the existing concept of toleration is inadequate to deal with contemporary controversies like the headscarf affair. The problem with the existing concept is that it views even the most intractable disagreements as a product of individual differences rather than as group differences. Group differences, she contends, have an "ascriptive" quality: that is, they are not simple matters of personal preference. Not only is the headscarf endowed with religious significance, it is a signifier of ones loyalty to a group, and not just any group, but a group that has been oppressed and marginalized in the larger society. Thus, when the right to wear the headscarf is taken away, it presents a grave threat to the integrity and dignity of the Muslim community in France.[71] Heightened tolerance by the majority is therefore needed in order to make the Muslim minority feel welcome in France. Whether one agrees or not with Galeotti's assessment of tolerance in France, the fact of the matter is that national ideologies enshrined in constitutions will guide the application of values in mainstream society.

A good example of how legal processes can blur the picture on religion in the public space is the recent issue of minarets in Switzerland. On 29 November, 2009, Switzerland approved the amendment of Article 72 of its Constitution in a referendum, including a specific section prohibiting the construction of minarets.[72] Abroad, the decision stirred outbursts of indignation. In Iran, for example, the Swiss ambassador was summoned to account for the decision of his people. In Europe, the dominant feeling was one of astonishment. This had happened in a country with an impressive political history of peaceful co-existence between people of different cultures; a state based upon a decentralised system of government and a constitution embodying fundamental rights, including both equality before the law and freedom of religion and conscience as well as a fair record of international human rights compliance. These arguments were also heard in the debate in both houses of the Federal Assembly in Bern, where the referendum had to be validated before it could be put to the popular vote. What exactly happened?

In the Swiss system of public-political decision-making, assurances against the popular whim are not sought in qualified majorities but in the authority of the Federal Assembly to validate or invalidate an initiative that had secured the requisite number of more than 100,000 signatures. When a referendum meets the formal requirements, the Federal Assembly discusses two proposals from its governing council: one on validation, i.e. does the proposed referendum comply with a number of national and international norms, and one on endorsement, i.e. whether the Assembly members actually support the idea. If the initiative is validated but not endorsed, it will be put to the popular vote with a recommendation from the Assembly to reject it. This is what happened in the case of the minarets. Both the validation and the recommendation to reject the referendum were accepted by the people who voted in the referendum. However, a closer look at the majority vote reveals that the referendum did not have the full backing of the Swiss people. The referendum had a turnout of 53% and received a majority of 57.5%. Hence, the initiative passed with less than one third of the electorate; more precisely, the vote represented just below 20% of the Swiss population. This is because, of the approximate 8 million inhabitants in Switzerland, 5 million are citizens with voting rights.[73] Thus, of the 5 million people 53%, or around 2.7 million turned out on the day of voting. Out of 2.7 million voters, 1.5 million vote to ban minarets. Thus, less than 20% made the decision for the nation. The point is, therefore, that the majority is not always the majority, at least in Switzerland, and public debates, including international organizations,[74] are not always informed.

Hate speech

With access to the public debate becoming less restricted through modern methods of communication, the power of right wing movements in the public space has been enhanced. This means that unrestricted messages can enter the public space rapidly and abundantly. Thus, negative and hurtful messages, such as hate speech may become part of everyday life for some minority groups. While international law regulations impose some rules, most governments are reluctant to regulate against free speech; the balance between safeguarding the right to free speech and the desire to promote respect for different cultures and traditions becomes very difficult. Moreover, even if the right to free speech is protected, it may not always be conducive to understanding that it be exercised at any cost. As noted by Robert Frost, "what is legally permitted is not [always] ethically advisable."[75] The tension between free speech and cultural respect came to the fore in 2005 when a Danish newspaper published twelve satirical drawings, called cartoons, of the Prophet Mohammad. The background to the publication of the drawings is complex, and the ramifications for a large number of individuals were devastating resulting in violence and death.[76] The handling of the case by the Danish government was far from ideal, and the entire process showed that diversity in faith, culture and moral views needs to be handled with care.

Some of the most astute academic commentaries highlight not the regulatory aspect of preventing hate speech but the ethical one. Thus, Tariq Ramadan argues that what is needed is a stronger sense of mutual trust. We need to nurture civic responsibility. And rather than imposing censorship, we need more respect. Freedom of expression is not absolute, Ramadan argues, and therefore the capacity to be free and rational, which most people would want, must at the same time encourage a capacity to be reasonable.[77] Sune Lægaard follows the same line of reasoning when suggesting that the issue comes down to a balancing act between the freedom of expression and toleration, i.e. the question as to whether group defamation should restrict the freedom of expression. Drawing on statements made by the editor of the Danish newspaper, Lægaard reiterates the need for both self-censorship and self-restraint in the right proportions and at the right time.[78] In other words, there is little chance that differences on values and morality will disappear within late modern societies. Debates and controversies will remain part of the public space. What is paramount is that we learn to "manage" our diversity and conflicts. This will be the focus of the remainder of this book.

Key Points

- Late modernity is characterized by a high rate of social change induced by numerous forces resulting in demands on people's adaptability for survival. Reflexive rationality and fluid identities become the foundation for new modes of coping, and these requirements are equally as important for minorities as majorities;
- Among the forces influencing social change, Europeanization, globalization and North-South politics are the most difficult to explain and quantify. They influence how governments must react to changes in society, and this means that minorities as well as majorities are expected to adapt. However, minorities are at risk of bearing the brunt of changes;
- As societies become more diverse due to hyper-mobility induced by late modern changes, cultures meet more often in the public space resulting in new processes of self-identification and inter-relation. If inter-relational identities negate differences and one another, there is a risk that dogmatization and resentment become dominant in the meeting of diverse cultures, and minorities are often the scapegoats;
- The constructivist notion of culture highlights the complexity of culture as a social phenomenon. Essentialized views of cultural groups may provide distorted pictures of human existence and especially of cultural and ethnic minorities; for this reason, many scholars encourage a balanced explanation of cultural practices taking into consideration both relativist and universalist views of culture;
- The problem of balancing divergent views of culture has become clear in the public debates on culture both at the international and domestic level. Fears that cultures may clash in a world of hyper-mobility and that governments have failed to properly govern the increased cultural exchanges have been lodged by academics and politicians alike. In these debates cultural and ethnic minorities seldom get a positive reading;
- The inability to govern and understand diversity in the public space has had ramifications for minorities, especially religious minorities wishing to exhibit their religion publicly. Europe has witnessed a number of controversial cases about religion in the public space, and the public debate has grown increasingly harsh in this respect. The balance between freedom and respect is difficult to legislate, and often politics and law are inflexible in the fostering of toleration and respect.

Further reading

BARRY, BRIAN. *Culture and Equality: An Egalitarian Critique of Multiculturalism*. Polity Press, 2000.
BAUMAN, ZYGMUNT. *Identity*. Penguin Books, 1991.
BENHABIB, SEYLA. *Democracy and Difference*. Princeton University Press, 1996.
BENHABIB, SEYLA. *The Claims of Culture*. Princeton University Press, 2002.
CARENS, JOSEPH H. *Culture, Citizenship and Community*. Oxford University Press, 2000.
MENDUS, SUSAN, ed. *The Politics of Toleration*. Edinburgh University Press, 1999.
OKIN, SUSAN MOLLER. *Is Multiculturalism bad for Women?* Princeton University Press, 1999.
PAREKH, BHIKHU. *Rethinking Multiculturalism: Cultural Diversity and Political Theory*. Macmillan Press, 2000.
SAID, EDWARD W. *Orientalism: Western Conceptions of the Orient*. Penguin Books, 1978.
TARAS, RAYMOND. *Xenophobia and Islamophobia in Europe*. Edinburgh University Press, 2012.
TAYLOR, CHARLES. *Multiculturalism: Examining the Politics of Recognition*, expanded version. Princeton University Press, 1994.
YOUNG, IRIS MARION. *Justice and the Politics of Difference*. Princeton University Press, 1990.

Notes

1. Jean-Marie Guehenno, *The End of the Nation-State*, trans. Victoria Elliott (Minneapolis: University of Minnesota Press, 1995).
2. Francis Fukuyama, *The End of History and the Last Man* (Free Press, 1992).
3. Samuel Huntington, "The Clash of Civilizations", *Foreign Affairs* (1993).
4. Ulrich Beck, *Risk Society. Towards a New Modernity* (London: Sage, 1992).
5. Jacob Torfing, *New Theories of Discourse. Laclau, Mouffe and Zizek* (Oxford: Blackwell Publishers, 1999).
6. Lawrence Stone, "The Revival of Narrative: Reflections on a New Old History", *Past and Present* 85 (1979), pp. 3–24.
7. Ibid, pp. 3–24 at p. 13.
8. Gerard Delanty, "Modernity", in *Blackwell Encyclopedia of Sociology*, accessed June 1, 2013, subscription only, http://www.sociologyencyclopedia.com/public/tocnode?id=g9781405124331_yr2012_chunk_g978140512433119_ss1-117.
9. Hans Blumenberg, *The Legitimacy of the Modern Age* (MIT Press, 1983).
10. John Scott and Gordon Marshall, *A Dictionary of Sociology* (Oxford: Oxford University Press), p. 484.
11. Ira J. Cohen, "Anthony Giddens" in *Key Sociological Thinkers*, 2nd ed, ed. Rob Stones (Basingstoke: Palgrave Macmillan, 2008).
12. Jürgen Habermas, *The Philosophical Discourse of Modernity*, tr. Frederick Lawrence (Polity Press, 1985).

13 Anthony Giddens, *The Self and Society in the Late Modern Age* (Stanford University Press, 1991).
14 Ibid.
15 *Risk Society*. op.cit. note 4.
16 See also, accessed July 26, 2013, http://www.nextreformation.com/wp-admin/resources/risk-society.pdf.
17 Zygmunt Bauman, *Liquid Modernity* (Polity, 2000).
18 Robert Ladrech, "Europeanization of Domestic Politics and Institutions: The Case of France", *Journal of Common Market Studies* 32 (1994), pp. 69–88;
19 Tanja A. Börzel, "Towards Convergence in Europe? Institutional Adaptation to Europeanization in Germany and Spain." *Journal of Common Market Studies* 39 (1999) pp. 573–96.
20 Thomas Risse, Maria Green Cowles, and James A. Caporaso, "Europeanization and Domestic Change: Introduction", in *Transforming Europe: Europeanization and Domestic Change*, eds. Maria Green Cowles, James A. Caporaso and Thomas Risse (Ithaca, NY: Cornell University Press, 2001), pp 1–20 at p. 3.
21 Adrienne Héritier et al., *Differential Europe. The European Union Impact on national Policymaking* (Lanham, MD: Rowman & Littlefield, 2001).
22 Claudio M. Radaelli, "The Europeanization of Public Policy", in *The Politics of Europeanization*, eds. Kevin Featherstone and Claudio M. Radaelli (Oxford: Oxford University Press, 2003), pp. 27–56 at p. 30.
23 Ian Manners, "The normative ethics of the European Union", *International Affairs* 84 (2008), pp. 45-46. See also, Ian Manners, "Normative Power Europe: a Contradiction in Terms?" *Journal of Common Market Studies* 40 (2002), pp. 235–258.
24 David Held, Anthony McGrew, David Goldblatt and Jonathan Perraton, *Global Transformations* (Polity, 1999).
25 The Brandt Report (MIT Press, 1980).
26 William E. Connolly, *Identity\Difference. Democratic Negotiations of Political Paradox*, expanded ed., (Minneapolis: University of Minnesota Press (2002[1991]).
27 Connolly, op. cit., note 26, p. xix.
28 Ibid, pp. 65–68.
29 Ibid, pp. 198–200.
30 Ibid, pp. 25–26.
31 Ibid, p. 26.
32 Andreas Wimmer, "Facing Ethnic Conflicts", *Facing Ethnic Conflicts. Toward a new Realism*, eds. Wimmer et al (Rowman & Littlefield Publishers, 2004).
33 William E. Connolly, *The Ethos of Pluralization* (Minneapolis: University of Minnesota Press, 1995).
34 Anne Phillips, "Dealing with Difference: A Politics of Ideas, or a Politics of Presence", *Democracy and Difference. Contesting the Boundaries of the Political*, ed. Seyla Benhabib (Princeton: Princeton University Press, 1996), pp. 139–52 at p. 143.
35 Roger Ballard, "Race, Ethnicity and Culture" in *New Directions in Sociology*, ed. Martin Holborn (Ormskirk: Causeway, 2002), p. 13.
36 Anne Phillips, *Multiculturalism without Culture* (Princeton University Press, 2007).
37 Ibid, p. 14.
38 Rogers Brubaker, *Ethnicity without Groups* (Harvard University Press, 2004).
39 Ibid, pp. 3–4.
40 "Media Center – Female genital mutilation Fact Sheet", *World Health Organization* (WHO), No. 241, February 2013, accessed August 9, http://www.who.int/mediacentre/factsheets/fs241/en/, accessed August 9, 2013 ; "Female Genital Mutilation in the United States" *Sanctuary for Families*, March 2013, p. ii, accessed August 9, 2013, http://www.sanctuaryforfamilies.org/storage/sanctuary/documents/report_onfgm_w_cover.pdf; "European campaign to end FGM. Facts and Figures about female genital mutilation", Amnesty

International, accessed August 9, 2013, http://www.endfgm.eu/en/ and Ben Mathews, "Female genital mutilation: Australian law, policy and practical challenges for doctors", *The Medical Journal of Australia* (MJA) 194 (2011), pp. 139–141.

41 Henry K. Lee, "Japanese diplomat admits to beating wife", *San Francisco Chronicle*, December 20, 2012, accessed August 9, 2013, http://www.sfgate.com/crime/article/Japanese-diplomat-admits-to-beating-wife-4135864.php.

42 Jack Donnelly, "Cultural Relativism and Universal Human Rights",*Human Rights Quarterly* 6 (1984), pp. 400–409 at p. 400.

43 Samuel P. Huntington, "The Class of Civilizations?" *Foreign Affairs* 72 (1993), pp. 22–49.

44 Ibid, p. 39.

45 See also our discussion in Chapter 5.

46 *Indochina Migration and Refugee Act* of 1975 adopted by the Ford Administration.

47 Edward W. Said, "The Clash of Ignorance: Labels like 'Islam' and 'the West' serve only to confuse us about a disorderly reality" in *The Nation*, October 4, 2001; M. Shahid Alam, "Peddling Civilizational Wars: A Critique of Samuel Huntington" in *CounterPunch Newsletter*, 28 February 2002, accessed July 26, 2013, http://www.univie.ac.at/linguistics/forschung/wittgenstein/critics/huntington-kritik.pdf; For a good synopsis of the reactions to Huntington's thesis, see Darian Swan, "A Criticism of Huntington's 'Clash of Civilizations'" accessed July 26, 2013, http://www.academia.edu/1416654/ A_Criticism_of_Huntingtons_Clash_of_Civilizations_.

48 Matthew Weaver, "Angela Merkel: multiculturalism has 'utterly failed'" The Guardian, 17 October 2010.

49 "State multiculturalism has failed, says David Cameron", *BBC News Channel*, 5 February 2011.

50 *White Paper on Intercultural Dialogue "Living Together as Equals in Dignity"* Council of Europe Ministers of Foreign Affairs, 118th Ministerial Session, 7 May 2008, accessed August 9, 2013, www.coe.int/dialogue.

51 "Investing in Cultural Diversity and Intercultural Dialogue", UNESCO World Report, 2009, accessed June 30, 2013, http://www.unesco.org/new/en/culture/resources/report/the-unesco-world-report-on-cultural-diversity/.

52 Tove H. Malloy, "Conceptualizing Democratic Diversity Management for Multicultural Societies: Theories of Society and Law" *European Yearbook of Minority Issues* 6 (2006).

53 Phill Wood et al., *Cultural Diversity in Britain: a toolkit for cross-cultural co-operation* (Rowntree, 2006).

54 Leonard M. Hammer "Foreword" in *Interculturalism exploring critical issues*, eds. Diane Powell and Fiona Sze (Oxford: Interdisciplinary Press, 2004).

55 Christian Joppke, "The retreat of multiculturalism in the liberal state: theory and policy", *British Jounal of Sociology* 55 (2004), pp. 237–257.

56 Randal Hansen, "The Danish cartoon controversy: a defence of liberal freedom", *International Migration* 44 (2006), pp. 7–16.

57 Nasar Meer and Tariq Modood, "How does Interculturalism Contrast with Multiculturalism?" *Journal of Intercultural Studies* 33 (2012), pp. 175–196.

58 For a view on the role of traditional and national minorities in multiculturalism, see Tove H. Malloy, "Beyond the Limits of Multiculturalism: The Role of Europe's Traditional Minorities", *ECMI Issue Brief* 28 (2013), Flensburg: European Centre for Minority Issues.

59 Will Kymlicka, "Comment on Meer and Modood" *Journal of Intercultural Studies* 33 (2012), pp. 211–216.

60 Jean Tillie and Boris Slijper, "Immigrant political integration and ethnic civic communities in Amsterdam" in *Identities, Affiliations, and Allegiances*, Chapter 9, eds. Seyla Benhabib et al (Cambridge University Press, 2007).

61 Oxford Standard English Dictionary (OED) (Oxford Press, 2004).

62 Andreas Wimmer, "Explaining xenophobia and racism: A critical review of current research approaches, " *Ethnic and Racial Studies* 20 (1997), pp. 17–41.

63 Thomas McArthy, "Introduction" to Jürgen Habermas, *The Structural Transformation of the Public Sphere* (MIT Press, 1991/1961). See also Nancy Fraser, "Rethinking the Public Sphere: A Contribution to the Critique of Actually Existing Democracy", *Social Text* 25/26 (1990), pp. 56–80.

64 James Tully, *Strange Multiplicity: Constitutionalism in an Age of Diversity* (Cambridge University Press, 1995).

65 Ibid, p. 117.

66 Ibid, p. 122.

67 Ibid, p. 125.

68 "French law on secularity and conspicuous religious symbols in schools bans wearing conspicuous religious symbols in French public (i.e. government-operated) primary and secondary schools" of 15 March 2004.

69 *Chain v. France* (5.12.2007) and *Bessam v. France* (5.12.2007).

70 *Dogru v. France* (application no. 27058/05) and *Kervanci v. France* (no. 31645/04).

71 Anna E. Galeotti, *Toleration as Recognition* (Cambridge University Press, 2005).

72 See discussion in Bas de Gaay Fortman, "Minority Rights: A Major Misconception?", *Human Rights Quarterly* 33(2011), pp. 265–303 (based on Fortman's Valedictory Address as Chair in Political Economy of Human Rights at Utrecht University, delivered on 10 September 2010 in the Dom Church, Utrecht, The Netherlands).

73 STATPOP, Swiss Federal Statistics Office, "Ständige Wohnbevölkerung nach Alter, Geschlecht und Staatsangehörigkeitskategorie" 2010/11, accessed June 28, 2013, http://www.bfs.admin.ch/bfs/portal/de/index/themen/01/02/blank/key/frauen_und_maenner.html.

74 See press release from the European Commission on Racism and Intolerance (ECRI), accessed June 28, 2013, http://www.coe.int/t/dghl/monitoring/ecri/activities/35-Declaration_minarets/Declaration_en.asp.

75 Robert Frost, "Religion and Freedom of Speech: Portraits of Muhammad, " *Constellations* 14 (2007), pp. 72–90 at p. 72.

76 See a good detailed description by David Keane, "Cartoon Violence and Freedom of Expression", *Human Rights Quarterly* 30 (2008), pp. 845–875. See also, Sune Lægaard, "The Cartoon Controversy: Offence, Identity, Oppression?" *Political Studies* 55 (2007), pp. 481–498.

77 Tariq Ramadan, "Cartoon Conflicts" *The Guardian*, Monday 6 February 2006.

78 Lægaard, op. cit., note 76 at p. 496.

PART III

Chapter 8: Conflict mitigation policies

Kiryl Kaścian

Summary

Many international organizations have contributed to the mitigation of conflicts involving minorities. Three major ones have contributed through specific approaches and mechanisms that are not legally binding; these are the United Nations (UN), the Organization for Security and Co-operation in Europe (OSCE) and the North Atlantic Treaty Organization (NATO). Following in the footsteps of the League of Nations, the UN did not, however, initially adopt any minority protection mechanisms. The OSCE, on the other hand, has become one of the major players in the area of minority issues and conflict mitigation. Drawing on legal standards set by the Council of Europe and the UN, the OSCE promotes minority norms through several mechanisms, most notably the High Commissioner on National Minorities (HCNM) established in 1992. The mandate of the HCNM builds on three key concepts: impartiality, confidentiality and co-operation and is promoted through quiet diplomacy as well as through best practice examples compiled in thematic recommendations. NATO has also been actively involved with the design of relations between states and their minorities even though it does not create its own mechanisms on minority protection.

Introduction

Having examined concepts related to the understanding of minority issues and diversity in Part II, we now turn to how international organizations and public authorities have chosen to deal with diversity in societies that are permanently multicultural. Part III will examine mechanisms and policies that are in place in societies that for a fact are diverse. As the Permanent Court of International Justice stated as early as 1930, the existence of a minority is a matter of fact, not a question of law.[1] Societies of nearly every country in Europe are to various degrees ethnically and culturally diverse.[2] That is why ethnicity is not only one of a person's identity markers but it is also an undeniably important factor of population mobilization. There are various approaches which have been made within the field of political studies towards identifying the definition, nature, origins and typology of the ethnic conflicts (see further Chapter 5). Ethnic conflict has been referred to as "one particular form of social conflict, namely that in which the goals of at least one conflict party are defined in (exclusively) ethnic terms and in which the primary fault line of confrontation is one of ethnic distinctions."[3] While such conflicts are usually confined to the confines of a state, the role of international organizations as "conflict managers" provides the institutional perspective on approaches towards the resolution of conflicts.[4] Therefore, "in the initial stage of such a conflict, the leading role is [often] assigned to the regional organization" to draw "international institutions into resolving ethnic conflicts stage by stage."[5] As such, conflict mitigation mechanisms on minority issues available within the UN and the OSCE framework, as well as the NATO approach towards the mitigation of minority conflicts, are the main focus of this chapter. The chapter provides a general descriptive overview with the purpose of providing students with the basic understanding of how the mechanisms and approaches for minority protection available within the UN, the OSCE and the NATO function. Each organization's mechanisms and approaches towards minority protection are described in the separate sections of this chapter, starting from the UN, followed by the OSCE and NATO.

UN mechanisms

Since its foundation in 1945, the UN was determined to maintain international peace and security. Towards the fulfilment of these ends the UN committed itself in Art. 1 of the UN Charter to taking

effective collective measures for the prevention and removal of threats to the peace, and for the suppression of acts of aggression or other breaches of the peace, and to bring about by peaceful means, and in conformity with the principles of justice and international law, adjustment or settlement of international disputes or situations which might lead to a breach of the peace.[6]

Since any ethnic conflict regardless of its origin, scale, phase or scope represents a potential or actual threat to peace, the UN aims to channel any of such threats to peace towards the peaceful settlements of tensions or conflicts. Given that most of the countries in the world are heterogeneous in the composition of their populations, and insofar that ethnic affiliations often does not coincide with state borders is a matter of fact, the issue of power is often linked with the ethnic factor and minority-majority relations. However, when it comes to minority protection, the UN record is not glamorous. The UN approach has shown "little interest to adopt the minority protection system of the League [of Nations] or to develop a new system for the protection of minorities."[7] Rather, since the beginning of its activities, the UN has paid major focus on human rights in general, considering that "individual rights and the principle of non-discrimination were the appropriate means of protecting every one, members of minorities included" and hence making no direct reference to the rights of minorities in the UN Charter.[8]

The initial development of the UN approach towards minority issues was determined by the general human rights framework dominated by individual rights and the principle of non-discrimination. Such a stance, on the one hand, guaranteed the equal treatment of everyone, while, on the other hand, it was still quite ineffective in ensuring the collective rights of minority groups. As for collective rights which are minority rights, the general perception of these was based on the idea "group rights would be taken care of automatically as the result of the protection of the rights of individuals."[9] As a result, "minority groups find themselves in the position of having to individually claim overtly 'group' or community 'minority rights' as individual rights: the right to speak a minority language as an individual rather than a collective right exercisable by the minority group."[10] The UN competence in the sphere of minority issues and more broadly human rights includes two types of mechanisms, the Charter-based mechanisms, and the treaty-based mechanisms.

The Charter-based mechanisms are grounded on UN authority as outlined in the UN Charter and as agreed upon by all UN Member States. The competences of the bodies created are regulated by the resolutions adopted by the representative body in question which then further creates each particular mechanism. The treaty-based mechanisms are based on the provisions of the legally binding international treaties concluded within the scope of the UN system and dealing with the issues of human rights in general and minority issues in particular. Contrary to the Charter-based mechanisms which are potentially applicable towards all the UN member states, obligations of each country under the scope of each treaty-based mechanism may arise only if this country has ratified the treaty.

Another significant difference between these two mechanisms can be exemplified in the capacities of the actors involved. With regard to the treaty-based mechanisms, independent experts are involved as an intrinsic aspect of part of the mechanism itself, acting in their full capacity and independent from government influence, while the members of the Charter-based bodies act as representatives of their respective governments. Hence, they not only take instructions from them in taking a particular position but speak on their behalf. The following part of this section will provide a description of these mechanisms and will focus on the role and status of the Independent Expert.

Charter-based mechanisms

The UN authority to maintain these mechanisms is based on the provisions of the Organization's Charter while the competences of the bodies created thereupon are regulated by the resolutions which create each particular mechanism. The Sub-Commission on the Prevention of Discrimination and Protection of Minorities is now history, as it was terminated in 2006. It dates back to 1947, when the Commission on Human Rights was established, and the Sub-Commission on the Prevention of Discrimination and Protection of Minorities was launched. The Sub-Commission's scope of responsibilities was to make recommendations on minority-related issues. Over the years the Sub-Commission expanded its mandate to address other human rights issues, gradually reducing its focus on minorities. At the same time, the Commission committed itself to minority issues as one of its numerous thematic areas, although not as a priority. During the 1990s, the role of the Sub-Commission, therefore, changed.

In 1992 the UN Declaration on the Rights of Persons Belonging to National or Ethnic, Religious and Linguistic Minorities was adopted by the General Assembly. This document entitles persons belonging to minorities with the rights to:

- Participate effectively in cultural, religious, social, economic and public life (Art. 2(2)),
- Participate effectively in decisions on the national and, where appropriate, regional level concerning the minority to which they belong or the regions in which they live, in a manner not incompatible with national legislation (Art. 2(3)).[11]

Thus, the UN Declaration stipulated that it is not enough for the state to guarantee the formal participation of minorities. It is necessary to ensure their effective participation so that minority representatives can substantially influence the decision-making process and share ownership and responsibility for all relevant decisions made. However, a major flaw with the Declaration is that it "does not have a monitoring or implementation procedure and has not been referred to by the treaty bodies in their country reviews."[12] Perhaps as a consequence of this, a further step in changing the role of the Sub-Commission was taken in 1995 with the foundation of the Working Group on Minorities, as a subsidiary organ of the Sub-Commission, as it became clear that the Sub-Commission on the Prevention of Discrimination and Protection of Minorities had finally shifted towards the protection of human rights. Eventually, in 1999 the Sub-Commission was renamed the Sub-Commission on the Promotion and Protection of Human Rights.

The UN compares the Sub-Commission's role to a "think-tank" aimed primarily at studying the minority problems and making recommendations based on the results of these studies to be considered by the UN during the process of the adoption of appropriate and necessary measures aimed at the protection of minorities.[13] This approach has its background in the UN General Assembly resolution 217C(III) known as Fate of Minorities. Through this the UN General Assembly

request[ed] the Council to ask the Commission on Human Rights and the Sub-Commission on the Prevention of Discrimination and the Protection of Minorities to make a thorough study of the problem of minorities, in order that the United Nations may be able to take effective measures for the protection of racial, national, religious or linguistic minorities.[14]

The Sub-Commission consisted of 26 individual experts nominated by their respective governments and elected by the Commission. The composition of the Sub-Commission provided roughly equal geographic representation of each continent. The Sub-Commission was comprised of eight working groups that focused their work on the various aspects of human rights and minority-related issues. At the same time, "individual Sub-Commission members serve[d] as 'rapporteurs' who prepare[d] studies for the Sub-Commission on particular topics."[15] The work of the Sub-Commission "include[d] general debates—mainly thematic, recommendations for action forwarded to the Commission on Human Rights, and the adoption of resolutions." Finally, the

Sub-Commission also provided the function of a forum for the many non-governmental organizations working within this thematic field.

The Working Group on Minorities, which after 1995 became the central body within the UN to deal directly with minority issues, was thought to serve the role of a mechanism for "hearing suggestions and making recommendations for the peaceful and constructive solution to problems involving minorities, through the promotion and protection of their rights."[16] The main effect of the Working Group activities may be summarized as having been the publication of a number of papers conceptualizing various significant aspects of minority-related issues. Their topics may roughly be divided into the following categories:

- The rights of persons belonging to minorities,
- Good practices, and
- Other measures for the promotion and protection of minorities.[17]

In September 2007, the UN Human Rights Council adopted resolution 6/15 creating the Forum on Minority Issues which has substituted the Working Group as the main UN platform in serving minorities' needs and demands. The main goals of the Forum are set out as follows:

- To encourage collaboration and dialogue on the matters related to national, ethnic, religious or linguistic minorities,
- To assist in providing expertise and contribution to the activities of the Independent Expert on minority issues, and
- To identify and analyze best practices, challenges, opportunities and initiatives for the further implementation of the Declaration on the Rights of Persons Belonging to National or Ethnic, Religious and Linguistic Minorities.[18]

The Forum's activities are guided by the Independent Expert on minority issues whose responsibilities also include preparation and organization of the Forum's annual meetings and reporting on the Forum's thematic recommendations submitted to the Human Rights Council. The Independent Expert on minority issues is one of three dozens holders of a specific UN mandate who work independently on behalf of the UN on certain country-specific or theme-specific issue. The Independent Expert's mandate was adopted in 2005 and later renewed in 2008 and 2011. The mandate of the Independent Expert encompasses the following issues:

- Encouraging the implementation of the Declaration on the Rights of Persons Belonging to National or Ethnic, Religious and Linguistic Minorities with the reference of domestic legislation and international standards,
- Promoting the collaboration with the Office of the United Nations High Commissioner for Human Rights,
- Use of a gender perspective in the Independent Expert's work,
- Comprehensive collaboration with the appropriate regional organizations, UN bodies, mechanisms and mandates,
- Consideration of the NGO views on the minority-related issues covered by the Independent Expert's mandate,
- Guidance of the activities of the Forum on Minority Issues, and
- Preparation and submission of the Independent Expert's annual reports to the Council which should include "recommendations for effective strategies for the better implementation of the rights of persons belonging to minorities."[19]

While fulfilling her tasks, the Independent Expert obtains information from various actors involved into minority-related issues, ranging from states and international organizations to non-governmental organizations and members of the civic society. This information provides the basis for the Independent Expert's communication with the states which concerns the Declaration on the Rights of Minorities and its implementation into the domestic law of UN Member States. Within the scope of its mandate the Independent Expert prepares annual reports on the various thematic aspects of minority issues. The Independent expert also pays country visits at the invitation of the national governments. Such visits are aimed at the further development of relations with the national governments in question, particularly in elaborating constructive dialogue and identifying areas for collaboration. Apart from this, the Independent Expert also notifies problematic issues and tracks domestic policies on minority-related issues, all the while "study[ing] national legislation, policy, regulatory frameworks and institutions and practices, in seeking to promote the effective implementation of the Declaration on the Rights of Minorities."[20] For instance, "the Independent Expert has been collecting good practices at local and national levels in relation to political participation of minorities and has often identified the lack of effectiveness of participation measures at the local level and under-representation of minorities in political bodies in all regions of the world."[21] Such an approach enables the Independent Expert to comprehensively analyze the relations between majority and minorities at the national level in order to monitor and identify positive and negative developments which may positively and negatively contribute to the management of the diverse societies.

The Office of the United Nations High Commissioner for Human Rights (OHCHR), which was established in 1993 "to promote and protect the enjoyment and full realization, by all people, of all rights established in the Charter of the United Nations and in international human rights laws and treaties" is the main body of the UN addressing human rights issues.[22] The work of the OHCHR is based on the mandate provided by the UN General Assembly. This mandate rests on

- The UN Charter (notably Articles 1, 13 and 55),
- The Universal Declaration of Human Rights,
- The Vienna Declaration and Programme of Action the 1993 World Conference on Human Rights, and
- The 2005 World Summit Outcome Document.[23]

The OHCHR is not the same entity as the UN Human Rights Council as these two bodies have different mandates. The OHCHR minority-related work is covered by its Indigenous Peoples and Minorities Section (IPMS). Its goal is

to improve human rights protection for indigenous peoples and minorities at the international and national levels through strategies such as strengthening relevant legislations, policies and practices, as well as through undertaking capacity building activities, while promoting the UN Declaration on the Rights of Indigenous Peoples, the UN Declaration on the Rights of Persons Belonging to National or Ethnic, Religious and Linguistic Minorities and other key human rights standards.[24]

Treaty-based mechanisms

UN treaty-based mechanisms are applicable if the country is a party to a relevant treaty, i.e. the state in question has taken upon it the responsibility to respect and observe the norms of the treaty. Otherwise, apparent violations of the treaty's provisions may not be addressed through this particular mechanism. However, as Klímová-Alexander notes, "the issue of effective participation by minorities in public life is not an easy one to address for treaty bodies as states are often reluctant to provide adequate information on this topic and do not accord it sufficient attention."[25] UN treaties related to minority protection are:

- International Covenant on Civil and Political Rights (ICCPR, 1966),
- International Covenant on Economic, Social and Cultural Rights (ICESCR, 1966),
- International Convention on the Elimination of All Forms of Racial Discrimination (ICERD, 1965),
- Convention on the Rights of the Child (1989),
- Convention on the Elimination of All Forms of Discrimination Against Women (CEDAW, 1979),
- Convention against Torture and Other Cruel, Inhuman or Degrading Treatment or Punishment (CAT, 1984).[26]

The fulfilment of each treaty is supervised through respective treaty bodies arranged in the form of committees. They consist of distinguished experts in the sphere of human rights who serve in their independent capacity and not as the representatives of their governments.[27] The following overview will focus exclusively on the minority-related clauses of the UN fundamental treaties which may be found in two of these six fundamental treaties. The International Covenant on Civil and Political Rights (ICCPR) holds the only universal special minority rights clause which is set out in Article 27 and as follows:

In those States in which ethnic, religious or linguistic minorities exist, persons belonging to such minorities shall not be denied the right, in community with the other members of their group, to enjoy their own culture, to profess and practise their own religion, or to use their own language.[28]

The wording of the Article refers to the individual rights of the persons belonging to minorities to take part and be involved in the activities which represent the cultural markers of this particular minority (i.e. culture, religion and language). The Article contains no mention with regard to political rights of minorities, including "no reference to self-government."[29] Moreover, despite the recognition of the possible existence of minorities, the very grammatical formulation of "persons belonging to... minorities" implies that the cultural rights mentioned above belong rather to individuals, but not groups. The subsequent phrase "in community with the other members of their group" rather underlines the nature of such rights which may be executed only within a group, but not the right of this group to enjoy and benefit from using such rights. At the same time, the Human Rights Committee in its General Comment 23 emphasized an apparent need to adopt "positive legal measures of protection and measures to ensure the effective participation of members of minority communities in decisions which affect them" (Art. 7).[30]

Important to notice is the Article's negative formulation 'shall not be denied' regarding the rights of the persons belonging to minorities, which implies that the jurisdiction of the state should not be restrictive. In this regard, the Human Rights Committee in its General Comment 23 has underlined that "positive measures of protection are... required not only against the acts of the State party itself, whether through its legislative, judicial or administrative authorities, but also against the acts of other persons within the State party."[31] At the same time it is unclear how far the state should implement these positive measures and whether it could always be effective in the protection of minorities against other persons within the state.

A positive element is the interpretation of the word 'exist' as written in the General Comment in regard to the non-denial of rights. First, the existence of a minority is a matter of fact and thus it "does not depend upon a decision by that State party but requires to be established by objective criteria" (Art. 5.2). Second, rights are also accordingly expanded to apply to migrant workers and visitors of the state. At the same time, despite its positive impact in regard to cultural expression of minorities, Article 27 "has not stopped states from rescinding funding for minority-language schools, abolishing traditional forms of local autonomy, or encouraging settlers to swamp minority homelands", as "none of these policies... violates the rights to cultural expression and association protected in Article 27."[32]

The Convention on the Rights of the Child, being the most widely ratified treaty covering human rights issues, contains a reference to minority issues. The Convention is focused on the rights of children, i.e. the persons under 18 years. Art. 30 of the Convention stipulates that

In those States in which ethnic, religious or linguistic minorities or persons of indigenous origin exist, a child belonging to such a minority or who is indigenous shall not be denied the right, in community with other members of his or her group, to enjoy his or her own culture, to profess and practise his or her own religion, or to use his or her own language.[33]

Moreover, Art. 17(d), while recognizing the role performed by mass media, urges parties to the convention to particularly consider "the linguistic needs of the child who belongs to a minority group or who is indigenous."[34] Hence, Art. 30 of the Convention repeats the wording and approach laid down in Art. 27 ICCPR extending to children the rights which represent cultural markers of particular minorities (i.e. culture, religion and language).

It should be emphasized that if a UN Member State has ratified one of these fundamental treaties without reservations, persons belonging to minorities and living within the borders of the country in question may enjoy the full scope of rights ensured by the respective treaty. Moreover, it should be noted that in case of four treaties (CAT, CEDAW, ICCPR and ICERD), individuals are entitled to file individual complaints to the respective committees if the individual believes his or her rights have been violated in some way, provided that the member state has not issue a statement of reservation regarding the respective article. The procedure for proper filing of these complaints is similar in all four cases. To be admissible, the complaint shall meet certain important criteria:

- The petitioner or where applicable petitioners must not be anonymous,
- S/he/they should be victims of the concrete human rights violation,
- All domestic remedies in the state concerned must have been exhausted, and
- Substantive allegations must be provided.[35]

Upon admission, the respective committee can provide the state concerned with the opportunity for a response, while the petitioner is entitled to a counter-response. The respective committee comes to a decision as to whether or not the petitioner's rights were violated. The committee's conclusions do not have legally binding effect and are thus not always effective. Moreover, the process starting from filing a complaint by the petitioner to the adoption of the view by the respective committee is usually quite slow. At the same time such rulings may serve as evidence that the state failed to abide by its international obligations under the respective treaty and if a country is found to be at fault in such a judgment, the result may be a reaction which could coalesce in a wave of international criticism directed towards the country concerned. With regard to minorities, the practice shows that "States do sometimes respond positively to the process, and the mere fact that a well-founded case is brought to one of the committees may encourage a State to re-examine its policies or begin a dialogue with minority representatives."[36] Thus, the effectiveness of the UN mechanisms for minority protection is largely complicated by two core aspects, the political configuration of the domestic institutions of UN member states and the complicated applicability of the UN mechanisms for minority protection that rests upon a rather generalized approach of the UN towards minority issues.

OSCE mechanisms

The most important feature of the OSCE is its geographic composition and thus territorial scope, which makes it the largest regional organization in the world. Having members located in Asia, Europe and North America, the OSCE is not only a European organization, but both a Euro-Atlantic and a Euro-Asian organization. The role of the OSCE is predominantly political and is focused on activities aimed at security and cooperation in the areas of

- Conflict early warning,
- Conflict prevention,
- Crisis management, and
- Post-conflict rehabilitation.[37]

"Preoccupied with human and minority rights issues from the very beginning",[38] the OSCE is one of the major players throughout wider Europe working in the area of minority issues and providing standards for the protection of minorities. Within the former USSR context it seems to be the major player. The OSCE does not generate legally binding instruments, but in fact does play one of the key roles in agenda-setting.

In case of the OSCE there is no one single definition on what a minority is, or what exactly constitutes a minority. Thus, in its minority related activities the OSCE refers to the 1990 Copenhagen Document of the Organization for

Security and Cooperation in Europe ("Copenhagen Document"). This is a fundamental document with regard to minority issues within the OSCE framework, which represents the comprehensive international standard for minority rights protection. Within this framework, the question of whether or not a particular individual may be considered as belonging to a minority group is determined by the individual's personal choice. Accordingly, the existence of a minority is determined not by the state but by the "decision of those individuals who collectively see themselves as different to the majority, on a sense of belonging to the group and a commitment to the preservation of the identity of the group."[39]

One more quality of OSCE minority protection is the fact that it is linked with democratic institutions and human rights. The current state of minority protection within the OSCE framework was evaluated by the Kyiv Declaration, which emphasizes "that democracy is based, among other fundamental rules, on the respect for the rights of persons belonging to minorities and the promotion of mutual respect and tolerance" (Art.149).[40] The Kyiv Declaration urges OSCE participating states "to increase efforts to work with their diverse communities to develop and implement practices to provide members of minority groups with equal access to and opportunities within social, political, legal, and economic spheres" (Art. 22), as well as that each Member States, despite the achieved progress made in the minority protection sphere, "considers that it is still necessary to safeguard the conditions for members of minority groups to be able to express their own ethnic, cultural, linguistic or religious identities within an integrated and cohesive society" (Art. 151). Europe is seen as "the global champion of the legal provision for minorities"[41] where "various international bodies have been created with the mandate of monitoring and treatment of minorities and of recommending changes needed to live up to European standards of minority rights."[42] Thus, Will Kymlicka has noted that the establishment of the Office of the OSCE High Commissioner on National Minorities (HCNM) was a crucial element in this process.[43]

The High Commissioner on National Minorities

In response to the challenge of ethnic conflicts that pose one of the most serious threats in the potential escalation of violence in the OSCE countries, the designation of the HCNM in 1992 was aimed "to maintain an instrument of conflict prevention at the earliest possible stage in regard to tensions involving national minority."[44] The HCNM acts in his/her independent capacity without permanent approval from the OSCE Permanent Council which is the appropriate organization's body for the HCNM to getting necessary political support for his/her activities.[45] Such organizational independence has two crucial consequences. First, it gives the HCNM a status of impartiality that enables him or her to engage as a third party during mediation processes in the resolution of conflicts resulting from ethnic tensions. Second, it enables the HCNM to save time, particularly during situations where the escalation of ethnic tensions requires immediate attention and timely reaction.

The phrase 'the earliest possible stage' with regard to the development of ethnic tensions and conflicts represents one of the most important aspects of the work of HCNM in the areas of conflict prevention, resolution and adjustment, so that these negative developments do not pose any threat for the principles of the OSCE aimed at peace, stability and friendly relations among its member states.[46] Moreover, the 'early warnings' and if necessary 'early actions' constitute the key responsibilities of the HCNM towards minority-related potential conflict situations "which have not yet developed beyond an early warning stage, but, in the judgement of the HCNM, have the potential to develop into a conflict within the OSCE area."[47] The need to issue 'early warnings' has emerged twice. The first dates back to May 1999 in reference to the developments in the FYR of Macedonia which arose from the emergence of "possible repercussions on inter-ethnic relations from the large influx of Kosovo Albanian refugees."[48] The second instance occurred in June 2010 with reference to the systematic tensions between ethnic Kyrgyz and Uzbeks in the southern part of Kyrgyzstan.[49] During such cases, the HCNM is obliged to inform the OSCE immediately should the development of tensions supersede the capacities and abilities of HCNM.

The HCNM activities have, however, their limitations. For instance, the mandate does not include individual cases of persons belonging to any national minority. Thus, the role of the HCNM is to assess the particular situations of the groups and to evaluate the situation of minorities within the perspective of human rights concerns. Furthermore, the scope of HCNM's mandate does not encompass the possibility of communication on minority related issues "in situations involving organized acts of terrorism" or with "any person or organization that practises or publicly condones terrorism or violence."[50] According to the HCNM Office, the work and interpretation of minority issues may be described by three keywords: impartiality, confidentiality and co-operation.[51]

The first notion, impartiality, is linked with the very title of the HCNM's activities, which may often be misinterpreted by the inappropriate use of one single preposition 'for' instead of 'on'. Should the HCNM's job be entitled the "high commissioner for national minorities",[52] the activities would have been favourable towards minorities resembling the role of their advocate which implies taking sides and, as such, partiality. At the same time, the proper title High Commissioner on National Minorities infers that the HCNM is impartial, and will consider the interests and arguments of both parties in cases involving apparent ethnic tensions or conflicts, and will be able to provide states with non-biased recommendations aiming at minimizing the emergence or further development of those interethnic tensions or conflicts. Moreover, such activities are conducted by the HCNM within the ambit of the obligations of OSCE member states under the Organization's framework. That is why, in cases where these obligations are not met by the state involved, the HCNM will urge the government of this state to implement policy changes aimed at conflict prevention, stability maintenance and securing of the full scope of rights for the persons belonging to a minority.[53]

Impartiality is linked with the second notion, confidentiality. Taking sides in a conflict can immediately produce a lack of trust held by at least one of the parties as well as being possibly costly in terms of further escalation of the conflict. Confidentiality thus gives parties to the conflict the full assurance that their positions will remain behind the closed doors and will not be swept out into public view, allowing for conditions of full disclosure relating to the positions of each party. Thus, it could be said that "rather than watching over rule-of-law-based implementation, the HCNM's mandate is focused on quiet diplomacy as a means of conflict prevention."[54] Moreover, "the strategy of the HCNM remains mediation characterized by pragmatism… designed to reach compromises rather than set standards."[55] As a result of this strategy, the HCNM is able to fully engage all of the parties to the conflict and make them more cooperative in endeavours to find a durable and effective solution in reducing tensions. The ability to find legitimate solutions is linked with the third key notion, co-operation. This is the stage which enables the parties of the conflict to work on conflict settlement by exchanging views and taking concrete measures on a durable basis. The reference to durability is linked with issues of peace and stability. In cases of a durable and effective solution the emergence of further tensions is lessened in the long-term perspective. Moreover, in cases of the effective adjustment of a conflict, this experience may successfully be used as best practices for further existing and possible conflicts.

All HCNMs have worked to provide guidelines in the area of minority issues as is evidenced in their recommendations. Recommendations formulated by the HCNM comply with international minority protection standards laid down in the major universal and regional treaty-based instruments (FCNM, ICCPR, ECHR, etc.), and encompasses proposals for alterations and amendments to domestic legislation and the implementation of new policies and approaches aimed at maintaining and strengthening peace between ethnic communities. In cases of interstate tensions related to a particular minority's kin-state involvement, they may deal with the promotion and development of the bilateral cooperation between two states in the sphere of diversity promotion and respect for minority rights.

The thematic recommendations are based on two interrelated core aspects: the promotion of integration, and the respect for diversity. The recommendations aim to "achieve an appropriate and coherent application of relevant minority rights in the OSCE area that could serve as a reference for policy- and law-makers on the OSCE member states."[56] They are not legally binding documents, however, they are "intended to reflect existing international legal standards and might be considered a kind of soft law."[57] Recommendations represent compendia prepared by distinguished international experts in minority issues aimed to cover various areas of life in diverse societies which might potentially cause difficulties or tensions. Being formulated for the purpose of "finding a balance between strengthening the unity of a society and protecting the rights and the identity of the minorities living in these States", these thematic recommendations "clarify the content of the relevant international standards and to provide practical guidance for States."[58] So far, the HCNM Office has prepared and published seven different thematic recommendations listed chronologically:[59]

- The Hague Recommendations regarding the Education Rights of National Minorities (1996),
- The Oslo Recommendations regarding the Linguistic Rights of National Minorities (1998),
- The Lund Recommendations on the Effective Participation of National Minorities in Public Life (1999),
- Guidelines on the Use of Minority Languages in the Broadcast Media (2003),
- Recommendations on Policing in Multi-Ethnic Societies (2006),

- The Bolzano/Bozen Recommendations on National Minorities in Inter-State Relations (2008),
- The Ljubljana Guidelines on Integration of Diverse Societies (2012).

In order to fulfil its goals, the guidelines consist of four parts:

- General principles such as freedom of expression and protection of identity,
- State policy on broadcasting in minority languages,
- Regulation (including the limits to regulation and translation restrictions),
- Measures and funding to promote broadcasting in minority languages.[60]

The guidelines provide a framework for

pertinent state policies which should, inter alia, include the establishment of independent regulatory bodies and be geared towards the inclusion of persons belonging to national minorities; deal with the issue of regulation by emphasising, among other things, that states may not prohibit the use of any language in the broadcast media and, while promoting the use of some languages, must not discriminate against minority languages; and assert that any regulation should take into account the factual situation and contain proposals for promoting the use of minority languages in the broadcast media.[61]

The role of HCNM recommendations is crucial for providing guidelines for dealing with minority issues in Europe. They are not setting new standards[62], but together with the FCNM they "are clearly based on an integrationist approach."[63] At the same time, "it is arguably questionable how effective the politically binding OSCE HCNM Recommendations have been in addressing the grievances of national minorities in Europe."[64] Nevertheless, as Ghebali emphasises, the recommendations have "developed a genuine normative function… [and] these norms are of a special nature: although fully sticking to internationally agreed standards and practical good practices, they are neither formal HCNM recommendations, nor official OSCE commitments."[65] Such a litmus test of to what degree a state follows recommendations such as these recommendations may therefore be used in measuring the effectiveness of domestic policies and laws with regard to domestic minority protection policies in OSCE member states.

NATO and minority-related conflict mitigation

The NATO involvement in minority issues may be traced back as early as 1955 and was connected with the membership application of the Federal Republic of Germany. This accession "was conditional on its working out a reciprocal minority rights agreement with Denmark, an agreement which is now seen as a model of how kin-states can work constructively through bilateral relations to help minorities in neighbouring states."[66] The end of the Cold War marked a huge step for the internalization of minority rights in the European context.[67] Along with other international organizations such as the OSCE, the Council of Europe and the EU, NATO was one of the main actors "actively involved in the decision-making about state-minority relations."[68] In 1991 it was set out that the respect for minority rights would become one of the criteria for prospective candidates to adhere to before obtaining full membership.[69] Even though NATO "did not [itself] create new monitoring bodies specifically focused on minority rights… [it has] made clear that [it] support[s] the work of the OSCE HCNM and the CoE and expect [its] candidate countries to cooperate with them as a condition of accession."[70] Therefore, two main dimensions of potential NATO involvement into minority-related issues can be defined: the politics of security in Europe, and the maintenance of bilateral cooperation among the countries as a condition for their membership in the organization.

Minority rights in Europe are related to the politics of security which includes NATO, although NATO is involved in minority issues to a somewhat lesser degree than other organizations which have been previously mentioned.[71] NATO, along with the EU and OSCE "ha[s] also been engaged in a parallel process of monitoring countries for their potential threat to regional security."[72] This format provides a space of organizational cooperation between NATO and OSCE, such as in the cases of the conflicts in Bosnia and Herzegovina and the conflicts in Kosovo. It should be emphasized that the OSCE HCNM mandate is attributed to the OSCE security basket and the early warnings and if necessary early actions belong to the main tasks of the HCNM towards minority-related situations. At the same time, "behind the OSCE… lies NATO, with its security mandate and its power to intervene militarily if necessary."[73]

In connection with the conditions for the membership in NATO one may observe two important issues. First, the membership conditionality is linked with the resolution of all possible territorial disputes with neighbouring states, which often have an interethnic component involved.[74] Second, in searching for a solution to these problems, the NATO candidate countries must comply with the principles set out by the OSCE.[75] These requirements illustrate another dimension of the NATO approach to minority issues—that the conditionality of NATO membership is related to minority standards set out by another international organization. Hence, this signifies not only the will of NATO to cooperate with other regional organizations on the matter of minority rights, but also signifies its readiness "to delegate monitoring and assessment of minority situation to other institutions, above all to the OSCE and Council of Europe."[76]

Furthermore, the maintenance of regional security within new NATO Member States may be more effective if "the institutional and normative adjustments induced by NATO's cooperative security arrangements would be associated with a democratic development of the political-military structures, as well as with non-nationalist and regionally cooperative attitudes."[77] The moderate success of NATO's ability to build capacities for regional cooperation on the basis of mutual trust and partnership may be observed in the cases of Hungary and Romania, both of which have a complex history of 20th Century bilateral relations with one another, full of mistrust and tensions. Bjola admits that "NATO's robust political and military engagement with Hungary and Romania has proved indeed conducive to the improvement of the bilateral relationships between the two countries at the level of foreign and military policy Directions."[78] However, the effectiveness and tempo of further progress in this area is still unclear and the minority factor remains one of the vital issues impeding significant institutional progress achieved under the NATO framework. As a result, "the issue of national minorities remains the main source of mistrust and political tension between the two countries"[79] reappearing from time to time on the national political agenda for one reason or another. Moreover, although there has been a general positive trend, "the sound political and military engagement between NATO and the two countries has not been yet rendered into similar vigorous patterns of bilateral cooperation between Hungary and Romania."[80] It can be expected that the framework set out (by NATO) may further positively influence progress in the improvement of bilateral relations among countries such as Hungary and Romania and may further contribute to the formation of a stable and secure CEE region, guaranteed by NATO.[81]

Thus, the NATO approach to minority issues stresses the ongoing trend of the internalization of minority rights in Europe.[82] Having not being directly involved in the development of the minority rights framework in Europe, NATO relies on those set out by other organizations, namely the OSCE and the Council of Europe.[83] These policies are pursued within the scope of the common goals of these two organizations to maintain stability and security throughout wider Europe. Such institutional cooperation enables the OSCE norms to serve a measurement tool to gauge the effectiveness of domestic policies and laws with regard to minority protection policies and instruments in OSCE and NATO member states, which makes their domestic application more effective, contrary to the rather general and complicated UN mechanisms.

Key Points

- When first addressing minority issues, the UN initially had no interest in implementing the framework adopted within its predecessor, the League of Nations, preferring to construct, implement and maintain its own system of minority protection.
- The initial focus of the activities of the UN was individual human rights and non-discrimination in general, and as such, the UN Charter contains no direct reference to minorities and their protection.
- The competence of the UN in the sphere of minority issues, and more broadly human rights, includes two types of mechanisms: Charter-based mechanisms and treaty-based mechanisms.
- The OSCE is one of the major players in the wider Europe on minority issues and the providing of minority norms.
- The Copenhagen Document is a fundamental document with regard to minority issues within the OSCE framework, which represents comprehensive international norms for minority rights protection; whether or not a person belongs to a minority is determined by individual choice.
- The distinguishing feature of OSCE minority protection norms is the fact that it is linked with democratic institutions and human rights.

- The goal to establish the post of the HCNM in 1992 was done so "to maintain an instrument of conflict prevention at the earliest possible stage in regard to tensions involving national minority"; the work of the HCNM and the interpretation of minority issues may be described as being guided by three key concepts: impartiality, confidentiality and co-operation.
- The OSCE promotes best practices by means of its thematic recommendations which are based on two interrelated core aspects: the promotion of integration, and the respect for diversity; the recommendations represent non-legally binding compendia prepared by distinguished international experts in minority issues aimed to cover the various areas of life in diverse societies which may potentially cause difficulties or tensions.
- Along with other international organizations such as the OSCE, the Council of Europe and the EU, NATO is one of the main actors which is actively involved with the design of relations between states and their minorities. Its involvement has two main dimensions related to minority-related issues: the politics of security in Europe, and the maintenance of bilateral cooperation among countries as a condition for their membership in the organization.
- Having not created its own monitoring bodies specifically focused on minority rights, NATO requires candidates for membership to comply with the principles set out by the OSCE, so that the conditionality of NATO membership is directly related to the minority standards set out by outside international organizations.

Further reading

ARP, BJÖRN. *International Norms and Standards for the Protection of National Minorities: Bilateral and Multilateral Texts with Commentary*. Leiden: Brill, 2008.

HANNUM, HURST, and EILEEN F. BABBITT. *Negotiating Self-Determination*. Lanham: Lexington Books, 2006.

HOROWITZ, DONALD L. *Ethnic Groups in Conflict*, 2nd ed. Berkeley: University of California Press, 2000.

JACKSON PREECE, JENNIFER. *Minority Rights: Between Diversity and Community*. Cambridge: Polity Press, 2005.

MOWBRAY, JACQUELINE. *Linguistic Justice: International Law and Language Policy*. Oxford: Oxford University Press, 2012.

OSCE HCNM Thematic Guidelines and other publications, at http://www.osce.org/hcnm/78053.

PENTASSUGLIA, GAETANO. *Minorities in International Law: An Introductory Study*. Strasbourg: Council of Europe Press, 2002.

PENTIKÄINEN, MERJA. *Creating an Integrated Society and Recognising Differences: The Role and Limits of Human Rights, with Special Reference to Europe*. Rovaniemi: Lapland University Press, 2008.

THIO, LI-ANN. *Managing Babel: The International Legal Protection of Minorities in The Twentieth Century*. Dordrecht: Martinus Nijhoff Publishers, 2005.

WHEATLEY, STEVEN. *Democracy, Minorities and International Law*. Cambridge: Cambridge University Press, 2005.

WOLFF, STEFAN and MARC WELLER. *Autonomy, Self-governance and Conflict Resolution: Innovative Approaches to Institutional Design in Divided Societies*. London: Routledge, 2008.

Notes

1 Anna Meijknecht, *Towards International Personality: the Position of Minorities and Indigenous Peoples in International Law* (Antwerp: Intersentia, 2001), p. 66.

2 *Ljubljana Guidelines on Integration of Diverse Societies*, 4, accessed July 15, 2013, http://www.osce.org/hcnm/96883.

3 Stefan Wolff, *Disputed Territories: the Transnational Dynamics of Ethnic Conflict Settlement* (New York: Berghahn Books, 2003), p. 8.

4 Emil Payin, "Settlement of ethnic conflicts in post-Soviet society", in *Ethnicity and power in the contemporary world*, eds. Kumar Rupesinghe and Valery A. Tishkov (United Nations University Press, 1996), accessed July 15, 2013, http://archive.unu.edu/unupress/unupbooks/uu12ee/uu12ee09.htm. According to Payin, institutional approach "presupposes the establishment of a network of organizations (i.e., a special infrastructure) for the prevention and adjustment of inner conflicts. Such an infrastructure should comprise institutions at the national, regional, and global levels, and have functions that will differ from level to level".

5 Ibid.

6 *Charter of the United Nations*, accessed July 15, 2013, http://www.un.org/en/documents/charter/.

7 Solomon Dersso, "Minorities and International Law", *SAIFAC Research Paper Series* 1 (Braamfontein: SAIFAC, 2006), p. 11.

8 Ibid., pp. 11–12.

9 Rhona K. M. Smith "The Fate of Minorities – Sixty Years On", *Web Journal of Current Legal Issues*, 1/2009, accessed July 15, 2013, http://webjcli.ncl.ac.uk/2009/issue1/smith1a.html.

10 Ibid.

11 *Declaration on the Rights of Persons Belonging to National or Ethnic, Religious and Linguistic Minorities*, accessed July 15, 2013, http://www.un.org/documents/ga/res/47/a47r135.html.

12 Ilona Klímová-Alexander, "Effective Participation by Minorities: United Nations Standards and Practice", in *Political Participation of Minorities: A Commentary on International Standards and Practice*, eds. Marc Weller and Katherine Nobbs (Oxford University Press, 2010), pp. 286–307 at p. 298.

13 *United Nations Guide for Minorities, Pamphlet No. 3*: The Charter-based system of the UN, 2, accessed July 15, 2013, http://www.ohchr.org/Documents/Publications/GuideMinorities3en.pdf.

14 Resolution adopted by the General Assembly[Part C of General Assembly resolution 217 (III). International Bill of Human Rights]217 C (III). Fate of Minorities, UN Documents, accessed July 15, 2013, http://www.un-documents.net/a3r217c.htm.
15 *United Nations Guide for Minorities*, Pamphlet 3, p. 2.
16 The Former Working Group on Minorities, OHCHR website, accessed July 15, 2013, http://www.ohchr.org/EN/Issues/Minorities/Pages/TheformerWGonMinorities.aspx.
17 Ibid.
18 Forum on Minority Issues, OHCHR website, accessed July 15, 2013, http://www.ohchr.org/EN/HRBodies/HRC/Minority/Pages/ForumIndex.aspx.
19 Independent Expert on Minority Issues, OHCHR website, accessed July 15, 2013, http://www.ohchr.org/EN/Issues/Minorities/IExpert/Pages/IEminorityissuesIndex.aspx.
20 Ibid.
21 Klímová-Alexander, op.cit., note 12, p. 302.
22 Who we are – Mandate, OHCHR website, accessed July 15, 2013, http://www.ohchr.org/EN/AboutUs/Pages/Mandate.aspx.
23 Ibid.
24 OHCHR Indigenous Peoples and Minorities Section, OHCHR website, accessed July 15, 2013, http://www.ohchr.org/EN/Issues/Minorities/Pages/OHCHRIndigenousPeoplesMinoritiesSection.aspx.
25 Klímová-Alexander, op. cit., p. 299.
26 United Nations Guide for Minorities, Pamphlet No. 4: Human Rights Treaty Bodies and Complaint Mechanisms, pp. 3–9, accessed July 15, 2013, http://www.ohchr.org/Documents/Publications/GuideMinorities4en.pdf. In this context, among the hard law sources we can also refer to the International Labour Organization Convention 169 which, as Chablais notes, contains several provisions on participation of indigenous and tribal people (see: Chablais, Alain, 'Legal Entrenchment and Implementation Mechanisms', in *Political Participation of Minorities: A Commentary on International Standards and Practice*, eds. Marc Weller and Katherine Nobbs (Oxford University Press, 2010), pp. 735–750 at pp. 738–9. However due to the fact that the ILO convention deals only with the rights of indigenous people it despite its importance does not fall into the scope of this textbook aims.
27 *United Nations Guide for Minorities*, Pamphlet 4, p. 1.
28 *International Covenant on Civil and Political Rights*, accessed July 15, 2013, http://www.ohchr.org/en/professionalinterest/pages/ccpr.aspx.
29 Ephraim Nimni, 'Cultural Minority Self-governance', in *Political Participation of Minorities: A Commentary on International Standards and Practice*, eds. Marc Weller and Katherine Nobbs (Oxford University Press, 2010), pp. 634–60 at p. 638.
30 Cited by: General Comment No. 23: The Rights of Minorities (Art. 27): 08/04/1994, CCPR/C/21/Rev.1/Add.5, General Comment No. 23, accessed July 15, 2013, http://www.unhchr.ch/tbs/doc.nsf/%28Symbol%29/fb7fb12c2fb8bb21c12563ed004df111?Opendocument.
31 Ibid.
32 Will Kymlicka, "The Evolving Basis of European Norms of Minority Rights: Rights to Culture, Participation and Autonomy", in *The Protection of Minorities in the Wider Europe*, eds. Marc Weller, Denika Blacklock and Katherine Nobbs (Basingstoke: Palgrave Macmillan, 2008), pp. 11–41 at p. 17.
33 Convention on the Rights of the Child, OHCHR website, accessed July 15, 2013, http://www.ohchr.org/en/professionalinterest/pages/crc.aspx.
34 Ibid.
35 *United Nations Guide for Minorities*, Pamphlet 4, pp. 13–14.
36 Ibid., p. 15.
37 *Who we are*, OSCE website, accessed July 15, 2013, http://www.osce.org/who.
38 Krzysztof Drzewicki, "The Enlargement of the European Union and the OSCE High Commissioner on National Minorities", in *The Protection of Minorities in the Wider Europe*, eds. Marc Weller, Denika Blacklock and Katherine Nobbs (Basingstoke: Palgrave Macmillan, 2008), pp. 154–170 at p. 157.

39 *Mandate – HCNM*, OSCE website, accessed July 15, 2013.
40 Here and further in this text cited by: *Kyiv Declaration of the OSCE Parliamentary Assembly and Resolutions Adopted at the Sixteenth Annual Session*, accessed July 15, 2013, http://www.oscepa.org/members/member-directory/doc_download/250-kyiv-declaration-english.
41 Marc Weller, "Introduction: The Outlook for the Protection of Minorities in the Wider Europe", in *The Protection of Minorities in the Wider Europe*, eds.Marc Weller, Denika Blacklock and Katherine Nobbs (Basingstoke: Palgrave Macmillan, 2008), pp. 1–7 at p. 1.
42 Kymlicka, op.cit., note 32, p. 13.
43 Ibid.
44 *Overview – HCNM*, OSCE website, accessed July 15, 2013, http://www.osce.org/hcnm/43199.
45 *Mandate – HCNM*, OSCE website, accessed July 15, 2013, http://www.osce.org/hcnm/43201.
46 *Overview – HCNM*, op. cit. note 44.
47 *Mandate – HCNM*, op. cit. note 45.
48 Early warning – *HCNM*, OSCE website, accessed July 15, 2013, http://www.osce.org/hcnm/43265.
49 Early warning to the (special) Permanent Council on June 2012: statement by Knut Vollebæk, OSCE High Commissioner on National Minorities, accessed July 15, 2013, http://www.osce.org/hcnm/68539.
50 *Mandate – HCNM*, op. cit. note 45.
51 *Overview – HCNM*, op. cit. note 44.
52 Written purposely in small letters in order to show an apparent terminology problem and not make the readers get confused.
53 *Mandate – HCNM*, op. cit. note 45.
54 Weller, op. cit., note 41, p. 3.
55 Tove H. Malloy, *National Minority Rights in Europe* (Oxford: Oxford University Press, 2005), p. 10.
56 Rainer Hofmann, "The Future of Minority Issues in the Council of Europe and the Organization for Security and Cooperation in Europe", in *The Protection of Minorities in the Wider Europe*, eds. Marc Weller, Denika Blacklock and Katherine Nobbs (Basingstoke: Palgrave Macmillan, 2008), pp. 171–205 at p. 176.
57 Ibid.
58 *Conflict Prevention – HCNM*, OSCE website, accessed July 15, 2013, http://www.osce.org/hcnm/44692.
59 See further, the HCNM website, accessed July 15, 2013, http://www.osce.org/hcnm.
60 *Media – HCNM*, OSCE website, accessed July 15, 2013, http://www.osce.org/hcnm/44688.
61 Hofmann, op.cit., note 56, p. 188.
62 Krzysztof Drzewicki, "OSCE Lund Recommendations in the Practice of the High Commissioner on National Minorities", in *The Protection of Minorities in the Wider Europe*, eds. Marc Weller, Denika Blacklock and Katherine Nobbs (Basingstoke: Palgrave Macmillan, 2008), pp. 256–85 at p. 267.
63 David J. Galbreath and Joanne McEvoy, *The European Minority Rights Regime: Towards a Theory of Regime Effectiveness* (Basingstoke: Palgrave Macmillan, 2012), p. 95.
64 Ibid., p. 89.
65 Cited by: Galbreath and McEvoy, *The European Minority Rights Regime*, Ibid.
66 Kymlicka, op.cit., note 32, p. 11.
67 Ibid.
68 Ibid.
69 Ibid., p. 12.
70 Ibid, p. 13.
71 Malloy, op.cit., note 55, pp. 2–3.
72 Kymlicka, op.cit., note 32, p. 26.

73　Ibid.
74　Spruds, Andris, 'Minority Issues in the Baltic States in the Context of the NATO Enlargement', NATO Research Fellowships 1999–2001, p. 14, accessed July 15, 2013, http://www.nato.int/acad/fellow/99-01/spruds.pdf.
75　Ibid.
76　Ibid.
77　Corneliu Bijola, "NATO as a Factor of Security Community Building: Enlargement and Democratization in Central and Eastern Europe", NATO Research Fellowships 1999–2001, p. 4, accessed July 15, 2013, http://www.nato.int/acad/fellow/99-01/bjola.pdf.
78　Ibid., p. 32.
79　Ibid., p. 57.
80　Ibid.
81　Ibid., p. 28
82　Kymlicka, op.cit., note 32, p. 11.
83　Ibid., p. 13.

Chapter 9: Democracy, participation, and empowerment

Andreea Cârstocea

Summary

There exist a number of normative and practical challenges concerning the full and effective participation of national minorities in public life. Main concepts, such as representative democracy, representation, participation, and empowerment relate to these challenges. Moreover, the normative debates on the justification, merits, categorization, as well as the advantages and risks inherent to the descriptive representation of marginalized groups are highly relevant. At the practical level of political representation and participation, there are important means through which the participation of national minorities to public life can be achieved. These include the establishment of ethnic parties and of electoral and institutional arrangements to promote inclusion and power sharing, whether territorially based or not. Less formal institutions, such as social movements are another means through which marginalized groups can advance their demands. Most challenging is Roma participation in public life across Europe.

Introduction

The effective participation of national minorities in public life is generally recognized as a fundamental condition for a peaceful and democratic society. This we established as a right of minorities in Chapters 2 and 8 and as a necessity in Chapter 5. In this Chapter, we examine how public authorities may implement these ideals at the domestic level. Often minority groups find themselves, by their very nature, in a non-dominant and usually numerically inferior position to the general population, thus running the risk of having their interests ignored—or sometimes even encroached upon—by the majority population. Their comparative numerical inferiority means that national minorities may have difficulties in gathering sufficient votes for being adequately represented in local or national parliaments or in decision-making bodies, and thus, in the absence of special representation or participatory mechanisms, decisions that might affect their livelihood could be taken without their consultation. It is, therefore, not surprising that the main instrument for the protection of national minorities in Europe, the Council of Europe Framework Convention for the Protection of National Minorities, includes an article dedicated precisely to the "effective participation of persons belonging to national minorities in cultural, social and economic life and in public affairs, in particular those affecting them."[1]

The Council of Europe is not the only organisation in Europe to concern itself with this matter; recognizing that in order to promote minority participation governments often need to establish specific arrangements, in 1999 the OSCE also adopted a set of recommendations describing the means through which they can ensure the effective participation of national minorities in public life.[2] This chapter will give the student the opportunity to reflect on the ongoing debates—both normative and practical—related to this issue. The chapter will start from clarifying some of the central concepts to the issue of minority participation, namely representative democracy, descriptive representation, participation, and empowerment. Then, after taking the student through some of the normative debates surrounding the issue of descriptive representation, the chapter will offer some insights into the challenges of translating the principles of descriptive representation into practice, including an outline of the challenges presented by the low levels of participation of the Roma minority in public life throughout Europe.

General Considerations

A discussion concerning the participation to public life of national minorities cannot take place without briefly reflecting on the nature of democratic systems and on the challenges presented by representative democracy. Obviously, a comprehensive overview of the implications of the concept of democracy is far beyond the scope of this chapter; however, there are a few points that should be made before embarking on a discussion concerning the justification, merits, and means of ensuring the effective participation of national minorities in public life.

Democracy: who rules and how?

The etymological roots of the concept of *democracy* are to be found in the Greek *dēmokratiā*, a term coined from *dēmos* ('people') and *kratos* ('rule'), and describing a political system existing in some Greek city-states, notably

Athens, around the 5th Century BC. With its emphasis on the people and their power to rule, over time the concept has found its practical realization in various forms—direct democracies, liberal democracies, participatory democracies, deliberative democracies, representative democracies, parliamentary democracies, presidential democracies, western democracies, transition democracies are just a few of the most frequently mentioned types of democracy. To make things even fuzzier, many countries like to call themselves 'democratic' even though their political systems do not fulfill the basic tenets of democracy (e.g. the Democratic Republic of Congo, the Democratic People's Republic of Korea).

Thus given its wide ranging variations, it is almost impossible to produce an all-encompassing definition of the concept of democracy. What can be safely said is that democracy generally denotes a political system in which the power to rule belongs to the people, who exercise this power either directly (as used to be the case in the Athenian democracy), or indirectly (through a body of representatives); liberal democracies are in addition governed by the rule of law, and freedom, equality, and human rights are fundamental values. As this is a rather wide definition, it requires a few further clarifications, especially with respect to who the 'people' are, how they can rule, and whether there are limits to their rule.

While the emphasis on the people as holders of power is central to any definition of democracy, at various historical stages and in various regions of the world the people did by no means mean the totality of a state's population. Even the most well-known historical form of democracy, the Athenian system of direct democracy, only allowed the participation in government of a small part of the population. Thus, the right to vote was restricted to the adult male Athenian citizens who had completed their military training; this entitlement did not extend to slaves, freed slaves, children, or women, and therefore excluded vast parts of the population. Closer to modern times, the people came to encompass more segments of a state's population, but—for instance—for a long time women were excluded from participation (the first state to enfranchise women was New Zealand in 1873, while Germany enfranchised women in 1918, the United Kingdom in 1928, France in 1945, and Switzerland in 1971). The United States allowed women to vote as early as 1920, but did not fully enfranchise African Americans until 1965, when the Voting Rights Act was adopted. Today, developed democracies extend the right to vote and be elected to most segments of society, but one should remember that certain categories are still excluded, e.g. children and underage young people, the mentally ill, or in some countries, convicted criminals.

As mentioned previously, Athenian democracy was a direct form of democracy, where citizens themselves voted on legislation; such a system would today be cumbersome and difficult to implement, due to the much larger size of societies and the greater complexity of issues. As such, most present-day democracies are a variant of representative democracy, with decisions being taken through elected representatives; however, many democracies retain certain elements pertaining to direct democracy, such as referendums or the possibility for citizens to initiate legislation. Representative democracies appear to be more suited to today's societies, with their large populations and complex issues, thus being a more practical arrangement for the number and kinds of decisions that need to be taken. Other arguments in favor of representative democracy touch upon the fact that through elections citizens can elect to office individuals with the expertise to govern adequately, thus relieving ordinary individuals of the burden of making decisions regarding the numerous and complex issues at hand. A further argument in favor of representative democracies is that they offer a better environment for negotiations and compromise across the different sectors and sometimes conflicting interests in society, thus favoring stability and peacefulness.

An important aspect to be discussed in relation to any form of democracy is the extent—or the limits—of the people's rule. Thus, one of the major critiques of democracy is that it favors the will of the majority over that of the minorities; Alexis de Tocqueville called the problem "the tyranny of the majority", drawing attention to the fact that groups who do not share the views of the majority may not have a say in decisions affecting their lives.[3] A particular problem is that of persistent minorities[4] (e.g. national minority groups), who may be locked out of decision-making processes regardless of the political configuration. Modern-day solutions to ensuring an adequate treatment of such minorities are the guarantees of civil liberties (e.g. freedom of speech, assembly, or association) and human rights; as shown in Chapter 1, the issue of the rights of national minorities has become increasingly prominent in the 20th Century. Finally, democracies cannot function as such without a strong rule of law, meaning that governments are obliged to abide by the law in their activities, thus placing necessary constraints on the discretion of governments to make decisions for the society at large. The organisation of free, fair, and regular elections is another way to make governments accountable to the people, allowing them to 'punish' underperforming governments by not renewing their mandate. It follows then that in democratic systems the people's rule is necessarily limited by a series of constraints, such as the government's obligation to act within the limits of the law, respect the human rights of its citizens, and ensure its accountability to the people. These limitations are necessary for the functioning and perpetuation of the democratic system, thus precluding arbitrary actions by governments and exclusion of minorities from enjoying the benefits of such a system.

Representative democracy: the delegate vs. trustee dilemma

Any representative democracy will have to grapple with a fundamental dilemma related to the role of the representative in decision-making bodies. Simply put, the question that arises is whether the representative, once elected, should act according to the instructions he receives from his constituency, or whether he should act in the interest of the community but according to his best judgment, even if this might mean acting against the wishes of the constituency. These two opposing standpoints are generally known as the mandate vs. independence controversy, or, alternatively, as the delegate vs. trustee debate.[5] Both perspectives have their own supporters, with theorists endorsing one or the other based on a range of arguments.

For instance, James Madison articulated a delegate conception of representation whereby the representative acts as the voice of those who are represented, while Edmund Burke argued that representatives should use their superior judgment and not yield to the desires of the masses: "Your representative owes you, not his industry only, but his judgment; and he betrays, instead of serving you, if he sacrifices it to your opinion."[6] Obviously, a representative taking either of the two extreme positions would find his or herself in a position where the act of representation has become void of meaning. Thus, a representative acting exclusively according to the wishes of his or her constituency, therefore purely as a delegate, without any consideration of the broader political, economic, or social context would render his or herself "functionless."[7] Conversely, a representative acting without any consideration to the desires of his constituency could no longer be said to 'make present' the opinions, wishes, or claims of his electors.

This classic debate has been approached by Hanna Pitkin—one of the foremost scholars writing on the topic of representation—by proposing that the mandate vs. independence controversy poses a logically insoluble puzzle, since it asks us to choose between two elements that are both component parts of representation. Thus, she claims that there is no rational basis for choosing between the representative's judgment and the constituency's wishes. Instead of generalizing one or the other standpoint, she proposes that when these two opposing positions fail to coincide, a resolution should be taken by identifying the reason for this disagreement on a case-by-case basis.[8] In this context, what appears to be central to any theory of representative democracy is the presence of an accountability mechanism, which would allow those represented a degree of control over the actions of their representatives. In this respect, Andrew Roberts argues that the quality of a democracy is equivalent to the degree to which citizens control their rulers or, alternatively, to the strength of linkages (understood as the power to sanction incumbents, the power to select new officials, and the power to petition the government in between elections).[9] Anne Philips, writing about the representation of marginalized groups, considers accountability to be "always the other side of representation, and, in the absence of procedures for establishing what any group wants or thinks, we cannot usefully talk of their political representation."[10]

Political representation of marginalized groups

This section will outline some of the challenges associated with the adequate political representation of marginalized groups; while scholars discussing this issue generally referred to the situation of African Americans in the US or to that of women, their theories are extremely relevant and generally applicable to the case of national minorities in Europe and elsewhere. Before embarking on a more detailed analysis of what representation of marginalized groups actually entails, we should first clarify the concept of 'representation'.

In a seminal study on representation, starting from the analysis of the Latin ('*repraesentare*') root of the word, Hanna Pitkin finds the basic meaning of representation to be that of making present "something that is *not* in fact present."[11] If we are to translate this meaning into the realm of political representation, it becomes clear that representation is the act of making citizens' voices, opinions, and perspectives 'present' in public policy making processes, even if they are not physically present in legislative and decision-making bodies.

As outlined above, a representative democracy has at its core several elements, among which the organization of free, fair, and regular elections ensuring that representatives reflect the wishes and aspirations of their constituencies in law-making processes and in the policies they create. While for majority populations this is a quite straightforward idea, it is a more complicated issue for marginalized groups. These are segments of society which—due to historical discrimination or marginalization (e.g. African Americans, the Roma, women, etc.), or to their low numerical proportion compared to the majority population (e.g. national minorities in Europe)—find it difficult to achieve an adequate level of political representation. In an attempt to define marginalized groups, Melissa Williams finds that they share four characteristic features: (1) patterns of social and political inequality are structured along the lines of group membership; (2) membership in these groups is not usually experienced as voluntary; (3) membership in these groups is usually not experienced as mutable; (4) generally, negative meanings are assigned to group identity by the broader society or the dominant culture.[12] Other definitions of marginalized groups—in particular those attempting to define ethnic or national minorities—sometimes add the numerical dimension to this definition, as an important obstacle in their path to achieving fair representation. Where such groups are underrepresented in legislative or policy-making bodies, one cannot speak of their fair legislative representation and the equality as citizens of the members of these groups.[13] As such, many scholars argue that the adoption of special measures for correcting this situation of underrepresentation is the most effective way to remove inequality and ensure these groups' fair representation.

Participation

In the political science literature, participation is usually understood as the capacity of the people to exert an influence over political, socio-economic, cultural etc. decisions. Indeed, 'participation' is a concept so central to democracy that democracy understood as the rule of the people through the maximum participation of all the people came to be considered the ideal form of democracy;[14] or, as another scholar puts it, "the more participation there is, the more democracy there is."[15] Looking at the ways in which people can participate in public life, Sidney Verba identified four types of political participation: (1) voting, which he describes as potentially the single most important act of participation; (2) election-related campaign activities, such as campaigning for a candidate, attending meetings, or contributing money to a candidate's campaign; (3) citizen-initiated contacts, where people who are concerned about an issue initiate contacts with government officials, (4) cooperative participation, by which he refers to group or organizational activities initiated by individuals to deal with social or political issues.[16]

Other scholars analyzing the concept of participation point towards the scope of participation as another indicator of the fairness of decision-making processes; thus it is important to look at who participates in decision-making (thus recognizing that some participatory processes are completely open to all, while others invite only elite stakeholders); at the mode of communication and decision by analyzing how participants exchange information and make decisions (therefore differentiating between public meetings where citizens simply receive information from officials, meetings where citizens can express their preferences, and meetings where citizens engage in an active debate, take positions, exchange reasons etc.); and finally at the extent of authorization, that is at the link between discussions and policy (analysing the extent to which the deliberations have an impact on decision making).[17] Participation in public life is closely linked to political representation; while direct democracy is a less viable option in modern societies, through active participation people can influence decisions that affect their lives. By taking part in consultations, meetings, referenda, or by supporting their preferred candidate in elections people can express their policy options and influence the decision-making process.

In the case of marginalized groups, the existence of special arrangements for participation in public life is of particular importance, as in their absence such groups may not have the resources to make their voices heard in policy-making settings. This in turn would mean decisions would be taken for them and not by them, which—as demonstrated by history—can have dire consequences. As such, recognizing the importance of the participation of national minorities in public life, the Council of Europe included this issue under Article 15 of the Framework Convention for the Protection of National Minorities. In addition, the OSCE has also issued the Lund Recommendations on the Effective Participation of National Minorities in Public Life, emphasizing that this is an essential component of a democratic society, and that in order to achieve the effective participation of these groups, governments need to institute special measures. The Recommendations lay out a series of options for promoting participation at the level of central government, in elections, at regional and local levels, as well as for setting up advisory or consultative bodies; in addition, the Recommendations include arrangements for self-determination through territorial and non-territorial arrangements. Section III of this chapter will discuss some practical options for enhancing the participation of national minorities in Europe.

Empowerment

Most of the debates—whether normative or practice-oriented—surrounding the rights of national minorities are framed around a top-down approach, wherein the state is seen as the main actor instituting regimes of protection for its minorities, while minorities are seen as objects of the law, and not possessing much control over the policies that directly affect them. In recent years, this understanding of minority rights has increasingly come under criticism due to its paternalistic approach and due to the fact that it appears to treat minorities as "objects rather than subjects of their own life."[18]

As such, the concept of 'empowerment' has emerged in the literature, challenging the classic perspective on minority rights and stressing the importance of including the beneficiaries of rights as actors and as subjects of their own lives. The World Bank defines empowerment as "the process of enhancing the capacity of individuals or groups to make choices and to transform those choices into desired actions and outcomes",[19] pointing towards individuals and groups as agents of change. From this perspective, the realization of an individual's potential as a full and equal member in a society is achieved through the individual's power to induce desired changes to policy and legislation. Empowerment is an emerging perspective on minority rights, with academics and policy makers debating various aspects in relation to it, such as how to achieve the transition from a protection-based to an empowerment minority rights regime, or to what extent one can measure the degree to which an individual or a community is empowered.

The following section will discuss descriptive representation as one of the most important ways in which minorities can obtain a greater say in legislative matters and policy-making; arguably, through descriptive representation, minorities have at their disposal an important tool for determining their own future, enabling them to engage in a dialogue with majorities, propose policies they wish to see instituted, and amend or reject those which they find detrimental to their wellbeing.

Descriptive representation

One of the most important ways through which minorities can make their voices heard in the policy and law-making process is known as 'descriptive representation'. This refers to a series of arrangements through which minorities are given greater representative weight in legislatures and policymaking bodies than they would normally be able to achieve.

Microcosmic vs. selective representation

In attempting to envisage a system of representation in which all parts of society are fairly represented, Jane Mansbridge points towards two systems which, should they find practical implementation, would achieve a reasonably accurate reflection of societies: microcosmic representation and selective representation. Microcosmic representation assumes that the legislative or decision-making body (e.g. the parliament) is formed in such a manner as to constitute a representative sample of the electorate. Microcosmic representation entails some form of randomized election to government; its proponents argue that such a system of representation would ensure a more democratic process of decision-making, enhanced legitimacy of government, and increased responsiveness to the needs of the constituency.[20] The cost of such a system, however, is quite high, as a randomized election of legislators carries the risk that these will possess less ability, expertise, or commitment to the public good than legislators chosen through election.[21] Selective representation on the other hand appears as a much more feasible option; this system of representation gives certain selected groups greater descriptive representation than that which they would be normally able to achieve under the existing electoral system.[22] It entails devising special electoral arrangements (whether special quotas on electoral lists, district boundary gerrymandering or a system of reserved seats in legislatures) for specific groups whose electoral performance would otherwise be much poorer. Indeed, many countries in the world adopt this system of representation, devising special mechanisms of representation for minorities living on their territory. This type of representation, while more easily implemented, presents the problem of defining and selecting the criteria specifying which groups should be descriptively represented; in other words, legislators must answer the question as to which minorities should be represented descriptively.

Criteria for descriptive representation

Melissa Williams is one of the scholars embarking on a normative discussion concerning the criteria a group must fulfill in order to qualify for selective representation. The attributes that she finds fundamental are on the one hand the group's contemporary inequality as compared to other social groups, and on the other hand a history of discrimination and oppression. She argues against understanding representation as compensation for past injustices, basing her argument instead on considerations of justice. With present justice her primary concern, she emphasizes that past discrimination may play a role in the present injustice experienced by the group.[23]

Jane Mansbridge proposes approaching the topic of the representation of marginalized groups from a contingency perspective, wherein the determination of the merits for special representation would be reached by following a step-by-step analysis. The reason why a specific group is underrepresented in the legislature would constitute a first step in the enquiry (with the expectation that underrepresentation is the result of historical discrimination), followed by the question of whether the members of the group consider they are able to represent themselves adequately. Finally—and here Mansbridge diverges from Williams—the third question is concerned with the possible intentionality of the dominant group in suppressing the marginalized group throughout history. Drawing on normative responsibility, Mansbridge then argues that if the answer to the final question is in the affirmative, then the group appears to be a good candidate for affirmative selective representation.[24]

In a similar vein, taking a normative approach to the representation of ethnic minorities, Will Kymlicka begins by distinguishing between national minorities (which he defines as groups whose homeland has been incorporated through conquest, colonization, or federation) and ethnic groups (immigrant groups).[25] In Kymlicka's view, immigrant groups do not usually recreate a separate societal culture in their host country, but rather contribute new perspectives to the dominant culture. National minorities, on the other hand, at the time of their incorporation into the larger culture, constituted an ongoing societal culture, separate from the dominant one, and their language and historical narratives were already embodied in a full range of social practices and institutions.[26] Based on these differences, Kymlicka argues that national minorities should be accorded special representation, while immigrant groups should enjoy protection through a range of polyethnic rights. Taking the argument further, Kymlicka distinguishes between two types of justifications that would entitle a particular national minority group to special representation. A first argument is based on countering contemporary discrimination, and leading to the institution of temporary affirmative action programmes, while a second justification sees special representation rights as a corollary to the right of national minorities to self-government.[27]

The functions of minority representatives

In her seminal work, *The Concept of Representation*, Hanna Pitkin distinguishes between four categories of representation. Descriptive representation, according to Pitkin, is most appropriate in those situations where the purpose of representation is to supply information about something which is not actually present; applied to the political realm, the function of representative institutions is, consequently, to supply information about those represented.[28] In this understanding, representation is a matter of accurate resemblance or correspondence, a function of substitution or "standing for."[29] Pitkin finds this aspect problematic, as she contends that descriptive representation, in the political realm, raises the question of which characteristics are politically relevant for reproduction. The assumption underlying the principle of descriptive representation is that a representative body which corresponds perfectly to the nation as a whole can be expected to act exactly as the nation itself would (recalling Mansbridge's microcosmic representation outlined above); problems begin to arise, however, when the correspondence between the nation and the representative body is less than perfect.[30] Pitkin's view of descriptive representation is supported by that of Iris Marion Young, who argues that this type of representation implies the "impossible requirement that a person is represented only if everything about her potentially has a voice in the political process."[31]

Likewise, Pitkin's category of symbolic representation does not refer to anything that a representative does for those s/he represents; instead, the focus is on the representative's symbolical 'standing for' someone or something (a people, people's opinion, etc.). Symbolic representation rests on people's beliefs, however engendered, involving no rational or objective connection between who or what represents and who or what is represented.[32] Scholars concerned with issues relating to ethnic identity and the formation of nations have constantly emphasized the importance of symbols for ethnic groups. Anthony Smith, for instance, argues that "myths, memories, values, and symbols" are all part of the "core" of ethnicity;[33] Eric Hobsbawm stresses the importance of "invented traditions" in the formation of nations, by arguing that these are practices of a ritual or symbolic nature implying continuity with the past.[34]

Substantive representation departs from the passive, descriptive and symbolic meanings of the concept and focuses instead on what the representative does for those s/he represents. Here, Pitkin distinguishes among three types of "acting for" the represented; "the idea of substitution or acting instead of, the idea of taking care of or acting in the interest of, and the idea of acting as a subordinate, on instructions, in accord with the wishes of another."[35] In Pitkin's view, formalistic representation refers to the institutional setting that allows the initiation and performance of representation. Since ancient times, this type of representation has been approached from two points of view—the authorization and the accountability view, respectively. Authorization theorists focus on the initiation of representation, by defining a representative as someone who has been elected (authorized), while accountability theorists focus conversely on the termination of representation, by defining the representative as someone who will be subject to election (held to account).[36] Pitkin, rather than endorsing one or the other of these views, argues that they are both partially right, but ultimately wrong, as they take what is merely a part of the concept of representation for the whole.[37] These views of representation are called 'formalistic' as they are not concerned with the activity of the representative itself, but rather with the procedures by which a representative is authorized to act, or respectively is held to account following the act of representing.[38] The relevance of formalistic representation has been emphasized by various researchers, being considered a fundamental indicator of the quality of a democracy.

The different categories of representation, as identified by Pitkin, invite the question as to which category is the most relevant in the act of representation. While Pitkin herself does not prioritize one category of representation over another, and nor does she explain how these concepts of representation fit together, Jane Mansbridge remarks that "the primary function of representative democracy is to represent the substantive interests of the represented through both deliberation and aggregation. Descriptive representation should be judged primarily on this criterion."[39]

Advantages of descriptive representation

One of the normative questions that scholars interested in descriptive representation had to address is related to the advantages brought by descriptive representation of a marginalized group. Mansbridge draws attention to the fact that "descriptive" as a modifier of representation does not only denote visible, external characteristics (such as for instance the color of one's skin, or one's gender), but that descriptive also refers to a certain "shared experience."[40] According to Mansbridge, it is this shared experience that triggers the expectation on the part of the represented that the interests that the representative will pursue will be common to that of the group. Consequently, the belief in common interests may furthermore increase the level of trust between the representative and the represented.[41]

Apart from the impact the representative's identity has in setting up relations of trust, an equally important role it may fulfill relates to the deliberative and aggregative functions of democracy. Thus, Mansbridge argues that in order to fulfill the aggregative function of democracy—that of producing legitimate decisions where interests conflict—representatives need not be necessarily descriptive. However, she argues that for the deliberative function of democracy, interests are best represented by descriptive representatives because "the open-ended quality of deliberation gives communicative and informational advantages to representatives who are existentially close to the issues."[42] In a similar vein, Iris Marion Young argues that it is a legitimate request from the constituency to be represented by a person who shares its descriptive attributes:

An Asian American man who grew up in a predominantly African American neighbourhood, who has many African American friends, and who now works for a community service in a neighbourhood with many African Americans, for example, might be able to represent an African American perspective in many discussions, but most Asian American men could not because they are rather differently positioned.[43]

These theories describing the positive role of descriptive representation, as determined by the identity of the representative, appear to be confirmed by studies researching the effects of the descriptive representation of African Americans. Whether focusing on participation,[44] electoral turnout,[45] or policy influence,[46] studies generally demonstrate the positive impact descriptive representation has had on African American communities.

Dilemmas of descriptive representation

The main criticism of descriptive representation is that the costs deriving from it outweigh the gains it produces.[47] The major cost of descriptive representation has been identified as a diminishing of the role of substantive representation; this is argued to occur because in descriptive representation the constituency tends to focus on who the representative is rather than on what the representative does.[48] This is explained in the literature by the fact that where voters select a member of their own group, the descriptive characteristics can "lull [them] into thinking their substantive interests are being represented even where this is not the case."[49] Pitkin argues against understanding representation as a mere 'mirror' of the constituency:

We tend to assume that people's characteristics are a guide to the actions they will take, and we are concerned with the characteristics of our legislators for just this reason. But it is no simple correlation; the best descriptive representative is not necessarily the best representative for activity or government. Griffiths points out that a lunatic may be the best descriptive representative of lunatics, but one would not suggest that they be allowed to send some of their numbers to the legislature. (…) Representing means being like you, not acting like you.[50]

Melissa Williams acknowledges that the mere presence in legislatures of members of a marginalized group, although often necessary, is not sufficient for the fair representation of the group.[51] Indeed, that this may be so is reflected by cases such as those of Clarence Thomas (US Supreme Court judge of African American descent, whose appointment was opposed by the NAACP due to his conservative stance on affirmative action) and Phyllis Schlafly (leader of a national campaign against the Equal Rights Amendment in the US). As acknowledged by Williams, descriptive representation needs an accountability mechanism to ensure that the representative does pursue the interests of the group; in her view, elections appear as the most important mechanisms of accountability in this respect.[52]

In addition, this type of representation presents the problem of defining and selecting the criteria specifying which groups should be descriptively represented. Such a process carries the cost of essentialising, as it entails selecting a single characteristic that binds all members of the group (e.g. language, national origin, religion, or celebration of specific holidays), and categorizing the respective characteristic as coinciding with the common interests of the group.[53] The problem is that such categorization obscures cleavages within the group; moreover, it may encourage the "assimilation of the minority or subordinate interests in those of the dominant group without even recognizing their existence."[54] Iris Marion Young emphasizes that the idea of an essential group identity that members share denies the possibility of differentiation within and across groups, giving the example of the category of Muslim, which is in fact differentiated at least by traits such as gender or nationality.[55] To conclude, the concept of the political representation of marginalized groups raises a number of interesting and—as yet—unanswered normative questions. In the words of Kymlicka, "to date, the ideals of mirror representation and democratic accountability have not yet been adequately integrated."[56]

Representation in practice

Due to their demographic situation or to other socio-economic circumstances, and in the absence of special policies to facilitate their representation in the legislative and policy-making bodies, national minority groups run the risk of being locked out of decision-making processes. To prevent such a situation, many countries have set up a number of institutional and legal arrangements aiming towards achieving the fair representation of national minorities in legislative bodies and policy-making institutions. This section will briefly outline the most common of these arrangements, taking stock of the main advantages and disadvantages each of them presents.

Inclusion on mainstream parties lists

Often times mainstream parties choose to include on their party lists members of national minorities. The reasons for this may be found in a belief in the values of cultural diversity, or an attempt to show a commitment to equal participation, or, more pragmatically, they may hope to attract votes or other forms of political support from that respective minority. This type of representation may occur in those countries that have not adopted any special arrangements for the representation of national minorities (e.g. Slovakia, Macedonia, the Czech Republic); in such cases, national minorities must either face the same electoral threshold as mainstream parties or, alternatively, their presence on mainstream party lists may permit representation in the legislature.

While such an arrangement provides the minority group with descriptive representatives present in the legislative bodies, which may in turn determine the minority's desired policy changes, a number of critiques point towards certain disadvantages of this system of representation. First, where elections take place on party lists, it may be that the minority itself has little control as to the representative who is nominated on the list; instead, it would be the party who would decide on this issue. Second, inclusion of one or more members of a national minority on a party list may be nothing more than a symbolic gesture without practical consequences for the minority group; if the nominees are inexperienced, or if their numbers are very low, their impact on policy may be insignificant. Lastly, inclusion of minority representatives on party lists may not work in the case of minorities which are negatively perceived by majorities (such as the Roma), as parties might not want to be associated with them. This has become particularly obvious in the countries of Eastern Europe, where despite the presence of significant Roma populations, there are very few nominees of Roma background included on mainstream party lists.

Ethnic parties

Fundamentally, all definitions of ethnic parties underscore the importance of the ethnic element in the electorate, leadership, electoral platform, or its external descriptors. For instance, Donna Lee Van Cott puts forward a comprehensive definition of an ethnic party, pointing towards several indicators; her definition includes the party's authorization to run in elections, the ethnic belonging of both party membership and leadership, and the centrality of ethnic or cultural demands in the party's electoral platform.[57] Indeed, a party may be ascribed to the category of 'ethnic party' based on its external descriptors. The most obvious of these is the party's name; if the name of a party includes a reference to an ethnic group, then we may safely assume that the party promotes the interests of that group and therefore classify it as an ethnic party.[58] The symbols associated with a party are also revealing: the flag, electoral logo, colors, and clothing.

Concerning the ethnic background of the leadership, Kanchan Chandra distinguishes between an ethnic identity as self-activated by the leader (where the leader declares to belong to a certain identity) and one activated by others (where the leader's ethnic identity is ascribed by other people).[59] In terms of the membership of an ethnic party, the literature on ethnic parties agrees that these parties primarily limit their appeal to a well-defined constituency, rather than seeking to broaden their appeal outside the ethnic group. In this respect, Donald Horowitz argues that since an ethnic party derives its support from a particular ethnic group, and in return serves the interests of that group, "the test of an ethnic party is simply the distribution of support",[60] while Gunther and Diamond conclude that "a purely ethnic party seeks only to mobilize the votes of its own ethnic group."[61]

Concerning the ideology promoted by ethnic parties, scholars observed that ethnic parties generally display a low level of ideological or programmatic commitment and that instead of promoting a particular ideology they focus on obtaining cultural, political, or material benefits for the ethnic groups they represent.[62] While widely recognized as one of the most important means through which ethnic minorities can pursue their interests, scholars have found that ethnic parties also present the risk of ethnic outbidding. Horowitz, in his discussion of ethnic outbidding, identifies the origins of this process in various sources of discontent inside the ethnic group: opposition factions inside the group may appear as a result of perceived lack of intra-ethnic competition,[63] or when members are no longer satisfied with the political direction of the leadership.[64] With little scope for new supporters outside the limits of the constituency, challenger parties are incentivized to claim they present a 'purer' ethnic alternative, thus producing a mechanism of ethnic outbidding.[65] This in turn presents the potential for ethnic conflict, as majorities may find the claims and requests of such challenger parties as threatening to the existing order of things.

Inclusion and power-sharing

As mentioned above, the 1999 OSCE Lund Recommendations on the Effective Participation of National Minorities in Public Life put forward a set of concrete options for improving the participation of these groups in the decision-making processes. Among these, one option which is much favored by governments is to set up advisory bodies, acting as channels for dialogue between national minorities and national governments. These bodies normally consist of representatives of national minorities, and are consulted on matters that impinge on the interests of these communities. As often the legislation provides that it is compulsory for governments to consult these bodies prior to instituting any policy that might affect the interests of national minorities, consultative or advisory bodies are an important means to ensure that national minorities have a say in policy making. However, critiques of this type of arrangement point towards the fact that sometimes such bodies are financially dependent on governments, making them less inclined to be critical of the decisions taken. Another criticism relates to the fact that governments sometimes perform these consultations only symbolically, without engaging in meaningful debate and negotiation with these advisory bodies.

Another option for increasing the level of political representation of national minority groups is to create reserved seats in legislatures for national minorities. In Eastern Europe this is a fairly common procedure, whereby certain minority groups are guaranteed parliamentary representation. As outlined in section II of this chapter, this type of descriptive representation raises the question of which minorities are to be included among those represented descriptively. For instance, Slovenia reserves two seats in the National Assembly for its Italian and Hungarian minorities, but not for the Roma minority, while Montenegro secures a reserved seat to those minorities amounting to between 1 and 5% of the total population, while minorities over 5% of the total population benefit from three reserved seats.

Reduced electoral thresholds are also a fairly common option, whereby parties representing ethnic minorities are allowed to enter legislatures under more relaxed conditions than mainstream parties. The electoral legislations in Denmark, Germany, Italy, Poland, and Romania present various exemptions to the general threshold for accessing national Parliaments; as in the case of the reserved seats option, this arrangement requires criteria for deciding which minority groups should be included.

In those cases where a minority group is situated within a specific geographical region, territorial autonomy may be a compromise solution whereby legislative and executive powers are shared between the central states and the respective national minority. Such a compromise on the one hand preserves the integrity of a state, while at the same time ensures the minority's self-government in the respective region. The classic example of a successful territorially autonomous region is that of South Tyrol in Italy, which is often presented as a model for settling interethnic conflicts and for the successful protection of linguistic minorities.

National cultural autonomy is a concept developed in the 19th Century by Otto Bauer and Karl Renner, as a proposed arrangement for managing the multiple and often conflicting claims of the nations living in the Austro-Hungarian Empire. Under the arrangement proposed by them, on the one hand, historic crown lands or provinces would be recognized as central elements in a system of territorial federalism. On the other hand, power would also be devolved to a national council (consisting of elected representatives) of each nation, particularly in matters pertaining to education, culture, the arts, sciences, museums.[66] While the practical application of their theories was limited, some of the arrangements proposed by Renner and Bauer appear to have become particularly useful in recent years as a means to accommodate ethnic diversity in modern societies in the form of non-territorial autonomy or cultural autonomy. Such an arrangement refers to a devolution of political powers to national minorities on a non-territorial basis and through voluntary individual affiliation, and presents a series of advantages: it can be used in the case of both regionally concentrated and dispersed groups; it protects minorities against coercive assimilation by regionally dominant groups; and it formally acknowledges the multinational character of a state without giving rise to territorial claims.[67] Examples of such non-territorial arrangements are the minority governments set up in Hungary or Serbia, wherein national minorities exercise a relatively high degree of control over political, educational, cultural, and socio-economic issues.

Social movements and Roma participation

Sometimes certain groups in society find themselves unable to achieve a desired outcome through conventional channels (e.g. by petitioning the government) and instead attempt to achieve their goals in an alternative manner, through grassroots activism. In this respect, social movements have occasionally emerged as a means through which marginalized groups could achieve their goals and induce the changes they desired in society.

Social movements

A social movement results from the more or less spontaneous coming together of people whose relationships are not defined by rules and procedures, but who pursue a common goal. While social movements are notoriously hard to define and analyze, they have been characterized as being neither a political party nor an interest group, which are stable political entities that have regular access to political power and political elites; but neither are they a mass fad or trend, which are unorganized, fleeting and without goals. Instead, they appear to be situated somewhere in between.[68]

Scholars have also attempted to discern the elements that are conducive to the formation of a social movement. In this respect, Jo Freeman identified four essential elements involved in movement formation: (1) the growth of a pre-existing communications network that is (2) cooptable to the ideas of the new movement; (3) a series of crises that galvanize into action people involved in a cooptable network, and/or (4) subsequent organizing effort to weld the spontaneous groups together into a movement.[69] All definitions of social movement reflect the notion that social movements are intrinsically related to social change, reflecting the belief that people can collectively bring about social change if they dedicate themselves to the pursuit of a common goal.[70]

The civil rights movement in the US is perhaps the best-known example of a social movement. The general goal of this movement, which was at its most active in the 1950s and 1960s, was to achieve equality for African Americans; in particular, the movement sought to obtain freedom from discrimination, equal access to public facilities, employment, education and housing, and the right to vote. The movement, although not entirely successful (i.e. while it managed to change legislation, it did not manage to entirely remove *de facto* inequality, such as economic inequality), did transform American society. Racial discrimination and segregation were abolished, African Americans obtained the right to vote and be elected to public office, and education became available to all regardless of race or ethnic background. As such, this social movement is a good example of how a marginalized group can reach its goals through grassroots activism, thus inducing the social changes it desires.

Participation of the Roma

A chapter focusing on the participation and empowerment of national minorities in Europe would not be complete in the absence of a brief discussion of the situation of the Roma minority. A heterogeneous minority with multiple cultural and socio-economic subgroups, highly dispersed geographically, facing high levels of marginalization, discrimination and sometimes segregation, the situation of the Roma minority presents some of the most difficult challenges to policy makers.

Political representation and participation of the Roma are at particularly low levels. Given the highly fragmented political environment of this minority, Roma parties have great difficulties in passing electoral thresholds, resulting in few—or, in some cases, zero—Roma representatives in national parliaments. The problem is compounded by the fact that the Roma do not have a kin state to help pressure governments to adopt more effective policies for this minority; as a result, even where governments have adopted policies to promote the participation of national minorities in public life, they are usually ineffective or insufficient for the adequate representation of the Roma minority.

With limited political participation and representation at the national level, there is a degree of organisation at a transnational level, with the Roma National Congress and the International Romani Union attempting to provide visibility and representation throughout Europe. Such organizations however have had limited success so far, facing criticism of being elitist and removed from the constituencies they claim to represent.[71] Most advocacy work at the European level is carried out by organizations such as the European Roma Rights Centre, the Open Society Institute—Roma Participation Programme, and the European Roma Information Office; while effective, these are not Roma grassroots organizations, and cannot be said to be representative of the Roma communities. As such, for the time being the prospects for improved Roma participation through conventional channels remain limited. The question that might be asked is whether there are sufficient grassroot actors, interest, and mobilization for the Roma to become a social movement and to push for social change in this manner. For now, although there are many grassroot organizations and initiatives advocating for Roma rights, issues of representation, political fragmentation, and lack of coordination render such a possibility to appear, at the present time, remote. We ask, therefore, in the last chapter how public authorities may ensure better participation and integration of groups that are not collectively strong.

Key points

- Representative democracy, while the most widespread form of democracy today, poses a number of dilemmas, such as determining the relationship between the representative and his/her constituency, or determining the best way to ensure the fair representation of marginalized groups.
- Representation, participation, and the empowerment of national minorities are interrelated concepts, fundamental for ensuring that national minorities have a voice in the legislative and policy-making process, enabling them to decide on important issues having an impact on their lives.
- Descriptive representation of marginalized groups appears as the most widespread arrangement for political representation of marginalized groups; while the advantages of such a system of representation have been widely emphasized, there are certain risks associated with it which need to be understood and addressed.
- In examining the role fulfilled by a minority representative, there are certain categories of representation (descriptive, symbolic, formalistic, substantive) that help us guide our analysis.
- Participation in public life can be achieved through a variety of practical arrangements, such as inclusion on mainstream party lists, eth-

nic parties, advisory or consultative bodies, reserved seats in legislatures, reduced electoral thresholds, non-territorial or territorial autonomy.
- Social movements represent a further option for advancing the interests of marginalized groups, with the civil rights movement in the US being one of the best-known examples.
- The Roma minority in Europe faces some of the most difficult challenges in ensuring fair representation and effective participation; so far, in the case of this minority, existing mechanisms for representation and participation have proved inadequate.

Further reading

BARANY, ZOLTAN D. *The East European Gypsies: Regime Change, Marginality, and Ethnopolitics*. Cambridge: Cambridge University Press, 2002.
BOCHSLER, DANIEL. "Electoral Rules and the Representation of Ethnic Minorities in Post-Communist Democracies", in *European Yearbook of Minority Issues*, edited by EURAC and ECMI 7 (2007/2008). Leiden and Boston: Martinus Nijhoff (2010), pp. 153–180.
BRUSIS, MARTIN. "The European Union and Interethnic Power-Sharing Arrangements in Accession Countries", *Journal on Ethnopolitics and Minority Issues in Europe* 4 (2003), pp. 1–19.
CHANDRA, KANCHAN. "Ethnic Parties and Democratic Stability", *Perspectives on Politics* 3 (2005), pp. 235–252.
DIAMOND, LARRY and RICHARD GUNTHER, eds. *Political Parties and Democracy*. Baltimore and London: The Johns Hopkins University Press, 2001.
ISHIYAMA, JOHN and MARIJKE BREUNING. "What is in a Name? Ethnic Party Identity and Democratic Development in Post-Communist Politics", *Party Politics* 17 (2011), pp. 223–241.
ISHIYAMA, JOHN T. and MARIJKE BREUNING. *Ethnopolitics in the New Europe*. Boulder: Lynne Riener, 1998.
MCGARRY, AIDAN. "Ambiguous nationalism? Explaining the Parliamentary Under-Representation of Roma in Hungary and Romania", *Romani Studies* 19 (2009), pp. 103–124.
STEIN, JONATHAN P., ed. *The Politics of National Minority Participation in Post-Communist Europe*. New York: M.E. Sharpe, 2000.
STEWART, MICHAEL., ed. *The Gypsy "Menace."* London: Hurst, 2012.

Notes

1. Council of Europe, Art. 15 of the 1995 *Framework Convention for the Protection of National Minorities*, accessed July 15, 2013, http://conventions.coe.int/Treaty/en/Treaties/Html/157.htm.
2. OSCE, *The Lund Recommendations on the Effective Participation of National Minorities in Public Life*, 1999. accessed July 15, 2013, http://www.osce.org/hcnm/32240?download=true.
3. Alexis de Tocqueville, *Democracy in America and Two essays on America* (London : Penguin, 2003).
4. See Thomas Christiano, "Democratic Equality and the Problem of Persistent Minorities", *Philosophical Papers* 23 (1994).
5. J. Roland Pennock, "Political Representation: An Overview", in *Representation*, eds. J. Roland Pennock and John W. Chapman (New York : Atherton, 1968), pp. 3–27.
6. Edmund Burke, "Speech to the Electors at Bristol at the Conclusion of the Poll", quoted in Jon Elster: *Deliberative Democracy* (Cambridge: Cambridge University Press, 1998), p. 3.
7. Pennock, op. cit., note 5, p. 15.
8. Hanna Fenichel Pitkin, *The Concept of Representation* (Berkeley, Los Angeles, London: University of California Press, 1972), p. 165.
9. Andrew Roberts, *The Quality of Democracy in Eastern Europe. Public Preferences and Policy Reforms* (Cambridge: Cambridge University Press, 2010), pp. 31–33.
10. Anne Phillips, "Democracy and Difference: Some Problems for Feminist Theory", The Political Quarterly 63 (1992), pp. 79–80.
11. Pitkin, op. cit., note 8, p. 92.
12. Melissa Williams, *Voice, Trust, and Memory. Marginalised Groups and the Failings of Liberal Representation* (Princeton: Princeton University Press, 1998), pp. 15–16.
13. Ibid., p. 3.
14. Carole Pateman, *Participation and Democratic Theory* (Cambridge: Cambridge University Press, 1970), p. 2.
15. Sidney Verba, *Democracy in America* (Chicago: University of Chicago Press, 1972), p. 1.
16. Ibid., pp. 46–47.
17. Archon Fung, *Varieties of Participation in Complex Governance*, "Theorizing Democratic Renewal." (workshop, University of British Columbia, Vancouver, Canada, June 10–11, 2005), p. 6.
18. Tove H. Malloy, "National Minorities between Protection and Empowerment: Towards a Theory of Empowerment", (Concept Paper Prepared for the *ECPR Joint Sessions*, Mainz, Germany, 2013), p. 3.
19. World Bank, *What is Empowerment?*, accessed July 15, 2013, http://web.worldbank.org/WBSITE/EXTERNAL/TOPICS/EXTPOVERTY/EXTEMPOWERMENT/0,,contentMDK:20272299~pagePK:210058~piPK:210062~theSitePK:486411~isCURL:Y,00.html.
20. Jane Mansbridge, "What Does a Representative Do? Descriptive Representation in Communicative Settings of Distrust, Uncrystallized Interests, and Historically Denigrated Status", in *Citizenship in Diverse Societies*, eds. Will Kymlicka and Wayne Norman (Oxford: Oxford University Press, 2000), p. 106.
21. Ibid.
22. Ibid., p. 105.
23. Williams, op.cit., note 12, pp. 176–177.
24. Jane Mansbridge, "Should Blacks Represent Blacks and Women Represent Women? A Contingent Yes", *The Journal of Politics* 61 (1999), p. 639.
25. Will Kymlicka, *Multicultural Citizenship* (Oxford: Oxford University Press, 1996), pp. 77–78.
26. Ibid.
27. Ibid., pp. 144–145.

28 Pitkin, op. cit., note 8, p. 81.
29 Ibid, p. 90.
30 Ibid., pp. 86–87.
31 Iris Marion Young, *Inclusion and Democracy* (Oxford: Oxford University Press, 2002), p. 133.
32 Pitkin, op. cit., note 8, p. 110.
33 Anthony D. Smith, *The Ethnic Origins of Nations* (Oxford: Blackwell Publishers, 1996), p. 15.
34 Eric Hobsbawm, "Introduction: Inventing Traditions, " in *The Invention of Tradition*, eds. Eric Hobsbawm and Terence Ranger (Cambridge: Cambridge University Press, 1983), pp. 1–14.
35 Pitkin, op. cit., note 8, p. 139.
36 Ibid., p. 58.
37 Ibid., p. 38.
38 Ibid., p. 59.
39 Mansbridge, op.cit., note 24, p. 630.
40 Mansbridge, op.cit., note 24, p. 629.
41 Claudine Gay, "Spirals of Trust? The Effect of Descriptive Representation on the Relationship between Citizens and Their Government", *American Journal of Political Science* 46 (2002), p. 718.
42 Mansbridge, op.cit., note 24, p. 635.
43 Young, op.cit., note 31, pp. 147–148.
44 See Banducci, Susan A. et al., "Minority Representation, Empowerment, and Participation", *The Journal of Politics* 66 (2004), pp. 534–556 ; Bobo, Lawrence and Franklin D. Gilliam, 1990. "Race, Sociopolitical Participation, and Black Empowerment", *American Political Science Review* 84 (1990), pp. 377–393.
45 See John D. Griffin and Michael Keane, "Descriptive Representation and the Composition of African American Turnout", *American Journal of Political Science* 50 (2006), pp. 998–1012.
46 See Robert R. Preuhs, "The Conditional Effects of Minority Descriptive Representation: Black Legislators and Policy Influence in the American States", *The Journal of Politics* 68 (2006), pp. 585–599.
47 See Charles Cameron, David Epstein, and Sharyn O'Halloran, "Do Majority-Minority Districts Maximize Substantive Black Representation in Congress?", *American Political Science Review* 90 (1996), pp. 794–812.
48 Mansbridge, op.cit., note 24, pp. 630–633.
49 Mansbridge, op.cit., note 24, p. 640.
50 Pitkin, op. cit., note 8, p. 89.
51 Williams, op.cit., note 12, p. 6.
52 Williams, op.cit., note 12, p. 7.
53 Mansbridge, op.cit. note 20, p. 108.
54 Ibid.
55 Young, op.cit., note 31, p. 88.
56 Ibid.
57 Donna Lee Van Cott, *From Movements to Parties in Latin America: The Evolution of Ethnic Politics* (Cambridge: Cambridge University Press, 2005), p. 3.
58 Kanchan Chandra, "What is an Ethnic Party?", Party Politics 17 (2011), p. 159.
59 Ibid., p. 165.
60 Donald Horowitz, *Ethnic Groups in Conflict* (Berkeley and London: University of California Press, 1985), p. 293.
61 Gunther, Richard and Larry Diamond, "Species of Political Parties: A New Typology", *Party Politics* 9 (2003), p. 183.
62 Ibid., p. 183.

63 Horowitz, op.cit., note 60, p. 335.
64 Ibid., p. 343.
65 Ibid., p. 293.
66 Otto Bauer, *The Question of Nationalities and Social Democracy* (Minneapolis and London: University of Minnesota Press, 2000), pp. 259–308.
67 Rainer Bauböck, "Territorial or Cultural Autonomy for National Minorities?." *IWE–Working Paper Series* 22 (December 2001), accessed August 1, 2013, http://eif.univie.ac.at/downloads/workingpapers/IWE-Papers/WP22.pdf).
68 Jo Freeman and Victoria Johnson, *Waves of protest: Social movements since the sixties* (Lanham, Maryland: Rowman & Littlefield, 1999).
69 Ibid., pp. 7–24.
70 Encyclopedia Britannica, Entry on "Social Movements", accessed August 1, 2013, http://www.britannica.com/EBchecked/topic/551335/social-movement.
71 Aidan McGarry, *Who Speaks for the Roma. Political Representation of a Transnational Minority Community* (New York: Continuum, 2010).

Chapter 10: Diversity management

Alexander Osipov

Summary

Diversity management is a concept highly relevant to minority studies. It is defined as a top-down policy tool deliberately aimed at shaping and regulating the ethnic, cultural or heterogeneity of societies and the social relations which result from diversity. The rather generic term, diversity management, concerns a variety of ways in which the governments perceive ethnic, racial or linguistic diversity and strive to manage it. Diversity policies are centred on social categories and the meanings that governments and societies assign to them. Diversity policies can be conceptualised and legitimised in different ways and are carried out for different purposes with different legal and political tools within numerous areas of public policy and administration. The effectiveness of diversity policies and their unintended outcomes are still underexplored areas and pose a challenge for academic analysis.

Introduction

Given that public authorities possess multiple resources and levers, which may be used to cause some kind of effect on respective societies, domestic policies must be regarded as a central issue within the broad domain of minority issues and ethnic relations. The topic of diversity management, or diversity policies, requires making use of a few related disciplinary outlooks and can be better grasped through synergies between political science, law and sociology. This Chapter seeks to provide a general overview of the topic, the major policy areas of primary interest for the study of diversity issues and of the major analytical perspectives involved therein. The explanation involves different disciplinary perspectives; since the core issue concerns the construction of social categories and the linkages between discourses and practices, it centres on the sociological approach. The issues to be addressed include considerations on the definition and scope of diversity management, the meaning of ethnicity or culture-based categories, the rationales, strategies and tools of diversity management, its context-dependence and the limits of its effectiveness.

Diversity management can be defined as a policy deliberately aimed at shaping and regulating social relations pertinent to the ethnic, cultural or racial heterogeneity of society. Such policies are pursued on different conceptual grounds, and the approaches employed cannot be confined to minority protection alone. There is a need for a broad generic term, and as such here we use both 'diversity management' and 'diversity policy' as synonyms. It should be made clear from the outset that there is yet no uniform and commonly accepted terminology for this area of public policy. Diversity management is also used in business administration referring to the recruitment and promotion of employees of different ethnic and cultural backgrounds for the purpose of increasing the corporate efficacy.[1] However, diversity management has, since the 1990s, increasingly come to refer to domestic policies aimed at and concerning societal ethnic or cultural heterogeneity. It is in this sense that the term is employed throughout the Chapter. Diversity management must be regarded thus as an artificial intellectual construct, an analytical tool, or an ideal type introduced to encompass politics with certain common features. There is no single or commonly accepted understanding what diversity management is about and no standard terminology.[2]

Policy-makers and legal professionals alike do not necessarily approach the regulation of diversity as a single and specific area of human activities. International treaties concerning non-discrimination, minority protection and cultural diversity oblige states to guarantee some rights and liberties crucial for minorities (such as the freedom of association or the right to private life) and to take certain proactive measures for the promotion of equality and the preservation of minority cultures. In sum, these obligations may be treated as a distinct type of policy, but international instruments as such remain silent on the issue of how these policies are comprehended, structured, developed and named. Accordingly, national constitutions and laws contain provisions that directly or indirectly envisage a proactive role of governments in the treatment of ethnic and cultural diversity, but few countries use special naming for such a policy. The idea of a comprehensive 'nationalities policy' was elaborated in the Soviet Union, which needed to mobilise its multi-ethnic population for the radical social and economic transformations it underwent.[3] Still today the idea persists in the USSR successor states and some other former socialist countries. Another example is Canada and Australia, which unite their aboriginal, immigrant and anti-discrimination policies under the tag of 'multiculturalism'.

Furthermore, a few scholars also address diversity policies as a specific and distinguishable set of practices or phenomena. Those who use this notion often understand it broadly, as the entire process of nation-building or the general guarantees of human and civil rights.[4] This lack of a uniform and clear vision is quite understandable. Many decisions and actions of public authorities may have an unequal effect on different ethnic or cultural groups; this (real or imaginary) unequal effect may be interpreted by external observers in different ways and quite often as outputs of deliberate strategies and measures. Correspondingly, the notion of diversity may gain a virtually unlimited scope of application. Conditionally we can regard diversity management (or diversity policy) as activities of public authorities which meet three criteria: (1) they are expected to shape ethnic, cultural or racial heterogeneity in a certain way; (2) they are aimed at this deliberately; (3) they are of a systematic and institutionalised character.

Activities, which we conventionally call diversity management, may vary in purposes, scope, form and content; the issues, important for one country, might be perceived as irrelevant for another one. The decisive factor is the agendas that the ruling elites recognise and which are eventually dependent on the given country's demographic composition, migration patterns, international relations, economic situation, political institutions and other circumstances. Diversity management in certain countries may rest on different values and aspirations, which may include or exclude certain areas of social relations and public management. Diversity can imply different attitudes towards heterogeneity as a problem or asset and may be subject to the idea of creating a culturally homogeneous society or to the maintenance or differences.

It is important when attempting to adequately describe diversity policies to draw a distinction between practical and analytical categories.[5] The former are used by policy-makers and other actors directly involved in the process; the latter are employed by external observers and analysts who are ideally supposed to distance themselves from the vocabulary of the observed social environment. The main difference between the two categories is that while scholars in principle agree to a certain term's meaning and on the modes and limits of its application, one cannot mediate and manage the meanings of practical categories. This is mainly because the latter reflect relations of power and authority, and are overloaded with implications dependent upon the given context. For example, the term 'minority' taken as an analytical category may depict a certain demographic composition (by juxtaposition to a large 'majority' and numerically smaller minorities). The term may also be used when analysing a pattern of domestic policy (a special treatment of designated groups). As a practical category, that which we label 'minorities' may bear numerous hidden meanings. For instance, when we analyse the right of a government to decide who is entitled to be an acknowledged as a (national) minority and who is not, in terms of the distinction between welcomed 'traditional minorities' and unwelcomed 'migrants' (or, conversely, 'indigenous populations'), as well as when we analyse the right to have a say in public space or not, and so forth. In the attempt to grasp the logic and aims of concrete agents' behaviour, analysts are to distance themselves from the practical vocabulary; otherwise they are likely to become constrained by it.

It is also important to note the difference between so-called instrumental and symbolic policies.[6] There is no clear boundary between the types; the principal distinction is that instrumental policies directly concern the distribution of power and wealth in a given society, while symbolic policies produce interpretations and descriptions of those relations. Naming or recognition of certain ethnic groups (a symbolic policy) does not necessarily mean that those groups will be treated differently and granted or denied certain privileges and resources (instrumental policies); on the contrary, actual discrimination in favour of or against certain categories or measures which are meant to support of certain cultures and languages (instrumental policies) will be publicly acknowledged, articulated or justified (symbolic policies).

Practical conceptualizations of diversity

There is no common or widely accepted—either practical or theoretical— understanding of what diversity is. One may say that a common feature of almost all approaches to the understanding and description of social heterogeneity apply the category of 'group'. In other words, diversity is usually understood (explicitly or tacitly) as the co-existence of different human collectives (peoples, minorities, races or nations), and this implies the existence of inter-group boundaries, individual affiliations with groups and intra-group cohesion. In practical terms, racial, ethnic, national, and linguistic categories are applied as changeable meanings which are dependent on the given social context, including a country or geographic region. Correspondingly, domestic policies are affected by the mainstream interpretations of how diversity is manifested.

Some countries (first and foremost the United States), but also international organisations, employ racial categories. In academia, for centuries, 'race' meant the division of humankind on the criteria of biological traits and features of human physical appearance. During the 20th Century, biology and anthropology rejected the idea of 'race' as a biologically distinct category, as all human beings belong to the same species, and certain minor genetic and physical differences do not overlap and create distinct collectives.[7] More often, the term race is used to serve as a practical category. During the times of the trans-Atlantic slave-trade, slavery within the Americas and later during colonialism, race was a tool to singling out subjugated and exploited groups and keeping them segregated and under social control. Since then the meaning of the term has changed. In the United States, it refers officially to a person's origin and delineates categories which need protection from discrimination. In international organisations, primarily within the United Nations (UN), race in the context of 'racial discrimination' or 'racism', serves as a generic term for the differentiation of people on a variety of criteria and also for the protection from discrimination.

The word 'nation' is understood in two major modalities: as *demos*, the population of a country or unity of its citizens regardless of their origin, or as a group based on kin or culture. The latter interpretation is usually called ethnic nationalism; it barely exists in pure forms,[8] but its elements are more specific to Eastern and Central rather than Western Europe or North America. The ethnic interpretation of nation also generated a certain understanding of 'nationality' which in Central and Eastern Europe and the former Soviet Union refers to ethnic affiliation. A similar meaning bears the term 'national origin' in the United States where it is used for statistical purposes and as a legal basis for prohibiting discrimination. Accordingly, the term 'people' bears two major meanings, and in its ethnic interpretation remains in use in the former Soviet Union and some successor states of the former Yugoslavia,[9] as well as in its reference to indigenous groups.

The word 'ethnicity' and the adjective 'ethnic' were introduced into European academic language during the 1960s, partly as a replacement for racial categories.[10] Since then, ethnic has become a broad term for naming multiple categories based on national origin, culture, traditions or language. Individual ethnic affiliation in some cases is ascribed by scholars or governments; in other cases it rests on self-identification. The adjective ethnic has been introduced within some international instruments: the 1992 UN Declaration on the Rights of Persons Belonging to Minorities refers to national, *ethnic*, linguistic and religious minorities, while the International Convention on the Elimination of All forms of Racial Discrimination prohibits discrimination based, among other grounds, on *ethnic* origin. At the national level, ethnic is more often used in the former communist countries, even in domestic legislation. In that region, it often serves to draw a distinction between national and ethnic minorities, i.e. those who do have a 'kin-state' outside their country of residence.

There is a common belief that language is the most visible and clearly identifiable attribute of an ethnic group. However, a single ethnic category may traditionally have more than one separate language (for example, Mordovians, a people living in Central Russia, speak two different codified Finnish languages; the Sami, who live in the Nordic countries, use ten different languages). Other ethnicities may share one common language. Moreover, an ethnic group may in practical terms be bi- or trilingual, and the mother tongue or the first language spoken by a person may differ from the language this person speaks at home or at the workplace. Nevertheless, the common sense assumption that a language is an attribute of an ethnic group persists even among policy-makers and experts. The categorization of people on linguistic criteria thus can be done on different grounds and mean different things. Sometimes, the designation of a 'linguistic community' may be a synonym for 'ethnic community' (Belgium and Finland are examples), and belonging to a language group may be recognized on the criteria of origin rather than language used in daily life (such as in the case of Francophone or Anglophone minorities in Canadian provinces and territories).

The word 'culture' also has multiple and changeable meanings, as discussed in Chapter 4. The social sciences have listed hundreds of definitions of what the term may mean.[11] Since the 1950–60s some sociologists offered culture as a replacement for racial categories, and since then the formulation of 'cultural group' is used as a denominator for ethnic, national, linguistic or religious categories.[12] This approach reflects a common belief that culture may be regarded as a sharply defined and specific substance affiliated with a certain group and distinguishable from similar substances of other groups. Cultural groups do not figure as legal terms, but this notion is, for example, widely employed during political debates. A major implication in this context is that limiting of ethnic or minority issues to narrowly understood issues of cultural affairs may also serve a certain purpose which may be designed to keep minorities outside the political domain.

Group categorization, i.e. the official naming and acknowledgement of groups, is always a complex and often a controversial issue. Some countries have set up a certain legally defined system of terminology (such as the US or

Canada); some use eclectic and unclear wording (like Russia or Ukraine); some list individually recognised minorities or draw clear distinctions between different types of categories (as the Nordic countries do) while some employ a flat and generic approach (as in Belarus, which does not distinguish between minorities and immigrant groups). There are numerous cases when governments will explicitly refuse to acknowledge the very existence of certain groups as separate ethnicities or minorities; for example, Turkey still refrains from recognizing Kurds as a distinct people or nation, and Ukraine avoids regarding Carpathian Rusyns (who speak a dialect of Ukrainian) as a minority group. Official recognition belongs to the domain of symbolic policies, but in practical terms it becomes important because it has a direct effect on the self-esteem of individuals and creates a platform for claim-making on behalf of minorities and for further negotiations.

The idea of a 'group' (notwithstanding whether it is defined as ethnic, racial or linguistic) implies something that consists of individuals whose membership must rest upon certain criteria and must manifest itself in some routine interactions. Public recognition of a group does not necessarily require and entail registration or acknowledgement of a person's ethnic affiliation. A mandatory record of an individual's ethnicity or race in official documents was practiced in the framework of colonial rule, apartheid, fascist and communist regimes. Currently, international legal norms in principle state that ethnic affiliation with or belonging to a national minority must be a matter of individual choice which shall not entail any negative consequences for a person. A number of national constitutions also contain similar provisions. In practice, governments gather general information about the composition of their populace for administrative purposes through impersonal censuses or surveys.

In modern societies, mandatory assignment of ethnicity is a rare exception; and is practiced for the most part in a few former communist countries (such as Kazakhstan). National legislation in a few countries also envisages the voluntary recording of an individual's ethnicity on the basis of self-identification. A specific case is registering persons belonging to indigenous populations in North America and South Pacific because this status entails certain privileges. Belonging to officially recognised racial statistical categories (Whites, Native Americans, Blacks, Pacific Islanders, Asians and in some contexts Hispanics)[13] is fixed on a voluntary basis, but recording of this information in numerous official forms has become a routine procedure which most people do not avoid. In Europe, fixation of individual racial or ethnic belonging, even in impersonal statistic databases, is generally viewed as non-acceptable. Exceptions are rare, and they concern post-conflict settlement such as the power-sharing arrangements and proportional allocation of jobs in public sector in Bosnia and Herzegovina[14] and South Tyrol. The Italian autonomous province of South Tyrol (Trentino—Alto Adidge, or Südtirol) has instituted the practice of keeping linguistic community registers for German- Italian- and Ladin-speakers, and all inhabitants of the province are obliged to make periodic declarations on which community they opt to belong to.[15]

Although maintaining lists or any other official recognition of individual ethnic or racial affiliation are rare cases, this does not mean that people are able to choose whatever ethnicity they may wish to identify with. This choice is usually restricted by non-official and informal mechanisms: all humans are dependent on their social environments and on the web of interactions they are involved in; the manifestation of this or that ethnicity a person may self-identify with makes little if any sense if the surrounding society does not recognise the person as such. Governments can nevertheless affect individual ethnic affiliations. In some rare cases there are formal qualifications set up for claiming membership of an ethnic group (in most cases it concerns belonging to indigenous groups). More often, official authorities can indirectly encourage or discourage affiliation with minorities, the respective tools being the recognition or non-recognition of certain groups and domestic educational and linguistics policies. An even more effective device on behalf of governments is deciding upon engaging in a certain level of cooperation with ethnic activists who often acquire the monopoly to speak on behalf of an entire ethnic group and to define who is entitled to participate in minority activities. For example, the governing bodies of the Hungarian and Italian minority self-governments in Slovenia are entitled to admit people as members of their minorities or deny membership.[16] In Hungary, only people nominated by minority NGOs may stand for the office at the elections to minority councils.[17]

Major frames of diversity management

There are no theories or comprehensive normative models of diversity management. A correct manner in which to bring the existing approaches in the system together is to do it through the notion of a 'frame'. This term, recently accepted by sociology and political science, still lacks a clear meaning. Usually, it refers to an angle for the viewing and contextualization of certain phenomena or the perspective to identify and set up an agenda.[18] One can conditionally single out several frames within diversity management, and the major ones are (1) minority protection, (2) non-discrimination, and (3) compounded statehood, such as federalism. There are also other ways to label and discursively organize diversity policies; these rest on eclectic or fuzzy approaches. The three major frames, although partly overlapping and lacking a uniform application, differ nevertheless in that the first two rest more or less upon clearly defined legal frameworks, while the third one is not only well elaborated within the field of political theory but is also a concept which is practiced by a number of individual states and international organizations.

Minority protection

Minority protection implies that the society in question can be divided into several distinct groups which exist in a state of asymmetric relations with each other.[19] Historically, the concept of national or ethnic minorities is derived from the idea of nation-state; minorities are in some way juxtaposed to 'nation' or 'majority', which constitutes the fundamental of the state. The notion of minority, when taken as an analytical tool, generates problems. As a descriptive model, it is supposed to reflect and lump together at least three completely different types of social relations, these being ethnic or similar categorization and statistics, power and wealth distribution and internal group cohesion and solidarity. In other words, the term minority means not only the dry numbers or arithmetic relating to people who differ from the majority, but also implies their weak or subordinate role in politics and in public life, as well as refers to the state of internal organisation of such minorities and their cohesion as a social entity. These three types of relations frequently do not go hand in hand; methods of minority categorisation are always a problem as mentioned above; it is never possible to completely disaggregate a given society into groups with fixed memberships and boundaries.

As a practical category, minority often engenders the use of power on behalf of governments. Minorities are those who the government allows to be minorities; those who are not recognised as such (for example, because they are allegedly recent migrants) are frequently denied the right to make certain claims. The idea of minority nevertheless remains in popular use, because it is already institutionalized in legal and political mechanisms and because it complies with some common sense assumptions. Indeed, when a political system is based on electoral democracy, a numerically small group cannot outvote the majority and thus has a certain need of some special protective and representative mechanisms. Along with this, if most of the population speaks one language, those who are not sufficiently fluent likely find themselves in a disadvantaged position and as such possess a need for some certain protective treatment.

Non-discrimination

According to the dominant contemporary approach, minority protection is comprised of three components; namely, that of non-discrimination, the protection and promotion of culture and participation in public life. Non-discrimination essentially refers to the enjoyment of equal rights and the equal treatment of individuals within a given society; it is widely considered to be insufficient without protecting the opportunity to preserve and promote minority identity or culture.[20] The third element, known as 'participation', refers to securing access of minority members or minority groups *per se* to public deliberations and decision-making on an equal footing with the majority.[21] Generally, the prevention and elimination of discrimination concerns many social categories, such as those based on gender, age, age or sexual orientation, along with those based on ethnicity or related grounds, but in fact non-discrimination has become one of the major frameworks of diversity management. Thus, non-discrimination overlaps partly with minority protection. A distinction can further be drawn between the two areas however, because they have different historical backgrounds, and generate discourses which place certain emphasis on different issues and evolve within different institutional environments. Most interpretations of discrimination can be summarized as distinctions made between people on certain grounds without justifiable reasons.[22] Yet, not every perspective involving an element of differentiation between people implies discrimination. Moreover, at times the identical treatment of individuals, who find themselves in substantively different positions, can be treated as certain cases of discrimination. European law, numerous national legislations, and discourse and commentary on the part of international organizations differentiate between two major types of discrimination; namely 'direct' and 'indirect' discrimination.[23] Direct discrimination occurs when individuals or organizations are treated differently due to belonging to different social categories; for example, to different ethnic or racial groups. The term 'indirect discrimination' a rule, practice or requirement that is facially neutral with regard to a certain characteristic but may in fact disadvantage people possessing certain characteristics. For example, a literacy test for voters (like the ones used in the past in the southern states of the United States) although it contains no racial qualifications would effectively bar, for example, a racial minority from politics if a high percentage of that racial group is illiterate.[24]

There is a ban on discrimination enshrined in international human rights law, in EU community law and in legislation across Europe, yet their application certainly varies greatly across states and within the wider international community. The social sciences additionally offer a broader and looser interpretation based on the idea of restricted access to resources for certain groups.[25] Non-discrimination is very important for diversity politics and policies not only because it generates certain legal instruments but also for reasons that it sets up certain public agendas and guides public discourses.

Case-law on discrimination and anti-racist civil activism in North America, and later in Europe and other parts of the world have led to the popularity of certain explanatory schemes. Social disparities between racial or ethnic categories are interpreted as being those relations between beneficiary and suppressed groups as such, also labeled as 'racism' and 'discrimination'.[26] The proposed solutions rest on the redistribution of resources and opportunities in favour of disadvantaged groups for the sake of achieving the state of so-called substantive equality understood as equality of opportunities (in a more radical version—of social outcomes). Recent interpretations of substantive equality acquire new dimensions such as the recognition, promotion and preservation of group identity, the promotion of groups' participation in public life and remedying past wrongdoings.[27]

Compound statehood

The phrase 'compound statehood' may be used for the addressing of ideas and policy devices resting upon the perception of ethnic categories as political entities and component parts of the statehood in question. Political systems based upon the recognition of several constituent groups (ethnic or otherwise) may fall apart into federalism, consociationalism or power-sharing,[28] no matter whether the constituent entities are territorially defined or not. Other frames may rest on what could be generically called 'container concepts' (such as 'multiculturalism', 'management of inter-ethnic relations', 'integration' and some others), which bear divergent or unclear meanings and implications dependent upon the particular context.

The first and the main concept, multiculturalism has pioneered recent policymaking efforts and debates on the accommodation of ethnic diversity.[29] Multiculturalism can mean different things to different people, such as a political programme, an official slogan, or a normative theory of ethno-cultural pluralism. A common element for all these kinds is rejection of the ethno-cultural homogeneity of a society as an ideal and implies the recognition of ethno-cultural diversity as an asset for social and political development. In most of its varieties, multiculturalism emphasizes culture as the essence of inter-group differences which are to be accommodated; it avoids explicit symbolic hierarchies of ethnicities and stresses the equal value of all cultures and offers public support to cultural pluralism.[30] Quite often, multiculturalism applies as an overarching term towards diversity policy in general, lumping together prohibition of discrimination, the support of multilingualism, the promotion of tolerance, the symbolic recognition of different ethnicities as founding entities of the nation-state, and other policies related to diversity. The second term, management of inter-ethnic relations, employed predominantly in some former communist countries, encompasses all possible types and areas of diversity management while offering no clear specifications. The notion of integration, which is increasingly achieving popularity, addresses predominantly immigrant issues and often has a multiplicity of implications and a variety of goals, while ultimately referring to the creation of a more cohesive and homogeneous society.[31] On integration, see further Chapter 5.

Goals and objectives

Diversity policies can be pursued for different purposes and respectfully rationalised and justified to the general public in a variety of ways. The concern voiced most often is the threat of conflicts, clashes, destabilization and ultimately the disintegration of a certain country; generically it is referred to in the literature as the "security agenda" or "securitization of minority issues."[32] Perceptions of threats and of their sources vary. Some countries may be concerned with territorial partition and separatism; others about violent clashes or the rise of radical political movements. For some, the challenge lies inside within their own borders while others fear international interference and foreign propaganda. Therefore, diversity management may be pursued for the reasons of reducing or eliminating perceived threats. A similar and partly overlapping goal can be referred to as 'nation building'. Ruling elites as a rule strive to increase the loyalty of the population to the political system and to attempt to foster compliance with some linguistic and cultural standard. In this sense, heterogeneity might be viewed as a challenge which may be approached either through homogenizing policies or by making the state system responsive and friendly to differences.

A third goal of diversity policies is closely linked with the first two described above and may serve as their extension at the practical level; it may be referred to as the pursuit of social cohesion. Countries need entire systems of governance and social institutions to be functional. This implies that members of the society can communicate with each other, that they have similar expectations in similar situations and behave according the same set of social rules; otherwise the society will likely split into segments and faces the danger of ultimate collapse. The meaning of social cohesion implies that the entirety of the populace shares the same basic values, can use a common language or languages, comply complies with the same rule of law and enjoys the same rights and opportunities. The emergence of poor, illiterate and marginalised minority groups, who are likely to become ultimately engaged in crime, or the loss of governmental control over certain localities, where the population does not speak the majority language or disrespects the official administration in favour of informal leaders, all pose a threat to the integrity and governability of society and, therefore, prompts pre-emptive or remedial measures.

Most modern countries swear allegiance to the rule of law, and some really follow this principle. Equality, first and foremost, everyone's equal status before the law, is the backbone of the modern legal systems. As described above, equality and non-discrimination are no longer interpreted exclusively as formal equality or equal treatment, but rather as fair treatment. The latter may envisage different attitudes towards individuals, groups and institutions in accordance with their actual social positions, needs or disadvantages. Those who are in a weak or vulnerable position may gain certain preferences for the enjoyment of genuine or substantive equality. This approach is advocated in modern scholarly and political debates mostly in Europe and North America and in some cases also materialise and develop in jurisprudence and positive action set up by legislative or executive power. However, there is no uniform understanding of what a weak or vulnerable position is and what the fair treatment of certain groups in a concrete situation shall be. In some cases, the government, particularly the judiciary, may lift previous restrictions or barriers detrimental to minorities and support vulnerable groups for the sake of implementing constitutional provisions on the basis of equal rights or of following the ideal of an open and tolerant society. In some cases, on the contrary, a government may justify restrictions against minorities for the sake of justice for allegedly suppressed or disadvantaged majorities. Countries which are guided by ethno-nationalist ideologies may create advantages for majority groups, and this as a rule justified as a remedy for perceived inequalities, the overcoming of illegitimate privileges undeservedly enjoyed by certain minorities. Rogers Brubaker coined the term "nationalising state" to refer to those regimes, which strive to bring multiethnic and multicultural societies in line with some ideal of a state dominated by its 'core' or 'titular' ethnicity.[33] There was a proliferation of such regimes located in Central and Eastern Europe as well as in the Middle East between the two World Wars. Today most former communist countries in Europe are pursuing such policies under the same banner.[34]

Another publicly acknowledged reason for the pursuit of diversity policies is 'restorative justice'. It refers to a return back to some ideal state of affairs or provision of compensations for previously disadvantaged categories. On the one hand, restorative justice manifests itself as an element of a nationalising state and as a way to legitimise pressure placed on minorities in one form or another; on the other hand, the same logic sometimes turns out to be favourable to minorities or vulnerable groups. Since 1960s, the executive and the judiciary in the United States has prescribed 'affirmative action' for disadvantaged racial groups, primarily African-Americans, on the grounds that such policies will help the remedying of past injustices.[35] In recent years, similar arguments have, for example, appeared in Canadian courts during presentations of cases regarding the linguistic rights of the French-speaking minorities.[36] Another case is legislation and policies aimed at the rehabilitation of ethnic groups forcibly relocated in 1930–40s (such as Crimean Tatars, Chechens or Germans) in most successor states of the former Soviet Union.

A final goal of diversity policies which is well worth mentioning here may be referred to as the objective of cultural preservation, or, in other words, the creation of conditions for the expression, maintenance and development of the cultures of certain groups. Culture, taken as an attribute of an ethnic group, is often perceived as a value in and of itself, and this means that the promotion and protection of a group's cultural features is regarded as a common agenda for the entire society in question or the whole humankind. The outcomes and concrete forms of the respective policies aiming at the protection and preservation of distinct cultures may also vary. They may target minorities or majorities and they may be dependent of how culture is understood. Cultural agendas quite often give room for political manipulation. On the one hand, those minority concerns and claims, which are unwelcomed by the ruling elite, can be bracketed and excluded from public deliberations, since they do not relate to cultural issues or do not reflect traditional cultural patterns; on the other hand, political claims may be portrayed as pertinent to the preservation of culture or identity, and this reinforces the positions of the claimants.[37]

Strategies, norms and policies

The same or similar goals of diversity accommodation can be pursued through different, even contradictory strategies. The typologies of diversity policies (however they are termed) elaborated in academia usually rest on singling out underlying strategies. The typological systems vary, but basically they are based at such dimensions as the pursuit of homogenization or at the acknowledgement and support of differences. Typologies in the scholarly literature are ranging from the full elimination or suppression of differences, to the marginalization and segregation of subordinate groups, to procedural neutrality of the state, to the acknowledgement of ethnically distinct segments and finally to the incorporation into the state of constituent autonomous elements.[38] In practice, real policies often combine elements of different strategies. This means that state agencies may treat different groups or social categories differently. For example, assimilative pressure on immigrants, or unrecognised minorities, can go hand in hand with showcasing the support for individual privileged minorities or indigenous peoples;[39] as well as generous official declarations in favour of cultural pluralism may not entail the respective practical measures, and so forth.

As a rule, the goals and strategies of diversity management are embedded within domestic legal norms. Most countries are parties to international human rights treaties which contain provisions pertinent to non-discrimination, the protection of minorities or the promotion of cultural pluralism. These provisions rarely apply directly, but they provide guidelines for national legislation processes. National constitutions stipulate the principle of equality and often the prohibition of discrimination; quite often they acknowledge the existence of minorities and the possibility to use different languages in private and sometimes in public sphere.

Normative regulation depends on the type of legal system. The continental system (to which most of the European and Asian countries belong) rests on codified law and the hierarchy of laws which set up legal norms while the norms are implemented by the executive and disputes over them are resolved in courts. In the common law countries, legal norms are created both through statutory legislation and through court decisions which set up binding legal precedents. This is particularly important in North America, the United Kingdom and the South Pacific. The U.S. Constitution and legislation lack clarity in many respects, particularly in definitions of race, discrimination or positive obligations of the state. Meanwhile, the courts have interpreted the meaning of discrimination, the limits of its prohibition, procedures for making claims about discrimination and the criteria and legitimate grounds for the imposition of affirmative action policies. The American judiciary contributed to the transformation of the dominant approaches towards discrimination: while initially it was interpreted as equal treatment of all individuals, later the emphasis was placed on remedial measures in favour of certain vulnerable groups labelled as a "protected class."[40] The American courts had a final say in deciding what types and forms of affirmative action can be allowed, and in many cases this type of measures were imposed by court orders.[41]

Far-reaching developments have recently taken place in Canada. Canadian courts have given interpretations of the grounds of discrimination, direct and indirect discrimination, and positive obligations. Moreover, the Canadian system of jurisprudence has adopted the notions of identity protection and cultural survival of language groups as legitimate grounds for making claims; it endorsed the doctrine of "institutional completeness" or the need to provide Francophone minorities with a full set of cultural, education and social institutions which would secure the group's viability as a social entity.[42] Courts in Canada and Australia have also developed a comprehensive case-law on public policies toward indigenous communities.[43]

In most other countries jurisprudence affects diversity policies to a smaller degree; diversity management is carried out by the executive plus the independent statutory and private-public bodies or non-governmental organisations which serve as public sector agents. All EU member states and almost all EU candidate countries have comprehensive anti-discrimination laws (or at least anti-discrimination provisions in sectoral laws) enacted in line with the EU Equality Directives.[44] Anti-discrimination statutes are in force in North America, the South Pacific and several countries of Africa and Asia. They cover several potential discriminatory grounds including race, skin colour and ethnic origin. Few countries have a minority-(or ethnicity) specific legislation. Canada has adopted a comprehensive Multiculturalism Act of 1988 which sets up general guidelines for diversity policies. Most countries of Central and Eastern Europe (such as Austria, Hungary, Poland, Belarus, Croatia) have laws on minorities which guarantee general human and civil rights of persons belonging to minorities and also stipulate positive obligations of the governments vis-a-vis minority institutions.

As mentioned above, few countries accept the idea of a comprehensive and co-ordinated diversity policy; respectively; there are rare cases when a country possesses an executive body with the full authority to guide all governmental activities pertinent to diversity. Several post-communist countries had instituted ministries of nationalities affairs during the first years of democratic transit after the end of the Cold War. To date, many ministries of nationalities have been transformed into lower-level departments within ministries of culture or migration affairs. There are also standalone executive bodies on minority issues (such as the Bureau of Interethnic relations in Moldova or the Plenipotentiary on Religious and Nationalities Affairs in Belarus) within the executive. Another model can be considered the development of liaison offices in between the government or the parliament on the one side, and minority associations, on the other (such as in Denmark, some German *Länder* or Austria). As a general rule, executive bodies in charge of diversity policy are agencies which do not coordinate other agencies' activities, but rather perform a consultancy role vis-a-vis the government, manage individual cultural programmes and serve as an interface between the authorities and minority organizations. Noteworthy is that responsible bodies can be established at different (national, provincial or local) levels; sometimes a relative inactivity of national authorities in ethno-cultural affairs is related to a higher degree of involvement on the side of regional or municipal authorities. Finally, some countries have developed the institution of minority ombudsperson (Finland, Hungary) or commissioner on indigenous rights (Australia); these agencies are established by the parliament and are suppose to provide general supervisory role regarding diversity policy, generate policy recommendations and consider individual complaints.[45]

The prohibition of discrimination is usually secured in courts under a civil procedure; some countries also have incorporated systems of administrative justice (the United Kingdom, Finland) or civil rights departments within executive agencies (the United States), which function under simplified procedural rules in comparison with courts of general jurisdiction. Anti-discrimination laws usually envisage the establishment of independent bodies (imbued with legal personality by the state), which exist to ensure that such laws relating to anti-discrimination and equality are properly enforced. Such bodies provide for the possibility of arbitration and reconciliation procedures instead of lawsuits wherever appropriate; they hold their own legal hearings on individual complaints; whenever possible or appropriate they represent individual litigants in courts; and finally, they engage in consultations and public awareness-raising.

Areas of application

As noted above, a wide range of legislative or administrative measures may ultimately have disparate effects on different groups. The authorities may structure their activities in a variety of ways, so one cannot say in advance that a given area can be placed within the domain of diversity management. Language policies in multi-lingual societies are probably the strongest tool that a government possess if it wants to create certain advantages or disadvantages for people because language regulations may influence political participation, access to civil service and to justice, educational opportunities, access to the labour market and so forth. Restrictive language regulations or policies of one-language-only in the public domain may bar linguistic minorities from enjoying effective participation in public life. Meanwhile, the promotion of the official language and teaching it to those who are not native speakers can be beneficial for the entire society as these measures contribute to integration and social cohesion. Policies sensitive to minority languages and the promotion of minority languages can be beneficial for political stability and may increase minorities' social mobility, but in certain circumstances such policies may also lead to the alienation or isolation of certain segments of society.

Models resting on one official language at the national level prevail in modern societies. Rarely do states intrude into the unofficial usage of minority languages in businesses or private associations. Those that allow communication in minority languages in the public domain do it in different areas, forms and degrees. For example, in some countries, people may claim and receive interpretation in their native tongue in the context of their communication with the executive or the judiciary. International human rights norms require the provision of interpreters in criminal justice system to be provided for detainees, suspects or defendants, and most countries comply with this requirement. Minority or regional languages may enjoy official status in certain autonomous regions or municipalities; they may also be present in media or in schools.

As noted, diversity policies are often subject to nation-building or the definition of how the nation or the population of the given country looks like. Citizenship and migration policies might be closely linked to diversity policies, but governments may not always portray them as culturally biased or selective. Some countries grant almost automatically citizenship rights (like Israel or Greece), or ease naturalisation procedures to those who are acknowledged by the state (in a variety of different ways) as belonging to the main or eponymous ethnicity (like Finland, Latvia or Poland). Those people may be exempted from visa and immigration requirements (Poland, Hungary) or may qualify as beneficiaries of support provided by the state to the country's ethnic diaspora (such policies are pursued by numerous countries such as Russia, Greece, Hungary, Poland, Bulgaria, Belarus). Immigration authorities may give preferences to people from certain countries which are regarded as culturally close to the recipient state (this is what the United States, Canada and Australia used to do until late 1960s or what the Netherlands or Spain are currently doing in some way). An important aspect of immigration and naturalisation processes in most countries requires the applicant's cultural and linguistic integration, i.e. command of the official language and knowledge of the country's legislation, history and culture. Ultimately, this tendency aims at maintaining the country's linguistic and cultural homogeneity.

Policies in public education are linked to diversity in two respects: the sensitivity of the educational system towards minorities' needs and the indoctrination of pupils. A government may opt for cultural pluralism in education; this may result in the official support of private or public minority schools, schools with multicultural curricula or where minority languages are taught. In its ultimate manifestations, cultural pluralism in education takes the shape of parallel or segregated school sub-systems which is often seen within compound statehoods, i.e. federations or consociational democracies. On the other hand, schooling may also be a device of cultural homogenization or assimilation. An important circumstance also to be considered relates to the dynamics of the school system since cultural or linguistic pluralism may be regarded as a transitional stage on the way to total mono-lingualism. A school curriculum may also be in danger of delivering a nationalist vision of the state if it is based on an ethnocentric interpretation of the country's history and culture without providing any room for minorities or immigrants. Having noted that, a system of teaching may also aim at the promotion of such values as tolerance, multiculturalism and human rights.

Another area is the particular administrative and territorial organization of the state. Territories inhabited with distinct ethnic or linguistic groups may under certain historical circumstances become constituent units of the federation or enjoy some degree of political, administrative or cultural autonomy. Administrative and political decentralization is often regarded by policymakers and academics as a way to make the state machinery more sensitive to minority needs and thus to help prevent or resolve conflicts whenever necessary.[46] A certain degree of territorial autonomy may allow for policies of official multilingualism, adjustment of the school curricula to the local needs, support to local cultural institutions and in some cases special representative rights within national institutions of government. Territorial arrangements based on ethnic or linguistic grounds also may bring about suspicion and criticism, if a local government of an autonomous region privileges its 'titular' ethnicity; this may potentially become a catalyst for separatist claims or may provoke new conflicts. Finally, a government can dilute or partition a compactly settled ethnic group through, for example, splitting it by redrawing internal administrative boundaries or by merging into a larger region (although such measures are prohibited, for example, by the Framework Convention for the Protection of National Minorities).

Anti-discrimination policies are usually confined to such areas as employment and labour relations, access to services, education, housing, health care and relations with public authorities.[47] As mentioned previously, the elimination of discrimination, the remedying of its consequences, the availability of compensation schemes for victims and sanctions for perpetrators are achieved though courts of general jurisdiction, administrative justice, and supervisory organs of the executive or independent anti-discrimination bodies. In addition, independent bodies may carry out general monitoring, consultancy and public awareness-raising. The configuration and competences of these subsystems vary from country to country. As a rule, the judiciary and the executive in North America and the Great Britain feature more opportunities than most of the EU member states in imposing positive obligations and affirmative action on businesses, educational authorities or public agencies in favour of disadvantaged groups.[48] EU law does not prescribe or mandate positive action to public or private institutions; positive action is recommended and exempted from the general prohibition of discrimination, but not specified. Not surprisingly, practices which fall under the definition of positive action and concern ethnic or racial groups are exceptionally rare cases in Europe.[49]

Some countries provide for the special representation of minorities or constituent ethnic groups. This is achieved through proportionate representation or, conversely, either reserved seats in parliaments (Romania, Slovenia), separate electoral lists, lowered electoral threshold for minority parties (Germany) or other electoral devices.[50] A large part of diversity policies are concerned with interactions between governmental bodies and civil society organizations. Ethnicity-based NGOs are salient manifestation of ethnicity in the public sphere, and some governments regard them as being genuine representatives or embodiments of ethnic groups. Quiet a number of countries have established consultative or advisory bodies, which as a rule are comprised of NGO spokespersons, elected on the bottom-up basis or appointed under through a top-down approach. These bodies serve as an interface between the government and ethnic groups; they are ideally supposed to deliver the concerns and views of their constituencies to official authorities and to contribute to joint decision-making processes.

Consultative and representative bodies are formed on a variety of grounds and work in different ways: there can be bodies serving one ethnic group (like Roma) or comprised of the representatives of many ethnicities; they may address all minority-related issues or a particular area of administration.[51] Some countries use a more sophisticated scheme of relationships with minority NGOs or private institutions. Hungary and the countries of Western Balkans, for example, have established minority councils which are elected by minority constituencies and which function as representative structures combining features of public bodies and non-governmental organizations; the Nordic countries apply a similar scheme for the Sami people. In some cases, public authorities delegate competences and financial resources to non-governmental organisations and other private institutions and thus authorise and empower them to perform public functions and to deliver services in the areas of culture, education and social security. Cultural projects and programmes for minorities are often carried out jointly by official bodies and minority NGOs.

Limits of state interventionism

Although there is no general or uniform model of diversity management or explanation of the reasons of minority-related policies, one may always ask the question of whether or not the presumed goals are achievable in reality. The general answer is that the theme is still underexplored and that there are no systems of measurements and indicators which would allow for the demonstration of and proving the causal linkage between the undertakings and outcomes in ethnic relations. Moreover, little scholarly attention has been paid so far to the unintended and unanticipated outcomes of diversity policies or individual measures, particularly in the long run. It would be incorrect therefore to assume the existence of a definite causal link between governmental activities within the area in question and that which has actually been achieved. Human society is too complex, and interventions on the part of public agencies will always have only limited effects. The example of 20th Century totalitarian communist regimes is illuminating in this respect. For example, the Soviet Union pursued a radical and far reaching diversity policy and its rulers had possessed strong instruments ranging from forced relocation of ethnic groups under Stalin to socio-economic planning and massive propaganda. The regime was however unable to overcome socio-economic disparities between ethnicities or to assimilate them.

Open societies which feature market economies and the rule of law are based on the freedom of individual choice and the separation of business and civil society from the government; this means that social mobility and stratification processes can be affected to a limited degree through the 'pulling and pushing of levers' that a government may choose to exploit according to its view and interpretation of, among other things, the national interest. Such processes may not easily be effectively governed in a realistic manner. Public authorities can prohibit discrimination, but they cannot effectively govern the behaviour of entrepreneurs, schools principals, police, judges, landlords and others who routinely make decisions concerning other people. Governments can promote tolerance through the education system and can punish hate speech (or designate the category of 'hate crimes' as being separate from normal 'crimes'), but they cannot brainwash the whole population. Law-makers and the executive can encourage the usage of certain language or persecute non-official languages in the public sphere, but they are technically unable to transform the system of social communication where different languages perform different functions and are valued differently. Agenda-setting and the creation of explanatory schemes as to what constitutes a nation and what diversity means are more visible and effective exercises. In other words, symbolic policies are the most salient and transparent part of diversity management. Instrumental policies still resist uniform explanations and require a thorough examination in each individual case. In short, there is no simple approach to understanding minority issues in diverse societies, but the diligent student must try.

Key points

- Governments have incentives and possess tools which can be used to affect social relations in one way or another around the ethnic, cultural or racial heterogeneity of their populaces.
- Diversity management, or diversity policies, depend upon official group categorizations which are made on a variety of grounds (ethnic, racial, linguistic) and have different social meanings and consequences in different contexts.
- Domestic policies are conceptualized in a variety of ways, and although major frames such as minority protection, non-discrimination, power-sharing, multiculturalism and others have their own histories, theoretical backgrounds and implications, they overlap and interact.
- Public authorities pursue different goals and operate in different social environments and under multidirectional political pressures; therefore, their choice of strategies and objectives depends on many circumstances. The major goal pursued can be conceptualised as either nation-building or as the creation and maintenance of a stable and cohesive society.
- Despite the strength of governmental institutions, many areas of social relations, such as language use, social mobility, and popular attitudes towards different groups are beyond the reach of governmental intrusion.
- Therefore, many undertakings in the domain of diversity management may be regarded as being merely symbolic policies which have no direct effect on social relations.

Further reading

ACKREN, MARIA. *Conditions for Different Autonomy Regimes in the World. A Fuzzy-Set Application.* Åbo: Åbo Akademis Förlag – Åbo Akademi University Press, 2009.

AGARIN, TIMOFEY and MALTE BROSIG, eds. *Minority Integration in Central Eastern Europe. Between Ethnic Diversity and Equality*. Amsterdam, New York: Rodopi, 2009.

AKTÜRK, ŞENER. *Regimes of Ethnicity and Nationhood in Germany, Russia, and Turkey*. Cambridge: Cambridge University Press, 2012.

BENEDIKTER, THOMAS, ed. *Solving Ethnic Conflict through Self-Government. A Short Guide to Autonomy in Europe and South Asia*. Bolzano/Bozen: Eurac Research, 2009.

BRUBAKER, ROGERS. "Nationalizing States Revisited: Projects and Processes of Nationalization in Post-Soviet States", *Ethnic and Racial Studies* 34 (2011), pp. 1785–1814.

DAFTARY, FARIMAH and FRANÇOIS GRIN, eds. *Nation-Building, Ethnicity and Language Politics in Transition Countries*. Budapest: OSI, LGI/ECMI, 2003.

JOPPKE, CHRISTIAN. "Minority Rights for Immigrants? Multiculturalism versus Antidiscrimination", *Israel Law Review* 43 (2010), pp. 49–66.

KINGA, GAL. *Minority Governance in Europe*. Budapest: LGI/ECMI Series on Ethnopolitics and Minority Issues, 2002.

KYMLICKA, WILL. *Multicultural Odysseys: Navigating the New International Politics of Diversity*. Oxford ; New York: Oxford University Press, 2007.

KYMLICKA, WILL. *Finding Our Way. Rethinking Ethnocultural Relations in Canada*. Toronto, Oxford, New York: Oxford University Press, 1998.

SKURBATY, ZELIM A. ed. *Beyond a One-Dimensional State: an Emerging Right to Autonomy?* Leiden/Boston: Martinus Nijhoff Publishers, 2005.

WELLER, MARC, BLACKLOCK, DENIKA and NOBBS, KATHERINE, eds. *The Protection of Minorities in the Wider Europe*. Basingstoke: Palgrave Macmillan, 2008.

Notes

1   John Wrench, "Managing diversity, fighting racism or combating discrimination? A critical exploration", in *Resituating Culture* (Strasbourg: Council of Europe, 2004), pp. 113–23.

2   Tove H. Malloy, "Conceptualizing Democratic Diversity Management for Multicultural Societies: Theories of Society and Law", *European Yearbook of Minority Issues* 6 (2007), pp. 281–306.

3   Walker Connor, *The National Question in Marxist-Leninist Theory and Strategy* (Princeton, NJ: Princeton University Press, 1984).

4   Joseph Marko, "The Law and Politics of Diversity Management: A Neoinstitutional Approach", *European Yearbook of Minority Issues* 6 (2007), pp. 251–80; Mitja Žagar, "Diversity Management and Integration: From Ideas to Concepts", *European Yearbook of Minority Issues* 6 (2007), pp. 307–27.

5   Rogers Brubaker, *Ethnicity Without Groups* (Cambridge, MA: Harvard University Press, 2006), p. 31.

6   Anne L. Schneider and Helen Ingram, *Policy Design for Democracy* (Lawrence: University Press of Kansas, 1997), pp. 150–88.

7   Thomas H. Eriksen, *Ethnicity and Nationalism. Anthropological Perspectives* (London and New York: Pluto Press, 3rd ed., 2010), pp. 4–9.

8   Brubaker, op.cit. note 5, 132–46.

9   Dejan Stjepanović, "Territoriality and Citizenship: Membership and Sub-State Polities in Post-Yugoslav Space", *CITSEE Working Paper* (2012), accessed 15 July 2013, http://www.law.ed.ac.uk/citsee/workingpapers/.

10 Steve Fenton and Stephen May, "Ethnicity, Nation and 'Race': Connections and Disjunctures", in *Ethnonational Identities*, eds. Steve Fenton and Stephen May (Houndmills: Basingstoke, 2002), pp. 1–20.

11 Seyla Benhabib, *The Claims of Culture: Equality and Diversity in the Global Era* (Princeton, N.J.: Princeton University Press, 2002); Anne Phillips, *Multiculturalism without Culture* (Princeton: Princeton University Press, 2007).

12 Ibid.

13 United States Census Bureau, accessed 15 July 2013, http://www.census.gov/population/race/

14 Florian Bieber, *Post-War Bosnia. Ethnicity, Inequality and Public Sector Governance* (Houndmills, Basingstoke: Palgrave Macmillan Ltd., 2006).

15 Jens Woelk, Francesco Palermo and Joseph Marko, eds., *Tolerance through Law. Self Governance and Group Rights in South Tyrol* (Leiden: Martinus Nijhoff, 2007).

16 Tamas Korhecz, "Democratic legitimacy and election rules of national and ethnic minority bodies and representation", *International Journal of Minority and Group Rights* 9 (2002), pp. 161–81.

17 Balazs Dobos, "The Development and Functioning of Cultural Autonomy in Hungary", *Ethnopolitics* 6(2007), pp. 451–69.

18 Robert Entman, "Framing: Toward Clarification of a Fractured Paradigm", *Journal of Communication* 43, (1993), pp. 51–8; David Snow and Robert Benford, "Master Frames and Cycles of Protest", in *Frontiers in Social Movement Theory*, eds. Aldon D. Morris and Carol McClurg Mueller (New Haven and London: Yale University Press, 1992), pp. 133–55.

19 Athanasia Spiliopoulou Åkermark, *Justifications of Minority Protection in International Law* (London; Boston: Kluwer Law International, 1997), pp. 88–93.

20 Kristin Henrard, *Devising an Adequate System of Minority Protection. Individual Human Rights, Minority Rights and the Right to Self-Determination* (The Hague, Kluwer Publishers, 2000).

21 Annelies Verstichel, *Participation, Representation and Identity: The Right of Persons Belonging to Minorities to Effective Participation in Public Affairs: Content, Justification and Limits* (Antwerp: Intersentia, 2009); Marc Weller and Katherine Nobbs, eds., *Political Participation of Minorities: A Commentary on International Standards and Practice* (Oxford: Oxford University Press, 2010).

22 *Non-Discrimination in International Law. A Handbook for Practitioners* (London: Interights, 2011).

23 Ibid.; Christa Tobler, *Indirect Discrimination. A Case Study into the Development of the Legal Concept of Indirect Discrimination under EC Law* (Antwerp, Oxford: Intersentia, 2005).

24 Roy L. Brooks, *Integration or Separation? : A Strategy for Racial Equality* (Cambridge, Mass.: Harvard University Press, 1996).

25 John Rex, *Race Relations in Sociological Theory* (London: Routledge & Kegan Paul, 2nd ed., 1983),pp. 117–18; Anthony Giddens, Sociology (London: Polity Press, 5th. edn, 2006), p. 1014.

26 Joe. R. Feagin and Vera Hernan, *White Racism. the Basics* (New York: Routledge, 1995); Howard Wynant, "Race and racism: Towards a global future", *Ethnic and Racial Studies* 29 (2006), pp. 986–1003.

27 Christopher McCrudden, "The new concept of equality", *ERA-Forum* 4 (2003), pp. 9–24; Olivier De Schutter, "Three models of equality and European anti-discrimination law", in *Northern Ireland Legal Quarterly* 57 (2006), pp. 1–56; Nancy Fraser, *Justice Interruptus: Critical Reflections on the "Postsocialist" Condition* (New York: Routledge, 1997).

28 Arend Lijphart, *Democracy in Plural Societies: A Comparative Exploration* (New Haven, CT: Yale University Press, 1977); Yash Ghai, "Constitutional Asymmetries: Communal Representation, Federalism, and Cultural Autonomy", in *The Architecture of Democracy. Constitutional Design, Conflict Management, and Democracy*, ed. Andrew Reynolds (Oxford: Oxford University Press, 2002), pp. 141–70.

29 Bhikhu Parekh, *Rethinking Multiculturalism: Cultural Diversity and Political Theory* (Cambridge, MA: Harvard University Press, 2000); Edward A. Tiryakian, "Assessing Multiculturalism Theoretically: E Pluribus Unum, Sic et Non", *International Journal on Multicultural Societies* 5 (2003), pp. 20–39.

30 Parekh, op.cit. note 30; Michael Wieviorka, "Is multiculturalism the solution?" *Ethnic and Racial Studies* 21 (1998), pp. 881–910; John Rex and Gurharpal Singh, "Multiculturalism and Political Integration in Modern Nation-States – Thematic Introduction", *International Journal on Multicultural Societies* 5 (2003), pp. 3–19.

31 Wolfgang Bosswick and Friedrich Heckmann, *Integration of migrants: Contribution on local and regional authorities* (Dublin: European Foundation for the Improvement of Living and Working Conditions, 2006); Christian Joppke, *The Role of the State in Cultural Integration: Tends, Challenges, and Ways Ahead* (Bern: Migration Policy Institute, 2012); Peter Scholten, *Framing Immigrant Integration. Dutch Research-Policy Dialogues in Comparative Perspective*, IMISCOE Research (Amsterdam: Amsterdam University Press, 2011).

32 Gwendolyn Sasse, "Securitization or Securing Rights? Exploring the Conceptual Foundations of Policies towards Minorities and Migrants in Europe", *JCMS: Journal of Common Market Studies* 43(2005), pp. 673–93.

33 Rogers Brubaker, N*ationalism Reframed. Nationhood and the National Question in the New Europe* (Cambridge: Cambridge University Press, 1996), p. 9.

34 Will Kymlicka, "The Internationalization of Minority Rights", *International Journal of Constitutional Law* 6 (2008), pp. 1–32, at pp. 26–9; Claus Offe, *Varieties of Transition* (Cambridge: Polity Press, 1996), pp. 50–81.

35 Fred Pincus, *Reverse Discrimination: Dismantling the Myth* (Boulder, Colo.: Lynne Rienner Publishers, 2003).

36 Stephanie Chouinard, "Is There a Right to Non-Territorial Autonomy in Canada? The Case of Institutional Completeness and Minority Language Rights", in *The Challenge of Non-Territorial Autonomy: Theory and Practice*, eds. Ephraim Nimni, Alexander Osipov and David J. Smith (Bern: Peter Lang, 2013), pp. 229–44.

37 Avigail Eisenberg, ed. *Diversity and Equality: The Changing Framework of Freedom in Canada* (Vancouver, Toronto: UBC Press, 2006).

38 Ghai, op.cit. note 29; John McGarry and Brendan O'Leary, *The Politics of Ethnic Conflict Regulation. Case Studies of Protracted Ethnic Conflicts* (London and New York: Routledge, 1996); Barbara Metzger and Marc Weller, eds., *Settling Self-determination Disputes: Complex Power-Sharing in Theory and Practice* (Leiden: Martinus Nijhoff, 2008).

39 Elke Winter, "'Immigrants Don't Ask for Self-government': How Multiculturalism is (De)legitimized in Multinational Societies", *Ethnopolitics* 10 (2011), pp. 187–204, at pp. 200–1.

40 Dinesh D'Souza, *The End of Racism: Principles for a Multiracial Society* (New York: Free Press, 1995), pp. 220–26.

41 Pincus, op.cit. note 35.

42 Chouinard, op. cit. note 36.

43 Brian Slattery, "What Are Aboriginal Rights?" *CLPE Research Paper* 1 (2007).

44 Council Directive 2000/43/EC of 29 June 2000 implementing the principle of equal treatment between persons irrespective of racial or ethnic origin; Council Directive 2000/78/EC of 27 November 2000 establishing a general framework for equal treatment in employment and occupation; see Erica Howard, *The EU Race Directive: Developing the Protection against Racial Discrimination within the EU* (London: Routledge, 2009).

45 Marnie Lloyd, ed., *Ombudsman Institutions and Minority Issues: A Guide to Good Practice* (Flensburg: ECMI, Bundesministerium des Innern, 2005).

46 Thomas Benedikter, *The World's Modern Autonomy Systems. Concepts and Experiences of Regional Territorial Autonomy* (Bozen/Bolzano: European Academy of Bozen/Bolzano, 2009); Marc Weller and Stefan Wolff, eds., *Autonomy, Self-governance and Conflict Resolution. Innovative approaches to institutional design in divided societies* (London and New York: Routledge, 2005).

47 *The Fight against Discrimination and the Promotion of Equality. How to Measure Progress Done* (Luxembourg: Office for Official Publications of the European Communities, 2008).

48 *International Perspectives on Positive Action Measures. A comparative analysis in the European Union, Canada, the United States and South Africa* (Luxembourg: Office for Official Publications of the European Commission, 2009).

49 Marc De Vos, *Beyond Formal Equality. Positive Action under Directives 2000/43/EC and 2000/78/EC* (Luxembourg: Office for Official Publications of the European Commission, 2007).

50 Brendan O'Leary, "The Logics of Power-sharing, Consociation and Pluralist Federations", in *Self-determination Disputes: Complex Power-Sharing in Theory and Practice*, eds. Barbara Metzger and Marc Weller (Leiden: Martinus Nijhoff, 2008), pp. 47–58; Benjamin Reilly, *Democracy in Divided Societies: Electoral Engineering for Conflict Management* (Cambridge, UK; New York: Cambridge University Press, 2001).

51 Marc Weller, "Minority Consultative Mechanisms: Towards Best Practices", *European Yearbook of Minority Issues* 7/8 (2010), pp. 425–47.

Bibliography

Agreement between the European Community and the Council of Europe on cooperation between the European Union Agency for Fundamental Rights and the Council of Europe, *Official Journal* L 186, 15.7.2008, pp. 7–11.

AL-ALI, NADJE and KHALID KOSER, eds. *New Approaches to Migration: Transnationalism and Transformations of Home*. London: Routledge, 2002.

ALFREDSSON, GUDMUNDUR. "A Frame with an Incomplete Painting", *International Journal on Minority and Group Rights* 7 (2000), pp. 291–304.

ANDERSON, BENEDICT. *Imagined Communities: Reflections on the Origins and Spread of Nationalism*. London: Verso, 1983.

ANDERSON, BENEDICT. *Imagined Communities: Reflections on the Origin and Spread of Nationalism*. London: Verso, 1991.

ANDERSON, JAMES and DOUGLAS HAMILTON. *National Conflict, Transnationalism and Democracy: Crossing borders in Ireland*; conference paper presented at Nationalisms and Identities in a Globalized World (17–22 August 1998), accessed 12 May, 2013, http://www.nuim.ie/staff/dpringle/igu_wpm/anderson.pdf.

ANDERSON, LIAM D. *Federal Solutions to Ethnic Problems: Accommodating Diversity* (London: Routledge, 2013).

ANDRIS, SPRUDS. "Minority Issues in the Baltic States in the Context of the NATO Enlargement", *NATO Research Fellowships* 1999–2001, p. 14, accessed July 15, 2013, http://www.nato.int/acad/fellow/99-01/spruds.pdf.

APPADURAI, ARJUN. "Disjuncture and Difference in the Global Cultural Economy", in *Global Culture*, ed. MIKE FEATHERSTONE. London: Sage, 1990, p. 295–310.

APPADURAI, ARJUN. "The Production of Locality", in *Counterworks: Managing the Diversity of Knowledge*, ed. RICHARD FARDON. London: Routledge, 1995.

APPADURAI, ARJUN. *Modernity at Large: Cultural Dimensions of Globalization*. Minneapolis: University of Minnesota Press, 1996.

ARENDT, HANNAH. *The Origins of Totalitarianism*. New York: World Publishing, 1972.

AUKERMAN, MIRIAM J. "Definitions and Justifications. Minority and Indigenous Rights in a Central/East European Context", *Human Rights Quarterly* 22 (2000).

BALLARD, ROGER. "Race, Ethnicity and Culture", in *New Directions in Sociology*, ed. MARTIN HOLBORN. Ormskirk: Causeway, 2002, p. 13.

BANDUCCI, SUSAN A. et al., "Minority Representation, Empowerment, and Participation", *The Journal of Politics* 66 (2004), pp. 534–556.

BANTING, KEITH, and WILL KYMLICKA. *Multiculturalism and the Welfare State. Recognition and Redistribution in Contemporary Democracies*. Oxford University Press, 2006.

BARRY, BRIAN. *Culture and Equality: An Egalitarian Critique of Multiculturalism*. Cambridge: Polity, 2001.

BAUBÖCK, RAINER. "Transnational Citizenship: Membership and Rights", in *International Migration*. Aldershot: Edward Elgar, 1994.
BAUBÖCK, RAINER. "Recombinant citizenship", in *Inclusions and Exclusions in European societies*, eds. MARTIN KOHLI and ALISON WOODWARD. London: Routledge, 2001.
BAUBÖCK, RAINER. "Territorial or cultural autonomy for national minorities?", *IWE-Working Paper Series* 22 (December 2001), accessed August 1, 2013, http://eif.univie.ac.at/downloads/workingpapers/IWE-Papers/WP22.pdf.
BAUBÖCK, RAINER. "Political Community beyond the Sovereign State: Supranational Federalism and Transnational Minorities", in *Conceiving Cosmopolitanism: theory, context and practice*, eds. Steven Vertovec and Robin Cohen. Oxford: Oxford University Press, 2002, pp. 110-136.
BAUER, OTTO. *The Question of Nationalities and Social Democracy*. Minneapolis and London: University of Minnesota Press, 2000, pp. 259–308.
BAUMAN, ZYGMUNT. *Liquid Modernity*. Cambridge: Polity, 2000.
BECK, ULRICH. *Risk Society. Towards a New Modernity*. London: Sage, 1992.
BELLONI, ROBERTO. "Peacebuilding and Consociational Electoral Engineering in Bosnia and Herzegovina", *International Peacekeeping* 11 (2004), pp. 334–53.
BENEDIKTER, THOMAS. *The World's Modern Autonomy Systems. Concepts and Experiences of Regional Territorial Autonomy*. Bozen/Bolzano: European Academy of Bozen/Bolzano, 2009.
BENHABIB, SEYLA. *The Claims of Culture: Equality and Diversity in the Global Era*. Princeton: Princeton University Press, 2002.
BENOIT-ROHMER, FLORENCE and HILDE HARDEMAN. "The Pact on Stability in Europe", in *Helsinki Monitor* 4 (1994), pp. 38–51.
BIEBER, FLORIAN. *Post-War Bosnia. Ethnicity, Inequality and Public Sector Governance*. Houndmills, Basingstoke: Palgrave Macmillan Ltd., 2006.
BIJOLA, CORNELIU. "NATO as a Factor of Security Community Building: Enlargement and Democratization in Central and Eastern Europe", *NATO Research Fellowships* 1999–2001, p. 4, accessed July 15, 2013, http://www.nato.int/acad/fellow/99-01/bjola.pdf.
BILLIG, MICHAEL. *Banal Nationalism*. London: SAGE Publications, 1995.
BLOED, ARIE and PIETER VAN DIJK, eds. *Protection of Minority Rights through Bilateral Treaties. The Case of Central and Eastern Europe*. The Hague: Kluwer Law International, 1999.
BLUMENBERG, HANS. *The Legitimacy of the Modern Age*. Cambridge, MA: MIT Press, 1983.
BLYTH, MARK. "Institutions and Ideas", in *Theory and Methods in Political Science*, eds. DAVID MARSH and GERRY STOKER. Basingstoke: Palgrave, 2010.
BOBO, LAWRENCE and FRANKLIN D. GILLIAM. "Race, Sociopolitical Participation, and Black Empowerment". *American Political Science Review* 84 (1990), pp. 377–393.
BÖRZEL, TANJA A. "Towards Convergence in Europe? Institutional Adaptation to Europeanization in Germany and Spain", *Journal of Common Market Studies* 39 (1999), pp. 573–96.
BÖRZEL, TANJA A. and THOMAS RISSE. "Conceptualizing the Domestic Impact of Europe", in *The Politics of Europeanization*, eds. KEVIN FEATHERSTONE and CLAUDIO RADAELLI. Oxford: Oxford University Press, 2003, pp. 57–80.

BÖRZEL, TANJA A. and Thomas Risse. "From Europeanisation to Diffusion: Introduction", *West European Politics* 35, 2012, pp. 1–19.
BOSSWICK, WOLFGANG, and FRIEDRICH HECKMANN. *Integration of migrants: Contribution on local and regional authorities*. Dublin: European Foundation for the Improvement of Living and Working Conditions, 2006.
BRAY, ZOE. *Boundaries and Identities in Bidasoa-Txingudi, on the Franco-Spanish frontier*, PhD-thesis, Florence: European University Institute, 2002.
BROOKS, ROY L. *Integration or Separation?: A Strategy for Racial Equality*. Cambridge, Mass.: Harvard University Press, 1996.
BROWN, MICHAEL E. *Ethnic Conflict and International Security*. Princeton: Princeton University Press, 1993.
BRUBAKER, ROGERS. "National Minorities, Nationalizing States, and External National Homelands in the New Europe", *Daedalus* 124 (1995), pp. 107–132.
BRUBAKER, ROGERS. *Nationalism Reframed. Nationhood and the National Question in the New Europe*. Cambridge: Cambridge University Press, 1996.
BRUBAKER, ROGERS. "The Manichean Myth: Rethinking the Distinction between 'Civic' and 'Ethnic'", in *Nation and National Identity. The European Experience in Perspective*, eds. HANSPETER KRIESI et al., Zurich: Ruegger, 1999.
BRUBAKER, ROGERS. "Ethnicity without Groups", *European Journal of Sociology* 43 (2002), pp. 163–189.
BRUBAKER, ROGERS, *Ethnicity Without Groups*. Cambridge, MA: Harvard University Press, 2006.
BRUBAKER, ROGERS, MARGIT FEISCHMIDT, JON FOX and LIANA GRANCEA. *Nationalist Politics and Everyday Ethnicity in a Transylvanian Town*. Princeton: Princeton University Press, 2006.
CAMERON, CHARLES, DAVID EPSTEIN, and SHARYN O'HALLORAN. "Do Majority-Minority Districts Maximize Substantive Black Representation in Congress?", *American Political Science Review* 90 (1996), pp. 794–812.
CAPORASO, JAMES. "Towards a Normal Science of Regional Integration", *Journal of European Public Policy* 6 (1996), pp. 160–164.
CAPOTORTI, FRANCESCO. "Study on the Rights of Persons Belonging to Ethnic, Religious and Linguistic Minorities", *UN Doc.* E/CN.4/Sub.2/384/Rev.1.
CARMICHAEL, CATHIE. *Ethnic Cleansing in the Balkans: Nationalism and the Destruction of Tradition*. London: Routledge, 2002.
CARSTOCEA, RAUL. "Uneasy Twins? The Entangled Histories of Jewish Emancipation and Anti-Semitism in Romania and Hungary, 1866–1913", *Slovo* 21 (2009), pp. 74–76.
CASTELLS, MANUEL. "End of Millennium", in *The Information Age: Economy, Society and Culture III*. 2nd ed., Cambridge and Oxford: Blackwell, 2000.
CHABLAIS, ALAIN. "Legal Entrenchment and Implementation Mechanisms", in *Political Participation of Minorities: A Commentary on International Standards and Practice*, eds. MARC WELLER and KATHERINE NOBBS. Oxford University Press, 2010, pp. 735–750.
Chain v. France (5.12.2007) and *Bessam v. France* (5.12.2007).
CHANDRA, KANCHAN. "What is an Ethnic Party?", *Party Politics* 17 (2011), p. 159.

Charter of Fundamental Rights of the European Union (2000/C 364/01), *Official Journal of the European Communities* C 364/1, 18.12.2000.

Charter of the United Nations, accessed July 15, 2013, http://www.un.org/en/documents/charter/.

CHECKEL, JEFFREY T. "The Europeanization of Citizenship?", in *Transforming Europe* (2001), pp. 180–197.

CHOUINARD, STEPHANIE. "Is There a Right to Non-Territorial Autonomy in Canada? The Case of Institutional Completeness and Minority Language Rights", in *The Challenge of Non-Territorial Autonomy: Theory and Practice*, eds. EPHRAIM NIMNI, ALEXANDER OSIPOV and DAVID J. SMITH. Bern: Peter Lang, 2013, pp. 229–44.

CHRISTIANO, THOMAS. "Democratic Equality and the Problem of Persistent Minorities", *Philosophical Papers* 23 (1994).

CLARKE, SIMON. "Culture and Identity", in *The SAGE Handbook of Cultural Analysis*, eds. TONY BENETT and JOHN FROW. London: SAGE Publications, 2008, pp. 510–28.

CLAUDE, INIS L. *National Minorities: An International Problem*. Cambridge: Harvard University Press, 1955.

COBBAN, ALFRED. *The Nation-State and National Self-Determination*. London: Collins, 1969.

COHEN, IRA J. "Anthony Giddens", in *Key Sociological Thinkers*, 2nd ed., edited by ROB STONES. Basingstoke: Palgrave Macmillan, 2008.

COHEN, ROBIN. *Global Diasporas; An Introduction*. London: UCL Press, 1997.

COMMERCIO, MICHELE E. *Russian Minority Politics in Post-Soviet Latvia and Kyrgyzstan: the Transformative Power of Informal Networks*. Philadelphia: University of Pennsylvania Press, 2010.

Conflict prevention – HCNM, OSCE website, accessed July 15, 2013, http://www.osce.org/hcnm/44692.

CONNOLLY, WILLIAM E. *The Ethos of Pluralization*. Minneapolis: University of Minnesota Press, 1995.

CONNOLLY, WILLIAM E. *Identity/Difference. Democratic Negotiations of Political Paradox*, expanded ed., Minneapolis: University of Minnesota Press (2002[1991]).

Constitution of Bosnia and Herzegovina (preamble), Constitutional Court of Bosnia and Herzegovina, accessed July 6, 2013, http://www.ccbh.ba/eng/p_stream.php?kat=518.

Convention for the Protection of Human Rights and Fundamental Freedoms, as amended by Protocols No. 11 and 14, European Treaty Series No. 5.

Convention for the Protection of Human Rights and Fundamental Freedoms, ETS No. 005, 4 November 1950, entered into force 3 November 1953.

Convention on the Rights of the Child, OHCHR website, accessed July 15, 2013, http://www.ohchr.org/en/professionalinterest/pages/crc.aspx.

CONVERSI, DANIELE. "Cultural Homogenization, Ethnic Cleansing and Genocide", in *The International Studies Encyclopedia*, ed. ROBERT A. DENEMARK. Oxford and Boston: Wiley-Blackwell, 2010, pp. 719–42.

Council Directive 2000/43/EC of 29 June 2000 implementing the principle of equal treatment between persons irrespective of racial or ethnic origin, Official Journal L 180, 19/07/2000 P. 0022 – 0026.

Council Directive 2000/78/EC of 27 November 2000 establishing a general framework for equal treatment in employment and occupation, Official Journal L 303, 02/12/2000 P. 0016 – 0022.

Council of Europe, Art. 15 of the 1995 Framework Convention for the Protection of National Minorities, accessed July 15, 2013, http://conventions.coe.int/Treaty/en/Treaties/Html/157.htm.

COWLES, MARIA GREEN et al. *Transforming Europe: Europeanization and Domestic Change*. London: Cornell University Press, 2001.

CRAIG, PAUL and GRAINNE DE BURCA. *EU Law: Text, Cases, and Materials*. Oxford: OUP, 2011.

CRYSTAL, DAVID. *Language Death*. Cambridge: Cambridge University Press, 2000.

CSERGO, ZSUZSA. "Beyond Ethnic Division: Majority-Minority Debate about the Post-Communist State in Romania and Slovakia", *East European Politics and Societies* 16 (2002), pp. 1–28.

DAVIES, NORMAN. *Heart of Europe: The Past in Poland's Present*. Oxford: Oxford University Press, 2001.

DE SCHUTTER, OLIVIER. "Three models of equality and European anti-discrimination law", in *Northern Ireland Legal Quarterly* 57 (2006), pp. 1–56.

DE VARENNES, FERNAN. "Language Rights as an Integral Part of Human Rights", *International Journal on Multicultural Societies* 3 (2001), pp. 15–25.

DE VOS, MARC. *Beyond Formal Equality. Positive Action under Directives 2000/43/EC and 2000/78/EC*. Luxembourg: Office for Official Publications of the European Commission, 2007.

DECHENES, JULES. "Proposal concerning a Definition of the term 'Minority'", *UN Doc.* E/CN.4/Sub.2/1985/31.

Declaration of the Rights of Man and of the Citizen (1789), accessed July 10, http://www.constitution.org/fr/fr_drm.htm.

Declaration on the Rights of Persons Belonging to National or Ethnic, Religious and Linguistic Minorities, accessed July 15, 2013, http://www.un.org/documents/ga/res/47/a47r135.html.

DELANTY, GERARD. "Modernity", in *Blackwell Encyclopedia of Sociology*, accessed June 1, 2013, subscription only, http://www.sociologycncyclopedia.com/public/tocnode?id=g9781405124331_yr2012_chunk_g978140512433119_ss1-117.

DERSSO, SOLOMON, "Minorities and International Law", *SAIFAC Research Paper Series* 1. Braamfontein: SAIFAC (2006), p. 11.

DEWITTE, BRUNO. "The Constitutional Resources for an EU Minority Protection Policy", in *Minority Protection and the Enlarged European Union: The way forward*, Budapest: Local Government and Public Service Reform Initiative, 2004.

DIEZ, THOMAS et al. "The European Union and Border Conflicts: The Transformative Power of Integration", *International Organization* 60 (2006), pp. 563–593.

DIMAGGIO. PAUL J. and WALTER W. POWELL. *The New Institutionalism in Organizational Analysis*. Chicago: Chicago University Press, 1991.

DOBOS, BALAZS. "The Development and Functioning of Cultural Autonomy in Hungary", *Ethnopolitics* 6 (2007), pp. 451–69.

Dogru v. France (application no. 27058/05) and *Kervanci v. France* (no. 31645/04).
DONNELLY, JACK. "Cultural Relativism and Universal Human Rights", *Human Rights Quarterly* 6 (1984), pp. 400–419.
DONNELLY, JACK. *Universal Human Rights in Theory and Practice*, 2nd ed., Ithaca: Cornell University Press, 2003.
DRZEWICKI, KRZYSZTOF. "A Constitution for Europe: Enshrining minority rights", *OSCE Magazine* (2005), pp. 19–21.
DRZEWICKI, KRZYSZTOF. "OSCE Lund Recommendations in the Practice of the High Commissioner on National Minorities", in *The Protection of Minorities in the Wider Europe*, eds. MARC WELLER, DENIKA BLACKLOCK and KATHERINE NOBBS. Basingstoke: Palgrave Macmillan, 2008, pp. 256–85.
DRZEWICKI, KRZYSZTOF. "The Enlargement of the European Union and the OSCE High Commissioner on National Minorities", in *The Protection of Minorities in the Wider Europe*, eds. MARC WELLER, DENIKA BLACKLOCK and KATHERINE NOBBS. Basingstoke: Palgrave Macmillan, 2008, pp. 154–170.
D'SOUZA, DINESH. *The End of Racism: Principles for a Multiracial Society*. New York: Free Press, 1995.
Early warning – HCNM, OSCE website, accessed July 15, 2013, http://www.osce.org/hcnm/43265.
EISENBERG, AVIGAIL ed. *Diversity and Equality: The Changing Framework of Freedom in Canada*. Vancouver, Toronto: UBC Press, 2006.
Encyclopedia Britannica, Entry on "Social Movements", accessed August 1, 2013, http://www.britannica.com/EBchecked/topic/551335/social-movement.
ENTMAN, ROBERT. "Framing: Toward Clarification of a Fractured Paradigm", *Journal of Communication* 43 (1993), pp. 51–8.
ERIKSEN, THOMAS H. *Ethnicity and Nationalism. Anthropological Perspectives*. London and New York: Pluto Press, 3rd ed., 2010
ERK, JAN. *Explaining Federalism: State, Society and Congruence in Austria, Belgium, Canada, Germany and Sw itzerland*. London: Routledge, 2008.
ERNEST GELLNER, *Nations and Nationalism*. 2nd ed. Malden: Blackwell Publishing, 2006.
ESTEBANEZ, MARTIN MARIA AMOR. "Council of Europe Policies Concerning the Protection of Linguistic Minorities and the Justiciability of Minority Rights", in *Minorities, Peoples and Self-Determination*, eds. NAZILA GHANEA and ALEXANDRA XANTHAKI. Leiden: Martinus Nijhoff Publishers, 2005, p. 269.
European Charter for Regional or Minority Languages, ETS No. 148, adopted 5 November 1992, entered into force 1 March 1998.
European Charter of Local Self-Government, European Treaty Series No. 122 open for signatures 15.10.1985.
European Outline Convention on Transfrontier Co-operation. European Treaty Series 106 opened for signatures 21.5.1980.
EVANS, ROBERT JOHN WESTON, and HARTMUT POGGE VON STRANDMANN, ed. *The Revolutions in Europe, 1848–1849: From Reform to Reaction*. Oxford: Oxford University Press, 2000.

FAIST, THOMAS. "International Migration and Transnational Social Spaces: Their Evolution, Significance and Future Prospects", in *InIIS-Arbeitspapier* 9/98, Institut für Interkulturelle und Internationale Studien, Universität Bremen (1998), p. 31.

FAIST, THOMAS. *Transnationalization in International Migration: Implications for the Study of Citizenship and Culture*; WPTC-99-08; (Institute for Intercultural and International Studies (InIIS), University of Bremen (1999), p. 2, accessed May 2013, http://www.transcomm.ox.ac.uk/working%20papers/faist.pdf.

FAIST, THOMAS. "The Transnational Turn in Migration Research: Perspectives for the Study of Politics and Polity", in *Transnational Spaces: Disciplinary Perspectives*, ed. MAJA POVRZANOVICĂ FRYKMAN. Malmö University: IMER, Malmö, 2004, p. 12.

FAIST, THOMAS. "Diversity – a New Mode of Incorporation?", in *Ethnic and Racial Studies* 32 (2009).

FAIST, THOMAS. "Diaspora and Transnationalism: What Kind of Dance Partners", in *Diaspora and Transnationalism: Concepts, Theories and Methods*, eds. RAINER BAUBÖCK and THOMAS FAIST. Amsterdam: Amsterdam University Press, 2010, p. 10.

FEAGIN, JOE. R. and VERA HERNAN. *White Racism: the Basics*. New York: Routledge, 1995.

FEATHERSTONE, KEVIN, and CLAUDIO M. RADAELLI. *The Politics of Europeanization*. Oxford: Oxford University Press, 2003, pp. 27–56.

FENTON, STEVE, and STEPHEN MAY. "Ethnicity, Nation and 'Race': Connections and Disjunctures", in *Ethnonational Identities*, eds. STEVE FENTON and STEPHEN MAY. Houndmills: Basingstoke, 2002, pp. 1–20.

Final Act of the Congress of Vienna/General Treaty (1815), accessed July 10, 2013, http://www.dipublico.com.ar/english/final-act-of-the-congress-of-viennageneral-treaty-1815/.

FINK, CAROLE. "The League of Nations and the Minorities Question", *World Affairs* 157 (1995), pp. 197–205.

FINK, CAROLE. "The Paris Peace Conference and the Question of Minority Right", *Peace and Change* 21 (1996), pp. 276–279.

FORTMAN, BAS DE GAAY. "Minority Rights: A Major Misconception?", *Human Rights Quarterly* 33(2011), pp. 265–303.

Framework Convention for the Protection of National Minorities, ETS No. 157, adopted 1 February 1995, entered in force 1 February 1998.

FRASER, NANCY. "Rethinking the Public Sphere: A Contribution to the Critique of Actually Existing Democracy", *Social Text* 25/26 (1990), pp. 56–80.

FRASER, NANCY. *Justice Interruptus: Critical Reflections on the "Postsocialist" Condition*. New York: Routledge, 1997.

FREEMAN, JO, and VICTORIA JOHNSON. *Waves of Protest: Social Movements since the Sixties*. Lanham, Maryland: Rowman & Littlefield, 1999.

FROST, ROBERT. "Religion and Freedom of Speech: Portraits of Muhammad", *Constellations* 14 (2007), pp. 72–90.

FRYKMAN, MAJA POVRZANOVICĂ. "'Transnational Perspective' in Ethnology: From 'Ethnic' To 'Diasporic' Communities", in *Transnational Spaces: Disciplinary Perspec-*

tives, ed. MAJA POVRZANOVICĂ FRYKMAN. Malmö University: IMER, Malmö, 2004, pp. 77–101.

FUKUYAMA, FRANCIS. *The End of History and the Last Man*. Free Press, 1992.

FUNG, ARCHON. "Varieties of Participation in Complex Governance, Theorizing Democratic Renewal". (Workshop, University of British Columbia, Vancouver, Canada, June 10–11, 2005).

GALBREATH, DAVID J. and JOANNE MCEVOY. *The European Minority Rights Regime: Towards a Theory of Regime Effectiveness*. Basingstoke: Palgrave Macmillan, 2012.

GALEOTTI, ANNA E. *Toleration as Recognition*. Cambridge: Cambridge University Press, 2005.

GAY, CLAUDINE. "Spirals of Trust? The Effect of Descriptive Representation on the Relationship between Citizens and Their Government", *American Journal of Political Science* 46 (2002).

GEERTZ, CLIFFORD. *The Interpretation of Cultures*. New York: Basic Books, 1973.

General Comment No. 23: The rights of minorities (Art. 27): 08/04/1994, CCPR/C/21/Rev.1/Add.5, General Comment No. 23, accessed July 15, 2013, http://www.unhchr.ch/tbs/doc.nsf/%28Symbol%29/fb7fb12c2fb8bb21c12563ed004df111?Opendocument.

GHAI, YASH. "Constitutional Asymmetries: Communal Representation, Federalism, and Cultural Autonomy", in *The Architecture of Democracy. Constitutional Design, Conflict Management, and Democracy*, ed. ANDREW REYNOLDS. Oxford: Oxford University Press, 2002, pp. 141–70.

GIDDENS, ANTHONY. *The Self and Society in the Late Modern Age*. Stanford, CA: Stanford University Press, 1991.

GIDDENS, ANTHONY. *Sociology*. London: Polity Press, 5th ed., 2006.

GILBERT, GEOFF. "The Council of Europe and Minority Rights", *Human Rights Quarterly* 18 (1996), pp. 160–90.

GLASS, ZIPORAH G. "Building toward 'Nation-ness' in the Vine: A Postcolonial Critique of John 15.1–8", in *John and Postcolonialism: Travel, Space, and Power*, eds. MUSA W. DUBE SHOMANAH and JEFFREY STALEY. London: Continuum – Sheffield Academic Press, 2002, pp. 153–169.

GOETZ, KLAUS and SIMON HIX. *Europeanised Politics? European Integration and National Political Systems*. London: Frank Cass, 2000.

GRABBE, HANS-JÜRGEN. *The EU's Transformative Power: Europeanisation through Conditionality in Central and Eastern Europe*. Basingstoke: Palgrave, 2005.

GRAHAM, SMITH. "Sustainable Federalism, Democratization, and Distributive Justice", in *Citizenship in Diverse Societies*, eds. WILL KYMLICKA and WAYNE NORMAN. Oxford: Oxford University Press, 2000, pp. 345–65.

GREWAL, INDERPAL and CAREN KAPLAN, eds. *Introduction to Women's Studies: Gender in a Transnational World*. New York: MacGraw Hill, 2002.

GREWAL, INDERPAL. "Transnational America: Feminisms, Diasporas, Neoliberalisms", in *Transnational America* 22–23 (2005).

GRIFFIN, JOHN D. and MICHAEL KEANE. "Descriptive Representation and the Composition of African American Turnout", *American Journal of Political Science* 50 (2006), pp. 998–1012.

GRIN, FRANÇOIS. *Language Policy Evaluation and the European Charter for Regional or Minority Languages*. Basingstoke: Palgrave Macmillan, 2003.
GUARNIZO, LUIS E. "The Emergence of a Transnational Social Formation and the Mirage of Return Migration among Dominican Transmigrants", *Identities* 4 (1997), pp. 281–322.
GUARNIZO, LUIS E., and MICHAEL PETER SMITH. "The Locations of Transnationalism", in *Transnationalism from Below, Comparative Urban and Community Research*, eds. MICHAEL PETER SMITH and LUIS E. GUARNIZO. New Brunswick, New Jersey, 1998.
GUARNIZO, LUIS E., ALEJANDRO PORTES and WILLIAM HALLER. "Assimilation and Transnationalism: Determinants of Transnational Political Action among Contemporary Migrants", in *American Journal of Sociology* 108 (2003), pp. 1211–1248; accessed 14 June, 2013, http://hcd.ucdavis.edu/faculty/webpages/guarnizo/AssimTrans.pdf.
GUEHENNO, JEAN-MARIE. *The End of the Nation-State*, trans. Victoria Elliott. Minneapolis: University of Minnesota Press, 1995.
GUGLIELMO, RACHEL. "Human Rights in the Accession Process: Roma and Muslims in an Enlarged EU", in *Minority Protection and the Enlarged European Union: The way forward*, Budapest: Local Government and Public Service Reform Initiative, 2004.
GUIBERNAU, MONTSERRAT. *The Identity of Nations*. Cambridge: Polity, 2007.
GUNTHER, RICHARD and LARRY DIAMOND. "Species of Political Parties: A New Typology", *Party Politics* 9 (2003), p. 183.
HABERMAS, JÜRGEN. *The Philosophical Discourse of Modernity*, tr. Frederick Lawrence. Cambridge: Polity Press, 1985.
HALL, STUART. "Old and New Identities, Old and New Ethnicities", in *Culture, Globalization and the World-System: Contemporary Conditions for the representation of identity*, ed. ANTHONY D. KING. Houndmills, Macmillan, 1991.
HAMMER, LEONARD M. "Foreword", in *Interculturalism Exploring Critical Issues*, eds. DIANE POWELL and FIONA SZE. Oxford: Interdisciplinary Press, 2004.
HANNUM, HURST. "Contemporary Developments in the International Protection of the Rights of Minorities", *Notre Dame Law Review* 66 (1991), pp. 1431–1460.
HANNUM, HURST. *Autonomy, Sovereignty, and Self-Determination: The Accommodation of Conflicting Rights*, 2nd edition. Philadelphia: University of Pennsylvania Press, 1996.
HANSEN, RANDAL. "The Danish Cartoon Controversy: a Defence of Liberal Freedom", *International Migration* 44 (2006), pp. 7–16.
HARTNEY, MICHAEL. "Some Confusions Concerning Collective Rights", in *The Rights of Minority Cultures*, ed. WILL KYMLICKA. Oxford: Oxford University Press, 1995.
HASAN, RUMY. *Multiculturalism: Some Inconvenient Truths*. London: Politico's, 2010.
HCNM website, accessed July 15, 2013, http://www.osce.org/hcnm.
HELD, DAVID, ANTHONY MCGREW, DAVID GOLDBLATT and JONATHAN PERRATON. *Global Transformations*, Polity, 1999.
HELFFERICH, TRYNTJE, ed. *The Thirty Years' War: A Documentary History*. Indianapolis: Hackett Publishing Company, 2009, pp. ix–xxi.
HENRARD, KRISTIN. *Devising an Adequate System of Minority Protection. Individual Human Rights, Minority Rights and the Right to Self-Determination*. The Hague, Kluwer Publishers and Martinus Nijhoff Publishers, 2000.

HENRARD, KRISTIN. "Ever-Increasing Synergy Towards a Stronger Level of Minority Protection between Minority-specific and Non-Minority-Specific Instruments", in *European Yearbook of Minority Issues* 3, eds. EURAC and ECMI (Martinus Nijhoff Publishers: Leiden, 2003).

HENRARD, KRISTIN, AND ROBERT DUNBAR eds. *Synergies in Minority Protection. European and International Law Perspectives*. Cambridge: Cambridge University Press, 2008.

HERITIER, ADRIENNE et al., eds. *Differential Europe. The European Union Impact on national Policymaking*. Lanham, MD: Rowman & Littlefield, 2001.

HITCHINS, KEITH. *Rumania: 1866–1947*. Oxford: Clarendon Press, 1994.

HOBSBAWM, ERIC. "Introduction: Inventing Traditions", in *The Invention of Tradition*, eds. ERIC HOBSBAWM and TERENCE RANGER. Cambridge: Cambridge University Press, 1983, pp. 1–14.

HOFFMEISTER, FRANK. "Monitoring Minority Rights in the Enlarged European Union", in *Minority Protection and the Enlarged European Union: The way forward*. Budapest: Local Government and Public Service Initiative, 2004.

HOFMANN, RAINER. "The Future of Minority Issues in the Council of Europe and the Organization for Security and Cooperation in Europe", in *The Protection of Minorities in the Wider Europe*, eds. MARC WELLER, DENIKA BLACKLOCK and KATHERINE NOBBS. Basingstoke: Palgrave Macmillan, 2008, pp. 171–205.

HOROWITZ, DONALD. *Ethnic Groups in Conflict*. Berkeley: University of California Press, 1985.

HOWARD, WYNANT, "Race and Racism: Towards a Global Future", *Ethnic and Racial Studies* 29 (2006), pp. 986–1003.

HOWARD, ERICA. *The EU Race Directive: Developing the Protection against Racial Discrimination within the EU*. London: Routledge, 2009.

HUGHES, JAMES and GWENDOLYN SASSE. "Monitoring the Monitors: EU Enlargement Conditionality and Minority Protection in the CEECs", *Journal on Ethnopolitics and Minority Issues in Europe* 4 (2003), p. 1–37.

Independent Expert on minority issues, OHCHR website, accessed July 15, 2013, http://www.ohchr.org/EN/Issues/Minorities/IExpert/Pages/IEminorityissuesIndex.aspx.

International Covenant on Civil and Political Rights, accessed July 15, 2013, http://www.ohchr.org/en/professionalinterest/pages/ccpr.aspx.

International Perspectives on Positive Action Measures. A comparative analysis in the European Union, Canada, the United States and South Africa (Luxembourg: Office for Official Publications of the European Commission, 2009).

ITZIGSOHN, JOSE, CARLOS DORE CABRAL, ESTHER HERNÁNDEZ MEDINA and OBED VÁZQUEZ. "Mapping Dominican Transnationalism: Narrow and Broad Transnational Practices", *Ethnic and Racial Studies* 22 (1999), pp. 316–339.

JACKSON, PETER, PHILIP CRANG and CLAIRE DWYER. *Transnational Spaces*. London: Routledge, 2004.

JONES, PETER. "Human Rights, Group Rights, and Peoples' Rights", *Human Rights Quarterly* 21 (1999), pp. 80–107.

JOPPKE, CHRISTIAN, ed. *Challenge to the Nation-State: Immigration in Western Europe and the United States* (Oxford: Oxford University Press, 1998).
JOPPKE, CHRISTIAN. *Immigration and the Nation-State: The United States, Germany, and Great Britain.* Oxford: Oxford University Press, 1999.
JOPPKE, CHRISTIAN and EWA MORAWSKA. *Towards Assimilation and Citizenship. Immigrants in Liberal Nation-States.* Basingstoke: Palgrave Macmillan, 2003.
JOPPKE, CHRISTIAN. "The Retreat of Multiculturalism in the Liberal State: Theory and Policy", *British Journal of Sociology* 55 (2004), pp. 237–257.
JOPPKE, CHRISTIAN. "Beyond National Models: Civic Integration Policies for Immigrants in Western Europe", *Western European Politics* 30 (2007), pp. 1–22.
JOPPKE, CHRISTIAN. *Citizenship and Immigration.* Cambridge: Polity Press, 2010.
JOPPKE, CHRISTIAN. *The Role of the State in Cultural Integration: Tends, Challenges, and Ways Ahead.* Bern: Migration Policy Institute, 2012.
KAMUSELLA, TOMASZ. "Poland and the Silesians: Minority Rights à la Carte?", *Journal on Ethnopolitics and Minority Issues in Europe* 11(2012), pp. 42–74.
KARDOS, GABOR. "Role for the Kin-States?", in *Beyond Sovereignty: From Status Law to Transnational Citizenship?* ed. OSAMU IEDA. Hokkaido: Slavic Research Center, 2006, pp. 127–137
KASTORYANO, RIVA. "Settlement, Transnational Communities and Citizenship", *International Social Science Journal* 52 (2000), pp. 307–312.
KEANE, DAVID. "Cartoon Violence and Freedom of Expression", *Human Rights Quarterly* 30 (2008), pp. 845–875.
KEATING, MICHAEL. *State and Regional Nationalism: Territorial Politics and the European State.* London: Harvester-Wheatsheaf, 1988.
KEATING, MICHAEL. *The New Regionalism in Western Europe. Territorial Restructuring and Political Change.* Cheltenham: Edward Elgar, 1998.
KEATING, MICHAEL, and JOHN MCGARRY, eds. *Minority Nationalism and the Changing International Order.* Oxford: Oxford University Press, 2001.
KEATING, MICHAEL. *Plurinational Democracy. Stateless Nations in a Post-Sovereignty Era.* Oxford: Oxford University Press, 2001.
KELLY, PAUL. "Introduction. Between Culture and Equality", in *Multiculturalism Reconsidered*, ed. PAUL KELLY. Cambridge: Polity, 2002.
KENNEDY, PAUL, and VICTORIA ROUDOMETOF. *Communities Across Borders under Globalising Conditions: New Immigrants and Transnational Cultures* (Institute of Social and Cultural Anthropology (ISCA) at the University of Oxford – Working paper WPTC-01-17, 2001), accessed 15 June, 2013, http://www.transcomm.ox.ac.uk/working%20papers/WPTC-01-17%20Kennedy.pdf.
KETTLEY, CARMEN. "Power-Sharing and Ethnic Conflict: The Consociational-Integrative Dichotomy and Beyond", *in European Yearbook of Minority Issues*, eds. EURAC and ECMI. Leiden: Brill, 2003, pp. 247–67.
KHAGRAM, SANJEEV and PEGGY LEVITT. "Constructing Transnational Studies", in *The Transnational Studies Reader*, eds. PEGGY LEVITT and SANJEEV KHAGRAM. London: Routledge, 2008.

KHIDASHELI, TINATIN. "Federalism and Consociationalism: Perspectives for Georgian State Reform", in *Federal Practice. Exploring Alternatives for Georgia and Abkhazia*, eds. BRUNO COPPIETERS et al., Brussels: VUB University Press, 2000, pp. 195-202.

KLATT, MARTIN. *Fra modspil til medspil? Grænseoverskridende samarbejde i Sønderjylland/Schleswig 1945-2005*. Aabenraa: Institut for Grænseregionsforskning, University of Southern Denmark, 2006.

KLÍMOVÁ-ALEXANDER, ILONA. "Effective Participation by Minorities: United Nations Standards and Practice", in *Political Participation of Minorities: A Commentary on International Standards and Practice*, eds. Marc Weller and Katherine Nobbs. Oxford: Oxford University Press, 2010, pp. 286-307.

KNILL, CHRISTOPH and DIRK LEHMKUHL. "The National Impact of European Union Regulatory Policy: Three Europeanization mechanisms", *European Journal of Political Research* 41 (2002), pp. 255-280.

KOHN, HANS. "Western and Eastern Nationalisms", in *Nationalism*, ed. JOHN HUTCHINSON and ANTHONY D. SMITH. Oxford: Oxford University Press, 1994, pp. 164-165.

KOHOUT, JOHN. "On Potacka's Philosophy on History", *Filosoficky Casopis* 47 (1999), pp. 97-103.

KORHECZ, TAMAS. "Democratic Legitimacy and Election Rules of National and Ethnic Minority Bodies and Representation", *International Journal of Minority and Group Rights* 9 (2002), pp. 161-81.

KRAUSS, MICHAEL. "The World's Languages in Crisis", *Language* 68 (1992), pp. 4-10.

KUKATHAS, CHANDRAN. "Are There Any Cultural Rights?", in *The Rights of Minority Cultures*, ed. Will Kymlicka. Oxford: Oxford University Press, 1995.

KYMLICKA, WILL. *Multicultural Citizenship. A Liberal Theory of Minority Rights*. Oxford: Oxford University Press, 1995.

KYMLICKA, WILL, and WAYNE NORMAN. *Citizenship in Diverse Societies*. Oxford: Oxford University Press, 2000.

KYMLICKA, WILL, and MAGDA OPALSKI eds. *Can Liberal Pluralism be Exported? Western Political Theory and Ethnic Relations in Eastern Europe*. Oxford: Oxford University Press, 2001.

KYMLICKA, WILL. *Politics in the Vernacular. Nationalism, Multiculturalism, and Citizenship*. Oxford: Oxford University Press, 2001.

KYMLICKA, WILL. *Multicultural Odysseys: Navigating the New International Politics of Diversity*. Oxford: Oxford University Press, 2007.

KYMLICKA, WILL. "The Evolving Basis of European Norms of Minority Rights: Rights to Culture, Participation and Autonomy", in *The Protection of Minorities in the Wider Europe*, eds. MARC WELLER, DENIKA BLACKLOCK and KATHERINE NOBBS. Basingstoke: Palgrave Macmillan, 2008, pp. 11-41.

KYMLICKA, WILL. "The Internationalization of Minority Rights", *International Journal of Constitutional Law* 6 (2008), pp. 1-32.

KYMLICKA, WILL. "Comment on Meer and Modood", *Journal of Intercultural Studies* 33 (2012), pp. 211-216.

LADRECH, ROBERT. "Europeanization of Domestic Politics and Institutions: The Case of France", *Journal of Common Market Studies* 32 (1994), pp. 69-88.

LADRECH, ROBERT. *Europeanization and National Politics*. Basingstoke: Palgrave, 2010.

LÆGAARD, SUNE. "The Cartoon Controversy: Offence, Identity, Oppression?", *Political Studies* 55 (2007), pp. 481–498.

LAGUERRE, MICHEL S. *Diasporic Citizenship: Haitian Americans in Transnational America*. London: Macmillan, 1998.

LAPIDOTH, RUTH. *Autonomy: Flexible Solutions to Ethnic Conflicts*. Washington: US Institute of Peace Press, 1997.

LAPONCE, JEAN A. *The Protection of Minorities*. Berkeley: University of California Press, 1960.

LEE, HELEN and STEVE TUPAI FRANCIS, eds. *Definitions of Transnationalism in Migration and Transnationalism: Pacific Perspective* – Pacific Transnationalism conference, La Trobe University in Melbourne, Australia, November, 2006), accessed June 15, 2013, http://epress.anu.edu.au/migration/mobile_devices/index.html.

LENIN, VLADIMIR I. "The Revolutionary Proletariat and the Right of Nations to Self-Determination", in *Collected Works* 21 (1974), pp. 407–414, accessed July 10, 2013, http://www.marxists.org/archive/lenin/works/1914/self-det/ch01.htm.

LIJPHART, AREND. "Self-Determination versus Pre-Determination of Ethnic Minorities in Power-Sharing Systems", in *The Rights of Minority Cultures*, ed. WILL KYMLICKA. Oxford: Oxford University Press, 1995, pp. 275–288.

LIJPHART, AREND. *Democracy in Plural Societies*. New Haven and London: Yale University Press, 1977.

Ljubljana Guidelines on Integration of Diverse Societies, 4, accessed July 15, 2013, http://www.osce.org/hcnm/96883.

LLOYD, MARNIE ed. *Ombudsman Institutions and Minority Issues: A Guide to Good Practice*. Flensburg: ECMI, Bundeministerium des Innern, 2005.

MACARTNEY, CARLILE AYLMER. *National States and National Minorities*. London: Oxford University Press, 1934.

MALLOY, TOVE H. "National Minority 'Regions' in the Enlarged European Union: Mobilizing for Third Level Politics?", *ECMI Working Paper* 24 (2005), Flensburg: European Centre for Minority Issues.

MALLOY, TOVE H. *National Minority Rights in Europe*. Oxford: Oxford University Press, 2005.

MALLOY, TOVE H. "Conceptualizing Democratic Diversity Management for Multicultural Societies: Theories of Society and Law", *European Yearbook of Minority Issues* 6 (2007), pp. 281–306.

MALLOY, TOVE H. "Forging Territorial Cohesion in Diversity: Are National Minorities Promoting Fourth-Level Integration?", in *The Protection of Minorities in the Wider Europe*, eds. MARC WELLER, DENIKA BLACKLOCK and KATHERINE NOBBS. Basingstoke: Palgrave Macmillan, 2008, pp. 54–91.

MALLOY, TOVE H., ROBERTA MEDDA-WINDISCHER, EMMA LANTSCHNER and JOSEPH MARKO. "Indicators for Assessing the Impact of the Framework Convention for the Protection of National Minorities in its State Parties" (report presented during the Conference Enhancing the Impact of the Framework Convention, 9–10 October, 2008, accessed July 23, 2013, http://www.coe.int/t/dghl/monitoring/minorities/6_Resources/PDF_IAConf_Report_Bolzano_en_12nov08.pdf.

MALLOY, TOVE H. "Creating New Spaces for Politics? The Role of National Minorities in Building Capacities of Cross-Border Regions", in *Regional and Federal Studies* 20 (2010), pp. 335–51.

MALLOY, TOVE H. "National Minorities in the 21st Century Europe: New Discourses, New Narratives?", *ECMI Issue Brief* 24 (2010), Flensburg: European Centre for Minority Issues.

MALLOY, TOVE H. "Beyond the Limits of Multiculturalism: The Role of Europe's Traditional Minorities", *ECMI Issue Brief* 28 (2013). Flensburg: European Centre for Minority Issues.

MALLOY, TOVE H. and UGO CARUSO. *Minorities, their Rights, and the Monitoring of the European Framework Convention for the Protection of National Minorities.* Leiden: Brill Publishers, 2013.

MALLOY, TOVE H. "National Minorities between Protection and Empowerment: Towards a Theory of Empowerment", *Concept Paper Prepared for the ECPR Joint Sessions.* Mainz, Germany, 2013, p. 3.

Mandate – HCNM, OSCE website, accessed July 15, 2013, http://www.osce.org/hcnm/43201.

MANN, MICHAEL. *The Dark Side of Democracy: Explaining Ethnic Cleansing.* Cambridge: Cambridge University Press, 2005.

MANNENS, WOLF. "The International Status of Cultural Rights for National Minorities", in *Minority Rights in the 'New' Europe*, eds. PETER CUMPER and STEVEN WHEATLEY. The Hague: Martinus Nijhoff Publishers, 1999, p. 186.

MANNERS, IAN. "Normative Power Europe: a Contradiction in Terms?", *Journal of Common Market Studies* 40 (2002), pp. 235–258.

MANNERS, IAN. "The Normative Ethics of the European Union", *International Affairs* 84 (2008), pp. 45–46.

MANSBRIDGE, JANE. "Should Blacks Represent Blacks and Women Represent Women? A Contingent Yes", *The Journal of Politics* 61 (1999), p. 628–657.

MANSBRIDGE, JANE. "What Does a Representative Do? Descriptive Representation in Communicative Settings of Distrust, Uncrystallized Interests, and Historically Denigrated Status", in *Citizenship in Diverse Societies*, eds. WILL KYMLICKA and WAYNE NORMAN. Oxford: Oxford University Press, 2000, p. 99–123.

MARCH, JAMES G. and JOHAN P. OLSEN. *Rediscovering Institutions: The Organization Basis of Politics.* New York: The Free Press, 1989.

MARKO, JOSEPH. *Effective Participation of National Minorities. A Comment on Conceptual, Legal and Empirical Problems.* Strasbourg: Council of Europe, 2006.

MARKO, JOSEPH. "The Law and Politics of Diversity Management: A Neoinstitutional Approach", *European Yearbook of Minority Issues* 6 (2007), pp. 251–80.

MARSH, DAVID and PAUL FURLONG. "A Skin not a Sweater: Ontology and Epistemology in Political Science", in *Theory and Methods in Political Science*, 2nd edition, eds. DAVID MARSH and GERRY STOKER. Basingstoke: Palgrave Macmillian, 2002, pp. 17–41.

MAZOWER, MARK. "The Strange Triumph of Human Rights, 1933-1950", *The Historical Journal* 47 (2004), pp. 379–98.

MCCRUDDEN, CHRISTOPHER. "The New Concept of Equality", *ERA-Forum* 4 (2003), pp. 9–24;

McGarry, John, and Brendan O'Leary. "The Political Regulations of National and Ethnic Conflict in Parliamentary Affairs", in *A Journal of Comparative Politics* 47 (1994), pp. 94–115.

McGarry, John, and Brendan O'Leary. *The Politics of Ethnic Conflict Regulation: Case Studies of Protracted Ethnic Conflicts.* London: Routledge 1997.

McGarry, John, and Brendan O'Leary. "Federation as a Method of Ethnic Conflict Resolution", in *From Power-Sharing to Democracy: Post-Conflict Institutions in Ethnically Divided Societies*, ed. Sidney John Roderick Noel. Toronto: McGill-Queens University Press, 2005, pp. 263–96.

McGarry, Aidan. *Who Speaks for the Roma. Political representation of a transnational minority community.* New York: Continuum, 2010.

Medda-Windischer, Roberta. "The European Convention on Human Rights and Language Rights: Is the Glass Half Empty or Half Full?", in *European Yearbook of Minority Issues* 7, Leiden: Brill, 2010, pp. 95–121.

Media – HCNM, OSCE website, accessed July 15, 2013, http://www.osce.org/hcnm/44688

Meer, Nasar and Tariq Modood. "How does Interculturalism Contrast with Multiculturalism?", *Journal of Intercultural Studies* 33 (2012), pp. 175–196.

Meijknecht, Anna. *Towards International Personality: the Position of Minorities and Indigenous Peoples in International Law.* Antwerp: Intersentia, 2001.

Mithum, Marianne. "The Significance of Diversity in Language Endangerment", in *Endangered Languages: Language Loss and Community Response*, eds. Lenore A. Grenoble and Lindsay J. Whaley. Cambridge: Cambridge University Press, 1998.

Modeen, Tore. *The International Protection of Minorities in Europe.* Åbo: Åbo Akademi, 1969.

Moravcik, Andrew. *The Choice for Europe: Social Purpose and State Power from Rome to Maastricht.* Ithaca: Cornell University Press, 1998.

Mulalic, Muhidin. "Multiculturalism and EU Enlargement: The Case of Turkey and Bosnia-Herzegovina", in *The Islamic World and the West: Managing Religious and Cultural Identities in the Age of Globalisation*, ed. Christoph Marcinkowski. Berlin: LIT and the Asia-Europe Institute, 2009, pp. 112–115.

Musschenga, Albert W. "Intrinsic Value as a Reason for the Preservation of Minority Cultures", *Ethical Theory and Moral Practice* 1(1998), pp. 201–225.

Narayan, Uma. "Undoing the 'Package Picture' of Cultures", *Signs* 25 (2000), pp. 1083–1086.

Nimni, Ephraim J. "Introduction for the English-Reading Audience", in *The Question of Nationalities and Social Democracy*, in Otto Bauer. Minneapolis and London: University of Minnesota Press, 2000, pp. xviii–xix.

Nimni, Ephraim J. "Cultural Minority Self-governance", in *Political Participation of Minorities: A Commentary on International Standards and Practice*, eds. Marc Weller and Katherine Nobbs. Oxford: Oxford University Press, 2010, pp. 634–60

Non-Discrimination in International Law. A Handbook for Practitioners. London: Interights, 2011.

Northedge, Frederick S. *The League of Nations: Its Life and Times, 1920–1946.* Leicester: Leicester University Press, 1986.

NYBERG SØRENSEN, NINA and KAREN FOG OLWIG, eds. *Work and Migration: Life and Livelihoods in a Globalizing World (Transnationalism)*. London: Routledge, 2002.

O'LEARY, BRENDAN. "The Logics of Power-sharing, Consociation and Pluralist Federations", in *Self-determination Disputes: Complex Power-Sharing in Theory and Practice*, eds. BARBARA METZGER and MARC WELLER. Leiden: Martinus Nijhoff, 2008, pp. 47–58.

OFFE, CLAUS. *Varieties of Transition*. Cambridge: Polity Press, 1996, pp. 50–81.

OHCHR Indigenous Peoples and Minorities Section, OHCHR website, accessed July 15, 2013, http://www.ohchr.org/EN/Issues/Minorities/Pages/OHCHRIndigenous PeoplesMinoritiesSection.aspx.

ONG, AIHWA. *Flexible Citizenship: The Cultural Logic of Transnationality*. Durham, NC: Duke University Press, 1999.

OSCE, The Lund Recommendations on the Effective Participation of National Minorities in Public Life, 1999, accessed July 15, 2013, http://www.osce.org/hcnm/32240?download=true

ØSTERGAARD-NIELSEN, EVA. "Transnational Political Practices and the Receiving State: Turks and Kurds in Germany and the Netherlands", *Global Networks* 1 (2001), p. 261–281.

Overview – HCNM, OSCE website, accessed July 15, 2013, http://www.osce.org/hcnm/43199.

PACKER, JOHN. "On the Definition of Minorities", in *The Protection of Ethnic and Linguistic Minorities in Europe*, eds. JOHN PACKER and KRISTIAN MYNTTI. Åbo: Institute for Human Rights, 1995.

PACKER, JOHN. "Problems in Defining Minorities", in *Minority and Group Rights in the New Millennium*, eds. DEIDRE FOTTRELL and BILL BOWRING. The Hague: Kluwer International Law, 1999.

PALERMO, FRANCESCO. "National Minorities in Inter-State Relations: Filling the Legal Vacuum?", in *National Minorities in Inter-State Relations*, eds. FRANCESCO PALERMO and NATALIE SABANADZE. Leiden and Boston: Martinus Nijhoff Publishers: OSCE, 2011, pp. 3–27.

PAREKH, BHIKHU. *Rethinking Multiculturalism: Cultural Diversity and Political Theory*. Basingstoke: Palgrave Macmillan, 2000.

PATEMAN, CAROLE. *Participation and Democratic Theory*. Cambridge: Cambridge University Press, 1970.

PAYIN, EMIL. "Settlement of Ethnic Conflicts in Post-Soviet Society", in *Ethnicity and Power in the Contemporary World*, eds. Kumar Rupesinghe and Valery A. Tishkov. United Nations University Press, 1996, accessed July 15, 2013, http://archive.unu.edu/unupress/unupbooks/uu12ee/uu12ee09.htm.

PEJIC, JELENA. "Minority Rights in International Law", *Human Rights Quarterly* 19 (1997), pp. 666–685.

PENNOCK, J. ROLAND. "Political Representation: An Overview", in *Representation*, eds. ROLAND J. PENNOCK and JOHN W. CHAPMAN. New York: Atherton, 1968, pp. 3–27.

PENTASSUGLIA, GAETANO. *Minorities in International Law: An Introductory Study*. Strasbourg: Council of Europe, 2002.

PENTIKÄINEN, MERJA. *Creating an Integrated Society and Recognising Differences: The Role and Limits of Human Rights, with Special Reference to Europe.* Rovaniemi: Lapland University Press, 2008.
PHILLIPS, ANNE. "Dealing with Difference: A Politics of Ideas, or a Politics of Presence", *Democracy and Difference. Contesting the Boundaries of the Political*, ed. SEYLA BENHABIB. Princeton: Princeton University Press, 1996, pp. 139-52.
PHILLIPS, ANNE. "Democracy and Difference: Some Problems for Feminist Theory", *The Political Quarterly* 63 (1992), pp. 79-90.
PHILLIPS, ANNE. *Democracy and Difference.* Cambridge: Polity, 2002.
PHILLIPS, ANNE. *Multiculturalism without Culture.* Princeton: Princeton University Press, 2007.
PINCUS, FRED. *Reverse Discrimination: Dismantling the Myth.* Boulder. Colo: Lynne Rienner Publishers, 2003.
PITKIN, HANNA FENICHEL. *The Concept of Representation.* Berkeley, London: University of California Press, 1972.
PORTES, ALEJANDRO. "Conclusion: Towards a New World – the Origins and Effects of Transnational Activities", *Ethnic and Racial Studies* 22 (1999), pp. 463-477.
PORTES, ALEJANDRO and RUBEN G. RUMBAUT. *A Portrait: Immigrant America*, 3rd ed. (Berkeley: University of California Press, 2006).
PORTES, ALEJANDRO, LUIS E. GUARNIZO and PATRICIA LANDOLT. "The Study of Transnationalism: Pitfalls and Promise of an Emergent Research Field", *Ethnic and Racial Studies* 22 (1999), accessed 16 June 2013, http://www.tandfonline.com/doi/pdf/10.1080/014198799329468.
PREECE, JENNIFER JACKSON. "Minority Rights in Europe: From Westphalia to Helsinki", *Review of International Studies* 23(1997), pp. 75-92.
PREECE, JENNIFER JACKSON. *National Minorities and the European Nation-States System.* Oxford: Clarendon Press, 1998.
PREECE, JENNIFER JACKSON. *Minority Rights: Between Diversity and Community.* Malden: Polity, 2005.
PREUHS, ROBERT R. "The Conditional Effects of Minority Descriptive Representation: Black Legislators and Policy Influence in the American States", *The Journal of Politics* 68 (2006), pp. 585-599.
PRODI, ROMANO. A Union of Minorities Seminar on Europe – Against anti-Semitism, For a Union of Diversity. Brussels, 19 February 2004, accessed August 8, 2013, http://europa.eu/rapid/press-release_SPEECH-04-85_en.htm.
PRODI, ROMANO. *The Impact of the Reforms and Enlargement on the Islands Regions, The Reasons for Island Status.* Convention of the Association of Industry of the Province of Sassari. Sassari, 24 January 2003, accessed August 8, 2013, http://europa.eu/rapid/ pressReleasesAction.do?reference=SPEECH/03/28&format=HTML&a
Protocol No. 12 to the Convention for the Protection of Human Rights and Fundamental Freedoms, European Treaty Series 177 of 4.11. 2000.
PUPAVAC, VANESSA. "Politics and Language Rights: A Case Study of Language Politics in Croatia", in *Minority Languages in Europe*, eds. GABRIELLE HOGAN-BRUN and STEFAN WOLFF. Basingstoke: Palgrave MacMillan, 2003, pp. 138-154.

RADAELLI, CLAUDIO M. "The Europeanization of Public Policy", in *The Politics of Europeanization*, eds. KEVIN FEATHERSTONE and CLAUDIO RADAELLI. Oxford: Oxford University Press, 2003, pp. 27–56.

RADAELLI, CLAUDIO M. and ROMAIN PASQUIER. "Conceptual Issues", in *Europeanization: New Research Agendas*, eds. PAOLO GRAZIANO and MAARTEN P. VINK. Basingstoke: Pallgrave Macmillan 2007.

RAMAGA, PHILIP VUCIRI, "The Bases of Minority Identity", *Human Rights Quarterly* 14 (1992), pp. 409–428.

Recommendation 43 on "Territorial Autonomy and National Minorities" of 27 May 1998; Resolution 52 on "Federalism, Regionalism, Local Autonomy and Minorities" of 3 June 1997 and Recommendation 70 on "Local law/special status" of 23 November, 1999.

REIDEL, LAURA. "What are Cultural Rights? Protecting Groups with Individual Rights", *Journal of Human Rights* 9 (2010), pp. 65–80.

REILLY, BENJAMIN. *Democracy in Divided Societies: Electoral Engineering for Conflict Management*. Cambridge: Cambridge University Press, 2001.

Resolution on a Community Charter of Regional Languages and Cultures and on a Charter of Rights of Ethnic Minorities (Rapporteur: Arfe).

REX, JOHN. *Race Relations in Sociological Theory*. London: Routledge & Kegan Paul, 2nd ed., 1983.

RISSE, THOMAS, MARIA GREEN COWLES, and JAMES A. CAPORASO. "Europeanization and Domestic Change: Introduction", in *Transforming Europe: Europeanization and Domestic Change*, eds. MARIA GREEN COWLES, JAMES A. CAPORASO and THOMAS RISSE. Ithaca, NY: Cornell University Press, 2001, pp 1–20.

ROBERTS, ANDREW. *The Quality of Democracy in Eastern Europe. Public Preferences and Policy Reforms*. Cambridge: Cambridge University Press, 2010.

ROBINSON, JACOB. *Were the Minority Treaties a Failure?* New York: Institute of Jewish Affairs, 1943.

ROSTING, HELMER. "Protection of Minorities by the League of Nations", *The American Journal of International Law* 17 (1923).

RUIZ VIEYTEZ, EDUARDO. *The History of Legal Protection of Minorities in Europe*, XVII–XX Centuries. Derby: University of Derby, 1999.

SANDERS, DOUGLAS. "Collective Rights", *Human Rights Quarterly* 13 (1991), pp. 368–386.

SASSE, GWENDOLYN. "Minority Rights and EU enlargement: Normative Overstretch or Effective Conditionality?", in *Minority Protection and the Enlarged European Union: The way forward*. Budapest: Local Government and Public Service Reform Initiative, 2004.

SASSE, GWENDOLYN. "Securitization or Securing Rights? Exploring the Conceptual Foundations of Policies towards Minorities and Migrants in Europe", *JCMS: Journal of Common Market Studies* 43 (2005), pp. 673–93.

SASSE, GWENDOLYN, and CLAIRE GORDON. *The European Neighbourhood Policy*. Bozen: EURAC Research, 2008.

SCHABAS, WILLIAM A. "Ethnic Cleansing and Genocide: Similarities and Distinctions", in *European Yearbook of Minority Issues* 3 (2005), pp. 109–28.

SCHALLER, DOMINIK J., and JÜRGEN ZIMMERER. "Late Ottoman Genocides: The Dissolution of the Ottoman Empire and Young Turkish Populations and Extermination Policies – Introduction", *Journal of Genocide Research* 10 (2008), pp. 7–14.

SCHILLER, NINA GLICK, LINDA BASCH and CRISTINA SZANTON BLANC. "From Immigrant to Transmigrant: Theorizing Transnational Migration", *Anthropological Quarterly* 68 (1995), pp. 48–63.

SCHILLER, NINA GLICK. "Transmigrants and Nation-States: Something Old and Something New in the U.S. Immigrant Experience", in *The handbook of international migration: The American experience*, ed. CHARLES HIRSCHMAN, PHILIP KASINITZ and JOSH DEWIND. New York: Russell Sage Foundation, 1999, pp. 94–119.

SCHIMMELFENNING, FRANK and ULRICH SEDELMEIER. *The Europeanization of Central and Eastern Europe*. Ithaca: Cornell University Press, 2005.

SCHIMMELFENNING, FRANK. "Europeanization beyond Europe", *Living Review in European Governance* 7 (2012).

SCHNECKENER, ULRICH. "Models of Ethnic Conflict Regulation: the Politics of Recognition", in *Managing and Settling Ethnic Conflicts: Perspectives on Successes and Failures in Europe, Africa and Asia*, eds. ULRICH SCHNECKENER and STEFAN WOLFF. London: Hurst & Co. Publishers, 2004, pp. 18–39.

SCHNEIDER, ANNE L., and HELEN INGRAM. *Policy Design for Democracy*. Lawrence: University Press of Kansas, 1997.

SCHOLTEN, PETER. "Framing Immigrant Integration. Dutch Research-Policy Dialogues in Comparative Perspective", *IMISCOE Research*. Amsterdam: Amsterdam University Press, 2011.

SCHWELLNUS, GUIDO. "The Adoption of Non discrimination and Minority Protection Rules in Romania, Hungary, and Poland", in *The Europeanization of Central and Eastern Europe*, eds. FRANK SCHIMMELFENNING and ULRICH SEDELMEIER. Ithaca: Cornell University Press, 2005.

SCOTT, JOHN, and GORDON MARSHALL. *A Dictionary of Sociology*. Oxford: Oxford University Press.

SEDELMEIER, ULRICH. "Europeanization", in *The Oxford Handbook of the European Union*, eds. ERIK JONES et al., The Oxford Handbook of the European Union. Oxford: Oxford University Press, 2012.

SEYLA, BENHABIB. *The Claims of Culture: Equality and Diversity in the Global Era*. Princeton, N.J.: Princeton University Press, 2002.

SHAW, STANFORD J. "The Dynamics of Ottoman Society and Administration", in *History of the Ottoman Empire and Modern Turkey* 1. Cambridge: Cambridge University Press, 1976.

SIGLER, JAY A. *Minority Rights: A Comparative Analysis*. Westport, Conn: Greenwood Press, 1982.

ŠKILJAN, DUBRAVKO. "From Croato-Serbian to Croatian: Croatian Linguistic Identity", *Multilingua* 19 (2000), pp. 3–20.

SLATTERY, BRIAN. "What Are Aboriginal Rights?", *CLPE Research Paper* 1 (2007).

SMITH, ANTHONY D. "The Ethnic Sources of Nationalism", in *Ethnic Conflict and International Security*, ed. MICHAEL E. BROWN. Princeton: Princeton University Press, 1993, pp. 27–41.

SMITH, ANTHONY D. *The Ethnic Origins of Nations*. Oxford: Blackwell Publishers, 1996.
SMITH, DAVID J. "Framing the National Question in Central and Eastern Europe: a Quadratic Nexus?", *Global Review of Ethnopolitics* 2 (2002), pp. 3–16;
SMITH, RHONA K. M. "The Fate of Minorities – Sixty Years On", *Web Journal of Current Legal Issues*, 1/2009, accessed July 15, 2013, http://webjcli.ncl.ac.uk/2009/issue1/smith1a.html.
SMITH, ROBERT. "Reflections on Migration, the State and the Construction, Durability and Newness of Transnational Life", in *Migration and Transnational Social Spaces*, ed. LUDGER PRIES (Aldersot: Ashgate, 1999), p. 187–219.
SNOW, DAVID and ROBERT BENFORD, "Master Frames and Cycles of Protest", in *Frontiers in Social Movement Theory*, eds. ALDON D. MORRIS and CAROL MCCLURG MUELLER. New Haven and London: Yale University Press, 1992, pp. 133–55.
SOYSAL, YASEMIN NUHOGLU. *Limits of Citizenship: Migrants and Post-National Membership in Europe*. Chicago: University of Chicago Press, 1994.
SPILIOPOULOU ÅKERMARK, ATHANASIA. *Justifications of Minority Protection in International Law*. London; Boston: Kluwer Law International, 1997.
SPILLMAN, KURT R. "Ethnic Coexistence and Cooperation in Switzerland", in *Ethnic Conflicts and Civil Society: Proposals for a New Era in Eastern Europe*, eds. ANDREAS KLINKE, ORTWIN RENN and JEAN-PAUL LEHNERS. Aldershot: Ashgate, 1997.
STATPOP, Swiss Federal Statistics Office, "Ständige Wohnbevölkerung nach Alter, Geschlecht und Staatsangehörigkeitskategorie 2010/11", accessed June 28, 2013, http://www.bfs.admin.ch/bfs/portal/de/index/themen/01/02/blank/key/frauen_und_maenner.html.
STAVENHAGEN, RODOLFO. "Cultural Rights and Universal Human Rights", in *Economic, Social and Cultural Rights. A Textbook*, eds. ASBJØRN EIDE, CATARINA KRAUSE and ALLAN ROSAS. Dordrecht: Martinus Nijhoff Publishers, 1995, p. 66.
STJEPANOVIC, DEJAN. "Territoriality and Citizenship: Membership and Sub-State Polities in Post-Yugoslav Space", *CITSEE Working Paper* (2012), accessed 15 July 2013, http://www.law.ed.ac.uk/citsee/workingpapers/.
STONE, LAWRENCE. "The Revival of Narrative: Reflections on a New Old History", *Past and Present* 85 (1979), pp. 3–24.
SUNY, RONALD GRIGOR, et al., eds. *A Question of Genocide: Armenians and Turks at the End of the Ottoman Empire*. Oxford: Oxford University Press, 2011.
TAWHIDA, AHMED. *The Impact of EU Law on Minority Rights*. Oxford: Hart Publishing, 2011.
TAYLOR, CHARLES. "The Politics of Recognition", in *Multiculturalism: Examining the Politics of Recognition*, ed. AMY GUTMAN. Princeton: Princeton University Press, 1994, pp. 25–6.
TAYLOR, CHARLES. *Philosophical Arguments*. Cambridge, MA: Harvard University Press, 1995.
The Brandt Report. MIT Press, 1980.
The Fight against Discrimination and the Promotion of Equality. How to Measure Progress Done. Luxembourg: Office for Official Publications of the European Communities, 2008.

The Thirty Years' War: A Documentary History, ed. TRYNTJE HELFFERICH. Indianapolis: Hackett Publishing Company, 2009, pp. ix–xxi.

THORNBERRY, PATRICK. *International Law and the Rights of Minorities*. Oxford: Clarendon, 1991, p. 164.

THORNBERRY, PATRICK and MARIA AMOR MARTIN ESTEBANEZ. *Minority Rights in Europe*. Strasbourg: Council of Europe, 2004.

TILLIE, JEAN, and BORIS SLIJPER. "Immigrant Political Integration and Ethnic Civic Communities in Amsterdam", in *Identities, Affiliations, and Allegiances*, eds. SEYLA BENHABIB et al.Cambridge: Cambridge University Press, 2007.

TIRYAKIAN, EDWARD A. "Assessing Multiculturalism Theoretically: E Pluribus Unum, Sic et Non", *International Journal on Multicultural Societies* 5 (2003), pp. 20–39.

TOBLER, CHRISTA. *Indirect Discrimination. A Case Study into the Development of the Legal Concept of Indirect Discrimination under EC Law*. Antwerp: Intersentia, 2005.

TOCQUEVILLE, ALEXIS DE. *Democracy in America and Two essays on America*. London: Penguin, 2003.

TOGGENBURG, GABRIEL N. "A Rough Orientation through a Delicate Relationship: The European Union's Endeavours for its Minorities", *European Integration Online Papers* 4 (2000).

TOGGENBURG, GABRIEL N. ed. *Minority Protection and the Enlarged European Union: The Way Forward*. Budapest: Local Government and Public Service Reform Initiative, 2004.

TORFING, JACOB. *New Theories of Discourse. Laclau, Mouffe and Zizek*. Oxford: Blackwell Publishers, 1999.

Treaty of Peace with Poland [Polish Minorities Treaty], Versailles, 28 June 1919, accessed July 10, 2013, http://www.macalester.edu/courses/intl245/docs/treaty_poland.pdf.

Treaty of Westphalia (1648), The Avalon Project, Yale Law School, Lillian Goldman Law Library, accessed July 10, 2013, http://avalon.law.yale.edu/17th_century/westphal.asp.

TRIFUNOVSKA, SNEZANA. "The Issue(s) of Minorities in the European Peace and Security Context", *International Journal on Group Rights* 3 (1996), pp. 283–299.

TULLY, JAMES. *Strange Multiplicity: Constitutionalism in an Age of Diversity*. Cambridge University Press, 1995.

TURI, JOSEPH-G. "Typology of Language Legislation", in *Linguistic Human Rights: Overcoming Language Discrimination*, ed. TOVE SKUTNABB-KANGAS. Berlin: Mouton de Gruyter, 1994.

UN Convention on the Prevention and Punishment of the Crime of Genocide, adopted 9 December 1948, accessed July 6, 2013, http://www.hrweb.org/legal/genocide.html.

United States Census Bureau, accessed 15 July 2013, http://www.census.gov/population/race/.

VAN COTT, DONNA LEE. *From Movements to Parties in Latin America: The Evolution of Ethnic Politics*. Cambridge: Cambridge University Press, 2005.

VAN DER STOEL, MAX. "Looking Back, Looking Forward: Reflections on Preventing Inter-Ethnic Conflict", in *Facing Ethnic Conflicts. Toward a New Realism*, eds. ANDREAS WIMMER, RICHARD J. GOLDSTONE, DONALD L. HOROWITZ, ULRIKE JORAS, and CONRAD SCHETTER. Lanham: Rowan and Littlefield Publishers, 2004, pp. 113–119.

VAN DYKE, VERNON. *Human Rights, Ethnicity, and Discrimination*. Westport, Conn: Greenwood Press, 1985.
VERBA, SIDNEY. *Democracy in America*. Chicago: University of Chicago Press, 1972.
VERHULST, STEFAAN. "Diasporic and Transnational Communication: Technologies, Policies and Regulations", *The Public* 6 (1999), accessed 12 June, 2013, http://Javnost-Thepublic.Org/Article/Pdf/1999/1/2/.
VERSTICHEL, ANNELIES. *Participation, Representation and Identity: The Right of Persons Belonging to Minorities to Effective Participation in Public Affairs: Content, Justification and Limits*. Antwerp: Intersentia, 2009.
VERTOVEC, STEVEN. "Conceiving and researching transnationalism", *Ethnic and Racial Studies* 22 (1999), p. 447–462, accessed 15 June, 2013, http://www.transcomm.ox.ac.uk/working%20papers/conceiving.PDF.
VERTOVEC, STEVEN. "Introduction", in *Migration and Social Cohesion*, ed. STEVEN VERTOVEC, Aldershot: Edward Elgar (1999).
VERTOVEC, STEVEN, and ROBIN COHEN, eds. *Migration, Diasporas and Transnationalism*. London: Edward Elgar, 1999.
VERTOVEC, STEVEN. "Minority Associations, Networks and Public Policies: Re-assessing Relationships", *Journal of Ethnic and Migration Studies* 25 (1999), pp. 21-42.
VERTOVEC, STEVEN. "Transnationalism and identity", *Journal of Ethnic and Migration Studies* 2001, p. 576, accessed June, 2013, http://www.ub.unimaas.nl/ucm/e-readers/HUM2018/Vertovec.pdf.
VERTOVEC, STEVEN. *Transnationalism – Key Ideas*. London: Routledge, 2009.
VUCINICH, WAYNE S. "Mlada Bosna and the First World War", in *The Habsburg Empire in the First World War*, ed. ROBERT A. KANN, BELA KIRALY, and PAULA S. FICHTNER. New York: Columbia University Press, 1977, pp. 45–69.
WALDINGER, ROGER, and DAVID FITZGERALD. "Transnationalism in Question", *American Journal of Sociology* 109 (2004), p. 1177, accessed 12 June, 2013, http://www.sscnet.ucla.edu/soc/faculty/waldinger/pdf/B7.pdf.
WALKER, CONNOR. *The National Question in Marxist-Leninist Theory and Strategy*. Princeton, NJ: Princeton University Press, 1984.
WATERBURY, MYRA A. "Bridging the divide: Towards a Comparative Framework for Understanding Kin-state and Migrant-Sending State Diaspora Politics", in *Diaspora and Transnationalism: Concepts, Theories and Methods*, eds. RAINER BAUBÖCK and THOMAS FAIST. Amsterdam: Amsterdam University Press, 2010, pp. 131–148.
WELLER, MARC. "Creating the Conditions Necessary for the Effective Participation of Persons Belonging to National Minorities: A critical Evaluation of the First Results of the Monitoring of the Framework Convention for the Protection of National Minorities 1998–2003". Paper submitted to the Council of Europe's Conference marking the fifth anniversary of the FCNM, 30–31 October 2003.
WELLER, MARC and STEFAN WOLFF, eds. *Autonomy, Self-governance and Conflict Resolution. Innovative Approaches to Institutional Design in Divided Societies*. London and New York: Routledge, 2005.
WELLER, MARC. "Introduction: The Outlook for the Protection of Minorities in the Wider Europe", in *The Protection of Minorities in the Wider Europe*, eds. MARC

WELLER, DENIKA BLACKLOCK and KATHERINE NOBBS. Basingstoke: Palgrave Macmillan, 2008, pp. 1–7.

WELLER, MARC. "Minority Consultative Mechanisms: Towards Best Practices", *European Yearbook of Minority Issues* 7/8 (2010), pp. 425–47.

WELLER, MARC, and KATHERINE NOBBS eds. *Political Participation of Minorities: A Commentary on International Standards and Practice* (Oxford: Oxford University Press, 2010).

White Paper on Intercultural Dialogue "Living Together as Equals in Dignity" Council of Europe Ministers of Foreign Affairs, 118th Ministerial Session, 7 May 2008, accessed August 9, 2013, www.coe.int/dialogue.

Who we are – mandate, OHCHR website, accessed July 15, 2013, http://www.ohchr.org/EN/AboutUs/Pages/Mandate.aspx.

WILLIAMS, MELISSA. *Voice, Trust, and Memory. Marginalised Groups and the Failings of Liberal Representation.* Princeton: Princeton University Press, 1998.

WIMMER, ANDREAS. "Explaining Xenophobia and Racism: A Critical Review of Current Research Approaches", *Ethnic and Racial Studies* 20 (1997), pp. 17–41.

WIMMER, ANDREAS et al., eds. *Facing Ethnic Conflicts: Toward a new Realism.* Rowman & Littlefield Publishers, 2004.

WINTER, ELKE. "'Immigrants Don't Ask for Self-government': How Multiculturalism is (De)legitimized in Multinational Societies", *Ethnopolitics* 10 (2011), pp. 187–204.

WOELK, JENS, FRANCESCO PALERMO and JOSEPH MARKO, eds. *Tolerance through Law. Self Governance and Group Rights in South Tyrol.* Leiden: Martinus Nijhoff, 2007.

WOLFF, STEFAN. *Disputed Territories: the Transnational Dynamics of Ethnic Conflict Settlement.* New York: Berghahn Books, 2003.

WOLFF, STEFAN "Conflict Resolution Between Power Sharing and Power Dividing, or Beyond?", *Political Studies Review* 5 (2007), pp. 377–393.

WOLFF, STEFAN, and MARC WELLER. *Autonomy, Self-governance and Conflict Resolution: Innovative Approaches to Institutional Design in Divided Societies.* London: Routledge, 2008.

WOOD, PHILL, et al. *Cultural Diversity in Britain: a Toolkit for Cross-Cultural Cooperation.* Rowntree, 2006.

World Bank, What is Empowerment?, accessed July 15, 2013, http://web.worldbank.org/WBSITE/EXTERNAL/TOPICS/EXTPOVERTY/EXTEMPOWERMENT/0,,contentMDK:20272299~pagePK:210058~piPK:210062~theSitePK:486411~isCURL:Y,00.html.

World War I Document Archive, President Wilson's Fourteen Points (1918), accessed July 10, 2013, http://wwi.lib.byu.edu/index.php/President_Wilson's_Fourteen_Points.

WRENCH, JOHN. "Managing Diversity, Fighting Racism or Combating Discrimination? A critical exploration", in *Resituating Culture*. Strasbourg: Council of Europe, 2004, pp. 113–23.

XANTHAKI, ALEXANDRA, "Multiculturalism and International Law: Discussing Universal Standards", *Human Rights Quarterly* 32(2010), pp. 21–48.

YOUNG, IRIS MARION. *Inclusion and Democracy.* Oxford: Oxford University Press, 2002.

ŽAGAR, MITJA. "Diversity Management and Integration: From Ideas to Concepts", *European Yearbook of Minority Issues* 6 (2007), pp. 307–27.

Index

A

AC (Advisory Committee) 10, 5–58, 60, 70, 113, 361
accession 51, 75, 77, 80–5, 100, 136–7, 195, 238
Action Plan 84–5, 92, 100
Adequate System of Minority Protection 22, 297, 310
Advisory Committee see AC
African Americans 41, 249, 252–3, 260, 267
agreements 39, 40, 46, 52, 63–4, 66, 78, 84, 100, 111, 139
  bilateral 66, 72, 139–40
  international 99, 108
alienation 113, 290
alterity 189, 198
Amsterdam Treaty 66, 70, 73, 83, 100
Anderson 126, 159, 170, 180, 185, 187, 301
antagonism 114, 118, 198
anti-discrimination 198, 274, 288, 290, 292
approaches 27, 52, 75, 83, 93, 95, 112, 131–2, 147, 150, 154, 161–3, 169–70, 177–8, 189, 201, 206, 209, 216, 221, 236, 274, 276, 280, 288, 298, 322–3
  inclusive 146
  multiculturalist 114
  normative 52, 257
  pan-European 69, 93
  political 52, 65
  top-down 161–2, 255, 293
arbitration 131, 147–9, 154, 290
Armenians 37, 142, 157, 177, 320
assimilation 21, 33, 36, 116, 128, 131, 137, 141, 144–6, 154, 161, 163, 168, 179, 182, 261, 266, 291
assimilation policies 145
Augsburg 30
Austria 17, 32–3, 35–7, 39, 42, 44–5, 149–50, 159, 289, 306
Austria-Hungary 33, 35–6, 44
authorities, public 56, 221, 247, 268, 273, 275, 292–3
autochthonous 16–7, 22, 179
autonomy 18, 23, 29, 33, 36, 38, 40, 55, 63, 71–2, 115–6, 119, 136–7, 150–3, 175, 178–9, 182, 191, 201, 230, 265, 318
  administrative 151
  national 36
  non-territorial 36, 151, 182, 265, 269, 350
  territorial 36, 145, 151, 182, 265, 269, 292, 362

B

Basingstoke 22–3, 49, 98–100, 127, 129, 184, 214, 243–4, 296–7, 302, 304, 306–8, 310–4, 316, 318, 323
Belarus 100, 279, 289, 291
Belgium 33, 38–9, 72, 151–2, 159, 278, 306
beliefs 78, 80, 110, 112, 124, 150, 169, 175, 195, 258
Berkeley 22, 155, 241, 270–71, 310, 313, 317
bilateral relations 142, 238–9
bilateral treaties 55, 66, 84, 132, 139
bodies 61, 81, 97, 161–2, 223–5, 227–9, 237–8, 241, 247, 251–4, 256, 262, 264, 269, 280, 288–9, 292–3, 297, 312
  advisory 264, 293

decision-making 125, 250, 254, 262, 264, 293
　representative 293
Bolzano/Bozen Recommendations 139–40, 237
Bolzano/Bozen Recommendations on National Minorities 139, 237
Bolzano/Bozen Recommendations on National Minorities in Inter-State Relations 139, 237
borders 16–7, 32–7, 41–2, 45, 69, 84, 133, 135–7, 150, 162, 165, 167–9, 171, 173, 175, 177–9, 181, 187, 195–6, 201, 203, 223, 231, 284, 301
　international 27, 46, 166, 177
boundaries, national 166, 183
Brubaker 115, 125, 138, 140, 148, 149, 201, 296, 303
Budapest 99–100, 296, 305, 309, 310, 318, 321
Bulgaria 17, 34, 37, 39, 42, 66, 72, 291, 361–2

C

Cambridge 22–3, 47–8, 70, 72, 126–7, 129–30, 155, 157–8, 184, 216–7, 241–2, 269–71, 296–9, 301–5, 308–11, 314–9, 321–2
Cambridge University Press 47–8, 72, 126–7, 129, 155, 157–8, 216–7, 242, 269–71, 296, 298–9, 303, 305, 308, 310, 314–6, 318–9, 321–2
Canada 118, 123, 129, 159, 197, 270, 274, 279, 288, 291, 296, 298, 304, 306, 308, 310
candidate countries 100, 238–9, 288
cantonisation 131, 149, 154
capital 162, 168, 170–1, 173–4, 179, 194, 196
Catholics 29, 30
Central and Eastern Europe 10, 32, 37, 39, 41, 45, 64, 66, 71, 73, 81–3, 100, 245, 277, 286, 289, 302, 308, 361

Central Powers 37–9
characteristics
　cultural 16, 138, 203, 204
　ethnic 60, 109, 111
Charter-based mechanisms 7, 223–4, 240
Charter of Local Self-Government 52, 62–3, 72, 306
citizens 21, 31, 40, 59, 68, 146, 211, 249–54, 277
citizenship 14, 20, 31, 40, 59, 99, 138–9, 141, 146, 161–2, 164, 167–8, 179–80, 182–4, 195, 198, 291, 302, 311, 320, 361
civilizations 189, 203–4
Claims of Culture 127, 214, 297, 302, 319
Clarendon Press 22, 47–9, 70–1, 125–8, 310, 317
clause 51, 53, 55, 91, 93, 229
CoE see Council of Europe
cohesion 13–4, 95–6, 103, 114, 175, 206, 276, 281, 285, 290
collaboration 226–7
collective identity 111, 132, 134, 175, 178, 199, 200
collective rights 108, 118–20, 162, 223
Commentary on International Standards and Practice 242–3, 297, 303, 312, 315, 323
Commission 58, 67–8, 72–3, 81, 83, 88, 90, 92–3, 97, 101–2, 138, 142–3, 197, 224–5
Commission on Human Rights 143, 224–5
committee, respective 231
Committee of Ministers 55, 57, 63, 205
communication 110–1, 118, 121, 165, 167, 169, 170, 173, 180, 190, 196, 206, 208–9, 212, 227, 234, 254, 290, 294
communities 19, 29, 41, 67, 109–10, 140, 145, 147, 163, 165–8, 170–1,

173–8, 180–2, 203, 207, 216, 233, 260, 264, 288, 321
imagined 169–70, 175
Community Charter of Regional Languages and Cultures 73, 318
competences, exclusive 78
complaints 42, 44, 231
individual 128, 231, 289–90
concept 6, 20–2, 75–8, 117, 135, 161–6, 169–71, 176–7, 186, 196, 198, 205–7, 210, 248–9, 252–5, 258, 261, 265, 273, 281, 284, 297, 315
key 161–2, 221, 241
Conceptualizing Democratic Diversity Management for Multicultural Societies 216, 296, 313
conditionality 14, 70, 77, 80–2, 84–5, 100, 239, 241, 318
conditionality of NATO membership 239, 241
confidentiality 60, 221, 234–35, 241
conflict mitigation 7, 221–2, 238
conflict prevention 88, 152, 233–5, 241
conflicts 13–4, 16, 29–31, 37–8, 45, 132, 134–5, 149, 180, 190, 197, 204, 207, 212, 221–2, 234–5, 238, 242, 265, 284, 292
Congress 5, 32–3, 35, 37, 39, 41–2, 48, 62–4, 69, 267, 271, 303, 307
Congress of Berlin 5, 33, 35, 39, 41–2
consociationalism 131, 145, 153–4, 283
constituency 63, 251–2, 256, 260, 263–4, 268
Constitution 22, 68, 73, 158, 211, 288, 304, 306
constitutions, national 274, 279
constructivists 82
continent 17, 21, 37, 89, 127, 203, 225
Convention 22, 53–6, 64, 71–3, 102, 121, 128–9, 142, 157, 229–31, 243, 304, 314, 317, 321
Copenhagen Criteria 65, 81–3, 195

Cornell University Press 47–8, 99–101, 128, 215, 305–6, 315, 318–9
Council 5, 10, 14, 22, 43, 51–8, 62–5, 67–73, 75, 81, 88, 92, 100–3, 122, 126–8, 130, 142, 157, 195, 205–6, 216, 221, 225–8, 234, 238–42, 244, 248, 254, 270, 296, 298, 301, 304–6, 308, 310, 314, 317, 321, 323, 362
Council of Europe (CoE) 5, 10, 14, 22, 51–8, 62–5, 68–73, 75, 122, 126–8, 130, 157, 205–6, 216, 221, 238–42, 244, 248, 254, 270, 296, 301, 305–6, 308, 310, 314, 317, 321, 323–24, 362
Council of Europe and Minority Rights 70, 72, 130, 308
countries 18, 29–30, 34, 37–8, 42–3, 45, 55, 58, 60, 72, 75, 78, 80, 82–4, 98, 100, 121–2, 140, 142, 150, 172, 174, 178–9, 181, 194–5, 197–8, 202–5, 207, 222, 233, 238–9, 241, 249–50, 256, 262–3, 274–6, 278–9, 284–5, 287–91, 293
Croats 33, 36–9, 43, 149
cultural autonomy 44, 58, 178, 265, 272, 292, 302
national cultural autonomy 265
Cultural Contestation in Ethnic Conflict 155
cultural diversity 36, 38, 62, 86, 131, 189, 197, 204, 262, 274, 284
Cultural Diversity and Political Theory 126, 157, 214, 297, 316
cultural exchanges 196, 198, 213
cultural heritage 89, 97, 102, 121, 138
cultural identities 169
cultural issues 89, 287
Cultural Logic of Transnationality 184, 316
cultural markers 145, 229, 231
cultural meetings 189
cultural practices 110, 119, 173, 213
cultural processes 162, 182, 201
cultural protection 27, 41

cultural rights 57–8, 108, 116–8, 120–1, 138, 202, 230
cultural specificities 169, 180
cultural traditions 116, 118, 201
cultural values 112, 116, 168, 201
culture policy 88, 91, 97
Culture Program 90
cultures 15, 89, 93, 95, 102, 107, 110, 113–5, 121, 123, 125, 150, 166, 182, 189, 198, 20–5, 209, 211–3, 276, 284, 286
  diverse 169, 213
  dominant 115, 253, 257
  group's 116, 209 286
Czechoslovakia 37–9, 41–2, 45, 144

D

decision-making processes 125, 250, 254, 262, 264, 293
Declaration 31, 48, 66, 217, 225–8, 233, 242, 244, 305
declarations 31, 59, 70, 80, 108, 120, 280, 287
degree of cultural protection 27, 41
democracy 31, 51–2, 6–5, 69, 73, 80, 97, 100–1, 127, 147, 181, 233, 248–53, 259–60, 268, 281
democratic systems 248, 251
Denika Blacklock 23, 243–4, 306, 310, 312–3, 323
descriptive representation 247–8, 255–6, 258–61, 265
Descriptive representation of marginalized groups 268
designation 233, 278
development 13, 19, 27, 29, 31, 36, 76, 82–4, 92, 94–6, 100, 111, 126, 135, 137, 152, 164, 167–9, 173, 175, 180, 182, 192, 194, 196, 197, 223, 227, 234–6, 239–40, 284, 286, 289
  cultural 54, 182
  levels of 95, 103
  regional 63, 93–5, 97–8

dialogue 14, 57–8, 70, 90, 108, 123, 125, 205–7, 216, 226–7, 232, 255, 264, 323
  inter-cultural 123, 205–7
diasporas 165, 169, 171, 175, 177–8, 180, 186
differences, elimination of 141–2
diffusion 70, 77–8, 98, 173, 195, 196
direct democracy 249–50, 254
disability 67, 73, 101
Disciplinary Perspectives 174, 183, 307
discourses 13, 21, 78, 80, 93, 99, 102, 190, 273, 282–3, 314
discrimination 15, 22, 29, 45, 53, 55, 66–7, 86–7, 97, 101, 111, 114, 129, 144, 146, 155, 198, 257, 267, 276–7, 282–3, 288–9, 292, 294, 296, 319, 323, 362
  combat 73, 87, 101
  elimination of 61, 282, 292
  historical 253, 257
  prohibiting 66, 87, 277
  prohibition of 56, 98, 284, 287, 289, 292
dispersal 176, 177–8
diverse societies 141, 158, 189, 198, 202, 207, 228, 236, 241, 295
diversity 8, 21, 27, 62, 86, 88–9, 91–2, 97, 102, 112, 114–5, 123, 125, 131, 137, 146, 151–2, 154, 161, 172, 180, 189, 196, 198, 203–6, 209–10, 212–3, 216, 221, 236, 241, 265, 273–6, 280, 282–91, 293–6, 323
  internal 114
  managing 154
diversity management 8, 21, 206, 273–5, 280, 282, 284, 287–8, 290, 293–5
diversity policies 273–5, 281, 285–8, 291, 293–5
divided societies 153, 199–200, 208, 298, 322
domestic change 76–7, 79, 86
domestic minority policies 80, 82

domestic policies 80, 82, 140, 227, 238, 240, 273–4, 276
dominant groups 38, 42, 190, 266
dynamics 6, 79, 85, 108, 116, 123, 162–4, 170–1, 176, 179–81, 191, 194, 291

E

Eastern Europe 9, 23, 33–5, 38–40, 47, 54–5, 66, 127, 195, 263–4, 270, 296, 312, 318, 320
ECHR 10, 52–5, 57–8, 62, 69–70, 97, 236
ECJ 10, 87–8, 93, 97–8, 102–3
ECRI see European Commission on Racism and Intolerance
ECRML (European Charter for Regional or Minority Languages) 10, 52, 58, 60–2, 68, 72, 97, 120, 123, 129, 306, 308
education 29, 57, 61, 90–1, 96, 102, 119, 121–3, 134, 139–40, 145, 265, 267, 288, 291–4
Education Rights of National Minorities 236
Effective participation of national minorities 247–8
Effective Participation of National Minorities in Public Life 236, 254, 264, 270, 316
Effective Participation of Persons belonging to National Minorities 72, 323
effectiveness 57–8, 66, 70, 98, 180, 228, 232, 237, 239–40, 273
Egalitarian Critique of Multiculturalism 127, 214, 301
EGTC (European Grouping of Territorial Cooperation) 10, 96–7, 103
elections 250, 252, 254, 261–3, 280
empires, multinational 27, 32, 35–6, 38, 42

empowerment 8, 19, 28, 161, 247, 248, 255, 267–8
empowerment of national minorities 267–8
Enlarged European Union 23, 99, 100, 101, 305, 309–10, 314, 318, 321
enlargement 75, 77, 80, 82–5, 95, 100, 102, 195, 317–8
Enlightenment 5, 31, 32, 192
ENP (European Neighbourhood Policy) 10, 80, 84, 100–1, 318
EP (European Parliament) 10–1, 68, 73, 88, 91–2, 97, 101–3
EP Intergroup 91–2
equality 29, 40–1, 51, 70, 73, 87, 97, 101, 114, 117, 119, 122–3, 125, 134, 137, 139, 147, 152, 197, 206, 208, 211, 249, 253, 267, 274, 283, 285, 287, 290, 297, 305, 315
 substantive 283, 285
establishment 5, 15, 27, 33–4, 37, 39, 45–6, 61, 67, 90–1, 97, 121, 165, 175, 182, 233, 237, 242, 247, 289
Estonia 37, 39, 59, 72, 82, 138
Ethnic 6, 10, 21–3, 73, 100, 108, 116, 127–9, 135, 137, 140, 154–9, 172, 182–4, 186, 215–6, 222, 224, 226–8, 236, 241–2, 269, 271, 296–8, 301, 303–5, 307, 310, 312–5, 317–20, 322–3
ethnic affiliation 223, 277, 279–80
Ethnic and Linguistic Minorities 22, 126
Ethnic and Racial Studies 172, 182–4, 186, 216, 296–8, 307, 310, 317, 322, 323
ethnic cleansing 37, 131, 141–3, 153–4
ethnic communities 135, 143, 145, 147–8, 152–3, 236
Ethnic Conflict and International Security 155–6, 303, 320
ethnic conflict regulation 6, 132, 140, 143, 153
ethnic conflicts 135, 143, 222, 233, 242, 316

ethnic groups 32, 38, 46, 109, 111, 123–4, 129, 131, 135, 137, 144, 150, 201, 257–8, 264, 276, 286, 293–4
Ethnic Groups in Conflict 155, 241, 271, 310
ethnic identity 111, 144, 164, 258, 263
ethnic minorities 14, 67, 143, 147, 213, 257, 264–5, 278, 281
ethnic origin 66, 73, 87, 101, 278, 288, 298, 304
ethnic parties 247, 263
ethnicity 20, 27, 29, 107–9, 112, 124, 128, 133, 135, 144, 163, 201, 206, 221, 258, 273, 277, 279, 280, 282, 286, 288, 291–3
  individual's 279
Ethnicity and Language Politics in Transition Countries 296
Ethnopolitics 156, 269, 296–8, 305, 320, 323
EU (European Union) 5–6, 10–1, 14, 19, 48, 51–2, 62, 64–70, 72–3, 75–103, 122, 174, 194–5, 206, 215, 238, 241, 243, 269, 283, 288, 292, 298, 301, 305–6, 308–10, 312, 314–5, 318–21, 362
EU institutions 76, 81, 83, 88–9, 91, 94
EU language policy 91
EU Law 99, 102, 305, 320
EU level 76–7, 86–7, 92
EU member states 77, 80, 89, 92, 95, 195, 288, 292
EU membership 77, 81–2, 84–5, 98
EU policies 75, 80, 95, 97
EU treaties 87, 88, 90–1, 95
Europe 9, 13–23, 27–32, 34–5, 37–8, 45–9, 51–6, 58, 60–5, 68–70, 73, 75, 82, 89, 91, 93, 99–103, 110, 128–9, 131, 135, 140, 150, 154, 156, 158, 177, 184, 189, 190, 197–8, 202–6, 209, 211, 213–6, 221, 232–3, 237–8, 240–2, 244, 247–8, 252–4, 267, 269, 277, 279, 283, 285, 293, 296, 301–3, 305–6, 310–1, 313–5, 317, 319, 320, 323, 362
European agenda 90–1, 102
European Agricultural Guidance and Guarantee Fund 95
European and International Law Perspectives 72, 310
European anti-discrimination law 297, 305
European Approach 5, 69
European Centre for Minority Issues 9–10, 99, 102, 216, 313–4, 361–2
European Charter for Regional or Minority Languages see ECRML
European Charter of Local Self-Government 52, 62–3, 72, 306
European citizenship discourse 14
European Commission 10, 67, 72, 81, 100–2, 217, 298–9, 305, 310
European Commission on Racism and Intolerance (ECRI) 10, 217
European Communities 65, 73, 298, 304, 321
European context 21, 87, 107, 238
European Convention 10, 52–3, 58, 71–2, 117, 129, 315
European Convention on Human Rights 10, 71, 117, 129, 315
European Convention on Human Rights and Language Rights 129, 315
European countries 65, 138, 140, 181, 195, 198, 205
European Court of Human Rights 53, 122, 210
European cultural heritage 91
European cultural policy 90
European decisions 195
European Framework Convention 22, 72, 314
European Grouping of Territorial Cooperation see EGTC
European History 5, 27
European Integration 76, 99–100, 103, 308, 321

European Integration and National Political Systems 99, 308
European integration processes 75
European International Law 5, 51
European Minority Rights Regime 70, 244, 308
European multinational empires 37
European Nation-States System 22, 48, 70, 127, 317
European Neighbourhood Policy see ENP
European organizations 64
European Outline Convention on Transfrontier Co-operation 52, 63, 72, 306
European Parliament see EP
European Parliament Intergroup for Traditional Minorities 102
European politics 20, 32-3, 43, 45, 51, 63
European regions 94, 96
European Social Fund 95-6
European societies 183, 198, 302
European states 18, 34, 181
European Treaty Series 10, 71, 72, 304, 306, 317
European Union see EU
European Yearbook of Minority Issues 101, 103, 129, 134, 136-7, 155-7, 216, 269, 296, 299, 309, 311, 313-5, 319, 323
Europeanisation 6, 75-85, 98, 100, 101, 103, 302, 308
Europeanisation literature 77-8
Europeanisation mechanisms 76-7, 85
Europeanisation process of transnational diffusion 86
Europeanisation processes 77, 80, 98
  horizontal 77, 80
Europeanisation research 79
Europeanization 20, 85, 98-101, 189-90, 194-6, 213, 215, 302, 304-5, 312, 318-9, 362-3

Europeanization and Domestic Change 100, 215, 305, 318
Europeanization and National Politics 98-9, 312
Europeanization of Central and Eastern Europe 99, 101, 319
Europeanization processes 195
Euro-regions 19, 64
Europe's history 14, 28, 37
events 18, 20, 90, 115, 141-3, 172, 175, 190, 196, 201
Evolving Basis of European Norms of Minority Rights 243, 312
examination 180, 294
exchanges 61, 143, 164-6, 169, 174-5, 177, 181, 196, 198, 213
experts, international 236, 241
Explanatory Report 72, 119, 128-9
expression 31-2, 61, 108-11, 114, 116-7, 120,-1, 145, 212, 230, 286
  cultural 113, 179, 230
external protections 119

F

Facing Ethnic Conflicts 73, 215, 322-3
factors 17, 35, 109-10, 149, 153-4, 162, 173, 175-6, 181-2, 203
fair representation 253, 261-2, 268-9
Faist 163-4, 173-5, 178-9, 182-3, 185-6, 307, 322
Faist, Thomas 174, 179, 182, 307
Fate of Minorities 225, 242-3, 320
FCNM 10, 52, 56-2, 66, 68, 70, 72, 97, 113-4, 117, 119-23, 127, 128, 129, 130, 236-37, 323
federalism 145, 150, 152, 265, 281, 283
federalisation 131, 141, 149-50, 154
female genital mutilation 119, 215
field 13-4, 19-20, 52, 64, 76-8, 83, 87, 89-90, 92, 102, 161-2, 164-6, 169, 172, 179-81, 183, 208, 221, 226, 281, 317, 362
  particular 162-3

fight 13, 204, 207, 209
Finland 37, 39, 149, 278, 289, 291
First World War 49, 108, 143, 322
forces 28, 32, 81, 153, 168, 189, 190, 192–6, 213
  external 189, 193, 194
formation 51, 109, 111, 135, 164, 170–1, 178, 181, 185, 190, 194, 199, 202, 240, 258, 266, 309
Former Working Group on Minorities 243
Forum on Minority Issues 226–7, 243
Fourteen Points 37–9, 49, 323
FRA (Fundamental Rights Agency) 10, 68, 97
Framework Convention 10, 52, 56, 72, 113, 127, 128, 248, 254, 270, 292, 305, 307, 314, 323, 361
France 17, 21, 30, 32, 36, 38–9, 42–3, 68, 72, 103, 122, 138, 145, 156, 210, 215, 217, 249, 297, 303, 306, 312, 316, 323
Frank Schimmelfenning 99, 101, 319
freedom 13, 53, 73, 97, 101, 113, 115, 120, 137, 144, 175, 193, 199, 202–3, 206, 209–13, 216, 237, 249–50, 267, 274, 294, 309
  individual 116, 118
  religious 5, 27–8, 32, 41, 46
freedom of expression 53, 120, 212, 237
fundamental freedoms 100, 129
Fundamental Rights Agency see FRA

G

General Comment 119, 230, 243, 308
genocide 37, 131, 141–3, 153, 154, 157, 321
Germans 38, 42, 45, 286
Germany 9, 17, 23, 33, 35, 37, 39, 42, 44–5, 144, 150, 159, 183, 205, 215, 238, 249, 265, 270, 293, 296, 302, 306, 311, 313, 316, 363
globalisation 163, 167–8, 182

globalization 62, 165, 168, 189, 190, 196, 213, 362
goals 21–2, 64, 82, 85, 92, 109, 135, 156, 222, 226, 237, 240, 266–7, 284, 287, 294–5
governments 44, 52, 55–7, 60, 62, 64, 70, 72, 79, 131, 149, 161, 163, 170–2, 177, 195, 198, 207, 212–3, 224–5, 227, 229, 248, 250, 254, 264, 266–7, 273–4, 277, 279–81, 289, 291, 293
Great Powers 32–6, 39, 42, 47
Greece 13, 37, 39, 41–2, 48, 72, 103, 138, 143, 291
group differences 20, 125, 210
group identity 111, 133, 201, 202, 253, 261, 283
group members 115,–6, 124, 253
group membership 253
group rights 117–8, 124, 223
group-differentiated rights 119–20, 124
groupism 115, 200–1
groups 16–9, 21, 27, 28, 32, 34, 38, 42, 44–5, 59, 61, 72, 76, 93–4, 107, 110, 112–5, 117–21, 123, 125, 129, 131, 133–5, 138, 141–2, 146, 152, 154, 162, 167, 169, 172, 174–5, 177–9, 181–2, 189–90, 197–8, 200–1, 206–9, 212–3, 223, 225, 230, 234, 247, 250, 253–7, 261, 264, 266, 268, 276–8, 280–1, 283, 285–7, 290, 292–3, 295
  cultural 115, 118, 201, 206, 213, 275, 278
  cultural/linguistic 114
  disadvantaged 283, 292
  diverse 206, 208
  indigenous 277, 280
  individual 135
  majority 177, 286
  marginalized 247, 253–4, 266, 268–9
  nationalist 177
  particular 111, 114, 134, 177
  sub-national 95

subcultural 179
various 114, 123
Guarnizo, Luis E. 168, 172, 183–5, 309, 317

H

Hague 22, 70, 73, 125, 128, 236, 297, 302, 310, 314, 316
HCNM (High Commissioner on National Minorities) 7, 10, 59, 68, 146, 154, 221, 233–8, 241–2, 244, 304, 306, 309, 314–6
headscarves 210
hegemonic control 131, 147, 154
High Commissioner on National Minorities see HCNM
history 13-4, 16, 19–20, 27–30, 37, 39, 41, 45, 62, 66, 76–7, 86, 109, 111, 121, 127, 131, 142, 189, 191, 192, 199, 211, 224, 239, 254, 257, 291
History of Legal Protection of Minorities in Europe 22, 318
history of religious minorities 28–9
homeland 17, 132, 134, 138, 140, 167, 169, 171, 174–5, 177–8, 183, 186, 257
  external national 138, 156
homogeneity, ethno-cultural 112, 284
homogenization, cultural 291
human rights 14–5, 20, 45, 47, 51, 53-4, 58, 65, 67 9, 73, 80, 84, 87, 97–8, 100–1, 117–22, 124, 128–9, 132, 168, 171, 174, 202, 206, 211, 223–5, 228–31, 233–4, 240, 249–50, 283, 290, 292, 362
  individual 54, 83, 87, 240
Human Rights Committee 60, 119, 129, 230
Human Rights Quarterly 70, 72, 126–30, 216–7, 301, 306–8, 310–1, 316, 318, 323
Hungary 36–7, 39, 42, 45, 48, 66, 71, 73, 101, 103, 138, 144, 239, 266, 269, 280, 289, 291, 293, 297, 303, 305, 319
Huntington 203–4, 214, 216
hybridity, cultural 169, 177

I

ICCPR (International Covenant on the Civil and Political Rights) 51, 71, 117, 119–20, 122, 128, 145, 229, 231, 236
ICESCR (International Covenant on Economic, Social and Cultural Rights) 10, 120, 229
identities 60, 79, 88–9, 94, 98, 109, 112, 116, 132, 135–6, 138, 145–7, 165, 167–70, 176, 178–81, 190, 195, 198, 200, 213, 233, 362
  discourse 190
  group's 111, 121
  multiple 170, 180–1
  personal 13, 198–200
ideology, nationalist 35, 164, 286
IMER 10, 174, 183, 307
immigrant groups 17, 62, 257, 279
immigrants 17, 19, 22, 123, 161, 164, 166, 168, 172, 179, 181, 287, 291
impartiality 221, 234–5, 241
implementation 41, 43, 62– 3, 73, 76, 79, 81, 84–5, 87–90, 94–6, 139, 161, 225–7, 235–6, 256
inclusion 14, 19, 21, 55, 68, 96, 133–4, 237, 247, 262, 268
independence 17, 32, 34, 36, 39, 45, 48, 111, 150, 234, 251
Independent Expert 67, 88, 101, 224, 226–7, 243, 310
indigenous peoples 60, 118, 228, 287
Indigenous Peoples and Minorities Section (IPMS) 10, 228
indirect discrimination 282, 288
individualists 117, 124
individuals 19, 21, 31, 45, 107, 112, 115, 117, 124, 129, 141, 151, 162–3,

165–8, 172, 180–1, 193, 198, 201, 203, 208, 212, 223, 23–1, 233, 250, 253, 255, 279, 282, 285, 288
influence, group/minority identities 198
InIIS see Institute for Intercultural and International Studies
injustices 119, 200, 257, 286
Innovative Approaches to Institutional Design in Divided Societies 156, 242, 323
Institute for Human Rights and Minority Rights Group 71
Institute for Intercultural and International Studies (InIIS) 10, 179, 185–6, 307
Institute of Social and Cultural Anthropology see ISCA
institutionalisation 19, 171–3, 175
instrumental policies 276
integration 14, 19–21, 62, 7–7, 84, 86, 88, 90, 93, 96, 125, 131, 137, 141, 144–6, 153–4, 158, 161, 164, 177–9, 190, 194, 199–200, 205–6, 216, 236, 241, 268, 283–4, 290–1, 321, 362
  multicultural 145–6
integration policies 145–6
intensity 59, 85, 164–6, 173, 175, 196
inter-culturalism 205–6
inter-group 6, 108, 123, 125, 136, 144, 276, 284
inter-state relations 18, 139
Intercultural Dialogue 205, 216
interests 45, 61, 79, 117, 119, 140, 150, 152, 167, 203, 208, 235, 247, 250, 259–61, 263–4, 269, 361–3
  national 42, 203
Intergroup for Traditional Minorities 91, 102
international bodies 139, 233
International Convention 129, 229, 277
International Covenant 10, 51, 108, 120, 126, 206, 229, 243, 310

International Covenant on Economic, Social and Cultural Rights see ICESCR
International Covenant on the Civil and Political Rights see ICCPR
international human rights laws 228
international human rights system 120, 124
international human rights treaties 287
International Journal of Minority and Group Rights 297, 312
International Journal on Group Rights 73, 321
International Journal on Minority and Group Rights 101, 301
International Journal on Multicultural Societies 129, 297–8, 305, 321
International Law 48, 71, 126, 129, 241, 297, 316, 318, 321
International Law and Language Policy 241
International Legal Protection of Minorities 242
international migration 164, 184, 319
International Minority Protection 47
international norms 107, 211, 240
international organizations 32, 51, 211, 221, 227, 238, 241, 281–2
international peace 27, 31, 222
International Protection of Minorities in Europe 22, 315
international recognition 46, 136, 142
international relations 13, 18, 20, 30, 38, 42, 44, 46, 47, 76, 147, 186, 275
International Security 155–6, 303, 320
international standards 139, 227, 236
International Status of Cultural Rights for National Minorities 128, 314
international treaties 28, 32, 65, 87, 223
Interpretation of Cultures 23, 126, 308
intra-group 108, 123, 125, 276
IPMS see Indigenous Peoples and Minorities Section

Iris Marion Young 258, 260-1, 271
ISCA (Institute of Social and Cultural Anthropology) 11, 182-3, 311
issue networks 174, 175
Italy 17, 33, 36, 38-9, 43, 72, 149, 151, 265
Ithaca 47, 48, 99, 128, 215, 306, 315, 318-9

J

Jackson-Preece 115, 126-9
Jewish minorities 40, 44
Jews 29, 38-9, 45, 47, 177
Joppke, Christian 23, 184, 216, 296, 298, 311
Journal 4-9, 7-2, 98-9, 101-2, 125-7, 157, 184-6, 215-6, 242, 269-71, 297-8, 301-3, 306, 308-12, 314-5, 317-20, 322, 361
Journal of Common Market Studies 101, 215, 298, 302, 312, 314, 319
Journal of Intercultural Studies 216, 312, 315
Journal of Politics 270-1, 301, 314, 317
Journal on Ethnopolitics and Minority Issues in Europe 72, 127, 269, 310-1, 361
judiciary 151, 285-6, 288, 290, 292
justice discourses 19
Justification of Minority Protection in International Law 70
justifications 257
Justifications of Minority Protection in International Law 297, 320

K

kin-states 42, 44, 132, 138, 139-40, 149, 238
Kluwer International Law 22, 70, 316
Kluwer Law International 70, 73, 297, 302, 320

Kymlicka 16, 22-3, 49, 70, 116, 119, 125, 128-30, 141, 145-7, 155-9, 206, 216, 233, 243-5, 257, 262, 270, 296, 298, 301, 308- 9, 312-4

L

language death 121
language groups 288
  separate 61
language learning 92
language policies 111, 121
Language Politics 127, 318
language rights 57-8, 119, 202
languages, dominant group's 111
late modernity 189-93, 198, 201, 202, 204-5, 209
League 5, 14, 28, 30, 32, 39-5, 47-9, 51, 54, 108, 132, 206, 221, 223, 240, 307, 316, 318
League of Nations 5, 14, 28, 32, 39-45, 47-9, 51, 54, 108, 132, 206, 221, 240, 307, 316, 318
levels 77, 92, 94-5, 103, 140, 145-6, 171, 176, 182, 204, 242, 248, 254, 267, 289
  domestic 77-9, 203-4, 213, 247
  international 161, 176
  national 227-8
  supranational 90-1
liberal democracies 119, 149, 249
Liberal Theory of Minority Rights 22, 128, 155, 312
limitations 5, 28, 31, 41, 122-3, 234, 251
linguistic diversity 89-93, 97-8, 101-2, 108, 121, 273
  promotion of 92
linguistic minorities 40, 71, 108, 121, 124, 225-6, 229, 231, 265, 290
Linguistic Rights of National Minorities 236
Lisbon Treaty 13, 67-9, 87, 100

M

Maastricht Treaty 14, 65, 88
majority 18, 27, 31, 36, 38, 47, 57, 61, 69, 87, 101, 107, 110–1, 114, 116, 119, 121–3, 125, 131, 134–6, 138, 143, 145, 147, 150–1, 161–2, 177, 182, 194, 200, 210–1, 223, 228, 233, 247, 250, 252, 275, 281–2, 285–6
majority population 61, 110, 123, 138, 247, 252
Malloy 9, 13, 21, 23, 51, 71–2, 99, 102–3, 126, 129–30, 159, 189, 216, 244, 270, 296, 313–4, 361
Malloy, Tove H. 71, 99, 313–4
Malmö University 174, 183, 307
Managing Religious and Cultural Identities 48, 315
Mansbridge, Jane 256–60, 27–1, 314
marginalised groups 200
  political representation of 252, 261, 268
  representation of 252, 257
Marko, Joseph 72, 103, 130, 134, 136–7, 145, 155–7, 296–7, 314, 323
Martinus Nijhoff 22, 70, 101, 103, 125–6, 128, 156, 242, 269, 296–9, 306, 309, 310, 314, 316, 320, 323
Martinus Nijhoff Publishers 22, 101, 103, 125–6, 128, 156, 242, 296, 306, 309–10, 314, 316, 320
McGarry and O'Leary 140, 143–5, 147–9, 153, 157–9
mechanisms 7, 27, 32, 35, 38, 42, 52, 75, 77–8, 82, 85, 89, 94, 98–9, 121, 123, 164, 167, 182, 221–4, 227–8, 232, 240, 247, 256, 261, 269, 280–1, 312
  common 77, 78
  international human rights 139
  particular 223–4, 229
  treaty-based 7, 223–4, 228, 240
  vertical 77–8
media, broadcast 208, 237

member states 14, 54–9, 64–7, 72, 75, 77–, 83, 86–8, 90–2, 95, 98, 102, 122, 195, 223, 232, 234, 240
  new 55, 58, 64, 195
member states governments 57–8
Michael Keating 22, 103
migrants 61, 112, 163–5, 167, 174, 176–7, 181, 197, 276, 281, 298, 303
Migrants and Postnational Membership in Europe 186
migration 17, 62, 112, 161, 163, 165, 167, 169, 172, 177, 179, 184–5, 196–7, 203, 209, 275, 289, 291, 309, 313
minarets 209–11, 217
Ministers 55, 68, 205, 216, 323
minorities 13–8, 20–1, 27–9, 38, 40, 43–4, 51–4, 56, 58–60, 65, 67–9, 71–3, 75, 81, 83–8, 91–2, 94–6, 101, 103, 107–8, 110–1, 113–7, 119–23, 125, 128, 131–2, 134, 136–41, 144–5, 149–50, 154, 161–3, 177, 179–80, 190, 194–6, 198, 200, 207–8, 213, 221, 223–36, 238, 240–1, 243, 247, 250, 253, 255–7, 262–6, 274–6, 278–81, 285–91, 293, 308, 314, 317–8
  accommodation of minorities 18, 89, 114, 147
  benefit 121–2
  defined national 59
  history of 28, 31
  language 13, 61
  members of 20, 67, 125, 194, 196, 198, 207, 223
  national/ethnic 140
  new 15, 17, 123
  old 16, 17
  particular 231
  persistent 250
  problems in defining 22, 126, 316
  protecting 15, 52
Minorities and Human Rights 70
Minorities and International Law 242, 305

Minorities and Migrants in Europe 298, 318
Minorities in International Law 22, 71, 128, 157, 242, 317
minorities per se, national 56
Minority and Group Rights 22, 125, 128, 316
minority communities 139, 161, 230
minority cultures 119-20, 122-4, 189, 274
minority demands 136, 137
minority differences, eliminating 140-1, 154
minority existence 13, 18, 20-1, 107, 189-90, 193, 198, 209
minority group participation 96
minority groups 13-4, 27-8, 32-4, 36, 41, 43, 61, 75, 77, 87-8, 90, 93-4, 107, 113, 119-24, 135, 147, 162, 178, 181, 201, 205, 212, 223, 233, 247, 264-5, 282
  cultural minority groups 13
  degree of protection of 27-8, 46
  ethnic 205
  increasing recognition of 28, 46
  linguistic 93
  marginalised 285
  members of 119, 233
  national 38, 43, 76, 93, 250, 262, 264, 362
  ossify 125
  particular 90
  particular national 257
  promotion of 75, 94, 96
  protection of 28, 46
  surrounding particular 90
minority groups per se 282
minority groups subject 32
minority issues 9, 13, 20-1, 42, 53, 64, 81, 90, 93, 139, 161-2, 176, 179, 180, 190-1, 196, 202, 204-5, 221, 223-4, 226-7, 230, 232-4, 236-41, 243, 273, 278, 284, 289, 295, 310
  analyzing 161-2
  national 35, 58, 64, 66

studying 18-9
minority language groups 61
minority language use 93
minority languages 40, 61, 91-3, 97, 107, 113, 120, 122, 129, 237, 290-1
most national 61
Minority Languages in Europe 127, 318
minority membership, national 60, 87
minority protection 14, 20-1, 41, 51-2, 64, 66, 69-70, 81, 83, 86-7, 97, 121, 195, 198, 221-3, 229, 232-3, 238, 240, 274, 281-2, 295
  addressing national 55
  expanding national 55
  national 51-2, 55, 63-4
  system of 132, 240
minority-related issues 224-7, 238, 241, 293
minority rights 5-6, 14, 20-21, 27, 32-5, 39, 41-2, 44-7, 51, 53-5, 58, 62, 65, 68-9, 73, 75, 77, 80-1, 83-7, 97-8, 108, 114, 116- 7, 119-22, 125, 127, 132, 141, 155, 161-2, 198, 202, 223, 229, 232-3, 236, 238-41, 255, 306, 361-2
  domestic 75, 80
  evolution of 28, 46
  protection of 44, 80-1, 85-6
Minority Rights in Europe 48, 71, 317, 321
minority rights obligations 5, 28, 33-5, 39, 42, 46
minority rights regime 20, 27, 41, 44, 46-7, 51, 75, 82, 121, 198, 202, 255, 361
minority studies 9, 13, 15, 18-21, 85-7, 161, 180, 182, 189, 273
Minority Treaties 5, 36, 39, 41, 43, 49, 206, 318
MIT Press 155, 214-15, 217, 302, 321
mobility 13, 17, 20, 90, 167-8, 175, 178, 189-90, 196, 203, 209, 213, 290, 294-5
models, consociational 152-3

modern societies 21, 183, 206, 212, 254, 265, 279, 290
modernity 109, 135, 189–93, 198, 201–2, 204–5, 209, 213
monitor 62–3, 65, 228
monitoring 41–3, 47, 57, 61, 64–5, 67, 69, 72, 81, 83, 217, 225, 233, 238–9, 241, 292, 314, 323
Montenegro 33–4, 144, 265
multicultural 20, 61, 145–6, 179, 206–7, 210, 221, 286, 291
Multicultural Citizenship 22, 49, 70, 128, 155, 270, 312
Multicultural Odysseys 129, 296, 312
multicultural societies 206, 286
multiculturalism 36, 110, 114, 163, 205–7, 216, 274, 283–4, 292, 295, 298, 311
Multiculturalism and International Law 127, 323
Multiculturalism and Political Integration in Modern Nation-States 298
multilogue, inter-cultural 208
multinational corporations 165–6, 172
Muslim minorities 41, 110

N

nation building 150, 284
nation-state 17, 27, 32, 34–5, 37, 46, 109, 112, 135–6, 167, 173, 177, 179, 184, 189, 281, 284, 319
 new 33, 35, 37, 38
nation states 69, 171
national borders 76, 166–7, 170, 173
National Communities and Languages 91, 102
national governments 51, 166, 171, 227, 264
national groups 17, 36, 46, 95, 141, 178
national identity 114, 135, 172
national law 78, 119, 151, 168

national minorities 16– 7, 19, 27, 33, 35, 38, 40–1, 43–5, 52, 54–61, 63, 65, 68–9, 84, 88, 94, 111, 113, 117, 121, 128–9, 138–9, 180, 216, 235, 237, 239, 247–8, 250, 252–5, 257, 262, 264–5, 268, 272, 302, 361
 defined 59
 effective participation of 247–8
 members of 57, 60, 262
 participation of 247, 254, 267, 361
 protection of 41, 46, 56, 65, 84, 127
 recognized 59–60
 representatives of 84, 264
 respective national 265
 single 58
National Minorities and Cross-border Cooperation 96
national minorities exercise 266
National Minorities in Inter-State Relations 156, 316
National Minorities Promoting Fourth-Level Integration 23, 313
National Minorities/Sapientia Hungarian University of Transylvania 103
national minority rights 41, 43, 45, 51, 55– 6, 58, 65, 69
National Minority Rights in Europe 21, 23, 71, 126, 159, 244, 313–4, 361
national minority rights protection 65
National Models 184, 311
national movements 33, 35, 41
national origin 261, 277
national Parliaments 265
national politics 138, 170, 194
National Question 158, 296, 298, 303, 322
national self-determination 32, 37
 principle of 35, 39
national-socialist groups 45
national states 38, 177, 180, 207
National States and National Minorities 22, 47, 313
nationalising state 286

nationalism 32, 35, 37, 109, 111, 127, 133-4, 136, 150, 199, 269, 361
  civic forms of 113, 127
  emergence of 5, 28, 31, 46
  ethnic 277
Nationalism Reframed 158, 298, 303
nationalities 36, 49, 274, 289
Nationalities and Social Democracy 49, 272, 302, 315
nationalizing states 138
nationals 16, 40, 42, 198
nationhood 115, 133, 170
nations 31, 36, 41, 81, 109, 111, 123, 166, 168, 181, 183, 258, 265, 276
Native Americans 118, 279
NATO (North Atlantic Treaty Organization) 7, 11, 221-2, 238-41, 245, 301, 302
NATO approach 222, 239, 240
neglect, benign 121, 122
neighbourhood 75, 77, 80, 84-6, 98, 114, 260
networks 162, 166, 168-71, 173-82, 186, 194, 196, 201, 322
New Europe 156, 158, 269, 298, 303
New Immigrants and Transnational Cultures 182, 183, 311
New International Politics of Diversity 129, 296, 312
New Nation-States and National Minorities 155
Nobbs, Katherine 23, 155, 242-4, 296-7, 303, 306, 310, 312-3, 315, 323
non-discrimination 21, 51, 53, 57, 67, 73, 81, 87, 97, 101, 117, 122, 139, 240, 274, 281-2, 285, 287, 295, 362
  principle of 34, 223
non-discrimination legislation 87
non-recognition 113, 280
Nordic countries 278-9, 293
Norman 47, 49, 145-7, 157, 158-9, 270, 305, 308, 312, 314
Normative Power Europe 101, 215, 314

norms 8, 28, 60, 75, 77-81, 85, 98, 110, 118, 141, 145, 149, 162, 173, 193-5, 209, 211, 221, 229, 237, 240, 279, 287-8, 290
  broader European-level 77, 85
  international human rights 290
North Atlantic Treaty Organization see NATO
notions 27, 31, 35-6, 38, 46, 76, 83, 107, 132, 144, 162, 163, 167-8, 177, 288
notions of ethnicity 107
number 9, 14-5, 19-20, 37, 42-3, 51, 54-8, 60, 68-9, 72, 86, 91-3, 123, 135, 143, 153, 165, 167-9, 181, 189, 197, 203, 209-13, 226, 247, 250, 262, 268, 279, 281, 293, 362

O

objectives 8, 62, 85, 87, 89-91, 95-6, 98, 141, 284, 295
objects 13, 42, 200, 255
obligations 34, 40-1, 43, 48, 57, 122, 154, 174, 223, 235, 274
  international 58, 232
  positive 122, 288-9, 292
Official Journal 73, 301, 304-5
OHCHR 11, 228, 243, 304, 310, 316, 323
OHCHR Indigenous Peoples and Minorities Section 243, 316
OHCHR website 243, 304, 310, 316, 323
O'Leary, Brendan 316
option 85, 114, 116, 254, 256, 264-5, 269
organisation 42-3, 45, 102, 170, 173, 175, 178, 248, 250, 267, 281
  international 28, 39, 41, 45, 47, 276
Organization for Security and Cooperation in Europe see OSCE
organizations 44, 57, 69, 70, 165, 171, 173, 197, 201, 203, 205, 208, 211,

222, 226–7, 238–40, 242, 267, 282, 289, 293
non-governmental 11, 57, 226–7, 288, 293
OSCE (Organization for Security and Cooperation in Europe) 7, 11, 14, 51–2, 59, 66, 73, 75, 114, 129, 139, 146, 154, 156, 158, 221–2, 232–44, 248, 254, 264, 270, 304, 306, 310, 314–6
OSCE High Commissioner on National Minorities 114, 139, 146, 158, 233, 243–4, 306
OSCE member states 146, 235–6, 238
OSCE website 243–4, 304, 306, 314–6
Ottoman Empire 17, 29–30, 33–4, 37, 46, 48–9, 144, 157, 319–20
Outline Convention 52, 62–4, 71
Overcoming Language Discrimination 126, 321
Oxford 11, 21–3, 47–9, 70–1, 98–101, 109, 125–9, 155–9, 165, 182–4, 191, 214–6, 241–4, 270–1, 296–7, 301–15, 317–21, 323
Oxford English Dictionary 11, 109, 165, 183, 184
Oxford University Press 21–3, 47–9, 71, 99–101, 125–6, 128–9, 155, 157–9, 214–5, 241–4, 270–1, 296–7, 301–3, 305–9, 311–5, 318–20, 323

P

Packer, John 22, 71, 108, 117, 126, 128, 316
Palgrave Macmillan 23, 70, 129, 184, 214, 243–4, 296–7, 302, 304, 306, 308, 310–3, 316, 323
Pamphlet 242–3
parliament 111, 121, 256, 289
Parliamentary Assembly 55, 62–3, 127, 244
participation 8, 14, 21, 53, 57, 63, 68, 94, 96, 98, 102, 108, 123, 125, 146, 155, 167–8, 170, 181, 225, 227, 229–30, 243, 247–9, 253–4, 260, 262, 264, 266–9, 282–3, 290, 361
active 146, 154, 254
particularists 190
parties 144, 148, 152, 171–2, 231, 235, 262–3, 265, 267, 269, 287, 293
challenger 264
partition 32, 131, 141, 143–4, 149, 154, 284, 292
Party Politics 269, 271, 303, 309
peace 13–4, 21, 30, 37–9, 42, 45, 56, 127, 137, 147, 148, 171, 203, 222, 234–6
Peace of Augsburg 13, 30, 48
peace process 37
peace treaties 30
people 17, 30, 37, 49, 58, 96, 110, 112–3, 121, 133, 142–3, 146, 162, 166–70, 173–6, 178, 180, 183, 190–3, 196–7, 200–1, 204, 207, 209, 211–3, 228, 243, 248–50, 253–4, 258, 261, 263, 266, 277–82, 284, 290–1, 293–4
Peoples and Minorities in International Law 70
people's rule 250–1
perceptions 110, 112, 116, 163, 201
Permanent Court of International Justice 43, 221
persons 40, 56, 67–8, 71, 73, 84, 86, 88, 101, 107–8, 110, 115–7, 121–2, 124, 128, 142, 145–6, 173–4, 177–8, 209, 224, 226–7, 229–31, 233–5, 237, 248, 279, 289, 298, 304
Persons Belonging 297, 322
Persons Belonging to Minorities to Effective Participation 297, 322
perspectives 20, 80, 121, 161, 178, 251–2, 257, 273
historical 27–8, 171, 177
petitioner 231
petitions 42–4, 57
phenomena 18, 162–6, 170, 176–8, 201, 203, 274, 280

phrase 91, 204, 230, 234, 283
Pitkin 251-2, 258-9, 261, 270-1, 317
pluralism, cultural 107, 112, 124, 163, 284, 287, 291
Poland 32, 36, 37-40, 42, 45, 49, 66, 72, 101, 127, 138, 265, 289, 291, 305, 311, 319, 321, 362
Poles 32-3, 45
policies 7-8, 21, 30, 35, 75-6, 78, 80, 81-2, 84, 89, 91, 94-5, 98, 103, 107, 109-10, 114, 120-2, 125, 131, 134-5, 137-8, 145-7, 152, 154, 170-1, 173, 180, 182, 195, 207, 221, 228, 230, 232, 236-8, 240, 252, 255, 262, 267, 273-4, 276, 280, 283-4, 286-95
  anti-discrimination 274
  cultural 89-91
  nationalizing 138, 140
  regional 94-6, 97
  regional development 94, 98
  symbolic 276, 279, 294, 295
policy fields 82, 87, 90, 92
Political Participation of Minorities 155, 242-3, 297, 303, 312, 315, 323
political representation 31, 33, 131, 247, 252-4, 261, 264, 268, 361
Political representation of marginalized groups 252, 261, 268
political rights 27, 32, 34, 40-1, 132, 229
political science 9, 15, 21, 76, 107, 186, 253, 273, 280
political struggles 42, 190
political systems 164, 249
politicians 205, 213
politics
  global 55, 189, 195-7, 204
  international 28, 33-4, 168, 176
  rights-based understanding of 27, 44, 46
Politics of Europeanization 99-100, 215, 303, 307, 318

Politics of National Minority Participation in Post-Communist Europe 269
polity 76-7, 164, 190
Polity Press 23, 70, 214, 241, 297-8, 308-9, 311, 316
population 16, 31, 37-8, 61, 87, 121, 123, 131-2, 134, 138, 140-4, 151, 153-4, 176, 179, 205, 211, 221, 247, 249, 253, 265, 274, 277, 282, 285, 291, 294, 297, 321
  civilian 37, 143
Portes 22, 166, 168, 170-3, 183-6, 309, 317
Portes, Alejandro 172, 317
Position of Minorities and Indigenous Peoples in International Law 242, 315
positive action 56, 61, 285, 292
positive measures 21, 55, 57, 68, 230
power 19, 30, 32-3, 35-6, 41-2, 45, 70, 79, 109, 111, 119, 131, 141, 145, 147, 152, 154, 190, 194-6, 204, 208, 212, 223, 238, 242, 247, 249, 252, 255, 264-5, 275-6, 280-1, 283, 285, 295, 316
  political 149, 171, 265-6
pre-determination 15
Pre-Determination of Ethnic Minorities in Power-Sharing Systems 22, 313
Preece, Jackson 16, 22, 48-9, 70, 127-8, 241, 317
preservation 35-6, 75, 87-8, 90, 93, 97-8, 121, 124, 129, 131, 151, 233, 274, 283, 286
Prevention of Discrimination 15, 224-5
Prevention of Discrimination and Protection of Minorities 15, 224-5
Princeton 126-8, 155-6, 214-5, 270, 296-7, 302-3, 317, 319-20, 322-3
Princeton University Press 126-8, 155-6, 214-5, 270, 296-7, 302-3, 317, 319-20, 322-3

principles 28, 31, 34–5, 42, 46, 53, 56, 61, 63, 82–3, 86–8, 92, 94, 100, 119, 139, 147, 152, 175, 222, 234, 237, 239, 241, 248
processes 19, 28, 75–80, 82, 85, 93, 97, 143, 145, 149, 161–3, 168, 176–7, 179–80, 182, 195–6, 198–200, 210, 213, 234, 252, 254, 287, 291, 294, 361
programs 90, 92–4
promotion 41, 44, 61, 64–5, 75, 80, 83–4, 87, 90–4, 96–8, 120, 122, 124–5, 128, 131, 140, 151, 154–5, 177, 226, 233, 236, 241, 274, 282, 283–4, 286–7, 290, 292
promotion of minorities 93, 98
protection 20, 27, 38–41, 43–7, 51–2, 54, 56, 59, 61, 63–6, 69, 75, 80–1, 83–7, 89, 97–8, 100, 102, 108–9, 116–7, 119–20, 122, 124, 127, 129, 131, 139–40, 151–2, 154–5, 174, 177, 195, 198, 202, 206, 221–3, 225–6, 228, 230, 232–3, 237, 240, 255, 257, 265, 277, 281–2, 286–8
Protection of Ethnic and Linguistic Minorities in Europe 22, 71, 126, 316
Protection of Human Rights 52–3, 71, 128, 225, 304, 317
Protection of Human Rights and Fundamental Freedoms 52, 71, 128, 304, 317
Protection of Linguistic Minorities 126, 306
protection of members 46, 52
protection of minorities 27, 39, 44, 46–7, 65, 75, 80, 83, 87, 98, 100, 117, 122, 132, 195, 223, 225–6, 230, 232, 287
Protection of Minorities 22–3, 48, 58, 72, 224–5, 243–4, 296, 306, 310, 312–3, 318, 323
Protection of National Minorities 10, 22, 52, 56, 72, 113, 127, 128, 241, 248, 254, 270, 292, 305, 307, 314, 323, 361
Protection of National Minorities and Explanatory Report 72
protocol 55, 64
provisions 17, 29, 31–2, 35, 39, 40, 45, 48, 52, 55, 57–8, 68–9, 73, 75, 89, 101, 102, 117, 129, 138, 150, 161, 223–4, 229, 243, 274, 279, 285, 287, 288
public life 57, 63, 224, 229, 247–8, 253, 254, 267–8, 281–3, 290, 361
public policies 186, 195, 288, 322
public space 21, 189, 203, 207, 209–10, 212–3, 276
public sphere 180, 189, 198, 208, 287, 293–4
purposes, analytical 15, 17

R

race 40, 53, 67, 78, 101, 109, 164, 267, 276, 279, 288, 297, 321
Racial Discrimination 10, 121, 129, 229, 277, 298, 310
racial groups 282, 286, 293
Radaelli, Claudio M. 99–100, 195, 215, 302, 307, 318
Rainer Bauböck 158, 183, 186–7, 272, 307, 322
recognition 30, 33–4, 40–1, 60–1, 107, 110, 113, 125, 134, 137–8, 143, 149, 152, 200, 208, 230, 276, 279–80, 283–4
 federalising minority group 151
recommendations 55, 57, 63–4, 68, 81, 101, 148, 197, 224–7, 235–7, 241, 248, 289
 thematic 221, 226, 236, 241
referendum 211
reforms 43, 72, 80, 82, 102, 317
regional authorities 63, 298, 303
regional languages 62, 290
regions, minority-inhabited 94, 96
Reidel 110, 118, 126, 128–9, 318

relations 6, 19–21, 27, 44, 47, 56–7, 61, 64, 71, 80, 100, 107, 113, 135–40, 145, 149, 161–2, 164–7, 174, 176, 178, 182, 189–92, 194–6, 198, 208, 221, 223, 227, 234, 238–9, 241, 260, 273, 275–6, 281, 283–4, 289, 292, 294, 363
  external 75, 80, 84–5, 195
  inter-ethnic 137, 234, 283, 284
  inter-group 136, 144, 145
relativism, cultural 202
religion 16, 27–9, 31, 34, 40, 46, 53, 56, 67, 71, 73, 101, 108–9, 117, 121, 124, 126, 131, 133, 141, 206, 209–10, 213, 229, 231, 261
  freedom of 13, 53, 210, 211
  wars of 29–30
religious communities 29
religious garments 210
religious groups 32, 175, 177
religious minorities 13, 28, 30–1, 34, 46, 154, 177, 213, 277
religious symbols 209–10, 217
reports 57, 63, 68, 73, 81, 88, 97, 113, 227
representation 8, 32, 36, 121, 152, 185, 225, 228, 247–8, 251–3, 255–62, 264, 267, 269, 272, 293, 297, 309, 312, 315
  categories of 258–9, 268
  microcosmic 256, 258
  system of 124, 256, 262, 268
Representation of Ethnic Minorities in Post-Communist Democracies 269
Representation of national minorities 262
representative democracy 181, 247, 248, 250–2, 259
representatives 30, 33, 36, 43, 54, 63, 68, 73, 84, 166, 172, 224–5, 229, 232, 249, 250–2, 258, 260, 262, 264–5, 267, 293
resentment 42, 134, 200, 202, 213
residence 40, 112, 132, 134, 136, 138–40, 151, 154, 156, 166, 178, 278

resolutions 91, 97, 223–5
responsibilities 107, 108, 120, 151, 224, 226, 234
Rethinking Multiculturalism 126, 157, 214, 297, 316
revolutions 33, 37, 192
Rights of Minorities 71, 126–7, 227, 309, 321
Rights of Minority Cultures 125, 128–9, 309, 312
Rights of National Minorities 71
Rights of Persons Belonging 21–2, 108, 128–9, 224, 226–8, 242, 277, 303, 305
Rights of Persons Belonging to Minorities 277
risks 197, 247, 268
Risse, Thomas 100–1, 194, 215, 302, 303, 318
Rogers Brubaker 127–8, 138, 156, 158, 201, 215, 286, 296, 298
role 18, 42, 45, 69, 76–7, 79, 89–90, 93–4, 115, 125, 133–4, 139, 148–50, 180, 195, 204, 216, 222, 224–6, 231–2, 234–5, 237, 251, 257, 260, 268, 274, 281, 289
Role of National Minorities in Building Capacities 23, 313
Role of National Minorities in Building Capacity 99, 103
Role of National Minorities in Building Capacity of Cross-border Regions 99, 103
Roma 7, 8, 45, 100, 140, 161, 181, 247–8, 253, 263, 265–7, 269, 272, 293, 309, 315
Roma communities 140, 181, 268
Roma minority 248, 265, 267, 269
Romania 16, 33–4, 37–40, 42, 45, 48, 58–9, 66, 72–3, 100–1, 138, 239, 265, 269, 293, 303, 305, 319
Romanian Institute for Research on National Minorities/Sapientia Hungarian University 103
Rosting 48–9, 318

Routledge 103, 155–7, 159, 183–5, 242, 297–8, 301–3, 306–7, 310–1, 315–6, 318, 322–3

S

sanctions 47, 88, 292
scenarios 136, 144, 189
Schimmelfenning 99–101, 319
scholars 15, 18, 58, 77, 85, 91, 94–6, 120, 147, 161–3, 165, 167–9, 176, 189, 194, 213, 251–4, 256, 259, 263, 274–5, 277
scope 29–30, 48, 63, 66, 87, 93, 95–6, 138–40, 151, 176, 178, 181, 222–4, 227, 231–2, 234–5, 240, 243, 248, 254, 264, 273, 275
seats, reserved 256, 264–5, 269, 293
secession 35, 131, 137, 140–1, 143–4, 153–4
security 13, 19, 21, 27, 29, 38–9, 42, 52, 65, 73, 127, 135, 141, 190, 203, 205, 210, 222, 232, 238–40, 284, 293
  politics of 238, 241
selective representation 256–7
self-determination 15, 35, 38, 49, 118, 131, 140–1, 143–4, 154, 171, 193, 254
Self-Determination 22, 48–9, 126, 241, 297, 304, 306, 309–10, 313
self-determination principle 49
self-governance 118, 150, 152–3
self-government, full 151
shared meanings 110, 112
signatures 72, 211, 306
Slovakia 16, 45, 66, 71, 81, 100, 138, 262, 305
Slovaks 17, 33, 36, 38, 43
Slovenes 33, 37–8, 39
social change 20, 189, 193–4, 213, 266–8
social integration 116, 164, 199–200
social movements 178, 247, 266
social relations 128, 167–8, 171, 192, 196, 273–5, 281, 295

socialization 78–9, 82, 85–6
societies 13, 16, 20, 76, 114, 124, 132, 141, 146–8, 154, 165, 175, 181, 183, 189, 193, 197–200, 202–9, 212–3, 221, 250, 256, 273, 290, 294
  given 276, 281–2
  international 34, 40
  mainstream 205, 210
  multinational 36
  risk 189, 192, 214–5, 302
  wider 107, 114, 119, 125
solidarity 16, 35, 73, 101, 132–4, 164, 174–5, 179, 207, 281
sovereignty, national 44, 47, 56
spaces 97, 111, 162–3, 165, 168, 170, 173, 175–7, 179, 181, 207, 210
  segmented cultural 179
special representation 118–9, 247, 257, 293
Stability Pact 65–6, 71
standards, international minority protection 236
state institutions 135, 199
state multiculturalism 205
strategies 60, 84, 94, 98, 123, 197, 227–8, 273, 275, 287, 295
students 9, 13, 21, 27, 77, 189, 210, 222
Sub-Commission 224–5
subsidiarity, principle of 63–4
subunits 150
successes 51
successor states 37, 39, 42–3, 274, 277, 286
support 42, 52, 87, 89–92, 94, 98, 102, 122, 134, 138, 170, 177, 193, 211, 234, 238, 262–3, 276, 284–5, 287, 291, 292
Supranational Federalism and Transnational Minorities 158, 302
Switzerland 59, 114, 127, 151–2, 159, 210, 211, 249, 320
symbolic representation 258
symbols 72, 110, 175, 209, 210, 217, 258, 263

system 14–5, 29, 31–2, 44–5, 57–8, 63, 69–70, 110, 116–20, 122, 124, 128, 131–2, 147–8, 152–3, 164, 195, 197, 200, 208, 210–1, 223, 240, 242, 248–51, 256, 262, 265, 268, 278, 280–1, 285, 287–8, 290–1, 294
millet 29, 46

T

tensions 27, 30, 36, 111, 114, 137, 143, 149, 222, 233–6, 239, 241
  ethnic 114, 234–5
  religious 30
terms 18, 20–1, 38, 42, 65, 69, 84, 94, 110, 135, 139–40, 143, 151, 154, 164, 166, 168, 173, 178, 194, 201–2, 204, 208–10, 222, 235, 263, 276, 278
  generic 273–4, 277
  practical 42–3, 167, 276, 278–9
Territorial Autonomy and National Minorities 72, 318
territorial cooperation 94, 96–7, 103
territory 15–7, 30, 37, 40–1, 46, 59, 109, 131–8, 142–3, 151, 167, 170, 193, 204, 256
TEU 11, 83, 86, 88–9, 91, 95, 97, 100–2
TFEU 11, 78, 87–9, 91, 94–7, 99, 101–3
Thornberry 71–2, 108, 126, 128, 321
threats 143, 199–200, 222, 233, 284
ties 31, 109, 113, 135, 164, 167, 173–4, 177–8, 180–1, 193, 256
  symbolic 173, 175
Toggenburg 99–102, 321
toleration 199, 210, 212–3
traditional minorities 13, 276
traits, cultural 94, 96, 109, 121
Transforming Europe 100, 215, 304–5, 318
transnational 14, 77, 85, 90, 92, 96, 103, 161–5, 167–8, 170–1, 173–81, 183–6, 196, 267, 272, 309, 311, 315, 317
transnational activities 170–1, 173, 184, 317

socio-cultural 171
transnational actors 161–5
Transnational America 161, 185–6, 308, 313
transnational approach 176, 180–1
Transnational Citizenship 156, 183, 187, 302, 311
transnational communities 163, 167, 170, 175–6, 178, 180–1, 184, 311
  contemporary transnational 180
transnational cooperation 96
transnational diffusion 85
transnational discourse 163, 176
Transnational Dynamics of Ethnic Conflict Settlement 156, 242, 323
transnational identities 180
transnational kinship groups 174
transnational levels 169
transnational migration 163–4
Transnational organisations 175
transnational perspective 167, 173, 177–8
transnational relations 165, 167, 186
Transnational Social Spaces 179, 183, 186, 307, 320
transnational spaces 164, 173–4, 177
transnational ties 164
transnationalism 20, 161, 163–6, 168–73, 175–6, 178, 180–4, 186, 189, 317, 322
  socio-cultural 171
  term 164, 169
Transnationalism and Minority Issues 7, 176
treaties 14, 28, 30, 33, 39–41, 44, 48–9, 55, 66, 68, 90–1, 96, 108, 154, 228–9, 231, 274
  fundamental 229, 231
trust 209, 212, 235, 239, 251, 260
Tully 127, 208, 217, 321
Turkey 18, 37, 39, 42, 48, 72, 142–3, 157, 279, 296, 315, 319
types 18–9, 112, 142, 148, 171–4, 180, 196, 223, 240, 249, 253, 257–8, 276, 279, 281–2, 284, 288

typology 79, 141, 165, 171-2, 222

U

UDHR (Universal Declaration of Human Rights) 11, 45, 51, 54 120, 228
Ukraine 16, 84, 100, 279
Ukrainians 33, 38, 43, 44
Ulrich Sedelmeier 99, 101, 319
UN (United Nations) 7, 11, 14-5, 21-2, 32, 45, 51, 54, 60, 108, 118-9, 121-2, 126, 128-9, 142, 148, 157, 195, 197, 221-9, 231-2, 240, 242-3, 277, 303-5, 312, 316, 321
UN approach 223
UN Charter 118, 222-3, 228, 240
UN Declaration 22, 108, 128-9, 224-5, 228, 277
UN mechanisms 7, 222, 232, 240
UN Member States 223, 227
Union 9, 11, 37, 42, 45-6, 51, 66-8, 73, 81, 86-7, 89, 92, 95, 99-103, 194, 205, 267, 274, 277, 286, 294, 317, 319
United Nations see UN
United Nations Guide for Minorities 242-3
United Nations High Commissioner for Human Rights 227-8
United States 23, 37, 41-2, 49, 197, 203-4, 215, 249, 276-7, 283, 286, 289, 291, 297-8, 310-1, 321
unity 6, 20, 111-2, 114, 118, 131-2, 135-6, 145, 151, 201, 236, 277
Universal Declaration of Human Rights see UDHR
Universal Minority Rights 71
universalism, cultural 202
University of California Press 22, 155, 241, 270-1, 310, 313, 317

V

values 19, 42, 68, 73, 77, 81-4, 86, 88, 100-1, 110, 112, 116, 150, 162, 194, 201, 209-10, 212, 249, 258, 262, 275, 285, 292
 intrinsic 121, 123, 125, 127, 315
Vertovec 158, 165-6, 168-70, 180, 183-7, 302, 322
votes 247, 262-3
vulnerable groups 197, 285-6, 288

W

warnings, early 234, 238
wars 29-30, 35, 37, 135, 142
Weller 23, 72, 155-6, 159, 242-4, 296-9, 303, 306, 310, 312-3, 315-6, 322-3
Westphalia 30, 48, 108, 190, 317, 321
White Paper on Intercultural Dialogue 205, 216, 323
Wider Europe 23, 243-4, 296, 306, 310, 312-3, 323
Williams 155, 253, 256-7, 261, 270-1, 323
Wolff 127, 136, 155-6, 158-9, 242, 298, 317, 319, 322-3
World War 5, 14, 16, 20-1, 27, 32, 34-6, 45, 47, 49, 52-4, 65, 144, 286, 322-3
World War II 14, 20-1, 27, 45, 47, 52-4, 65, 144

X

xenophobia 189, 205, 207, 216, 323

Y

Yugoslavia 37, 41-3, 46, 73, 111, 142-5, 148, 277

Notes on Contributors

Prof. Dr. Tove H. Malloy
Dr. Tove H. Malloy is Director of the European Centre for Minority Issues and teaches at the University of Southern Denmark and Flensburg University. Her research interests are minority citizenship, the European minority rights regime and international conflict management. Dr. Malloy is a member of the Advisory Committee on the Framework Convention for the Protection of National Minorities in respect of Denmark, and she sits on the editorial board of several international journals. She is the author of National Minority Rights in Europe (OUP, 2005) and has edited several volumes. She has published in numerous journals and edited volumes. She holds a PhD from the University of Essex, UK.

Dr. Andreea Cârstocea
Dr. Andreea Cârstocea is a Senior Research Associate at the European Centre for Minority Issues. Among her research interests are participation of national minorities to public life and political representation. In addition to her research activity, Andreea also acts as editor of the ECMI Working Papers series. Previously she has taught the seminars for a range of courses at the School of Slavonic and East European Studies, University College London, and Goldsmiths College, University of London. Dr. Cârstocea worked for six years as civil servant for the Department for Interethnic Relations of the Romanian Government. She holds a PhD from the School of Slavonic and East European Studies, University College London, UK.

Dr. Raul Cârstocea
Dr. Raul Cârstocea is a Research fellow at Vienna Wiesenthal Institute for Holocaust Studies. His research interests include anti-Semitism, Jewish History, nationalism and nation-building processes in nineteenth and twentieth century Central and Eastern Europe. Previously he has been teaching at American University of Bulgaria and University College London. He holds PhD in History from University College London, UK.

Dr. Alexander Osipov
Dr. Alexander Osipov is heading the Justice and Governance Cluster at ECMI. His research interests include ethnic and racial discrimination, non-territorial autonomy. For 14 years Dr. Osipov was a member of the Human Rights Centre

"Memorial", one of the leading Russian human rights NGOs where he coordinated the programme on ethnic discrimination. He holds a PhD in Ethnology from the Russian Academy of Sciences.

Dr. Zora Popova

Dr. Zora Popova is a Senior Research Associate at the European Centre for Minority Issues. She has been involved in number of research projects on topics like the New Security Challenges, Rise of the Extreme Right in Europe, Charismatic Leadership, Bulgaria and the European Political Values. She has acted as an Expert in the Unit for Alternative Prognoses, Analyses and Actions at the Administration of the President of Republic of Bulgaria. She holds a PhD degree in Political Science from the University of Bath, UK.

Dr. Federica Prina

Dr. Federica Prina is an Editor of ECMI Journal on Ethnopolitics and Minority Issues in Europe. Her main research interests are participatory and linguistic rights of national minorities. Previously she has headed ECMI Culture and Diversity Cluster, worked as Senior Programme Officer for the London-based NGO Article 19, and also, involved in the joint Council of Europe and EU programme "Minorities in Russia: Developing Culture, Language, Media and Civil Society". She holds PhD in Politics from University College London.

Ms. Tamara Hoch Jovanovich

Ms. Tamara Hoch Jovanovich is a Visiting Fellow at the European Centre for Minority Issues. Her main research interests are located within the field of European studies, European integration, EU policy making, human rights and how these features link to national minority groups in times of Europeanization, globalization and transnationalization. She is a PHD Fellow at the Institute of Society and Globalization at Roskilde University in Denmark, where she is also teaching within the EU Studies programme.

Mr. Kiryl Kaścian

Mr. Kiryl Kaścian is a Researcher in the areas of European and Comparative Constitutional Law. His research interests focus on constitutionalism, Europeanization and interethnic relations in the CEE. He recently completed a fellowship in the German Bundestag. Apart of his research, Kiryl is a website editor of the analytical English-language quarterly "Belarusian Review". He is expecting to obtain his PhD in Law from the University of Bremen, Germany.

Ms. Hanna Vasilevich
Ms. Hanna Vasilevich is a Project Research Associate at the European Centre for Minority Issues. Her research interests cover national identities, ideologies, and state-building. Ms. Vasilevich undertook a research on Principle of non-discrimination and application of collective minority rights: case of Belarusians in Poland and Lithuania. She initiated the process to recognize Belarusians as a national minority in the Czech Republic. Ms. Vasilevich is completing her PhD in International Relations and European Studies at the Metropolitan University/International Relations Institute in Prague.